D1095586

A HISTORY OF
Duchesne County

A HISTORY OF

Duchesne County

John D. Barton

1998
Utah State Historical Society
Duchesne County Commission

ISBN 0-913738-41-7
Library of Congress Catalog Card Number 97-62437
Map by Automated Geographic Reference Center—State of Utah
Printed in the United States of America

Utah State Historical Society
300 Rio Grande
Salt Lake City, Utah 84101-1182

Contents

General Introduction

Whaen Utah was granted statehood on 4 January 1896, twenty-seven counties comprised the nation's new forty-fifth state. Subsequently two counties, Duchesne in 1914 and Daggett in 1917, were created. These twenty-nine counties have been the stage on which much of the history of Utah has been played.

Recognizing the importance of Utah's counties, the Utah State Legislature established in 1991 a Centennial History Project to write and publish county histories as part of Utah's statehood centennial commemoration. The Division of State History was given the assignment to administer the project. The county commissioners, or their designees, were responsible for selecting the author or authors for their individual histories, and funds were provided by the state legislature to cover most research and writing costs as well as to provide each public school and library with a copy of each history. Writers worked under general guidelines provided by the Division of State History and in cooperation with county history committees. The counties also established a Utah Centennial County History Council to help develop policies for distribution of state-appropriated funds and plans for publication.

Each volume in the series reflects the scholarship and interpretation of the individual author. The general guidelines provided by the Utah State Legislature included coverage of five broad themes encompassing the economic, religious, educational, social, and political history of the county. Authors were encouraged to cover a vast period of time stretching from geologic and prehistoric times to the present. Since Utah's statehood centennial celebration falls just four years before the arrival of the twenty-first century, authors were encouraged to give particular attention to the history of their respective counties during the twentieth century.

Still, each history is at best a brief synopsis of what has transpired within the political boundaries of each county. No history can do justice to every theme or event or individual that is part of an area's past. Readers are asked to consider these volumes as an introduction to the history of the county, for it is expected that other researchers and writers will extend beyond the limits of time, space, and detail imposed on this volume to add to the wealth of knowledge about the county and its people. In understanding the history of our counties, we come to understand better the history of our state, our nation, our world, and ourselves.

In addition to the authors, local history committee members, and county commissioners, who deserve praise for their outstanding efforts and important contributions, special recognition is given to Joseph Francis, chairman of the Morgan County Historical Society, for his role in conceiving the idea of the centennial county history project and for his energetic efforts in working with the Utah State Legislature and State of Utah officials to make the project a reality. Mr. Francis is proof that one person does make a difference.

ALLAN KENT POWELL
CRAIG FULLER
GENERAL EDITORS

Introduction

In 1861 Brigham Young sent an exploring party to the Uinta Basin to determine the region's potential for Mormon settlement. Upon the expedition's return to Salt Lake City, its members reported in the *Deseret News* of 25 October 1861 that they had found "the fertile vales, extensive meadows, and wide pasture range so often reported to exist in that region, were not to be found . . . and [that the country] is entirely unsuitable for farming purposes." The exploring party found the region lying east of the Wasatch Mountains a "vast contiguity of waste, . . . measurably valueless excepting for nomadic purposes, hunting grounds for Indians and to hold the world together." The report was disappointing to Brigham Young and others. Reports from trappers and hunters earlier had described the Uinta Basin with unreserved praise, claiming that it was a beautiful valley and more to be desired than any they had seen in the Great Basin, not excepting that of Great Salt Lake.

The expedition's survey of the Uinta Basin was likely limited; and it probably explored no farther east than what is now called the Myton Bench. Ironically, the Myton Bench today is an important farming region of the Uinta Basin; in fact, much of the region the 1861 expedition surveyed is a productive agricultural region. The change in the productiveness of the land has occurred as the result of the human will to turn a "vast contiguity of waste" into a productive farming and ranching region.

The land of Duchesne County, Utah, has long been inhabited by Ute Indians; white interest in the Uinta Basin, beginning with the Domínguez and Escalante Expedition of 1776, has waxed and waned for more than two hundred years. Soon after the 1861 expedition's report to Brigham Young, much of the Uinta Basin and all of present-day Duchesne County was set aside as an Indian reservation by President Abraham Lincoln. From the 1860s until the turn of the century, the Ute Indians and their reservation were left for the most part undisturbed, protected in part by the region's geographical isolation. However, changes in federal Indian policy in the 1880s, the discovery of Gilsonite, the increasing demand of whites for virgin farm and grazing lands, and an interest in area water by the Wasatch Front communities brought increased attention of whites to the western portion of the Uinta Basin.

Today, Duchesne County, created in 1914 as the state's twenty-eighth county, is home to more than 12,500 people of various cultural backgrounds. The 1990 U.S. Census listed a total of 12,645 people living in the county. Of this total 11,807 were white, 10 African-American, 664 Native American, 39 Asian or Pacific Islander, 350 Hispanic, and 125 listed as other races. Of the twenty-nine counties in the state, Duchesne ranks fifteenth in population. It has a diverse economy and boasts six incorporated communities—Roosevelt, Duchesne, Myton, Altamont, Tabiona, and Neola—and several unincorporated regions of habitation.

Writing this history of Duchesne County has been one of the most rewarding experiences of my life. Many times as I read pioneer journals and stories tears came to my eyes as I realized the sacrifice and effort those early homesteaders endured to live in this great county. Their sacrifice and dedication to building good homes for themselves and future generations of Duchesne County residents should not be forgotten or taken for granted. One of my regrets with this brief history is that there is simply not room in this account for a number of stories worthy of publication. Other individuals, while mentioned briefly, deserve additional pages. Some, such as William Smart and A.M. Murdock, could require a full biography.

To those who, upon reading this book, feel that a story, individual, group, area, project, or community, has been slighted, please accept my sincere apology. Although I am the first to admit that it was often insufficiently done, I have tried my best to capture a feeling for the times and fit that into the larger historical picture of an era. The stories and accounts that are recorded are intended to provide a window to view the past that not only represents the lives and experiences of those told but hopefully is representative of the experiences of the majority of Duchesne County residents. If the reading of this history sparks old memories, and similar stories and experiences are then remembered and shared with friends and family, this study will have been successful.

Readers will note that Uintah has come to be spelled two different ways, depending on its usage. Uinta spelled without the "h" indicates a natural or geographical feature, such as the Uinta Mountains or Uinta Basin. Uintah spelled with the "h" indicates a cultural or human creation; for example, Uintah County or Uintah Basin Medical Clinic. Early chroniclers and narrative writers did not always make these distinctions, and thus the reader will find some examples of what at first glance might seem to be inconsistent usage but which have been left in their original form in the interests of historical accuracy.

My sincere appreciation and heartfelt thanks go to the Utah State Legislature, which had the foresight and wisdom to pass House Bill 100 that called for the writing of county histories for the 1996 Utah statehood centennial; the Utah State Historical Society staff, especially Kent Powell and Craig Fuller; the Duchesne County commissioners; and willing help and critiques from several individuals and librarians for time and research, particularly Michelle Miles, Jeannie Hokett, J.P. Tanner, Melva Allred, Donna Barton, and Doris Burton of the Uintah County Library.

My love of history and many stories of the past I owe to my father, Jack D. Barton. From my earliest childhood I remember stories he told me of his experiences and those of other early Duchesne

County residents. Thanks, Dad, for telling me stories of meaning, not fairytales. I am forever grateful to my beautiful wife, Patricia, for her love and support and occasional demands that I get to work on this book. To my children, who missed many weekends and evenings with their father in order that this book could be researched and written, I hope that as they read the history and stories recorded herein they will feel that their sacrifice was worth it.

I feel privileged to have grown up in Duchesne County and heard personally many of the stories told here. I am a Westerner through and through, and I hope that I am living up to the expectations of my forebears and the heritage they left me. Duchesne County, in all its communities and regions, is a wonderful place to live and raise a family. I hope that readers of this work can look to the future as our pioneer forerunners did and appreciate their efforts to make Duchesne County a unique and wonderful place to live.

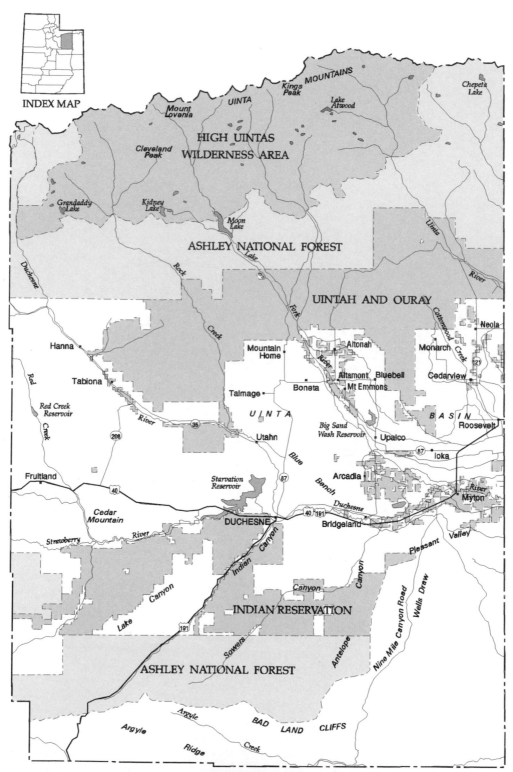

INDEX MAP

Chepeta Lake

Kings Peak

UINTA MOUNTAINS

Lake Atwood

Mount Lovenia

HIGH UINTAS WILDERNESS AREA

Cleveland Peak

Grandaddy Lake

Kidney Lake

Moon Lake

ASHLEY NATIONAL FOREST

Rock

Fork

Creek

Lake

UINTAH AND OURAY

Uinta

River

Neola

Duchesne

Cottonwood Creek

Hanna

Mountain Home

Altonah

Monarch

121

Tabiona

Altamont

Bluebell

Cedarview

River

Boneta

Mt Emmons

Red Creek Reservoir

Red

Creek

River

U I N T A

B A S I N

208

35

Talmage

Big Sand Wash Reservoir

Roosevelt

Utahn

Blue

Upalco

87

Ioka

Fruitland

40

Starvation Reservoir

87

Arcadia

River

Myton

Cedar Mountain

Bench

Duchesne

40 191

DUCHESNE

Bridgeland

Valley

Strawberry

River

Canyon

Indian

Canyon

Canyon

Pleasant

Lake

Canyon

Canyon

Nine Mile Canyon Road

Wells Draw

INDIAN RESERVATION

191

Sowers

Antelope

ASHLEY NATIONAL FOREST

Argyle

BAD

LAND

CLIFFS

Argyle

Ridge

Creek

DUCHESNE COUNTY

CHAPTER 1

BEFORE IT WAS CALLED DUCHESNE

Geography

Duchesne County is located in the western portion of the Uinta Basin, rimmed on three sides by mountains and high plateaus. This unique region, located in the northeastern section of Utah, possesses a variety of notable geographic features and is geographically different from the Great Basin portion of Utah. The settlement and development of Duchesne County has been shaped in part by its geography.

The Uinta Mountains and Uinta Basin are part of two larger physiographic regions identified by geographers as the Rocky Mountain and Colorado Plateau provinces, respectively. The Uinta Mountains are the dominant feature of the region and form the northern rim of the Uinta Basin. The Uintas are a rugged range of mountains that trend east-west, unlike most mountain ranges in the world that run north-south. The Uinta Mountains are about 150 miles long and 30 miles wide.

The central core of this broad range of mountains was formed by sedimentation of mostly quartzite strata of more than 20,000 feet in thickness laid down by ancient oceans over the course of hundreds of millions of years. During much of that time, a great part of the area that would become the western United States, including future Duchesne County, was covered by seas. At other times, the seas subsided or the land rose, leaving dry land, some of which was walked by dinosaurs some 150–100 million years ago. Throughout this time the deposition of sediment continued, either from the oceans or as soil or sand washed down or blown in from neighboring highlands.

About 55 million years ago the strata that had formed from the deposition of sediment was compressed and squeezed upward and outward to form the Uinta Mountains. Several mountain-building episodes—especially the Rocky Mountain, or Laramide, Orogeny, which occurred over 37 million years ago—thrust up the Uinta Mountains as we know them to heights greater than at present. The Uintas are the highest range in Utah, with several peaks over 12,000 feet; the highest, Kings Peak, is 13,528 feet above sea level.[1] Unlike many other mountains in the state and the region, the Uinta Mountains lack igneous rock of any consequence; this explains why no significant ore deposits have been found there.

During the Great Ice Ages of the past million years, the Uinta Mountains were covered with deep ice and snow. Glacial action carved and cut many depressions that later filled with water, creating hundreds of high alpine lakes. The pristine beauty found in the Uinta Mountains provides Uinta Basin residents and tourists both recreation opportunities and scenic enjoyment.

The Uinta Mountains are a significant geographical feature of the northern portion of the state, and they have generated tales and stories by Ute Indians and whites alike. The Utes relate the story of Norita, or Sleeping Princess Mountain, which lies on the west end of the county overlooking Rock Creek. To many, this mountain clearly resembles a woman lying on her back. Many people who first look at the mountain comment that the mountain resembles in detail the women's silhouette, from her face to her feet. The legend tells of a Ute maiden who was known throughout the region for her beauty and kindness. Enemy Indians, hearing of her great beauty, came to capture her. Upon seeing the enemy warriors, she fled to a high cliff.

Kings Peak in the Uinta Mountains is the highest point in the state of Utah at 13, 528 feet. Photo taken from the west side of the peak. (Utah State Historical Society)

Rather than be captured, she jumped to her death. Due to her bravery the Great Spirit sent wind and rainstorms which carved the mountain into her likeness so she would be remembered by all who looked at the mountain.

Local folklore also includes stories about Moon Lake, the largest natural lake in the county. Fed by Lake Fork Creek, Moon Lake was a deep, cold mountain lake until it was changed to a regulated reservoir in the 1930s. The lake is shaped like a crescent moon, and there have been many local stories about sightings of a mysterious monster in Moon Lake. Indian legends tell of canoes being capsized and floundering men attacked and dragged beneath the surface, never to be seen again. More recently, boaters have claimed that they were pursued and bumped by an ugly monster. Over the years there have been drownings in Moon Lake, and several of the bodies have never been recovered, which adds to the mystery of Moon Lake.[2]

The Uinta Mountains receive over thirty inches of precipitation annually, with the higher peaks receiving more than forty inches annually. The mountains are the source of several important drainage systems for northern Utah. The Bear, Provo, and Weber rivers deliver critical stream flows to northern Utah and the Wasatch Front. In the west end of the Uinta Basin, in Wasatch and Duchesne counties, flow several major streams. The Strawberry River flows eastward and is joined by the Duchesne River just east of the city of Duchesne. As the Duchesne flows eastward, the Uinta, Whiterocks, Yellowstone, and Lake Fork rivers as well as Current, Rock, and other creeks add to the Duchesne River, which becomes a major tributary of the Green River. The Green River also has other tributaries originating on the north face of the Uinta Mountains.

The Wasatch Mountains form the west rim of the Uinta Basin. The Wasatch Mountains along with the high southern Utah plateaus form what some call the "Wasatch backbone of Utah." This Wasatch backbone divides the state into the Basin and Range Physiographic Province, which extends westward to the Sierra Nevada, and the Colorado Plateau Physiographic Province, which includes most of eastern Utah. One prominent Utah historian has suggested that the Wasatch Mountains and the high southern Utah plateaus have shaped the economy and culture of eastern Utah including Duchesne County, making eastern Utah's history different from that of the rest of the state.[3] In historic times, the Wasatch and the Uinta Mountains presented a geographical barrier to anyone wanting to travel into the Uinta Basin and eastern Utah. The geographic isolation of the region was a major factor in Duchesne County being the last-settled area of the state.

The southern rim of the Uinta Basin is formed by the Tavaputs Plateau, named after a Uintah Ute chief. The Tavaputs Plateau extends from the Wasatch Mountain Range in a generally southeasterly direction for about 200 miles. A significant part of the Tavaputs Plateau is the Book Cliffs mountainous region. The plateau slopes northward and generally exceeds 8,000 feet in elevation, with several locations in the county exceeding 9,000 feet. Within the plateau is a series of rugged canyons, some accessible only by foot, horse, or four-wheel-drive vehicles. The southern escarpment of the Tavaputs Plateau is located in Carbon County. In its southern cliffs coal has been mined for more than a hundred years.

Rock Creek, one of the several streams in Duchesne County that provide breathtaking scenery, recreation, and economic opportunities. (John D. Barton)

Unlike the majestic Uintas, the Tavaputs Plateau is semiarid, with only a few intermittent seasonal streams. Notable streams in Duchesne County's portion of the plateau are the Avintaquin, Indian

Canyon, Argyle Canyon, and Nine Mile Canyon streams. Except for Minnie Maud Creek in Nine Mile Canyon, which flows directly into the Green River, the other streams from the north slope of the Tavaputs Plateau flow into the Duchesne River. Access to the Uinta Basin from the south has been primarily through Indian and Nine Mile Canyons. Evidence of early Indian use of Nine Mile Canyon is seen in panels of Native American rock art there.

The eastern rim of the Uinta Basin is formed by the Rocky Mountains of western Colorado. The huge Uinta Basin is approximately 125 miles long and varies between 40 and 60 miles in width.[4]

The rivers and streams of the Uinta Basin are its lifeblood in addition to serving as important transportation corridors. The historically important Domínguez and Escalante expedition of 1776 followed the Duchesne and Strawberry rivers through much of the Uinta Basin and future Duchesne County to reach Utah Valley. The Green River provided the means for William Henry Ashley and John Wesley Powell, among many others, to gain access to the Uinta Basin from Wyoming. The rivers and streams of the county and of the Uinta Basin attracted many fur trappers and traders to trap and trade for beaver pelts beginning in the 1820s. And, at the turn of the twentieth century, water from the untapped streams of Duchesne County was highly sought after by farmers and ranchers from Utah County and the Wasatch Front.

Plant and Animal Life

The flora of the Uinta Basin is much like that found elsewhere at its elevation and climate in Utah and throughout the Intermountain West. The valley floor is covered with sagebrush, rabbitbrush, greasewood, Indian ricegrass, needle-and-thread grass and other vegetation of semiarid regions. Found along the larger meandering streams in the county is a more diversified riparian plant life. Willows, cottonwoods, birch, and evergreens, along with various flowers and shrubs, are found adorning the streams' channels. Berries such as chokecherry, elderberry, bull berry, snow berry, wild strawberry, and raspberry provide a treat for humans and many other animals. Pinyon and juniper trees cover the foothills of the Uinta Mountains and the Tavaputs Plateau. At higher elevations Ponderosa pine, white

Norita or Sleeping Princess Mountain. (John D. Barton)

pine, lodgepole pine, Douglas fir, blue spruce, and aspen can be found. Common vegetation in the region at the present time includes Chinese elm, Russian olive, kosher weed, and tumbleweed, none of which is native to the Uinta Basin. All have been introduced and have become problem plants for farmers and ranchers.

Thick vegetation along the various rivers and streams was noted by the Spanish expedition led by Catholic friars Francisco Atanasio Domínguez and Silvestre Velez de Escalante in September 1776. On 18 September, while the expedition was following the Duchesne River upstream a few miles east of present-day Myton, the members were forced to change their course of march because they encountered "a grove or thicket of almost impenetrable rockrose and . . . marshy creeks."[5]

The two Catholic priests were always on the lookout for good land and possible settlement areas. While traveling along the Duchesne River in what is now Duchesne County, Escalante wrote: "Along these three rivers [one of which was the Duchesne River] we have crossed today there is plenty of good land for crops to support three good settlements, with opportunities for irrigation, beautiful cottonwood groves, good pastures, with timber and firewood nearby."[6]

The county's mountains, foothills, plains, and river valleys provide habitat for many species of birds and mammals. Moose, elk, mule deer, antelope, black bear, cougar, bobcat, and coyote are common. Smaller animals such as beaver, raccoon, fox, prairie dog, mink, and muskrat thrive in the area as well. The region's beaver brought fur trappers and traders to the Uinta Basin and the Uinta Mountains beginning in the 1820s. Many rodent and reptile species also make the area their home. Interestingly, there are very few rattlesnakes in the area, but some are occasionally seen in the southern hills. Old-time residents of the county claim that the many, and often very large, blowsnakes of the region keep the rattlesnake population down.

Many species of birds are commonly seen in the region, both migratory and nonmigratory varieties. Eagles, both golden and bald, red-tailed hawks, goshawks, night hawks, falcons, and many other raptors dot the summer skies. Migratory mallards, teal, Canadian geese, curlews, snipe, blue cranes, and sandhill cranes are common in the fall and spring. Smaller birds such as robins, swallows, blackbirds, crows, sparrows, killdeer, and meadowlarks are seen daily.

Early travelers in the region also encountered grizzly bear, buffalo, wolves, wolverines, otters, pine martins, mountain goats, and bighorn sheep.[7] Thousands of wild horses roamed the Uinta Basin at the time of white settlement and there are still significant numbers of mustangs on Johnny Starr Flat and in the Book Cliffs.

In the streams and high lakes cutthroat trout are native; rainbow, brook, and lake trout all were introduced early in the twentieth century. Domínguez and Escalante were so impressed with the fish in the Strawberry River and other streams that they made special note of their findings: "We descended to a fair-sized river in which there is an abundance of good trout, two of which the Laguna, Joaquin, killed with an arrow and caught, and each one of which would weigh somewhat more than two pounds."[8]

Walleye, bass, and bluegill have been introduced into lower elevation lakes in the county in recent years. In some of the high Uinta lakes grayling and golden trout have been planted. Several species of suckers and chubs, including the endangered humpback chub, are found in the Duchesne River. Carp were brought to Utah by Mormon immigrants from Germany. They were introduced to Utah rivers in the hope that they would augment the game fish and add to the food supply. They now are considered trash fish and cause many problems in the rivers throughout the state including the Duchesne River.

Fishing on the many lakes and streams in the county provided an important source of food for the Ute Indians both before and after the coming of whites. During the last half of the twentieth century fishing in the county has been an important sport and recreational activity for county residents and visitors from the Wasatch Front and elsewhere.

Climate and Weather

The geography of Duchesne County and the Uinta Basin makes the region cold in the winter and warm in the summer, with the average precipitation at lower elevations between eight and twelve inches annually; twenty-five or more inches of preceipitation falls on the Uinta Mountains. The normal yearly average maximum temperature in the county rarely exceeds the mid-60° Fahrenheit range, and the normal average minimum temperature hovers around 30 degrees.[9] The elevation of the airport at Duchesne is 5,815 feet; it has an annual precipitation measure of 8.71 inches. The mean annual temperature at the airport is 43.2 degrees, with an average of 115 frost-free days. Roosevelt's airport elevation, which is more than 700 feet lower than the airport at Duchesne, receives 7.44 inches of precipitation annually. The average yearly temperature at the Roosevelt airport is 46.5 degrees, and it has an average of 125 frost-free days.

The county experiences four well-defined seasons. Spring comes two or three weeks behind its arrival along the Wasatch Front and is usually accompanied by intermittent snowstorms, which are common until mid- April. The warming of daytime temperatures in mid-March begins to melt winter snows. Most years, gusty spring winds make it seem colder than temperatures indicate. The last frost generally occurs in mid-to-late May at Roosevelt, Duchesne, and Myton, and all three communities usually experience their first frosts in mid-to-late September.[10] In the upper country of Altamont, Tabiona, and

Glacial action thousands of years ago created many depressions that filled with water and formed the many small alpine lakes found in the Uinta Mountains. (Utah State Historical Society)

Fruitland there are even fewer frost-free days.[11] Most of the agricultural sections of the county have fewer than 120 freeze-free days a year.

Daytime temperatures during the summer months in the county reach the upper eighties and low nineties, with the evenings cooling to the upper fifties. Roosevelt is the hot spot in the county, with official record temperatures of 105 degrees set twice—in August 1958 and in July 1985.[12] Late afternoon summer thunderstorms occur frequently. Some have been severe, resulting in crop damage and damage to barns and other outbuildings. In July 1957 lightning struck the LDS chapel at Montwell, and nearby lightning knocked a boy unconscious and over a fence. On 20 August 1963 a severe hail and lightning storm struck Duchesne City, killing a woman and stunning her son as they were herding cows on the highway. Thunderstorms frequently drop a great amount of rain in a very short time. At least two drownings have occurred from summer flash floods. In late August 1909 a mail carrier drowned when he attempted to cross a swollen stream near Myton; and on 16 August 1928 a sheep rancher drowned from torrential rains in Nine Mile Canyon.[13]

Daytime temperatures during the fall months of September and early October range from 55 to 70 degrees; nighttime temperatures are brisk, often dropping to the thirties. Fall is a pleasurable season; there is usually an Indian summer after the first frost. The Uinta Mountains experience the first frost as early as late August or early September. Late November usually bring snowstorms and colder temperatures that turn fall into winter.

Winter temperatures are usually the coldest in January, when temperatures drop to as low as forty-three degrees below zero.[14] At several unofficial weather stations, winter temperatures have dropped to as low as fifty-eight degrees below zero. This intense period of cold is often accompanied by a low layer of fog which can last several weeks. Daytime temperatures during these intense cold spells reach the high twenties and low thirties. When there is no fog, winds often blow, making the county one of the coldest regions in the state. Most of the winter precipitation falls as snow, with snow depths of more than a dozen feet and more in the Uinta Mountains.

The climatic conditions and the short growing season in the county limits farmers to raising mostly forage crops and livestock, although home gardens are common, with many types of fruits and vegetables raised for domestic consumption.

Early Occupation

Anthropologists generally believe that humans crossed the Bering Strait area during the great Ice Ages of the past 20,000 years and that people then gradually spread throughout the North and South American continents. The archaeological record is scanty, but evidence does suggest that early humans were in the Intermountain West by at least 12,000 years ago. These earliest people were hunters, following the great prehistoric beasts of the era, including mammoths, mastodons, cave bears, giant sloths, ancient camels, and sabretooth cats. They are known as Paleo-Indians and have been classified by the types of projectile points they used to hunt their prey.

It can be assumed that the area of future Duchesne County was traversed by these early hunters as well as by the hunting people that succeeded them throughout the West, the Archaic people. The Archaic culture has been divided into regional variants based on the general ecological areas they inhabited as well as by the artifacts they produced. The Desert Archaic culture of the Great Basin is well known and artifacts have been found at numerous locations in the Great Basin, including a famous habitation of some 10,000 years ago, Danger Cave near Wendover.

Again, evidence of early humans in Duchesne County is not extensive and archaeologists generally can only assume that the early hunting and gathering people made use of the resources of the area, particularly during the warmer times of the year. The Archaic culture flourished from about 6,000 to 2,000 years ago, and it is with the time near the beginnings of the Christian era that researchers have found more extensive evidence of human habitation of the region. These people either assimilated or replaced the Archaic people, probably due to their improved methods of surviving on the land, including the beginnings of horticulture and more sedentary lifestyles. They are known as the Fremont culture, and the Fremont people also have been classified according to the various regions of the Intermountain West that they occupied, including the Uinta Basin.

The prehistoric society identified as the Fremont culture occupied the Uinta Basin for many centuries, from A.D. 300 to 1300. At its zenith, about A.D. 1000, the Fremont culture occupied a wide geographical area from eastern Nevada to western Colorado, and from southern Idaho to southern Utah. These early occupants' architecture, artifacts, and rock art are found at various archaeological sites throughout the Uinta Basin and the county.

Elk in Indian Canyon. (John D. Barton)

The Fremont people were hunters and gatherers who at different times and in different parts of the region developed horticulture, cultivating corn and other plants.[15] They also manufactured pottery and one-rod-and-bundle baskets to carry and store seeds, ground corn, and other harvested plants; used shaped grinding tools, the mano and metate; fashioned unique moccasins; and made trapezoidal-shaped clay figurines.[16] The Fremont people were roughly contemporaries with the more famous Anasazi culture of the Four-Corners region of Utah, Colorado, New Mexico, and Arizona, known for their cliff dwellings in much of the Southwest.

Archaeologists have identified several variants of the Fremont culture, identified with geographical regions of Utah: Great Salt Lake, Sevier, Parowan, San Rafael, and Uinta. Members of these geographical variants of the culture developed or adopted various agricultural, architectural, and other cultural elements at different times, making further differences among the several culture variants.

The Uinta Fremont people occupied the Uinta Basin sometime later, about A.D. 600, than other Fremont people occupied other areas of the Great Basin region. The Uinta Fremont cultivated corn and other plants later than did people of the two southern Utah Fremont culture variants. The geographical isolation of the area may have been the primary reason for the Fremont people occupying the Uinta Basin at a later date; the climate and availability of other resources may explain their later cultivation of corn and other plants.[17] The architecture of the Uinta Fremont was also different from other Fremont culture architecture. The Uinta Fremont constructed shallow, saucer-shaped pithouses or surface structures with off-centered fire pits. Surface storage structures were generally absent. Unique to the Uinta Fremont people was their use of Gilsonite to repair their clay wares.[18]

Collectively, the many Fremont Indian sites in Duchesne County and in the Uinta Basin, including the rock art panels, have provided a great deal of information and added to a growing body of knowledge about the Fremont people. Archaeologists have identified phases within the Uinta Fremont variant. These are commonly known as the Cub Creek and the Whiterocks phases and generally differentiate based on the adoption of corn, the use of pottery, and other cultural, economic, and architectural characteristics.[19]

Perhaps the most significant Fremont cultural sites in the county are in Nine Mile Canyon on the Duchesne-Carbon county line. Archaeologists have identified and investigated nearly 300 archaeological sites in the Nine Mile Canyon area, with additional sites still occasionally being discovered. Recent extensive study by archaeologists indicates that the Tavaputs Fremont people adapted well to the geographical features and natural resources of the Tavaputs Plateau. Late in arriving to the plateau country, the Tavaputs Fremont Indians adopted dry-laid masonry in the construction of their structures. They also were heavily concentrated in canyon drainages, which provided the best local environmental conditions for raising corn. They lived in the rugged Tavaputs Plateau country on a short-term or seasonal basis.[20]

Rock Art of the Fremont Indians in Nine Mile Canyon such as this famous *Goat Panel* are recognized as some of the best representations of Fremont Culture by experts throughout the world. (John D. Barton)

Elsewhere in the county, the Fremont people developed a simple system of irrigation to water their small gardens of corn, squash, and beans. In some places their irrigation ditches, hand dug with wooden or stone tools, appear to have been several miles long. Sometimes these ditches were chiseled through hardpan and even sandstone.[21]

The Uinta Fremont Indians built small granaries of stone and adobe, mortared with mud. They lived in small rock structures, with ten to twelve individual family dwellings making a village. Ruins in the Uinta Basin and elsewhere reveal that they constructed masonry buildings on the surface but also built stone-lined semisubterranean pit houses. Small villages frequently were located along dependable water sources and near tillable land. On the Tavaputs Plateau, dry-laid masonry towers were built, probably for defensive purposes. [22]

For several hundred years the Fremont Indians occupied the region, living a semisedentary life, cultivating small plots of land, drawing or carving rock art on the smooth sandstone canyon walls.

Painted and carved symbols probably represent something of their social activities, their religious thoughts, their views of their world, and other lifeways. The rock art in Nine Mile Canyon is some of the finest in the world and scholars from many research institutions have traveled to the area to study, photograph, and marvel. Fremont Indian rock art in great part remains a mystery to modern scholars and curious laymen alike.

Answers to why the Fremont people left the region are speculative at best and are topics of spirited debate among archaeologists; but, whatever the reason, the Uinta Fremont Indians began mysteriously abandoning the Uinta Basin as early as A.D. 1050, as much as 200 years earlier than other Fremont Indians disappeared from their homes in Utah.[23] The Nine Mile, or Tavaputs, Fremont disappeared later, around A.D. 1200. Perhaps they were driven out by the Numic-speaking ancestors of the Ute and Shoshoni Indians. There is some speculation that remnants of the Fremont people were absorbed by the Ute or Shoshoni Indians. Another theory suggests the Fremont Indians of the Uinta Basin suffered a fate similar to that thought to have befallen the Anasazi to the south: a long period of severe drought forcing them to abandon their homeland of generations and move elsewhere.[24] Contemporary Indian legends of the area tell of a time when there was so little rain or snow that the springs dried up and many of the watercourses nearly did the same. The Ute Indians of the nineteenth century living in the upper benches of the county traveled as far as the junction of the Lake Fork and Yellowstone rivers to obtain water. The fate of the Uinta Fremont remains unclear, but archaeologists agree that the Numic-speaking Shoshoni, Paiute, and Ute Indians inhabited the Great Basin and the Uinta Basin early in the fourteenth century, less than a century after the Fremont culture disappeared.[25]

The Shoshonean Stage

Anthropologists and others call the period from about A.D. 1300 (when the Fremont people disappeared and the Numic-speakers arrived) to about the year 1600 (the date European contact was made with the Indians of Utah and western Colorado) the Shoshonean era. These ancestors of the Shoshoni and Ute people abandoned the more

This stacked rock wall offered the Fremonts added protection from both the elements and enemies. (John D. Barton)

sedentary horticultural lifeways of the earlier Fremont Indians for that of hunting and gathering.[26] They lived in brush wickiups rather than the stone and masonry buildings of the Fremont people. The Indians spoke Numic languages and occupied a wide range of territory, from the Great Basin to the Uinta Basin and Colorado Plateau to the Front Range of the Rocky Mountains in Colorado, and from the Wind River Mountains of Wyoming to southern Utah, Colorado, and Nevada.[27]

Over time these Numic speakers settled in their respective locales known in historical time and were later identified by Anglo-Europeans as Northern and Southern Paiute tribes; Western, Northern, Eastern, and Western Shoshoni tribes; and Colorado and Utah Ute tribes. Still smaller bands or tribes were also noted, including the Timpanogots Utes of Utah Valley, the Uintah Utes of northern Utah and the Uinta Basin, the Sanpits and Moanunts of central Utah, the Pahvants of west-central Utah; and in Colorado, the

Parusanuch, Yampa, Sabuaganas, Tabeguache, Weeminuche, Muache, and Capote Ute bands.

Beginning around A.D. 1650 some of these Colorado and Utah Utes acquired the horse, and this and other interaction with Euro-Americans radically altered their lifestyles. Raiding between bands of Utes and Shoshoni Indians and jockeying for position for prime hunting and foraging territories was practiced and there was increased contact with Euro-Americans. The Uintah Utes of the Uinta Basin expanded their trade and hunting territory to reach the plains of Wyoming, the Front Range of Colorado, and the Spanish missions of northern New Mexico.

Euro-American Contact

The first historical contact of Euro-Americans with the Uintah Utes was made by the Domínguez-Escalante expedition, which traversed the Uinta Basin and parts of Utah in 1776. Catholic friar Francisco Atanasio Domínguez led the party and was assisted by Fray Silvestre Velez de Escalante. Because Escalante kept the journal of the expedition, his name has gained greater fame than that of Domínguez. The small party consisted of the two priests and eight other Spaniards, including Don Bernardo Miera y Pacheco, the cartographer, or mapmaker, for the expedition. The Domínguez-Escalante expedition planned to leave Santa Fe on 4 July but was delayed for several weeks, including one delay due to illness of Father Escalante. Later in July the expedition began its historical trek to Utah and the Great Basin.

The expedition's goals were to open a northern route from Santa Fe to newly settled Monterey, California, and to contact friendly Ute Indians along the way who might be ready for conversion to Christianity and Spanish ways of life. Other Spaniards had previously attempted to take a more direct route westward through Arizona, but deserts and hostile Indians made the Arizona route difficult and hazardous at best. The expedition members also explored northwest from Santa Fe into southwestern Colorado and southeastern Utah. Earlier, in 1765, an enterprising Spanish trader or military reconnaissance man, Juan Maria de Rivera, had led a small group to southwestern Colorado and southeastern Utah. With the exception of the

Rivera expedition, no other possible pre-Domínguez-Escalante expedition to southern Utah left known written records.

The Domínguez-Escalante expedition left Santa Fe and traveled north through southwestern Colorado, following streams and rivers. The expedition eventually found its way to the Gunnison River. After becoming lost and discouraged, they encountered a friendly Ute encampment. Here they acquired the services of two Ute boys, whom the padres called Silvestre and Joaquin. These youths agreed to guide them to Utah Lake and the home of the Laguna (Uintah) Utes.[28]

By 16 September the expedition had crossed the Rio de San Buenaventura (Green River) near the present-day town of Jensen, Utah. It is interesting to note that they killed buffalo in both the Colorado and Utah portions of the Uinta Basin.[29] After crossing the Green River, the party journeyed up the Duchesne River, traveling in a westerly direction. The padres noted that the Indian boy Silvestre exhibited great fear while in the region after seeing tracks of other horses and smoke from nearby fires. Silvestre informed the padres that enemy Indians, "Comanches" as Escalante called them, were in the area. The "Comanches" were most likely a small group of Shoshoni hunters who frequented the Uinta Basin from southern Wyoming or southeastern Idaho. Farther west in today's Duchesne County the expedition witnessed more smoke. Silvestre was less fearful of these wisps of smoke, believing the people in the area were either "Comanches or some Lagunas who usually came hunting hereabouts."[30]

Information is thus gained from the Domínguez-Escalante expedition that the Uinta Basin in 1776 was utilized by both Ute and Shoshoni Indians and that there was hostility between the two tribes. Hostility between the two tribes was probably a result of competition for hunting grounds, including those of the Uinta Basin.

Near the confluence of the Duchesne and Uinta rivers the Catholic friars wrote that they "saw ruins . . . of a very ancient pueblo where there were fragments of stones for grinding maize, of jars, and pots of clay. The pueblo's shape was circular . . . "[31] Modern researchers of the Domínguez-Escalante Trail have been unable to locate this ancient pueblo, which was most likely located near the Duchesne-Uintah county line. On 17 September 1776 the expedition camped about twenty miles east of Myton, calling the campsite La Ribera de San Cosme. The next day, they traveled west to the junction of the Strawberry and Duchesne rivers (called by them Rio de Santa Catarina, de Sena, and Rio de San Cosme) and camped for the night in a meadow about a mile above the present-day town of Duchesne. Reporting on the land seen that day, Escalante wrote: "There is good land along these three rivers [the Strawberry, Lake Fork, and the Duchesne] that we crossed today, and plenty of it for farming with the aid of irrigation—beautiful poplar groves, fine pastures, timber and firewood not too far away, for three good settlements."[32] Following the Strawberry River upstream, they camped the next night, 19 September, near present Fruitland, and the next day crossed Current Creek and continued their journey westward. When the expedition reached the Strawberry Valley, approximately where Strawberry and Soldier Creek reservoirs are now located, Silvestre informed the padres that some of his people had lived there earlier, but had withdrawn out of fear of the "Comanches."[33]

The expedition left the future Duchesne County, traveled through Strawberry Valley, descended Diamond Fork to the Spanish Fork River and entered Utah Valley on 23 September 1776. There the expedition members found the Utes very friendly and, after visiting for several days, the padres promised to return the next year to build a settlement. Utah history would likely have been different had the padres returned. Catholic missions rather than Mormon chapels might have dotted Utah's landscape. Also, if Brigham Young had received this report of the area, perhaps Duchesne County's history would read very differently today and the area may never have become part of the Ute Indian Reservation.

Anxious to reach the Spanish settlements in California, the Domínguez-Escalante expedition members left Utah Valley heading south rather than west. The Laguna Utes informed Domínguez and Escalante about the desert to the west and that crossing it would be very difficult. After a few days travel, near present-day Milford snow and cold weather settled on the expedition. Discouraged and tired, they drew lots to determine God's will they then returned to Santa Fe, enduring numerous hardships along the long way home. The expedition was not successful in finding a new route to California, but it did provide those who followed with important information and also was the first documentation of Europeans visiting Duchesne County. Along with the first map of the region, they left a valuable record of the geography and inhabitants of the region they traversed.

Years later, following the Domínguez-Escalante expedition to Utah, it is likely that other Spanish expeditions followed segments of the Domínguez-Escalante Trail and discovered other Indian trails through Utah. Various segments of the Domínguez-Escalante Trail became branches of the Old Spanish Trail linking Santa Fe with California through Utah.[34] Legends of Spanish mines buttress the likelihood that other Spanish exploring parties came to the Uinta Basin and Duchesne County before the 1820s when Mexican, English, French, and American fur traders began trapping and trading for beaver.

Local stories tell of the Spanish discovering gold and forcing the Indians to work mines in the Uinta Basin. According to several legends of the Utes, the oppressed workers eventually rebelled and killed all the Spaniards. This local lore is bolstered by claimed discoveries of cannonballs, bridle bits, old diggings, rock smelters, rusted Spanish helmets and breastplates, and tree and rock inscriptions. However, no scholarly confirmation from written records or studies of extant Spanish artifacts and presumably Spanish diggings and smelter works has yet confirmed the local lore of Spanish presence and their development of gold mines. Like much of the lore of the Spanish in the West, Duchesne County has tales of lost treasure and gold which, if found, would make the discoverer fabulously rich. The continued life of these stories of gold and lost Spanish mines makes for lively conversations at summer campfires and at family dinner tables.[35]

Closely related to lost Spanish gold mines is the county's most famous gold story—the Lost Rhoades Mines. A common version of the story tells of Ute chief Wakara (Walker), who went to Brigham Young not long after the Mormons arrived in Salt Lake Valley. Wakara, according to the legend, had been chosen by right of succession guardian of gold mines located in the Uinta Mountains. These gold mines had been made sacred by the forced labor and sacrifice there of past generations of Ute Indians. In some of the accounts the Spanish treatment of Utes was so brutal that the Utes revolted and drove the Spanish back to New Mexico. After some time, perhaps generations, the Spanish came back and again forced the Utes to work the mines. This led to another revolt near Rock Creek sometime in the mid-1800s. As the story goes, all the Spaniards were killed and the mine entrances buried.[36]

Wakara supposedly was told in a dream that when the big hats (Americans) came he was to tell them of the gold. The first Americans in the region, the mountain men, would not listen to him. When he told Brigham Young, Young agreed that only one man would be chosen to go and get the gold, which was so pure that smelting was not necessary. Knowledge of the gold's existence and location was to be a secret. Thomas Rhoades was selected to get the gold. The gold was only to be used by the Mormon church and not to profit any individual, and the Ute chief warned that Rhoades would be watched while in the mountains and no other would be allowed to come. If any others tried to do so they would be killed.

After a few years, Thomas Rhoades passed the responsibility to his son Caleb, and, with the death of Wakara in 1855, his brother Aropene assumed leadership and responsibility for watching the mines.

As the stories go, gold from the Rhoades mines was used by the Mormon church to mint its gold coins and to plate the statue of the angel Moroni atop the LDS temple in Salt Lake City. Although no known records exist in church archives, Brigham Young supposedly promised Wakara and Aropene, in the name of the Lord, that the gold would not be discovered by anyone and would be kept secret until the "last days," when it would come forth to benefit the Mormon church and the Utes in a time of great need. Many of the folktales on the subject contain warnings of supernatural power and heavenly intervention preventing anyone from finding the gold stores and mines. Other stories tell of people who have found one of the several mines and were suddenly stricken with heart attacks or other ailments, or were warned by ghostly Ute warriors to leave and never return.

The truth of these stories will possibly never be determined, but many people in Duchesne County believe them, and they are retold by each new generation of county residents. Regardless of the veracity of the stories, hundreds of people each year go to Rock Creek and other locations in the Uinta Mountains in search of the gold and the lost mines. To date no significant finds of gold have been discovered; but, of course, if the stories are true, that is to be expected. Thus the legends of the Lost Rhoades Mines are passed down, and many of those who believe the stories will not look for the gold, believing it will not be found until the hand of providence directs; others believe the parts of the stories about the gold's existence and seek for the mines and hidden caches hoping they can find and keep the gold for themselves regardless of the legends' warnings. Despite the absence of corroborative evidence of Spanish mining in Duchesne County, accounts of the lost mines continue to be a part of Uinta Basin folklore.[37]

The Mountain Men

Following the Domínguez-Escalante expedition of 1776, the next documented visitors to the Uinta Basin were Euro-American mountain men and fur traders, beginning in the 1820s. European men's fashion of the time demanded a supply of beaver to make felt hats. The American fur industry and the American West provided the beaver pelts. The economic profit to be gained from the export of American beaver was an important element in America's interest in the American West.

After the famous Lewis and Clark expedition of 1804–06 that explored to the Pacific Northwest coast lands of the Louisiana Purchase, American fur trappers and traders, in search of furbearing animals, extended their search into the upper Missouri River country of Montana and the central Rocky Mountains of Wyoming, Utah, and Colorado. Included in their search for beaver was the area of the Uinta Basin.

American fur traders adopted the earlier French trading system, establishing forts or trading posts to exchange goods for furs and pelts brought in by Indian fur trappers. Fur trading posts were located on navigable waterways, which were used to transport the furs, trade items, and supplies inexpensively. The lack of navigable waterways in the central Rocky Mountains and in the Intermountain West, however, soon forced the American fur traders to adopt a different system of doing business with the Indian trappers and growing numbers of white trappers. An organizer of this new fur-trading system was St. Louis fur entrepreneur William H. Ashley and his partner Andrew Henry.

Ashley hired white trappers and organized annual rendezvous at various locations in the central Rockies, including southwestern Wyoming and Bear Lake Valley. The now-famous rendezvous was where supplies for the next season were brought in on horses and mules, allowing the trappers to remain in the mountains. Furs and supplies were exchanged and paid for and mountain men and Indians congregated socially. The rendezvous quickly became times of relaxation and celebration, with liquor and high spirits both in great abundance. The annual rendezvous occurred at various locations in the Mountain West between the mid-1820s and the early 1840s when the beaver trade was at its zenith.

It was during the decades of the 1820s and 1830s that the mountain men discovered and explored many nooks and crannies in the American West and became more familiar with secluded locations, including the Uinta Basin. The fur trade in the Uinta Basin was an important chapter in the larger economic story of the fur trade, and at least one trading post was established near the Whiterocks River in future Uintah County.

It is likely that some French-Canadian fur trappers entered the area that would become Duchesne County even before the 1820s, perhaps as early as 1818. In 1970 archaeologist Polly Shaafsma, conducting a study of Indian rock art in Nine Mile Canyon, discovered the inscription "J.F. 1818" near the Nutter Ranch. She contacted the Nutter family regarding her discovery and reported her discussion with the Nutters: "According to the Nutters, this is the date when the first French trappers appeared in the area, and the carvings might well be authentic. The initials are also done in a style that could date from the early 19th Century."[38] To date, no other historical documentation or information about the 1818 rock inscription has been found, however.

Documented records in 1824 reveal that three different expeditions from Santa Fe, led by William Huddard, Antoine Robidoux, and Etienne Provost, were in the Green River country of eastern Utah

Antoine Robidoux, the most significant fur trader in the Uinta Basin, operated a fur trade post in the eastern portion of the Uinta Basin until 1844.
(Palace of the Governors, Santa Fe, New Mexico)

trapping beaver. Of the three, certainly Provost, and possibly the others, found his way into the county. Provost's small party traversed the county following nearly the same route Domínguez and Escalante had followed forty-eight years earlier. Provost reached Utah Valley from the Uinta Basin by a more circuitous route, however. From the Strawberry Valley Provost traveled north to the Weber River and then down to the Ogden area before turning south to Utah Valley.

In Utah Valley they were met by a band of Shoshoni Indians led by Chief Bad Gocha or "Bad Left-Handed One." Believing they were on friendly and peaceful terms with the Shoshoni, Provost and his men met with Bad Gocha and his band of Shoshoni; however, the Indians attacked the small party of fur trappers, killing six or seven of Provost's trappers. Provost and three or four others managed to escape with their lives.[39]

Traveling by way of either Provo Canyon or Spanish Fork Canyon, Provost and the other survivors made their return to the Uinta Basin by way of Strawberry Valley before moving on to the Green River, where they found refuge among some friendly Ute Indians. Later, during the winter of 1824–25, Francois LeClerc, Provost's trading partner from Taos, New Mexico, along with additional men and supplies, joined Provost and the survivors at their winter encampment.[40]

The following spring Provost left the friendly confines of the Uinta Basin and returned to the Great Basin by way of the Weber River to trade for fur with the more friendly Utes. Following his brief sojourn there, Provost made his way back to the Uinta Basin by way of Weber Canyon. Near present-day Mountain Green in Morgan County, on 6 June 1825 Provost and his trappers met a company of British trappers under the leadership of Peter Skene Ogden. Ogden had been ordered by his employer, the British Hudson's Bay Company, to trap out the beaver in the upper Snake River country, thereby creating a territory void of beaver. This plan, it was hoped, would discourage Americans from further activities in the disputed Oregon country, which both America and Britain wanted to possess as their own.

Later that day, Provost's and Ogden's companies encountered a third, but smaller, group of American fur trappers employed by

William Henry Ashley and led by Johnson Gardner. Gardner pro-voked Ogden to anger when he argued that Ogden and his company of British fur trappers were illegally in American territory.[41] Gardner was wrong, however, in his argument with Ogden and his under-standing of the territory. All of them were actually in Mexican terri-tory. Territory south of the present Utah-Idaho border did not become part of the United States until after the Mexican War.

The following day, 7 June, Provost and his men, while returning to the Uinta Basin, met the American fur trader William H. Ashley somewhere in present-day western Duchesne County. Ashley had come from St. Louis following the Platte River across Nebraska to southwestern Wyoming and northeastern Utah for the purpose of resupplying his company of fur trappers headed by Jedediah Strong Smith. Ashley planned to meet Smith and his party of trappers on Henry's Fork of the Green River on the north slope of the Uintas for the first of many rendezvous in the Intermountain West.[42]

Before the rendezvous, Ashley intended to explore the country south of the Uinta Mountains for beaver. By mid-April 1825, Ashley and his companions had arrived on the Green River and set about building several "bull boats" made of buffalo hide stretched over wil-lows to float down the Green River. A month later, Ashley had entered the valley that now bears his name.

Deciding not to go any farther down the often wild river, Ashley cached some of his supplies and traded for some horses with some Utes, whom Ashley described as being well clothed in "sheep skin & Buffalloe robes superior to any band of Indians in my knowledge west of Council Bluffs." Some of the Ute Indians also were "well armed with English fuseeze" guns.[43] The Uintah Utes, a band of Northern Utes, most likely had occupied the Uinta Basin sometime after the departure of the Domínguez-Escalante expedition and before extensive contact was made with the fur traders and trappers. Many of the Utes, including the Uintah Ute band, had acquired the horse and become expert horsemen. The Utes' acquisition of horses and guns from Spanish and later Mexican traders gave the Native Americans more power to deal with their neighbors the Shoshoni, to take advantage of the unmounted Goshutes and other bands and tribes, and to expand their trade activities. Ashley noted some of the

Utes were adorned with seashells, which suggests an extensive trade system among Native Americans.[44]

Now mounted, Ashley and his men traveled west, following the Duchesne River, which Ashley called the "Euwinty" River. Shortly after entering Duchesne County, Ashley sent out hunters to replenish the company's dwindling supply of meat. The hunters were successful, and the company's meat supply was momentarily well stocked.

Ashley, like some other fur trappers and explorers, kept notes of the country through which he traveled. His observations of the Uinta Basin ranged from "barren rocky land" to land along the Duchesne River bottoms that was described as "wooded with Willow & Cotton wood." The river itself was said to be "about 150 yds Wide [with] rapped current."[45] Several days' travel west of Myton on the Strawberry River, near present-day Fruitland, Ashley met Provost and his party of twelve men, who were returning from the Weber River and their encounter with Peter Skene Ogden.

Ashley prevailed upon Provost, who had pack animals, to take one of his men and return to Ashley Valley to retrieve the goods Ashley had cached there. Ashley and the rest of his men waited at Red Creek for Provost's return. Not wasting time, Ashley and some of his men trapped three beaver and caught between fifteen and twenty fish. Beaver trapping in the area was poor, however, and not to the liking of Ashley. Earlier, Ashley had written: "no game was killed to day, my party begins to feel severely the want of food . . . this Country continues almost entirely destitute of game."[46]

When Provost returned, the combined parties continued their journey northwest to the Strawberry Valley. Ashley wrote of the valley: "we traveled over a beautiful fertile valley last Evening through which runs a great number of small streams."[47] Crossing the valley, they turned north and traveled across the Kamas Valley. They then continued north and east by way of Chalk Creek to Henry's Fork of the Green River, where the first rendezvous was held.

The activities of Provost and Ashley in 1825 were the beginnings of a regular fur-trading business in the Uinta Basin. However, interest in the Uinta Basin also came from another direction and from another country. By the mid-1820s Santa Fe and Taos in New Mexico were becoming important commercial towns for trade between the Mexicans and Americans using the Santa Fe Trail. Part of this bustling trade included American and French-Canadian fur trappers and traders operating under Mexican authority. However, there were occasions in the 1820s when their relations with Mexican authorities became strained.

Francois Robidoux, a French-Canadian, and Sylvestre Pratte, an American trapper, and their men were particularly active trapping and trading for fur in northern Utah in the mid-1820s. They were also caught in political turmoil with Mexican government officials in Taos and for a brief time had the beaver pelts they had trapped in northern Utah confiscated; however, the beaver was later returned to them.

Both Robidoux and Pratte had met with some success in northern Utah, although, only a few years earlier, William Ashley had found the number of beaver there to his disliking. In 1827, Antoine Robidoux, brother of Francois, along with a small party of trappers, returned to Ute country to retrieve a cache of beaver pelts they had trapped earlier. Sylvestre Pratte also sent a small group back to the "outside of the boundaries of the Mexican Federation" to retrieve a stash of beaver trapped the previous year.[48] Included in this group of twenty-two mostly French-Canadian trappers was Ceran St. Vrain. The exact destinations of these two companies are unclear; however, it seems likely that one or both groups of trappers made its way to the Uinta Basin.

A rich legacy of lore, skill, geographical knowledge, and place-names was left by the hearty fur trappers. The name Duchesne, for example, given to various cultural and natural elements of the Uinta Basin, may have been left by trappers working for Pratte and St. Vrain. A French-Canadian, one Duchaine, was one of the twenty-two trappers who were dispatched by Pratte in January 1827 to trap beaver on the northern frontier of the Mexican empire. David Weber, noted Western historian, suggests that the Duchesne River was named for Duchaine and that the spelling evolved over time from Duchaine to Duchesne.[49]

Another possibility for the name's origin was that a French-Canadian trapper by the name of Duchesne reportedly was a member of Etienne Provost's fur trapping party. A very likely explanation, however, is that the name is in honor of a Catholic nun, Mother Rose Philippine Duchesne, who had come to St. Louis from France to work with the Indians in the West. Mother Duchesne was highly respected for her work in founding several schools on the frontier near St. Louis. She was well known to several trappers and traders, including William Ashley and Antoine Robidoux, and it is likely that someone from one of their parties named the Duchesne River in her honor.

Some confusion over geographical locations and names is a result of poor, inaccurate early maps. For example, in 1861 President Abraham Lincoln set aside much of the western section of the Uinta Basin for an Indian reservation. Government officials at that time incorrectly identified the Duchesne River as the Uinta River. By the 1870s and 1880s the name Duchesne was used more frequently. Later, other places in the Uinta Basin incorporated the name Duchesne— including Fort Duchesne, the town of Duchesne, and the future county.[50]

Other important fur trappers, government explorers, overland travelers, and Indians visited the Uinta Basin in the 1830s and 1840s. In 1834 Warren A. Ferris, while employed by the British Hudson's Bay Company, spent several weeks in the Uinta Basin trapping and hunting. Ferris avoided camping near Fort Robidoux and instead made a temporary encampment on benchland that was likely near present-day Altonah. Ferris wrote:

> Our camp presented eight earthen lodges, and two constructed of poles with cane grass, which grows in dense patches to the height of eight of ten feet, along the river [Lake Fork?]. . . . Our little village numbers 22 men, nine women and 20 children; and a different language is spoken in every lodge . . . though French was the language predominant among the men, and Flat-head among the women . . . [51]

Ferris noted the basin's streams and abundant game but strangely neglected to mention Antoine Robidioux's trading post on the Whiterocks River. Although he was favorably impressed with the area, Ferris did not remain long, nor did he ever return to the Uinta Basin.[52]

The Reed Trading Post and Fort Uintah

The Uinta Basin became an important crossroads for fur trappers, traders, and overland travelers. To take advantage of the growing
fur trading and trapping activities of northeastern Utah, Kentuckian
William Reed, his nephew James (Jimmy) Reed, and Denis Julien
established the Reed Trading Post in 1828 near the confluence of the
Whiterocks and Uinta rivers. The Reeds operated the post until 1832,
when Antoine Robidoux purchased the business and location from
them.[53] The Reed's enterprise was the first fixed Euro-American economic enterprise in the Uinta Basin and in Utah. Other trading posts
and permanent outposts were later established in Browns Hole and
on the Ogden River near present-day Ogden.

After buying out Reed, Robidoux expanded the fur-trading business, keeping an average of twenty trappers employed at the fort.
Robidoux was a prominent trader and entrepreneur who operated
his fur-trading business from his headquarters in New Mexico. For
the next twenty-two years he dominated trading activities in northeastern Utah and northwestern Colorado. Numerous fur trappers,
overland travelers, and Indians from far distances visited Robidoux's
trading post.

The relationship between the Ute Indians living in the Uinta
Basin and the Mexican, American, British, and French-Canadian
newcomers was for a time cordial if not friendly. However, as the
whites' presence expanded disputations occurred from time to time
between the Ute people and their new neighbors. On one occasion,
a California Indian, probably on a trading expedition to the Green
River country, was believed to have stolen one of Robidoux's prized
horses. Robidioux asked another visitor, Christopher "Kit" Carson, to
track down and retrieve the stolen horse. Carson and his partner
Stephen Louis Lee had journeyed to Ashley Valley to trade with the
Utes but had found that Robidoux had already acquired the bulk of
furs trapped that season.

Carson agreed to help find the missing horse. The tracks of the
horse and its apparent thief headed west. After two days of tracking
the horse and the California Indian, Carson located the missing horse

and its new owner in what was likely eastern Duchesne County. A fight ensued and Carson killed the Indian.[54]

During its existence, several important visitors visited Robidoux's trading post. Several months before Robidoux finally was forced to abandon the Uinta Basin in 1844, topographical engineer and U.S. Army captain John C. Frémont and his expedition paid a brief visit to the Uinta Basin. A year earlier, Frémont and a thirty-man expedition, which included guides Thomas Fitzpatrick and Kit Carson and cartographer Charles Preuss, were ordered west to conduct further surveys of the western interior. Frémont's journey of 1843–44 took him to the big bend of the Bear River near Soda Springs and south to the Great Salt Lake, where he rafted out to Fremont Island before continuing his journey west to California. Frémont returned to Utah on his way east from California, following segments of the Old Spanish Trail and the Domínguez-Escalante Trail. Upon his arrival at Utah Lake, Frémont continued east, backtracking the Domínguez-Escalante Trail to the Uinta Basin.

By 30 May 1844 Frémont had reached the Strawberry River, which he called the Red River. He was impressed with the country, describing the mountain passes and high country as "extremely rugged" land that provided the Ute people with security from "the intrusion of their enemies."[55] Frémont and his expedition generally followed the course of the Duchesne River eastward.

Frémont found the banks of the Duchesne River thick "with fine grass" and the river running clear. During the course of several days travel Frémont's expedition had to ford the Duchesne River several times. He found the river to be unpredictable. One day the expedition forded the Duchesne River "without any difficulty"; however, when forced to ford the river twice the following day, Frémont found the river had risen from the previous day's melt of mountain snow to the point that "it was almost everywhere too deep to be forded."[56]

Leaving the Duchesne River, Frémont turned to the Uinta Mountains and Robidoux's trading post. Before reaching the trading post, Frémont encountered yet another swiftly flowing stream, which earlier trappers called Lake Fork. Frémont wrote that, according to the Ute Indians, the Indian name for Lake Fork meant "great swiftness"; it was similar in meaning to the description of the speed of a racehorse.[57] The river was too swift and too deep in some places to be forded in safety, and it was with great difficulty that the expedition successfully forded Lake Fork.

By the afternoon of 3 June Frémont reached Robidoux's trading post. He described Robidoux's trappers living there as a "motley collection of Canadian and Mexican engages and hunters, with the usual number of Indian women."[58] Frémont was able to replenish his dwindling supply of coffee, sugar, and dry meat at the trading post. Frémont also hired Auguste Archambeau at the trading post to guide him eastward. Frémont described Archambeau as "an excellent voyageur and hunter, belonging to the class of Carson and Godey."[59] By 7 June, Frémont had reached Browns Hole, well known to many trappers of the region.

A few months later Robidoux was forced to abandon his outpost permanently. Continued difficulties with whites at the trading post mounted as others came to challenge or trade with the Ute Indians and with Robidoux. Robidoux was able to keep an upper hand in the region's highly competitive fur trade until 1844, at which time the Ute Indians had reached a breaking point. They attacked and burnt Robidoux's fort late in the year, forcing Robidoux permanently to abandon his trading post on the Whiterocks River.[60] The fort was either burnt by the attacking Ute Indians or was later set afire by Jim Baker, possibly an employee of Robidoux, to prevent renewed competition for beaver.[61] Other factors contributing to the attack included the sale of whiskey to the Indians, the cheating of them on the price of furs, and the kidnapping of Indian women into slavery and prostitution. This was perhaps the most successful attack by Indians of a fur-trading post during the era of the North American fur trade.[62]

With the expulsion of Robidoux, the Utes regained sole possession of the Uinta Basin, and the land remained unsettled by whites until the early 1870s when independent Mormon farmers and a handful of others began to trickle into Ashley Valley to farm and ranch. For nearly twenty years following the settlement of the Great Basin by Mormon colonizers, the Uinta Basin remained virtualy isolated and unwanted by whites. Exploring parties to the Uinta Basin in 1852 and in 1861 indicated that the Uinta Basin was less than desirable to colonize. Early in 1852 Mormon Indian interpreter, scout, and explorer

George Washington Bean, accompanied by Stephen B. Rose, Fayette Granger, Farley Granger, Bill Hendricks, and a Ute named Kihuanuts, explored the Uinta Basin. Discouraged by the inaccessibility of the basin, Bean wrote a mixed review on 29 February 1852 of the possibilities for settlement: "In the evening all agreed that the finest timber was here but not much land in a body suitable for cultivation. Water privileges were Excellent: Game plenty as deer antelope rabbits & sagehens."[63] This evaluation was echoed nearly a decade later when the second exploring party found the land undesirable and suited only for Indians and to hold the world together.

Real interest in the Uinta Basin came from Utah territorial and federal government Indian officials following the negative report Brigham Young received in 1861, however. Since the Walker War (1853–54) and the later Tintic War (1856) in Juab and Millard counties, Indian policies in the new territory were not working to the full satisfaction of either the Ute people or the Mormon settlers. In the minds of territorial officials removal of the Utes from the Great Basin appeared to be the best solution. The 1861 report confirmed the idea that the territory west of Ashley Valley was a suitable a place to relocate the Ute Indians away from Mormon settlements in western Utah. Later it was also favored as an abode for "troublesome" Ute Indians living in western Colorado when white settlers there wanted Ute lands.

The establishment of the Uintah Valley Indian Reservation in 1864 combined with the geographical barriers that isolated the western portion of the Uinta Basin to hinder its settlement and development by whites until the turn of the twentieth century.

ENDNOTES

1. Kings Peak was named after Clarence King, early director of the U.S. Geological Survey. See John W. Van Cott, *Utah Place Names* (Salt Lake City: University of Utah Press, 1990), 214. For further discussion of the geology of the Uinta Basin and Mountains see G.E. Untermann and B.R. Untermann, *Geology of Uintah County* (Salt Lake City: Utah Geological and Mineralogical Survey, June 1964), and William Lee Stokes, *Geology of Utah* (Salt Lake City: Utah Museum of Natural History/Utah Geological and Mineral Survey, 1986).

2. Donna Barton, compiler, *Memoirs of the Once Silent Uintah Mountains* (Roosevelt, UT: Altamont High School, 1996), 81, 84, 85. This book is a collection of local folk tales.

3. Charles S. Peterson, *Utah: A History* (New York: W.W. Norton & Company, 1976), chapter 8.

4. Many Duchesne County residents are unaware that nearly half of the Uinta Basin is located in Colorado. With the eastern rim of the basin formed by the Rocky Mountains, Steamboat Springs, Meeker, and surrounding areas actually are part of the Uinta Basin.

5. Herbert E. Bolton, *Pageant in the Wilderness: The Story of the Escalante Expedition to the Interior Basin, 1776* (Salt Lake City: Utah State Historical Society, 1972), 173.

6. Ibid., 173–74.

7. Some animals that were found in the Uinta Basin during its early history but were absent for several decades, such as mountain sheep, goats, and river otters, have been reintroduced into the region in recent years by wildlife officials.

8. Bolton, *Pageant in the Wilderness,* 175.

9. R. Clayton Brough, Dale L. Jones, Dale J. Stevens, *Utah's Comprehensive Weather Almanac* (Salt Lake City: n.p., 1987), 275, 323, 344, 356, 396, 400, 403, 407, 428.

10. Ibid., 20.

11. The Soil Conservation Service and the Central Utah Project based their determination for the need of irrigation and the potential impact this would have on Duchesne County farming on these averages. See United States Department of Agriculture and the Soil Conservation Service, "Final Environmental Impact Statement: Uintah Basin Unit Expansion," December 1991.

12. Brough, *Utah's Weather Almanac,* 428.

13. Ibid., 175, 199, 208.

14. Ibid., 323.

15. Jerry D. Spangler, *Paradigms & Perspectives: A Class I Overview of Cultural Resources in the Uinta Basin and Tavaputs Plateau* (Salt Lake City: Bureau of Land Management, 1995), 453.

16. Jesse D. Jennings, *Prehistory of Utah: The Eastern Great Basin,* University of Utah Anthropological Papers, No. 98 (Salt Lake City: University of Utah Press, 1978), 155, 162.

17. Spangler, *Paradigms & Perspecitves,* 473.

18. Ibid.

19. Ibid., 474–76.

20. Ibid., 472–73.

21. Lester Maxfield, an old-time resident of Altonah who came with his family into the county to settle, claimed that some of the canals in Altonah and Talmage were already in place and only needed cleaning out and headgates installed to be serviceable to modern farmers.

22. Spangler, *Paradigms & Perspectives,* 501. Several such towers are found in Nine Mile Canyon, and other stone towers are found elsewhere in Duchesne County.

23. Ibid., 599–602. See also *Handbook of North American Indians,* Warren L. D'Azevedo, ed., vol. 11, William C. Sturtevant, *Great Basin* (Washington, D.C.: Smithsonian, 1986), 171.

24. Spangler, *Paradigms & Perspectives,* 599–602.

25. James H. Gunnerson, *The Fremont Culture* (Cambridge, MA: Peabody Museum, 1969), 182–84. See also Barnes and Pendleton, *Prehistoric Indians,* 87; Jennings, *Prehistory,* 235; Sturtevant, *Great Basin,* 171–72.

26. Spangler, *Paradigms & Perspectives,* 600.

27. Ibid., 599.

28. Bolton, *Pageant in the Wilderness,* 41, 43.

29. Ted J. Warner, ed., *The Dominguez-Escalante Journal* (Provo: Brigham Young University Press, 1976), 42, 44. Neither the mountain men in the area nor the early settlers of the Uinta Basin mention seeing buffalo in the region; what few there were probably having been hunted out between 1776 and the 1820s.

30. Warner, *Dominguez-Escalante Journal,* 47. Escalante's use of "Comanche" is not entirely incorrect. The Comanche and Shoshoni tribes had the same origins. Comanches were descendants of Shoshoni who had left the mountains of Wyoming and migrated to the Texas plains. See Arrel Morgan Gibson, *The American Indian; Prehistory to Present* (Norman: University of Oklahoma Press, 1980), 78.

31. Warner, *Dominguez-Escalante Journal,* 47.

32. Ibid., 48.

33. Bolton, *Pageant in the Wilderness,* 62.

34. See LeRoy R. Hafen and Ann W. Hafen, *Old Spanish Trail* (Glendale, CA: Arthur Clark Company, 1954).

35. For more information on Spanish mining and Indian legends on the subject see Gale R. Rhoades and Kerry Ross Boren, *Footprints in the Wilderness; A History of the Lost Rhoades Mines* (Salt Lake City: Dream Garden Press, 1980). See also Gale R. Rhoades, *Lost Gold in the Uintah: The Rest of the Story* (Duchesne: Benziol Oil, 1995). Neither of these books are

considered by historians credible sources; however, they contain the most complete details of the many stories and folk tales of the lost Rhoades mines and other stories of gold finds in the Uinta Mountains.

36. Gale R. Rhoades, "Lost Gold of the Uintahs," *Western Treasures* 3, no. 4: 14–19.

37. Ibid. Local lore of Spanish miners being in the Uinta Basin in the mid-1800s has little historical possibility. In 1821 the people of Mexico revolted against Spain in their own war of independence. A decade later the young Mexican nation faced a series of diplomatic disputations and wars with Americans, first with Texans and later with the United States in the Mexican War, in which 500 Mormon soldiers participated. Neither Spanish nor Mexican mining entrepreneurs were in favorable positions to mine gold in the Uinta Basin and to use Indian labor.

38. See Spangler, *Paradigms and Perspectives,* 785.

39. Warren A. Ferris, *Life in the Rocky Mountains* (Denver: Old West Publishing Company, 1968), 134. The sources differ on the number of survivors of this attack; some say three or four survived, while others claim only Provost and one other escaped the treachery of Gocha. See Dale Morgan, *Jedediah Smith and the Opening of the West* (Lincoln: University of Nebraska Press, 1953), 149; and David Weber, *The Taos Trappers* (Norman: University of Oklahoma Press, 1968), 76.

40. For details on Provost's activities in Utah see LeRoy R. Hafen, "Etienne Provost," *Utah Historical Quarterly* 36 (March 1968): 99–112.

41. Dale M. Morgan, *The West of William Ashley* (Denver: Old West Publishing Company, 1964), 115, 116. With the Treaty of Ghent that ended the War of 1812, the United States entered a joint occupancy agreement of the Pacific Northwest with Great Britain. The Hudsons' Bay Company was operating out of the Columbia River region and trying to keep Americans from pushing any farther west from St. Louis. The British recognized that in the 1820s fur traders were the only Americans who were going westward to challenge the British for possession of the Northwest. To try and stem the tide of American traders pushing farther west, the Hudson's Bay Company had issued a policy called "Beaver Desert." Hudson's Bay trappers were to try and trap and trade for every beaver in the Rocky Mountains, creating a situation where the American traders would have no reason to continue westward. As impossible as it seems to create a "beaver desert," the task was virtually completed by the early 1840s. So intense was the competition between countries and companies involved in the fur trade that beaver were nearly trapped to extinction; only in the last decades have they made a significant comeback.

42. For additional information about the rendezvous see Fred R. Gowans, *Rocky Mountain Rendezvous* (Layton, UT: Peregrine Smith, 1985).

43. Morgan, *The West of William H. Ashley,* 114.

44. Ibid., 115 n. 171.

45. Ibid., 116.

46. Ibid., 115.

47. Ibid., 116.

48. Weber, *The Taos Trappers,* 109.

49. Ibid., 110.

50. For various sources dealing with the possible origins of the Duchesne River's name see Cecil J. Alter, "W.A. Ferris in Utah 1830–1835," *Utah Historical Quarterly* 9 (1941): 81–108; and Morgan, *The West of William Ashley,* 280 n. 160.

51. Quoted in Alter, "W.A. Ferris in Utah," 102.

52. See Alter, "W.A. Ferris in Utah," 81–108; and Ferris, *Life in the Rocky Mountains.*

53. John D. Barton, "Fort Uintah and the Reed Trading Post," *Montana Magazine of Western History* 43 (Winter 1993): 50–57. See also Julius Orn Murray, interview with John D. Barton, 3 October 1988, Alteria, Utah, transcript in possession of author.

54. Milo Milton Quaife, ed., *Kit Carson's Autobiography* (Chicago: R.R. Donelly and Sons, 1935), 34, 35.

55. Donald Jackson and Mary Lee Spence, eds., *The Expeditions of John Charles Fremont, Travels from 1838 to 1844* (Urbana: University of Illinois Press, 1970), 1:704.

56. Ibid., 705.

57. Ibid.

58. John C. Fremont, *Narrative of the Exploring Expedition to the Rocky Mountains* (London: Wiley & Putnam, 1846), 305.

59. Jackson and Spence, *Expeditions of John Charles Fremont,* 706.

60. John D. Barton, "Antoine Robidoux—Buckskin Entrepreneur," *Outlaw Trail Journal* 3 (Summer/Fall 1993): 35–40. See also the *Missouri Democrat,* 17 September 1845; and the *St. Louis Republican,* 6 March 1845. Both newspapers contain articles detailing the attack and burning of Robidoux's forts.

61. Jackson and Spence, *Expeditions of John Charles Fremont,* 706 n. 177.

62. Barton, "Antoine Robidoux," 35–40.

63. George W. Bean, Diary 3, p. 4, transcript at Utah State Historical Society Library, Salt Lake City.

CHAPTER 2

UTE LANDS
AND PEOPLE

Early Ute History

The Ute people traditionally have claimed large portions of the states of Utah and Colorado as their native homeland. The Utes' territorial claim by the middle of the sixteenth century included the territory west of the Front Range of the Rocky Mountains in Colorado to the territory surrounding Utah and Sevier lakes in present-day Utah. The northern boundary of Ute territory was at about the Wyoming border and the southern boundary in Colorado was in the region of the New Mexico border. From the Four Corners region, the southern boundary of Ute territory in Utah extended northwest to Sevier Lake. In this two-state region, the Ute people occupied as diversified a geographical region as any Indian tribe in North America.

The larger Ute tribe was divided into smaller tribes, bands, and family groupings in the two-state region. Adaptation to various regions and the natural resources there led to different lifestyles of many Ute bands. Europeans were quick to recognize differences of the various bands of Utes. Catholic priests Domínguez and Escalante, for example, called the Ute Indians living around Utah Lake Timpanogotzis, or Fish Eaters—a name those Ute people called themselves. The Timpanogotzis, unlike the Yampa band of Utes living in northwestern Colorado who regularly hunted deer and other game, utilized the local abundance of fish and waterfowl for their major source of food.

Ethnographers, historians, anthropologists, and other scholars have carried on the process of studying and identifying the various bands of Ute people. The commonly recognized bands of Utes in Colorado were the Muache, Capote, Weeminuche, Taviwach, Yampa, and Parusanuch.[1] In Utah the five bands of Ute people were the Uintah, Timpanogots, Sanpits, Moanunts, and Pahvant. By the early 1860s most of the Utah bands of Ute Indians resided in the Uinta Basin; by the 1880s they were joined there by several bands of Colorado Ute Indians.

Before contact with the Europeans, the Uintah Utes used the bow and arrow to hunt small game and the Timpanogots Utes used bows and arrows as well as spears to fish. Travel was done by foot. However, with the Spanish expedition of Francisco Vasquez de Coronado into the region in 1540 significant changes began to occur for the Ute Indians. Slowly, the Ute people acquired the horse from the Spanish, and by the middle of the seventeenth century the Utes living in Colorado and several of the bands in Utah had horses. By the middle of the eighteenth century virtually all Ute Indian bands possessed the horse and had become expert horsemen.

The Ute Indians also acquired iron items from the Spanish, using them in place of stone tools. They also obtained woven cloth, which replaced fur and hide clothing and was a highly sought after trade item. Guns and horses were symbols of power among the Ute people.[2] The horse made the Ute people very powerful compared to their poorer neighbors. The Utes made good use of the horse, extending their hunting grounds to the plains of Wyoming, where once again buffalo became an important source of food, shelter, and clothing for those Utes. Several Ute bands turned to slave trading, raiding other tribes in Utah and trading captured women and children in particular as slaves to Spanish and (later) Mexican traders. Horses

Ute Warrior and his bride, photo taken in the Uinta Basin circa 1873. (Utah State Historical Society)

also were an important trade commodity. Horses were acquired in California, trailed to Utah, and then traded for goods to the Spanish and Mexicans from Santa Fe.

The political and cultural organizations of the Utes centered on family groupings and bands and remained distinct until the acquisition of the horse. An elder or chief was chosen by each band based on wisdom gained and proven leadership. Chiefs or elders were men with strong personalities who could usually sway others to their points of view. Once counsel was given and opinions rendered, however, there was no mandate for others to follow decisions made by the chiefs, and the leaders had no authority to enforce their decisions.[3]

The transmission of culture and tradition fell to the older men and women of the tribe who had reputations for wisdom, spiritual power, healing ability, and success in hunting or war. It was they who taught cultural traditions to the children of the tribe. Ute bands came together from far distances to participate in various cultural activities including the annual Spring Bear Dance, a celebration of renewal and the promise of summer and times of plenty. One of the Ute cultural elements acquired from the Plains horse culture was the Sun Dance. The Sun Dance united human life with the domain of the spiritual, or other world, through mortification of the flesh. The Sun Dance also was believed to restore health and promote the spiritual and physical well-being of the participant. Dancing often lasted several days and, in combination with several days of fasting, individual dancers could receive a vision showing their path in life.

At the time of the arrival in Utah of the Mormon settlers in the mid-nineteenth century, several bands of Utes were concentrated along the Wasatch Front, especially in Utah Valley; others were in the Pahvant and Sanpete valleys as well as the lower Sevier Valley. Because of their fluid nature, it is difficult to determine the exact size, territory, and leadership of the various bands. Wakara was one of several chiefs of the Timpanogots Utes, and he claimed the territory from the Sevier River to the Green River in the Uinta Basin as his horse pasture.[4] Wakara was a very successful horse trader. In one of the most successful acquisitions of horses in western history, Wakara and mountain man Peg-Leg Smith stole more than 1,000 horses from California ranchers at San Luis Obisbo and drove them swiftly across the desert to the mountain valleys of Utah to escape pursuit and to pasture them before trading them to Mexicans in Santa Fe or along the Old Spanish Trail.

Some of the other tribal chiefs of various bands of Utah Utes in the mid-nineteenth century included Peteetnet, Ankatwest, Kanosh, Saweset, Tintic, Sanpitch, Sooksoobet, Merikahats, Anthrow (Antero), Sowysett, and Tabby-to-kwanah (Tabby).[5] They were all referred to by other Utes as brothers; some were true brothers, others half-brothers, and others cousins.

Indian population figures at mid-nineteenth century vary according to sources. Utah Indian agent Jacob Forney reported to the Commissioner of Indian Affairs in 1859 that there were 1,000 Utes living in the Uinta Basin.[6] In 1855 it was reported that the Pahvant band, which included the smaller group of Tintic Utes, numbered between 1,000 and 1,500.[7] Perhaps as many as several thousand Ute Indians resided in Utah when the Mormons set foot in the Great Salt

Ute lifestyle rapidly changed after they acquired horse, including use of lodges (tepees) instead of the smaller wickiup. Photo taken in the Uinta Basin circa 1873. (Utah State Historical Society)

Lake Valley in 1847. Fourteen years later, the Commissioner of Indian Affairs in a report to the Department of Interior in 1861 indicated that there were 20,000 Indians living within the Utah superintendency.[8]

At mid-nineteenth century the Ute Indians collectively were at the pinnacle of their strength and power. They had become noted throughout the Mountain West for their horses and riding ability.[9] George Brewerton, a guide who worked with Kit Carson, said of the Utes in 1848: "The Eutawa are perhaps the most powerful and war-like tribe now remaining of this continent."[10] The Ute people had carved out a territory and maintained their territorial integrity from encroachment from the Navajo, Comanche, Cheyenne, Shoshoni, and Bannock tribes as well as occasional incursions into Ute territory from Sioux and Blackfeet Indians. Two centuries of interaction with the Spanish, sometimes as the enforcement arm of Spanish domination of other tribes, coupled with their own frequent aggressive forays against neighboring tribes, brought them to this lofty contemporary position.

Ute-Mormon Relationships

The small trickle of white involvement with the Ute people of Utah and Colorado grew into a flood following the permanent settlement of the Great Salt Lake Valley by Mormon settlers and the discovery of gold and silver in Colorado in the 1850s. When the Mormons first settled the valley of the Great Salt Lake most Utes felt little or no concern. The valley was the unofficial border between the Utes and their Shoshoni rivals to the northwest. Both groups of people occasionally hunted in the Great Salt Lake Valley and the nearby Wasatch Mountains to the east. Neither Indian tribe resisted the permanent settlement of the Mormon pioneers in the valley.

However, as Mormon settlements expanded southward into Utah and San Pete valleys, the heartland of Ute territory, the Ute people understandably felt threatened. From the Mormons' point of view, the Utes neglected to make full use of the land; instead, they hunted, fished, and harvested seeds and berries. Little did the newcomers understand that the Utes followed seasonal cycles, camped in the same places, hunted and fished the same valleys and streams, and harvested at the appropriate times what nature provided year after year. The Mormon colonizers failed to understand that their occupation of the eastern valleys of the Great Basin dangerously disrupted both the fragile ecology and the traditional subsistence patterns of the Ute people.

Brigham Young promised the Utes that the Mormons would not

Utes in the Uinta Basin circa 1873. (Utah State Historical Society)

drive them from their lands or interfere with their lifestyle. However, Mormon cattle grazed the same grassy areas that the Ute horses grazed. Competition for the same resources intensified, and the Ute Indians demanded payment for the loss of their land and wild game. Payment to the Utes for the land settled or loss of game was not part of Brigham Young's colonizing policy. "The land belongs to our Father in Heaven," Brigham Young said in August 1847, "and we calculate to plow and plant it; and no man shall have the power to sell his inheritance for he cannot remove it; it belongs to the Lord."[11]

Especially important to the Utah Valley Timpanogots Utes was the abundant supply of fish found in Utah Lake and in the region's various waterways. However, when Mormon fishermen began catching large numbers of fish from the Provo and Spanish Fork rivers, the Utes' important food supply was seriously threatened. In a matter of a few short years the Timpanogots Utes were near starvation.

To fend off starvation and the loss of their land, individual Ute Indians turned to taking unattended Mormon livestock as compensation for their lands and the loss of game and fish. Mormon settlers responded by pursing the presumed thieves; when caught, the Indians were whipped or killed without the benefit of a trial. The Indians sought retribution. In turn, retaliatory raids were made by the Mormons on Ute camps. Tensions mounted. In an attempt to resolve the problem, the Utah Territorial Indian Agency was created by Congress in February 1851.

The territorial Indian agency, headed by Brigham Young, attempted to isolate the Ute Indians from Mormon colonizers and at the same time provide them a place to camp and learn the ways of agriculture. Several small Indian farms or reservations were created in the territory: at Corn Creek in Millard County, in the Sanpete Valley, and later in Utah County. However, clashes of economic and cultural values continued, and tension between the Utes and Mormons remained high. Little support was given to the Indians to teach them agriculture, and Mormon livestock continued to encroach on the Indian farms.

For years, the Utes had dealt in the Indian slave trade. Goshute and Paiute women and children abducted were traded to Mexican traders on the Old Spanish Trail. Chief Wakara was a key figure in the slave trade business. The slave trade repulsed Brigham Young and others, and in 1852 the Utah Territorial Legislature passed a law banning all slave trade within the territory, effectively putting an end to lucrative trade between the Utes and New Mexican slave traders.[12]

The combination of the loss of land, game, fish, and other resources, Mormon interference in the lucrative Indian slave trade,

Ute women weaving baskets circa 1870. (Uintah County Library–Regional History Center)

and the not-too-successful Indian farm program coalesced Ute anger against the Mormons.

The Walker War

In the summer of 1853, while Wakara's band was camped on Spring Creek near Springville, an ugly incident occurred between Wakara and the Mormon settlers. A trade altercation between Mormon settler James Ivie and some of Wakara's band touched off full-blown hostilities known as the Walker War.[13] Wakara and Arapeen undertook a campaign of raids against Mormon settlements. During the next ten months, raids, theft, and retaliation took place between the Utes and the settlers. About twenty Mormons and at least as many Utes were killed. Victory for the Utes was futile, however. The Mormons, at Brigham Young's direction, "forted up" throughout the territory, and trading with the hostile Utes—especially guns and ammunition—was prohibited. A peace agreement was reached between Brigham Young, then acting Indian

Superintendent of the territory, and Wakara in May 1854 at Chicken Creek (Nephi). In January 1855, a few months after agreeing to end the war, Wakara died, leaving the leadership of the Utes to his brothers, particularly Arapeen.[14]

Ending the Walker War peacefully did not resolve the underlying problems between the Mormon settlers and the Ute Indians. Brigham Young attempted to revive the Indian farm system at Corn Creek, at Twelve Mile Creek, and at other locations, and he also established a farm on the Spanish Fork River in Utah Valley. However, the federal government failed to provide financial support or other means of assistance to Young's Indian farm program. In 1855 federal Indian agent Dr. Garland Hurt began to undermine Young's Indian program. Indian agent T.W. Hatch reported that the Indian farms were in a "destitute condition, stripped of their stock, tools, and moveable fences, and no one [was] living upon either of them."[15] Most of the Utes refused to settle on the farms, preferring to live according to traditional ways. Also, Mormon settlers encroached on the land which had been set aside for these Indian farms as they fell into disuse.

The Ute Indian population suffered from poverty, ill-treatment, and declining numbers due to conflict and white man's diseases. Their plight forced Brigham Young and federal Indian officials to find another solution to the Indian problem. A large isolated region for the Ute people became the solution preferred by Brigham Young and the federal Indian agency.

Setting Aside the Uinta Valley Reservation

For all its vast acreage, Utah has only a few valleys that are highly desirable for farming and have a sufficient supply of water, and these valleys were highly desirable to Mormon settlers. From the mid-1850s to the early 1860s, the most desirable land in the Great Basin portion of Utah was being settled. Garland Hurt was forced by federal government policy to abandon the Indian farms in part because these lands were increasingly valuable as grazing and farming grounds for Mormon settlers. The idea of separating the Utes from the Mormons and removing them to some isolated region of the territory remained with Hurt and other federal territorial officials. A search was undertaken to locate such an area in the territory.

In 1861 Brigham Young sent a second small expedition to the Uinta Basin to investigate its suitability for settlement. The negative report of the earlier expedition of George Washington Bean had postponed Mormon entry into the Uinta Basin for nine years, and Young wanted a second look at that region. Shortly after the 1861 expedition's return to Salt Lake City the *Deseret News* printed its report:

> The fertile vales, extensive meadows, and wide pasture ranges were not to be found; and the country, according to the statements of those sent thither to select a location for a settlement, is entirely unsuitable for farming purposes, and the amount of land at all suitable for cultivation extremely limited.
>
> After becoming thoroughly satisfied that all the sections of country, lying between the Wasatch Mountains and the eastern boundary of the Territory, and south of Green River Country, was one vast "contiguity of waste," and measurable valueless excepting for nomadic purposes, hunting grounds for Indians and to hold the world together.[16]

This discouraging report solidified the notions of Brigham Young and federal Indian officials that the Uinta Basin was undesirable for Mormon settlement. Territorial Indian officials thus believed that the expedition had located a place considered of little value and isolated geographically; this rendered it, by government standards, an ideal location for an Indian reservation. That same year, President Abraham Lincoln issued an executive order establishing the Uintah Valley Indian Reservation.[17] This new Indian reservation included all of the territory within the drainage of the Duchesne River, mistakenly named in Lincoln's executive order as the "Uintah" River. The reservation included all the land on the south side of the Uinta Mountains to the Tavaputs Plateau, and from the summit of Daniels Canyon to the confluence of the Duchesne and Green rivers, an area of slightly more than 2 million acres. In 1864 the United States Congress voted to approve President Lincoln's action and make the Uinta Basin the permanent homeland for the Utah Utes. There was, however, nothing in Lincoln's order to force the removal of the Utes to the Uinta Basin, and the Timpanogots band of Utes and the other Ute bands resisted being relocated to the basin.

An Uneasy Decade 1855–1865

Following the Walker War, the Utah Utes remained on their traditional homelands, but they increasingly were forced to give way to growing numbers of Mormon settlers and watch the depletion of their food sources. The Tintic War soon resulted—a brief conflcit localized in the Juab, Tooele, and Millard counties area. The outburst of hostilities was clearly seen as evidence of a persistent problem simmering among the Ute people.

The presence of the federal troops known as Johnston's Army during and after the so-called "Utah War" of 1857–58 further reminded the Utes of their inferior position. The withdrawal of the troops in 1861 with the beginning of the Civil War renewed the possibilities of further confrontation between the Utes, Shoshonis, and Mormon settlers. Squeezed onto less desirable lands to live, the Indians of the territory threatened the uneasy coexistence with the Mormons as well as vital national transportation routes through the territory. Worsening conditions among the Ute people forced some of them to resort once again to stealing cattle and other food from the Mormons to stave off wholesale starvation.

To safeguard the overland trail from Indian raids at the outbreak of the Civil War, Colonel Patrick Connor and a group of volunteers from California were assigned to Utah to maintain peace with the Indians of the territory and to keep a watchful eye on the Mormons. To demonstrate his leadership, Colonel Connor and his men without provocation attacked and massacred several hundred Shoshoni men, women, and children at their winter encampment on the Bear River near the Utah-Idaho border early in January 1863.

The continued tension between Mormons and Utes and the massacre of the Shoshoni Indians at the Bear River prompted Indian Superintendent O.H. Irish to hold a council with Ute leaders at the mouth of Spanish Fork Canyon in 1865 for the purpose of persuading them to relocate to the Uintah Valley Indian Reservation. In a later report to Washington about the urgency of holding a council with Ute leaders, Superintendent Irish wrote: "Owing to the Indian difficulties in the adjoining territories which were having a bad influence upon our Indians and that they were very uneasy about the

Chief Tabby of the Utes was the first tribal leader to move his followers to the Uintah Reservation. He lived to be over one-hundred years old. (Utah State Historical Society)

reports . . . I thought it dangerous to delay negotiations."[18] In the surrounding territories within the years just prior to the Spanish Fork

Treaty the Shoshoni were attacked at Bear River, the Navajo were forced on the "Long Walk" to Fort Sumner, and the Cheyenne were massacred at Sand Creek. Although these tribes were enemies of the Utes, the Utes took little joy in seeing their foes defeated by armies of volunteer soldiers, for they could see, all too clearly, what might happen to them.

At the council the Utes were asked to abandon their claims to Utah and San Pete valleys and accept permanent settlement in the Uinta Basin. Several Ute chiefs and leaders advised against the treaty. However, Brigham Young, holding no official capacity but having the trust of many Indians, advised the Indians to accept the government's offer. He told them that the Indians should take what the government offered and go to the Uinta Valley, otherwise the government would simply take their land and give them nothing for it. After much discussion among themselves, twelve Ute leaders including Sow-e-ett, Kan-osh, An-kar-aw-keg, and Tabby agreed to the terms of the treaty. Sanpitch was one of several chiefs who opposed the treaty. To make things more difficult among some of the Utes, Sanpitch was a relative of Chief Tabby of the Uintah Utes.

The Spanish Fork Indian Treaty granted to the Utes a $25,000 annuity each year for ten years, $20,000 a year for the next twenty years, and $15,000 annually for the last thirty years. In addition to the annual annuities, the Ute people were to be supplied with staple goods, homes, and schools.[19] After the signing of the Spanish Fork Treaty it was understood that the Utes would move immediately to the Uinta Basin. However, only a few bands of Utes did so. The federal government was also neglectful in complying with the mutually agreed-upon terms of the treaty. Congress, facing the problems of Reconstruction after the Civil War and the recent assassination of President Lincoln, failed to ratify the treaty, and the expected annuities were never delivered to the Utes. The Utes once again were left without assistance and understandably felt betrayed.

The Black Hawk War

The lack of food, poor treatment, and the loss of resources and land led to the continued desperation of the Ute people; led by Black Hawk in the summer of 1865 some Utes attempted to recapture land,

Chief Antero suggested that the Indian agency be moved from the junction of the Duchesne River and Rock Creek to Whiterocks where it remained until Fort Duchesne was built in 1886. (Utah State Historical Society)

steal livestock, and drive the Mormon settlers from their traditional homeland. Many areas of the territory of Utah were victims of the raids either led by or attributed to Black Hawk and his followers and allies. The Black Hawk Indian War was the most costly of the Indian difficulties in Utah history.

Reacting to the lack of food and the unratified Spanish Fork Treaty, some Utes resumed making raids on Mormon settlements. With estimates of only about 100 followers, some of whom were Paiutes, Goshutes, and Navajos, Black Hawk's warriors ran off as many as 5,000 head of cattle and killed dozens of settlers and territorial militiamen. Towns, ranches, and outlying farms in the territory were attacked by the disgruntled and hungry Utes under the leadership of Black Hawk. So effective were the Ute marauders that several small settlements in central and southern Utah were abandoned, including major settlements at Richfield, Circleville, Kanab, and Panguitch.[20]

Many Mormons' perception of the raids was that the entire Ute tribe was at war with them. The San Pitch, Elk Mountain, and Uintah bands did supply and occasionally reinforce Black Hawk's raiders, but most of the Utes were not actively engaged in hostilities. Territorial and LDS church officials reacted to the raids by mobilizing as many as 2,500 militiamen, primarily from the Mormon church's militia, the Nauvoo Legion, to combat the Indians. Most of the militia saw little action. Black Hawk and his band were rarely found, avoiding direct confrontation with troops. However, time and pressure from the territorial militia ultimately worked against Black Hawk. Suffering from a debilitating gunshot wound, in a meeting during the summer of 1867 at the Uintah Agency Black Hawk agreed to a peace treaty and a return to the reservation. Several of his more desperate or truculent followers continued making raids for two or three more years until most had been killed.[21] Considering the band's successes, it was fortunate for the Mormon settlers that the majority of Utes did not participate in the war.

Ute Agencies

The end of the Black Hawk War began in earnest the relocation of the Utes to the Uinta Basin. This placed additional strain on the limited resources available at the agency. The location of the Uinta Indian Agency was unsettled, which added to the agency's difficulties. The first location was at the head of Daniels Canyon, where, in 1865, soldiers under the command of Colonel Connor constructed a small log building to serve as the agency headquarters. This was a poor choice; heavy winter snows limited access to the new agency. The next summer, special Indian agent Thomas Carter relocated the Indian agency to the upper Duchesne River near present-day Hanna. The agency moved again in 1867 to the junction of Rock Creek and the Duchesne River, north of present-day Starvation Reservoir. This location, like the others, proved to be unsatisfactory. Chief Anterio urged Indian agent Pardon Dodds to move the agency a final time to Whiterocks.[22] This location was of considerable historical and geographic significance for the Utes; nearby had stood Antoine Robidoux's Fort Uintah, and most of the major Indian trails in the Uinta Basin converged at Whiterocks.[23] The change was made, and Whiterocks served as the agency headquarters until Fort Duchesne was built in 1886. Previous to Fort Duchesne's establishment, the army built Fort Thornburg in Ashley Valley near present-day Maeser, but it existed for only a short time and the Indian agency was never established there.

When the Ute Indian agency moved east to Whiterocks, most of the Utes moved east as well. Strawberry Valley and the Duchesne River and Rock Creek regions remained important for hunting and summer camping areas for the Utes, but few lived there.

The Indian agency at the outset was plagued with fraud, misappropriation of goods, mismanagement, and the lack of resources, which was almost disastrous for the Utes. For example, Indian Agent L.B. Kenney was fired for "gross neglect."[24] In 1866 Indian Superintendent F.H. Head, who had replaced O.H. Irish, complained bitterly that he had no money and that the Utes at the agency were desperately in need of flour and beef, farm implements, and other provisions.[25] In 1871 Agent J.J. Critchlow complained in his annual report that too little had been done for the Utes by his predecessors in procuring sufficient foodstuffs and clothing for the Utes.[26] On at least one occasion when the situation on the reservation was especially critical, Brigham Young hurriedly sent several wagonloads of food and supplies to feed the starving Utes.

As was the case with other Native Americans, during the last quarter of the nineteenth century reservation life for the Utes was a period of readjustment of culture, restriction of travel and personal freedoms, and loss of social and personal esteem. The government's

Utes at Calvert Trading Post at Bridge (Myton) circa 1906. (Uintah County
Library–Regional History Center Fred Todd Collection)

reservation policy forced Indians onto reservation lands which
stripped them of the ability to maintain control of their lifeways and
their traditional lands. The result was Euro-American occupation of
their lands.

By the early 1880s the various bands of Utah Utes that had relocated to the Uintah Reservation were collectively identified as the

Uintah Utes. Placed in a situation where they became dependant on the federal government for most of their needs, it is little wonder that the Ute population, like other tribes, declined under reservation life. Indian Agent Critchlow counted only about 800 Utes living on the Uintah Indian Reservation during the winter of 1872–73. That number was reduced each summer when many Utes left the reservation in search of food.[27]

In terms of real dollar value, the reservation policy more than justified the cost of feeding and clothing the Indians rather than campaigning against them militarily. All reservation Indians became "wards of the government." The government to a great extent treated Indians as children unable to care for themselves, and the Utes were no exception to this way of thinking.

Removal of the Utes from Colorado

In 1881 the Uintah Utes were forced to share their lands with Utes from Colorado. The Uncompahgre and White River Utes were removed from the western slope of the Rocky Mountains to eastern Utah after having been forced to relocate several times prior to 1881. The shrinking of Colorado Ute land began when gold was discovered on the floodplains of the Rocky Mountains at Cherry Creek (Denver), Colorado, in 1858. Within the next several months additional discoveries were made at Central City and Leadville. New towns sprouted up and thousands of miners sped to the new mine fields. During the next several decades the land claims of the Colorado Utes, which had initially been from the foothills of the Rocky Mountains on the east to the Colorado Plateau, were reduced and pushed westward by four different treaties. The last of these took the southwestern corner of Colorado from the Utes when new silver and gold discoveries were found in the San Juan Mountains. Not only did the Utes lose land, but as was the case with other Indian tribes, the Colorado Utes' population also dwindled.

By the late 1870s most of the Utes of Colorado were living on either the White River or Los Pinos (Uncompahgre) reservations.[28] As much as possible the Colorado Utes were trying to maintain their traditional lifestyle while adjusting to new ways. Many of the Uncompahgre band Utes had turned to the raising of sheep, cattle, and horses and were having some success. However, this ranching type of economic activity was not what some Indian agents wanted; Indians, some believed, must be turned to husbandmen, receiving their food from the crops they planted and harvested each year. A violent incident relating to this then occurred in the spring of 1878 which caused Coloradoans to demand the removal of the White River and Uncompahgre bands of Utes from western Colorado to the Uinta Basin.

The main player in the final act of the drama of the removal of the Utes from Colorado was Indian Agent Nathan C. Meeker. A former poet, novelist, newspaperman, churchman, and organizer of utopian agrarian cooperative colonies, at all of which he had been a virtual failure, Meeker through political connections was appointed in 1878 to the position of Indian agent for the White River Ute Agency. With missionary-type zeal Meeker set about to transform the Utes into what he thought to be a higher image, which he saw as being much like that of his own. Meeker was confident that he could bring the Native Americans out of a "barbaric and savage" stage to one of "enlightenment" within twenty years. He believed that instead of caring for their livestock the Utes should be making the ground ready to plant crops.

Shortly after his arrival Meeker moved the agency fifteen miles downriver to an area of beautiful meadows where the White River Utes could be better taught in the use of the plow and he could begin the process of transforming the Utes into farmers. These meadows, however, were a favored pasture for the Utes' herd of horses. When the Utes refused to plow the ground, Meeker hired non-Indian plowmen to perform the task. This usurpation of grazing land increased tensions between Meeker and the Utes. Determined Utes fired their rifles as a warning to Meeker and the white farmers.

In a confrontation with a Ute leader called Johnson by whites (Canalla was his Ute name), the hot-tempered Meeker told Johnson and the other Ute owners of the horses pasturing in the meadows that they had too many horses and must kill some of them. More words were exchanged between Johnson and Meeker; finally, before Johnson left, he reacted angrily by giving Meeker a shove. Meeker was not about to be shown-up by an Indian and was determined to have his way. Recognizing that he was outnumbered and fearing Johnson and the others might attack him, Meeker telegraphed Colorado governor Frederick Pitkin requesting protection from the army. Meeker in his appeal to the governor claimed that he had been assaulted by a leading chief, forced out of his house, and injured badly. Pitkin welcomed Meeker's request.

The Meeker-Johnson confrontation was the cause célèbre for Governor Pitkin and other white Coloradoans who had been demanding the removal of the Utes from the state. For some time Governor Pitkin and newspaperman William B. Vickers had been using their combined skills of political persuasion and the power of the press to campaign for the removal of the Utes from Colorado. The *Denver Tribune* in a short editorial outburst reflected the sentiments of Pitkin when it wrote, "The Utes Must Go." Throughout the year of 1877, Vickers continued his tirade against the Utes in many of the issues of the *Denver Tribune*. Meeker's request was the excuse opponents of the Indians needed to bring to culmination their goal of evicting the Utes from the state.

The governor and the army reacted quickly to Meeker's request. Several cavalry units were ordered to the reservation to maintain peace. When the disquieted Utes learned that soldiers were on the way to their reservation, Indians attacked the agency. Meeker and all of the white male agency employees were killed, and three women, including Meeker's wife, were taken hostage. The immediate Indian success in the killing of Meeker and the taking of hostages stopped the army's advance for several days at Milk Creek.

Meanwhile, the Uncompahgre Utes under the leadership of Chief Ouray held a council to persuade the other Utes to end the hostilities. Having been to Washington, D.C., on several earlier occasions, Ouray and others knew of the futility of fighting the army. They reasoned that if fighting continued the result would be the removal of all Utes from Colorado. If necessary, Ouray was prepared to fight on the side of the whites against his fellow Utes. Ouray's intercession and the arrival of reinforcements to the beleaguered cavalry units ended the fighting. The three captive women were released.

The Uintah Utes stayed out of the action in Colorado. Fearing retaliatory raids from the army, they made plans to seek refuge in the

Uinta Mountains, if necessary, and urged Agent Critchlow and his family and employees to join them.[29]

Using the "Meeker Massacre" as justification for removal of the Indians, a successful campaign of white Coloradans to take over Ute lands occurred during the next three years. Indian agents and state officials, overlooking the willingness of Ouray and other Uncompahgre Utes to fight their own tribal members to avoid war with the whites, ordered both the White River and the Uncompahgre Ute bands removed from Colorado. Beginning in August 1881 the Uinta Basin was to be their new home. Here the White River band, numbering about 650 individuals, joined the Uintah band, numbering about 800, at the Whiterocks agency. The smaller Uncompahgre band, numbering less than 375 people, was removed to a new agency at Ouray, named for Chief Ouray. The Uncompahgre Indian Reservation was established on land southeast of the Uintah Reservation on 5 January 1882 by order of President Chester A. Arthur on some of the most desolate land of the Tavaputs Plateau. The land extended to the Colorado line just north of present Grand County but could not support the number of Utes send there. Two years later the Commissioner of Indian Affairs reported that there were 1,400 Utes living on the Uncompahgre Reservation and 965 Uintah and White River Utes living on the Uintah Reservation.[30] The two Indian agencies remained separated until 1887 when Fort Duchesne was built and the agencies were combined. Most Indians at the Uncompahgre Reservation were transferred to the Uintah Reservation.

With the arrival of the White River Utes from Colorado, the Uintah Utes felt they were being unfairly treated by having to share their reservation lands. Several groups of Uintah Utes protested the overcrowded conditions at their agency, and more than 100 Uintah Utes moved to Hanna and the Strawberry Valley at the west end of their reservation. Their protest was short-lived, however; after several months, the disenchanted Uintah Utes returned to the agency at Whiterocks.

Fort Duchesne

Within five years following the arrival of the Colorado Utes to the Uinta Basin, it was decided that the two Indian agencies should be combined and that the United States military should be posted on the reservation. On 23 August 1886 Fort Duchesne was established to serve as a protector in the area and to keep peace. Initially the Utes opposed the fort and even planned an attack on the army. Cooler heads among the Utes prevailed, however, and they accepted the new fort and the soldiers who manned it.

Stationed at Fort Duchesne were approximately 250 men. The fort's roster included two companies of black cavalrymen, referred to by the Indians as "Buffalo Soldiers."[31] The first commander of the newly established fort was Major Frederick Benteen, survivor of the Reno-Benteen contingent of the bungled attack on Sioux villages in the valley of the Little Big Horn in July 1876, where General George Armstrong Custer was killed. Although the fort was in Uintah County, its existence greatly affected the development of what became Duchesne County. One of the most significant developments was the construction of a road to Price through Nine Mile Canyon to supply the fort; another was the building of a telegraph to link Fort Duchesne with military command headquarters elsewhere. More about the road will be found in a following chapter.

Ute Reservation Life

Life on the reservation was hard for the Utes to understand and accept. Within one generation's lifespan they had gone from days of little contact with whites, when the few white intruders there were posed very little real threat and the Utes enjoyed a life of autonomy, to a new lifestyle not of their own choosing where they were restricted and confined to a reservation and dependent on limited annuities of the whites.

Many tried to live according to the traditions of their forefathers, but that was nearly impossible in the confines of the limited reservation in the Uinta Basin. Hunting forays off the reservation during the summer months frequently created concern among Indian officials and white settlers. In 1887 a group of Uncompahgre and White River Utes left the Uinta Basin to hunt and fish in western Colorado. Local sheriffs attempted to arrest them for poaching and some were accused of stealing horses. The Ute people resisted; this brought about growing white hysteria in western Colorado, and the Colorado militia was ordered to put an end to the so-called "Colorow War." Outnumbered and destitute, the Ute hunting party finally capitulated and was accompanied back to the Uinta Basin by soldiers from Fort Duchesne.

The failure of the government to provide adequate annuities, the continued encroachment of white ranchers and Gilsonite miners on the two reservations, and the passage of the Dawes Act by Congress in 1887, which eventually eliminated the two reservations and distributed small amounts of acreage to Indian families, drove many Ute people into depression and despair. In a response to their collective despair, many Utes turned to the Ghost Dance religion.

In 1890 a reworked new religion, the Ghost Dance, swept through western tribes. The original Ghost Dance was begun in 1869, and in 1890 it was revived by a Nevada Paiute, Wovoka (Jack Wilson), who had been raised by Mormon settlers. A key element of the religion was the performance of circle dancing. The new Indian religion included a belief in an Indian messiah who would come and cleanse the land of whites and nonbelieving Indians, restore the buffalo and other game, and resurrect deceased ancestors, Indians of earlier generations. Leaders of the new religion promised that grass would grow again on the prairies and that all Native Americans would live the free, happy life of days gone by.

Some Indians believed that their faith would render them immune to white men's weapons, and this growing belief brought apprehension from many whites and their growing opposition to the religious movement. Matters came to a head at Wounded Knee in South Dakota, where scores of Indians were killed by U.S. troops in what Native Americans and others have long regarded as a tragic massacre. The tragedy of the Sioux at Wounded Knee in 1890 diminished the enthusiasm for the Ghost Dance; however, a few Utes and other Native Americans remain adherents of the Ghost Dance religion.

Many Ute Indians in the 1910s turned to the Peyote religion, which was imported from Indian tribes in Arizona, New Mexico, Texas, and northern Mexico. It involved the use of small quantities of a part of a small spineless cactus, peyote, whose hallucinogenic properties were claimed to promote communication with the spiritual world. The Peyote religion was an expression of spiritual power, which helped to compensate the participant for the loss of personal political and economic control fostered by the reservation system. Like the Sun Dance and Ghost Dance, the Peyote religion emphasized Indian traditions. Within one generation perhaps as much as 50 percent of the tribe was involved. Presently this religion is known as the Native American church.[32]

Christian churches also influenced the lives of Utes living in the Uinta Basin. In the 1850s and 1860s, some Utes converted to the Mormon church. However, when the Uintah Reservation was established and most of the Utes were removed to the reservation, many Indian Mormons became disaffected and no longer were adherents of the Mormon church. Difficult relations between the Mormon church and the federal government in the 1870s and 1880s further prevented formal missionary work by the church with the Utes on the two reservations. Informally, contact between church members and the Utes continued when Mormons living in Ashley Valley helped the Utes there construct several short irrigation ditches.

Early in the 1870s President Ulysses S. Grant instituted an Indian program, identified as the "Peace Policy," which for a few years dramatically altered the administration and management of Indian reservations. An important element of Grant's Indian policy was the encouragement of Christian churches to take an active part in teaching Indians the art of agriculture, in organizing schools for the Indians, and in providing teachers for the Indian schools.

Various Christian denominations were assigned to work with specific Indian reservations. However, for nearly ten years the United States Indian Commission ignored the Uintah and Uncompahgre Indian reservations; no churchmen were permitted to serve there as Christian missionaries. In the early 1880s the Board of Home Missions of the Presbyterian church was contracted for several years to operate a school at Whiterocks for the Ute Indians. Presbyterian teachers met with little success, however.

Meanwhile, on the Uncompahgre Reservation, the Episcopal church was invited through the efforts of Indian agent James Randlett to become involved with the Uncompahgre Indians. The first Episcopal church minister to the Indians was Reverend George S. Vest. Milton J. Hersey, Lucy Carter, and Sue Garrett, members of the Episcopal church, were also involved on the reservation in the 1890s.[33]

In the 1880s, after many of the Uncompahgre families accepted farmsteads on the Uintah Indian Reservation as a result of the Dawes Act—the new government Indian policy of termination of Indian reservations and Indian tribes—the Episcopal church continued to serve the Indians at Fort Duchesne and at Leland. In 1893 the Episcopal church established a mission to serve the Ute people at Whiterocks. A small chapel was built there later.

Following the opening of the Uintah Indian Reservation to white settlement in 1905, Christian churches became more active working with the Indian people in Duchesne and Uintah counties. In 1915 the Episcopal church built a church at Randlett. Presently there are Episcopal church congregations at Randlett and Neola, LDS wards at Randlett, Myton, and Whiterocks, as well as in other towns in Duchesne County, and the Ute Indian Baptist church on Indian Bench to serve the Indian population in the two counties.

ENDNOTES

1. For examples of different band or tribal names of Utes see Julian H. Steward, *Basin-Plateau Aboriginal Sociopolitical Groups,* Smithsonian Institution Bureau of American Ethnology Bulletin 120 (Washington, D.C.: U.S. Government Printing Office, 1938), 219–30; Julian H. Steward, *Ute Indians I: Aboriginal and Historical Groups of the Ute Indians of Utah* (New York: Garland, 1974), 50–104; and Donald G. Callaway, Joel C. Janetski, and Omer C. Stewart, "Ute," in Warren L. D'Azevedo, ed., *Handbook of North American Indians:* vol. 11, *Great Basin* (Washington, D.C.: Smithsonian Institution, 1986).

2. Ted J. Warner, ed., *Dominguez-Escalante Journal,* 26–38.

3. Fred A. Conetah, *A History of the Northern Ute People* (Fort Duchesne, UT: Uintah-Ouray Ute Tribe, 1982), 6, 9.

4. Omer Stewart, "Ute Indians: Before and After White Contact," *Utah Historical Quarterly* 34 (Winter 1966): 54.

5. Steward, *Basin-Plateau Aboriginal Sociopolitical Groups,* 224–25.

6. Part of the Forney report is found in Steward, *Ute Indians I,* 28.

7. Steward, *Ute Indians I,* 55.

8. *Report of the Commissioner of Indian Affairs, accompanying the Annual Report of the Secretary of the Interior, 1861* (Washington, D.C.: Government Printing Office, 1861), 218.

9. Osborne Russell, *Journal of a Trapper 1834–1843*, ed. by Aubrey Haines (Lincoln: University of Nebraska Press, 1965), 120–22. See also Warren E. Ferris, *Life in the Rocky Maintains* (Denver: Old West Publishing Company, 1968), 312.

10. George Brewerton, *Overland With Kit Carson* (New York: Coward-McCann, 1930), 99, 100.

11. Quoted in Howard A. Christy, "Open Hand and Mailed Fist: Mormon-Indian Relations in Utah, 1847–52," *Utah Historical Quarterly* 46 (Summer 1978): 219.

12. For further discussion of the Indian slave trade see William J. Snow, "Utah Indians and the Spanish Slave Trade," *Utah Historical Quarterly* 2 (July 1929): 67–73; Charles Wilkes, "Some Source Documents on Utah Indian Slavery: Indian Tribes of the Interior of Oregon, 1841," *Utah Historical Quarterly* 2 (July 1929): 73–75; Garland Hurt, "Indian Agents Report on Slavery," *Utah Historical Quarterly* 2 (July 1929): 86–87; and Joseph J. Hill, "Spanish and Mexican Exploration and Trade Northwest from New Mexico into the Great Basin, 1765–1853," *Utah Historical Quarterly* 3 (January 1930): 3–23.

13. Conetah, *Northern Ute People*, 39. For more detail on the beginnings of the Walker War see Peter Gottfredson, *Indian Depredations in Utah*, reprint (Salt Lake City: Merlin G. Christensen, 1969, 43–47.

14. See Snow, "Utah Indians"; Joseph J. Hill, "Spanish and Mexican Exploration and Trade"; Christy, "Open Hand and Mailed Fist"; Howard A. Christy, "The Walker War: Defense and Conciliation as Strategy," *Utah Historical Quarterly* 47 (Fall 1979): 395–420.

15. T.W. Hatch to Commissioner James D. Doty, September 1862, *Report of the Commissioner of Indian Affairs, 1862*, 205.

16. *Deseret News*, 25 September 1861.

17. A. Lincoln, Executive Order, 5 October 1861, in *Executive Orders Relating to Indian Reservations, 1855–1912* (Washington, D.C.: Government Printing Office, 1912), 169.

18. O.H. Irish to W.P. Dole, 14 February 1865, Bureau of Indian Affairs, Letters Received by the Office of Indian Affairs, Utah Superintendence, 1866–1869, Recrd Group 75, National Archives, Washington, D.C., microfilm copy at Brigham Young University Library.

19. O.H. Irish to Commissioner of Indian Affairs, 7 June 1865, Letters Received, Record Group 75, National Archives, microfilm copy at Brigham Young University Library.

20. Conetah, *Northern Ute People,* 86. See also Deloy J. Spencer, "The History of the Black Hawk War 1865–1871," (Master's thesis, Utah State University, 1969), 54–55.

21. Warren Metcalf, "A Precarious Balance: The Northern Utes and the Black Hawk War," *Utah Historical Quarterly* 51 (Winter 1989): 24–35.

22. Conetah, *Northern Ute People,* 90.

23. James Warren Covington, "Relations Between the Ute Indians and the United States Government, 1848–1900" (Ph.D. diss., University of Oklahoma, 1949), 138–43.

24. Conetah, *Northern Ute People* 90.

25. F.H. Head to D.N. Cooley, 31 March 1866, Bureau of Indian Affairs, Letters Received.

26. *Annual Report of the Commissioner of Indian Affairs to the Secretary of the Interior for the year 1871* (Washington, D.C.: Government Printing Office, 1872), 547.

27. Floyd A. O'Neil, "A History of the Ute Indians of Utah until 1890," (Ph.D. diss., University of Utah, 1973), 110.

28. The Ute Mountain and Southern Utes did not play an active part in the proceedings or in the removal from Colorado. For more reading of the removal of the Utes from Colorado see Conetah, *Northern Ute People,* 96–113; Dee Brown, *Bury My Heart At Wounded Knee* (New York: Holt, Rinehart & Winston, 1970), 349–67; Robert Utley, *Frontier Regulars: The United States Army and the Indian 1866–1891* (Lincoln: University of Nebraska Press, 1973), 332–43.

29. Conetah, *Northern Ute People,* 92.

30. *Annual Report of the Commissioner of Indian Affairs to the Secretary of the Interior for the year 1883* (Washington, D.C.: Government Printing Office, 1883), 280.

31. For more information of Fort Duchesne see Gary Lee Walker, *History of Fort Duchesne Including Fort Thornburg: The Military Presence in Frontier Uintah Basin, Utah* (Ph.D. diss., Brigham Young University, 1992). See also Ronald G. Coleman, "The Buffalo Soldiers: Guardians of the Uintah Frontier, 1886–1901," *Utah Historical Quarterly* 47 (Fall 1979): 421–39.

32. For more on the Ghost Dance religion see James Mooney, *The Ghost Dance Religion and the Sioux Outbreak of 1890* (Washington D.C., 1893); and Arrell Morgan Gibson, *The American Indian: Prehistory to the Present* (Lexington, MA: D.C. Heath and Company, 1980), 477–83. For Ute participation in the Ghost Dance religion see Conetah, *Northern Ute People,* 91. This book is the best study to date done by a Ute historian on his people. There are, however, some errors in the book and the date for the Ute par-

ticipation in the Ghost Dance is one of them. Conetah dates the Ghost Dance in 1872, but Wovoka did not start the new religion until the last part of 1899. See page 132 for additional information about the Peyote religion.

33. For further information about Episcopal church activities in the Uinta Basin see James W. Beless, Jr., "The Episcopal Church in Utah—Seven Bishops and One Hundred Years," *Utah Historical Quarterly* 36 (Winter 1968): 77–96.

CHAPTER 3

EARLY ROADS, GRAZING AND SCHEMERS, AND OUTLAWS

The geography of the Uinta Basin and the establishment of an Indian reservation kept the area isolated from the rest of Utah for much of the nineteenth century. Wagon roads and trails into the Uinta Basin were virtually nonexistent until the establishment of army posts. Unlike much of Utah Territory, where Mormon pioneers and later the territorial government built or funded road construction, roads in and out of the Uinta Basin were first built primarily to serve the transportation needs of the U.S. Army.

The first wagon road built into the Uinta Basin was built in 1882 when the army constructed Fort Thornburg in Uintah County. With the aid of William A. Carter, Jr., son of Judge William A. Carter of the Fort Bridger area of Wyoming, the army had built the Carter Road over the Uinta Mountains to Carter, Wyoming, to supply Fort Thornburg. When the army moved to the newly constructed Fort Duchesne, the Carter Road was extended to the new fort.

The Carter Road proved to be very difficult to haul heavy freight over from the railhead to the army posts in the Uinta Basin—especially during the fall, winter, and early spring seasons. Delays in moving army freight from Green River, Wyoming, to Fort Thornburg were frequent, and freight often piled up at Green River. The *Salt Lake Tribune* reported on the freight conditions at Green River:

> there seems to be much doubt regarding the route of transportation to be adopted for the new post. There is arriving at Carter station over one million pounds of freight to be sent forward, and the contractor, Mr. Winston, of Virginia, is pushing it forward as fast as he can, the distance being 130 miles.[1]

The army looked for an alternative route. Brigadier General George Crook of the Department of the Platte, headquartered in Nebraska, determined that a road from Park City to the Uinta Basin would be open longer during the year than the Carter Road. Soldiers were put to work in August to build the road from Park City to the Uintah Indian Agency. It is likely that this military freight road followed the south fork of the Provo River in Summit County over Wolf Creek Pass to the Duchesne River down past Hanna and then east to Fort Thornburg in Ashley Valley. Before the snows came in 1882, freight contractors Merrill L. Hoyt and Joseph Hatch were hauling military freight from the railroad depot at Park City to Fort Thornburg. Their rate was ten cents per hundredweight of freight.

Other routes to Fort Thornburg and later to Fort Duchesne were constructed across what was later to become Duchesne County. One of the alternative roads constructed and used was the Daniels Canyon-Strawberry Valley route, which is currently followed by U.S. Highway 40. Before it was made into a freight road, the Daniels Canyon-Strawberry Valley route was used by some of the first settlers to trail their cattle to Ashley Valley. Another alternative route was the Indian Canyon route, which became a popular road briefly following the construction of the Denver and Rio Grande Railroad tracks through Carbon County in 1883. These three roads over the Wasatch Mountains presented similar problems to the Carter Road for army freighters—deep snow, steep passes, and difficult terrain. Today, two of the early military freight roads, U.S. Highway 40 and the Indian Canyon road, are paved and heavily traveled. The Wolf Creek Pass road has been widened considerably, with a firm gravel roadbed in place.

Freighting on the Nine Mile Road, hauling supplies to Fort Duchesne from the railroad in Price was a major economic boon to early residents of the county. Freighters hauled supplies to the fort and Gilsonite from the mines to the railroad. The most common method was a double team of horses or mules and tandem wagons. (Uintah County Library–Regional History Center.)

One of the best trails into the Uinta Basin, however, was through Nine Mile Canyon. This canyon provided a natural access into the basin and had been used by prehistoric Indians, Utes, mountain men, and others. When Fort Duchesne was built beginning in the fall of 1886 because of increased Indian difficulties, it was immediately decided that a better access road was needed to haul supplies to the new and larger fort. Early on, 275 men and support personnel assigned to the six companies of Fort Duchesne, along with dozens of camp followers, required increased supplies and a better year-round road.

The Nine Mile Canyon Road

The route through Nine Mile Canyon to the railroad in Price was deemed the best route by the army. For the army's needs none of the

Freighters hauling Gilsonite to the railhead at Price before the Uintah Railroad was completed in 1904. The freighters route was from the mines in Uintah County through Fort Duchesne to Myton and then south on the Nine Mile Road. Notice the Gilsonite is sacked for easier handling. (Uintah County Library–Regional History Center, Neal Collection)

existing roads provided what Nine Mile offered: the shortest distance from Fort Duchesne to a railroad, a more moderate grade, and a low pass through the Roan and Book Cliff mountains. It was so heavily used for twenty years that the road was aptly named the "Lifeline of Uintah Basin."[2] However, the Nine Mile Road did have problems the other roads did not have—slippery rock and stretches without water and feed. Ironically, the Nine Mile Road, once the most-traveled road in northeastern Utah, is today the least used and poorest of the four military roads in Duchesne County.

In the fall of 1886 the army, likely aided by John A. Powell, one of the early settlers of Price, located the route from Price through Nine Mile Canyon and up Gate Canyon. The army immediately went to work to make the road passable. Starting in August 1886 army labor crews worked on both the road and a telegraph line through Nine Mile Canyon. By January 1887 the telegraph was completed and Fort Duchesne was connected with the rest of the world. A year later, a stage line was established to carry passengers and mail between

Price and the Uinta Basin. This was a welcome addition. Earlier a bi-weekly buckboard service had been established between Fort Thornburg and Green River, Wyoming.[3]

The discovery of Gilsonite and other hydrocarbons in the Uinta Basin led to even greater use of the Nine Mile route. Gilsonite, a rare hydrocarbon found in commercial quantities in only a few locations in the United States, has had many uses, including use as a sealant for beer barrels and as a base for paints, inks, and perfumes. The hauling of Gilsonite in 100-pound sacks provided a steady return-trip load for teamsters who were hauling freight to Fort Duchesne.[4]

An especially important hydrocarbon find occurred in 1888, and it promoted the Nine Mile Canyon Road as a general freight road. A small section of land about one mile east of Fort Duchesne subsequently was removed from reservation lands by an act of Congress. With the Indians' consent, obtained through questionable means, the 7,040-acre "Strip" was segregated from the Uintah Indian Reservation and opened to mine Gilsonite. A wild, lawless mining town quickly sprang up on the isolated Strip. Being outside the boundaries of the Uintah Indian Reservation and at the extreme western end of Uintah County, the Strip was a place where federal and county law officers were rarely seen.

The Strip was a short-lived town and was one of the favorite haunts of Butch Cassidy and the Wild Bunch, mainly because of the lack of organized law. In its heyday there were four saloons and at least that many "hog ranches," the frontier name for businesses in the red-light (prostitution) district. There were several deaths by gun-fights and a great deal of violence. The army tried unsuccessfully to keep its soldiers off the Strip in their spare time by posting guards on the bridge crossing the Uinta River. However, the soldiers swam the river to get to the Strip. Any soldier caught with a bottle of whiskey at the fort was in serious trouble. It soon became the usual practice of the returning soldiers from the Strip to consume all of their whiskey before crossing the river. A favorite location of the soldiers to get rid of their empty bottles was a small ravine or hollow near the eastern edge of the Strip. The Ute tribe later named a resort there Bottle Hollow Resort for the nearby hollow that contained evidence of the soldiers' discarded whiskey bottles.

Another early freighter circa 1910. Although the tandem wagons was the most common, anyone with a team and a sturdy wagon could contract loads to haul. Note the water barrel on the back of the wagon box, the route from Myton to Price had several long dry stretches and the hard-working teams needed water that had to be hauled. (Uintah County Library–Regional History Center)

The road from Fort Duchesne through Nine Mile Canyon to Price meandered southwest from Fort Duchesne, crossing the many area benches and gullies as it ascended the south slope of the Tavaputs Plateau. The summit, at 7,300-feet altitude, was an imposing barrier but not as difficult as the other mountain passes into the Uinta Basin. Gate Canyon, a steep, narrow, and winding canyon littered with boulders and prone to flooding, sliced downward from the summit's south side to give access to Nine Mile Canyon after descending almost 1,600 feet in seven miles. The hills and canyons were an imposition to travelers, but the most serious problem was lack of water between Fort Duchesne and Nine Mile Canyon. For thirty-seven miles, between Minnie Maud Creek and the Duchesne River, there was no water along the route. On this dry stretch of the

Open Gilsonite mine, The Duchesne Vein circa 1910. (Uintah County Library–Regional History Center, Don Snow Collection)

road freighters had to haul water for themselves and their animals. Wrote one historian: "The only drink for man and beast was in barrels the outfits carried. For men on horseback and light rigs, it was not so bad, but for the freighters it was different; too much of the heavy loads had to be barrels of water."[5]

Owen Smith, a frequent traveler on the Nine Mile Road from its

Smith Wells circa 1910. Smith Wells was the only stopping place between Nine Mile Canyon and Myton. Owen Smith hand dug the well and added the store and home shown here. It became an oasis for freighters, the stage-coach, and travelers. (Utah State Historical Society)

beginning, knew the problems of thirty-plus miles of the dusty road without water. About halfway in that long dry stretch between the Duchesne River and Minnie Maud Creek was Gamma Grass Canyon, named for the native gamma grass that grows in the region. Smith recognized that Gamma Grass Canyon offered some shelter and pasture and lacked only water to make a good way-station.

In 1891, with help from a well witcher, or water finder, from Price, Smith located a well site in Gamma Grass Canyon. He and others then hand dug a 180-foot hole before they found water. The water contained a high concentrate of salts and other minerals and was deemed fit only for use by animals. Even with this minor setback, Smith moved his family to the newly dug well and established his way-station, which was commonly known as Smith Wells. In time, Gamma Grass Canyon became known as The Wells Draw, the name by which the small valley is known today.

The well itself was six feet square, timbered from top to bottom with cedar trees. A sizeable storage tank was made by blasting into the solid rock at the bottom of the well. At the top of the well a whim powered by a horse hitched to a pole from a center capstan raised water from the bottom of the well.[6]

Smith Wells was essentially a collection of small stone and wooden buildings. Smith built his family a small frame house against the cliffs on the west side of the valley. His wife cooked daily meals of chili or stew for weary travelers, who also lodged at Smith Wells on their two-day journey between Price and Fort Duchesne or Vernal.

There was another distinct advantage for Smith's way-station. It was midway between Vernal and Price. For the first few years of stage service, the stage between Price and Fort Duchesne operated twice weekly, carrying both passengers and mail. In 1889 the Fort Duchesne Stage Line, owned by Tom Miles, upgraded its service to a daily service between Price and Fort Duchesne. The Price *Eastern Utah Telegraph* advertised the Fort Duchesne Stage Line service as being "First Class."[7] Years later, Frank Alger also operated a stage line between Fort Duchesne and Price.

On average it took twelve hours for the stage to travel from Fort Duchesne or Price to Smith Wells. Arriving in early evening after a hard day's travel, passengers and mail then transferred to a fresh team and stage to continue their journey. In 1891 the stage line contracted overnight accommodations with Smith.[8] For part of his payment from the stage company Smith was given a measure of potable water brought by the stages from the bridge at the Duchesne River and Minnie Maud Creek. Expanding his business, Smith afterwards added a general store and post office. For twenty-five years Smith Wells became a "refuge for all travelers of the Nine Mile Road."[9]

Prices for water and feed at Smith Wells varied over the years. For example, the price for water in 1910 for a team of six horses was $1.50; it was twenty-five cents per horse or cow, one cent per head of sheep, and ten cents to fill the radiator of a car. Dogs drank free.[10]

In its heyday, the Nine Mile Road was used so heavily that it was reported one could not travel for more than fifteen minutes without seeing another traveler on the road. The 100-mile trip between Vernal and Price took a teamster driving heavily loaded freight wagons an average of six days if the weather was good and much longer

Owen Smith family in front of their home at Smith Wells, circa 1910. (Uintah County Library–Regional History Center)

if the weather was poor. Most of the freight outfits used on the Nine Mile Road were four- or six-horse teams pulling two wagons hitched in tandem. This method made it possible to haul loads of three or four tons total weight. The impact of freighting was an important factor in establishing Price as a commercial center for eastern Utah.

In addition to poor feed and lack of water between Minnie Maud Creek and the Duchesne River, there were other stretches of the road in the county which lacked adequate feed for animals. This required teamsters to haul their own hay and grain for their horses. Other freighter campgrounds were established along the Fort Duchesne and Price road, and there were stage stops about every twenty miles as well. The first campground from Price was at Soldier Station. Two stage stops were located in Nine Mile Canyon, one at the Tom Taylor Ranch, later known as Lee Station, and the other at Brock's Ranch at the mouth of Gate Canyon. Most freighters pushed from Brock's to Smith Wells the third day. The fourth day's haul was from Smith

Mail Wagon/Stage Coach en route from Price to Vernal, circa 1910. (Uintah County Library–Regional History Center)

Wells to Myton, which was then called The Bridge. From Myton to Fort Duchesne was another day's journey; and, for those freighters hauling to Vernal, it was an additional day.

The road was constantly a problem; it was hot, dry, and dusty in the summer and fall, cold and icy during the winter months, and muddy and filled with deep ruts in the spring. Many teamsters narrowly escaped freezing to death. Occasional winter storms with drifting snow often stranded teamsters and the daily stages. In 1891 the stage was stranded for an entire week before rescuers could reach it.[11] Glazed ice made the passes especially treacherous during the winter months. In 1891 the newspaper in Price complained of the road conditions:

> We have heard a great deal of complaint in the last week in regards to the wagon road up Soldier Canyon. They say it is almost impossible for a team to get over it, as the road is a glare of ice, besides great danger of upsetting; and killing their teams and smashing their wagons to pieces.[12]

Not only were bad roads and weather conditions a concern to teamsters, so too were Indians. Rarely openly hostile, some turned to running off stock during the night, and the next morning they would offer to find the "lost" stock for a fee. Facing these challenges, the teamsters usually traveled in groups of two or more.[13]

The road was used to transport millions of pounds of freight and thousands of travelers and settlers between 1886 and the early 1900s. In January 1891 more than 1.6 million pounds of freight was hauled over the Nine Mile Road to Price.[14] Using conservative estimates, freighters hauled over 50 million pounds of freight over the Nine Mile Road between 1886 and 1915.[15] This represented over 14,000 one-way trips for a team pulling an average load of 3,500 pounds. Light wagons, stage runs, cattle and sheep drives, and horseback riders added to the traffic on the road, making it one of the most used roads in eastern Utah. The average shipping rate was just over a dollar for 100 pounds of freight for a one-way trip.

High freight rates caused shippers to find ways to reduce the freight costs. Generally, the merchants refused to pay freight charges on the shipping crates. They had the freight weighed without the shipping crates before repacking and shipping the freight. It was left to the freighters to absorb the difference of the extra weight of the shipping crates.[16]

A freighter with a good team and wagon who was successful in finding freight to haul both ways often grossed as much as eighty dollars a week. Expenses for horse feed and care, maintenance of wagons, and other road expenses were then deducted from the gross income, leaving the freighter's average wages from fifty to one hundred dollars a month. For many, hauling freight over the Nine Mile Road to and from the Uinta Basin was a profitable venture, although it required long days and hard work. Freighting of army and Indian supplies and Gilsonite added significantly to the overall economic development of both the Uinta Basin and Carbon County.

Nine Mile Settlement

The extensive use of the Nine Mile Road encouraged the first legal homesteading in Duchesne County. Most of the western section of the Uinta Basin was reserved as an Indian reservation by presi-

Stage arriving in Myton, circa 1915. (Uintah County Library–Regional History Center.)

dential proclamation in 1861. Abraham Lincoln's presidential proclamation specifically stated that all land drained by the Duchesne River was to be included in the reservation. Lands south of the divide that separates the drainage of the Duchesne River from Minnie Maud, Argyle, and the other creeks that are tributaries to Nine Mile Creek and are found just north of the Carbon County line were not included in the reservation.

When the Nine Mile Road was completed at about the same time Fort Duchesne was established in 1886, ranchers and settlers claimed land along the thirty miles of Nine Mile Canyon. A few ranchers had wandered into the area a few years earlier, but most came when the road was built and improved.

The center point, socially if not geographically, was Brock's Ranch, located at the mouth of Gate Canyon. Here the army established a relay station for the telegraph line that was manned by soldiers from Fort Duchesne. Brock's Ranch was also the last campground with good water before one left the canyon traveling

This peacock at the Nutter Ranch struts in front of the blacksmith shop and log building that was once the saloon where Pete Francis was killed in a shoot-out. (Utah State Historical Society)

towards Smith Wells. This Brock, whose first name is unknown, was one of the first ranchers in the Nine Mile area, but within a short time of settling there he killed a man named Foote in a dispute and fled the country. His place was taken over by Pete Francis, who opened a saloon and a twenty-five-room hotel. Shortly after the establishment of several new businesses, Francis was shot and killed in a gunfight in his own saloon in 1901.

Most Utah communities, at least those settled by Mormons in the nineteenth century, included a formal town site that had a religious, educational, and commercial center. The community of Harper, however, was a collection of scattered ranches and stopping places that developed in Nine Mile Canyon as the Price-Fort Duchesne Road grew in importance. The 1890 census listed the larger area known as the Brock precinct as having a population of fifty. Ten years later, the precinct (later renamed Minnie Maud) more than doubled, with a population of 121. The population of Harper reached its largest size in 1910 with 130 residents.[17] The popularity of the Price-Fort

Duchesne Road and increased ranching activities along the northern
Carbon County line contributed to the precinct's growth.

By 1896 there was sufficient population in Nine Mile Canyon
that residents established the Minnie Maud School District. The local
ranchers and their families and overnight-inn proprietors identified
themselves as a distinct and viable community; the only porblem was
that they lacked the physical trappings of a town.

The school district was the first organized educational effort in
what became Duchesne County, and it served students living on both
sides of the Carbon County line. The schoolhouse, located at Brock's
Ranch at the mouth of Argyle Canyon just across the county line in
Carbon County, was the closest thing to a community center that
existed. In addition to the school district, the people of Nine Mile
Canyon established the town of Harper in 1905.[18]

Perhaps the most significant and colorful resident of Nine Mile
Canyon was Preston Nutter. A Virginia-born opportunist, Nutter
made his first fortune with a Colorado freight company before he
turned his attention to cattle in 1886 when he sold his interest in the
freight company. He moved first to Grand Junction, Colorado, in
search of a range for upwards of 20,000 head of cattle.

His search for grazing ground eventually led him to the Uintah
Indian Reservation, where in the early 1890s he was successful in
securing a summer grazing lease of more than 665,000 acres. Nutter's
lease with the Ute Indians was located in the Duchesne River
drainage for a period of five years at $7,100 a year. However, lacking
the needed capital to pay for the five-year lease, Nutter was forced to
seek financial backing outside the territory. Since Utah was in the
depths of a serious economic depression, Nutter turned to Charles F.
Homer of New York City whom he had met earlier in Colorado. The
two formed the Strawberry Cattle Company; Nutter, with 50 percent
ownership, was named president.

Nutter was successful in securing a multiyear lease from the Ute
Indians because he had honored earlier restrictions imposed by the
reservation. Neither the Utes nor Indian agent Robert Waugh were
interested in leasing grassland to ranchers who had been known to
have trespassed on the reservation.[19]

As mentioned, Preston Nutter was not the first to recognize the

Preston Nutter branding a mule at the Nutter Ranch headquarters in Nine Mile Canyon circa 1920. (Utah State Historical Society)

value of large parts of the Uintah Indian Reservation as summer rangeland. For a number of years, neighboring cattle outfits had illegally grazed their cattle in the Strawberry Valley and in the Current Creek section of the reservation. In addition to neighbors who trespassed on the reservation, there were cattlemen from other parts of Utah who annually trailed their cattle across the reservation on their way to market in Cheyenne, Wyoming. Frequently the trail herds lingered on the reservation lands for several months before being trailed on to Cheyenne.

Despite efforts from the Indian agents and protests from the Indians, prohibiting the trailing herds from crossing the reservation or imposing a grazing fee on neighboring ranchers was nearly impossible. An exasperated Indian agent, T.A. Byrnes, wrote of the situation in 1887: "These cattlemen have given me more trouble than all my Indians or business of both agencies. For years they have controlled this reservation and most of its affairs. They have pastured their cattle for years on this reservation and swindled these Indians at every opportunity."[20] The money and political power of the cattlemen proved to be too much for the Utes to be able to protect their lands.

In 1892 Indian agent Robert Waugh and the Indian Office in Washington, D.C., agreed that Strawberry Valley should be leased to ranchers of the area. Their rationale was twofold: first, the Utes did not have sufficient stock themselves to fully use the grazing grounds; and, second, to try to prevent trespassing was virtually impossible without expending more money or using the army. Waugh and others reasoned that if Strawberry Valley was leased to neighboring livestock men the leases would ensure that Strawberry Valley would be kept free of transient cattle herds and other trespassers while at the same time raising money for the federal treasury.

Soon after Nutter obtained his lease, other grazing interests, specifically sheepmen, sought grazing leases from the Ute Tribe. For several decades the production of sheep and wool had grown steadily in Utah. As a result, there was keen competition between sheepmen and cattlemen for the little remaining virgin summer grazing grounds found in the eastern part of the state.

The leasing of grazing ground by the Ute Indian agent to sheepmen greatly disturbed Nutter. Like many other cattlemen of the time, Nutter viewed sheep and cattle as being incompatible on the same rangeland. In Nutter's view, sheep destroyed grasslands. Rather than risk a range war, Nutter moved his cattle to Nine Mile Canyon and the rangeland of the Tavaputs Plateau after his lease expired, and in 1902 he bought the Brock Ranch from the widow of Pete Francis.[21]

Nutter had little or no interest in running either a saloon or a hotel, and he converted the hotel into a bunkhouse for his cowboys. Cowboying was not always a lucrative profession; occasionally some cowboys did other kinds of work, which from time to time filled their pockets with more money than did their skills working cattle. Virginia Price, Nutter's daughter, explained:

> Between train and bank robberies, the outlaws often turned to rustling. Like a lot of other ranchers, Nutter often found it more practical to hire the outlaws to work as cowhands during their cooling off periods. Most of them were cowboys at one time or another and made top hands, but what was more important their code prevented them from rustling from an employer.[22]

Robert LeRoy Parker, alias Butch Cassidy, and several other outlaws frequented the Nine Mile region. (Uintah County Library–Regional History Center)

Nutter's ranch headquarters was more than a collection of buildings and cattle. When he bought the ranch he also acquired a lonesome peacock left by Mrs. Francis. Nutter, who preferred riding a mule to a horse, soon found a mate for the lonesome bird; as a result, a flock of peacocks was a distinctive feature of Nutter's ranch for the next several decades.

At the peak of Preston Nutter's cattle operation, his cattle ranged across public lands from Blue Mountain on the Colorado-Utah border to the west Tavaputs Plateau, and south to the Arizona Strip in extreme northwestern Arizona. He owned several thousand acres in the bottoms of Nine Mile Canyon as well as on the mountains to the south and east of the canyon. On this sprawling ranch Nutter ran upwards of 25,000 cattle, which made him one of the largest cattle barons in Utah at the turn of the century.[23]

Nutter continued raising cattle, operating out of his Nine Mile Canyon base for the next several decades. He had gained such notoriety and high regard that he was a consultant to Washington politicians on grazing issues and was a firm supporter of federal regulation of livestock grazing. Preston Nutter died in 1936; the ranch continued in operation under the direction of his daughter Virginia Nutter Price.[24]

Indian Water: Non-Indian Users

Illegal cattle grazing was not the only piracy of Ute Indian resources—water from the upper Strawberry River Valley and the Uintah Indian Reservation was a coveted prize beginning with the farmers from Heber Valley and then, at the turn of the century, with irrigators from Utah Valley. In 1879, farmers from Heber Valley stealthily constructed the Strawberry Canal to divert water from the Strawberry River into Daniels Creek to irrigate their thirsty farms. Four years later, the Strawberry Canal Company was formed with fifty stockholders, most of whom were the farmers who were using the water. Following the example of the Strawberry Canal Company, other farmers during the next several years dug additional canals. By 1904 some 991 acres of land were being irrigated by water diverted illegally from the Uintah Indian Reservation. In 1904 farmers from Utah Valley were planning the massive Strawberry Valley Reclamation Project, the largest of its kind planned in the state at the time.

Irrigators were aided by Utah Senator Reed Smoot in their plans to divert water from the reservation. Soon after being elected, Smoot began applying political pressure to permit the diversion of water from the reservation. In a response to an enquiry made by him in December 1904 regarding water use and canal construction in Strawberry Valley, Uintah Indian agent H.P. Myton replied: " . . . while these people [the users of the diverted water] have no legal right to this water, I would recommend if it is at all possible that you permit them to continue to use the water."[25] Myton's rationale was that there was only one Indian family living in the Strawberry Valley and the Utes were not using the water. The criminal behavior by white irrigators was never brought before a court of law.

These several early successful efforts to divert water from the Uintah Indian Reservation, the Uinta Basin, and later Duchesne County provided a framework for an even larger and much more costly reclamation project years later—the Central Utah Project—funded in large measure by the federal government and vigorously promoted and support by residents of the Wasatch Front and farmers of central Utah.

Stockmore: Boom-Town Busted

There were other whites who tried to take advantage of the resources found on the Uintah Reservation with a land scheme profitable to the promoters. This scheme involved land promoters who attempted to swindle greedy would-be miners. The mining hoax and land fraud began in a bar in Park City in the summer of 1905 prior to the opening to white settlement of the Uintah Indian Reservation. A stranger in Park City paid for his drink with a small gold nugget. Following several additional drinks, the Park City bar patron willingly told his tale of mining the small gold nugget from a discovery he had made in the upper Duchesne River Valley near the present-day community of Hanna. Within days, miners and others were in the valley wanting land. Two supposed owners of land in the valley, a Mr. Stockman and a Mr. Moore, were eager to sell lots in the new town they called Stockmore. Almost overnight a small town of tents and hastily built wooden buildings was established, including a general store, four saloons, a barber shop, a livery, and an assay office—all necessary businesses for a new mining town.

One of the saloons was owned and operated by Frank Defa, who later became well known for his homemade whiskey. It was not long, however, before the new townspeople and prospectors alike grew restless when the anticipated gold was not located. In such situations, tempers grew short and fights were common. It was clear that law and order was needed. By now the Uintah Indian Reservation had been opened to homesteading, and, as word reached county officials that land problems were occurring in Stockmore, a sheriff was sent to investigate. The two mining promoters, Moore and Stockton, took their leave of the valley before they could be questioned. The Stockmore residents and miners quickly came to the realization that they had been "sold" land that was at the time part of the Uintah Indian Reservation and that the land did not contain veins of gold. They soon abandoned their worthless claims and left the valley. Lumber from the abandoned buildings was later used by the legitimate homesteaders of Hanna.

Months later the story filtered back to the Uinta Basin that the swindlers had made a very small gold strike in the Klondike region in Alaska. However, their small hoard of gold was insufficient to keep them in funds for long and so they had hatched the scheme involving the land near Stockmore. Knowing the western portion of the former Ute reservation in far-off Utah was poorly policed, they planned to get rich selling mining claims and town lots to greedy prospectors.[26] The two remained outside of Utah and the reach of the law and were never caught or prosecuted.

Outlaws

There were other nefarious characters who used the Uintah Indian Reservation for their own illegal purposes. Robert LeRoy Parker, alias Butch Cassidy, and his gang of outlaws known as the Wild Bunch commonly traveled through Nine Mile Canyon en route from Price to the Strip, Vernal, or Browns Park. Many local tales are told of Butch Cassidy and other outlaws visiting, eating with, and being warned of coming lawmen by ranchers and homesteaders along Minnie Maud Creek.

One such story, told years later, tells of Butch and some of his men coming to the Nine Mile homestead where Mariah "Ma" Warren lived. The outlaws frequently stopped there while riding through the area and often traded trail-weary horses for fresh ones. On one such visit, Ma Warren gladly prepared a meal for the travelers before they departed. The travelers made camp for the night a mile or two from Warren's place. No sooner had they gone than a posse from Carbon County came asking about the outlaws. Ma Warren claimed not to have seen or heard the outlaws. Following western courtesy, a meal was offered to the posse members. While cooking her second meal of the evening, Ma Warren had one of the children finish the cooking chores. She slipped out the back door to the corral where she quickly bridled a horse and rode bareback a mile or two to the camp of Cassidy to warn him of the lawmen's presence. She then returned in time to serve the unsuspecting posse their meal.[27]

For years prior to the opening of the Uintah Indian Reservation, water users, ranchers, miners, swindlers, freighters, and others criss-crossed the reservation, legally and illegally. The extra-legal maneuverings to gain access to Indian reservation lands were sufficiently limited and quashed to prevent the outbreak of open hostilities between Indians and whites and between competing white interests.[28] However, public demand for prime land and other resources was sufficiently strong in the West that Indian reservation lands, including the Uintah Indian Reservation, were coveted. By the summer of 1905 Indian Office and U.S. Land Office officials had readied the Uintah Indian Reservation for white settlement and the eventual creation of Duchesne County, Utah's twenty-eighth county.

ENDNOTES

1. *Salt Lake Tribune,* 2 September 1886.

2. *Builders of Uintah: A Centennial History of Uintah County* (Vernal: Uintah County Daughters of Utah Pioneers, 1947), 260–63. The origin of the name Nine Mile is obscure. Many have thought that it was named for the Miles family who lived there and had seven daughters; they, when added with the two parents, totaled nine Mileses, but there is sufficient evidence to suggest that the canyon was called Nine Mile prior to the Miles family living there. For additional readings on the name of the canyon see Edward A. Geary, "Nine Mile: Eastern Utah's Forgotten Road," *Utah Historical Quarterly* 49 (Winter 1981): 42–55.

3. House Executive Documents No. 1, Report of the Secretary of War, 1882, 47th Cong., 1st sess., vol. 1, p. 113, Serial Set, 2010, University of Utah.

The annual reports of the Secretary of War for 1881 and 1883 also briefly discuss military roads in the western half of the Uinta Basin.

4. Gary Lee Walker, "Recollections of the Duchesne Strip," *Outlaw Trail Journal* 3 (Winter/Spring 1993): 2–11. See also Geary, "Nine Mile," 47–48.

5. George E. Stewart, "The Wells: Welcome Oasis Between the Duchesne and the Minnie Maud," *Salt Lake Tribune, Home Magazine,* 16 April 1972, H-8.

6. H. Bert Jenson, "Smith Wells: Stagecoach Inn on the Nine Mile Road," *Utah Historical Quarterly* 61, (Spring 1993): 182–97.

7. *Eastern Utah Telegraph* (Price, UT), 5 March 1891.

8. *Vernal Express,* 27 October 1948.

9. See Jenson, "Smith Wells," 182–97.

10. Ibid., 186.

11. Edward Geary, "Nine Mile: Utah's Forgotten Road," 50.

12. *Eastern Utah Telegraph,* 6 November 1891.

13. Edward A. Geary, "The Carbon County Freight Road to the Uinta Basin," in Philip F. Notarianni, ed., *Carbon County: Eastern Utah's Industrialized Island* (Salt Lake City: Utah State Historical Society, 1981), 138–43.

14. Ibid., 141.

15. This figure is a rough estimate based upon those figures that are available. In fall 1887, 2 million pounds of freight was transported in for the army; in 1895 the amount of freight hauled to Fort Duchesne dropped to 526,870 pounds. Averaging these two figures and then multiplying the years Fort Duchesne was in operation, and then doubling the amount again for hauling Gilsonite and other freight loads on the return trips leads to the figure of about 50 million pounds.

16. Jenson, "Smith Wells," 187.

17. See U.S. censuses for 1890, 1900, and 1910; see also Geary, "Nine Mile: Eastern Utah's Forgotten Road," 51.

18. H. Bert Jenson, "Minnie-Maud School District," paper, 1992, Utah State University, Uintah Basin Branch Campus.

19. Kathryn MacKay, "The Strawberry Valley Reclamation Project and the Opening of the Uintah Indian Reservation," *Utah Historical Quarterly* 50 (Winter 1982): 72.

20. T.A. Byrnes to Commissioner of Indians Affairs, 8 November 1887, Letters Received, RG 75 NA, quoted in MacKay, "Strawberry Valley Reclamation Project," 70.

21. See Virginia N. Price and John T. Darby, "Preston Nutter, Utah

Cattleman, 1886–1936," *Utah Historical Quarterly* 32 (Summer 1964): 232–252.

22. Ibid., 241.

23. Ibid., 232–51.

24. Spangler, *Paradigms and Perspectives,* 832.

25. H.P. Myton to Reed Smoot, 5 December 1904, quoted in MacKay, "Strawberry Valley Reclamation Project," 72n20.

26. Elden Wilken, "Stockmore—Boom Town Busted," *Outlaw Trail Journal* 2 (Summer/Fall 1992): 44–46.

27. This story was told to the author by Alma "Doc" Warren many years ago. Warren died in 1986 and was well into his nineties at that time.

28. In this era in other areas nearby range wars did erupt. In both Browns Park and the Blue Mountain region in western Colorado cattle-sheep wars raged for a short time.

CHAPTER 4

LAND RUSH IN THE UINTA BASIN

In 1861, when President Abraham Lincoln issued the executive order creating the Uintah Indian Reservation in Uinta (Duchesne) Valley to house relocated Ute Indians, the reservation was part of a federal policy of separating Indians from whites. This formal ethnocentristic policy of the federal government was rooted in earlier English colonial policy set forth in the Proclamation of 1763, which distinguished Indian territory and white territory in the British colonies in North America. The policy also attempted to prevent individual whites as well as individual colonies from dealing with the Indians politically and economically. All relationships with the Indians were to be conducted through the British crown.

A similar policy was adopted with the election of Andrew Jackson as president. The Indian Removal Act of 1830 attempted to remove all Indians east of the Mississippi River to the newly formed Indian Territory located west of the Mississippi. Over a span of several decades, Indian territory shrunk to much smaller areas and generally more isolated reservations. The purpose of these policies—formal or informal—remained the same, however: remove

Land Office in Vernal. Would-be homesteaders registered their claims for land in this office after they made their selection of land. (Uintah County Library–Regional History Center)

and isolate Indians from the march of white civilization and prevent conflicts between the two cultures.

The settlement of Utah by the Mormons occurred before the United States claimed or controlled the Great Basin and the West beyond Colorado. The reservation policy, or at least separation of the

Ute Indians and others from Mormon settlements, was not a high priority with federal officials in the tumultuous decades leading to the Civil War. As elsewhere in the West, conflicts occurred when Mormon settlers occupied Ute, Shoshoni, Goshute, and Paiute lands. As discussed, territorial governor and superintendent of Indian Affairs Brigham Young early on attempted to establish a similar program of segregation of the Indians from expanding Mormon settlements. Young's Indian farm system failed in part, however, because of lack of support by the federal government.

President Lincoln replaced Brigham Young's Indian farm system with the Uinta Valley Indian Reservation. Eventually, most of the Ute Indians from along the Wasatch Front and central Utah were forced to remove to the new reservation. For Mormon settlers, the threat of conflict was removed and unlimited access to the land and other resources was achieved. The Uintah Reservation did for a time effectively separate and isolate the two cultures.

The reservation program attempted to teach the Ute people the ways of the whites. But neglect by the federal government, some mismanagement of the reservation, dishonesty among Indian agents and others, and forced confinement wrought havoc among the Ute people, much as reservation life did among other Indian tribes in the West. The death rate soared, poverty was widespread among Indian families, and, in general, life for the Utes on the Uintah Indian Reservation was miserable. Added to the general despair of the Ute people was increased pressure from their white neighbors to acquire more of their land and water. The Ute people were not successful in adopting white culture in isolation, and their situation was typical of life on other reservations.

Deplorable living conditions at reservations and the rapid decline of the national Indian population gave rise to several Indian reform groups, located primarily in the eastern United States. Foremost among those calling for reform was Helen Hunt Jackson, whose book *Century of Dishonor* outlined the plight of the Indians and predicted that Native Americans under the reservation system were not going to survive into the twentieth century. [1] Equally concerned with the growing "Indian question" were eastern Protestant churches, which called for reforming the ailing Indian reservation system.

A homesteading family finds a place where they hope to build a home and make a living. (Uintah County Library–Regional History Center)

Representatives from these reform groups and various churches came together at Mohonk Lake, New York, beginning in the late 1870s to find a solution to the Indian problem. Meeting annually, the reformers eventually adopted a plan.

At the core of the Indian problem as they saw it was the reservation system and the collective control of land by the various tribes. This ran counter to the self-sufficiency and individualism preached and practiced by white Americans. To rectify the problem, the Mohonk Lake conference attendees called for a complete elimination of Indian reservations. Indian tribes would no longer be recognized, and reservations were to be replaced with individual ownership of land, which would encourage individuality. This would force assimilation of the Indians into white society.

The Dawes Act

The Indian reformers convinced Massachusetts Senator Henry L. Dawes, chairman of the Senate Indian Committee, to adopt their plan; and in 1887 Congress passed the General Allotment Act (Dawes Act), which reversed a century-old federal government policy of collective ownership of property by Indian tribes.[2] In its place was the new policy of Indian self-sufficiency, with the key element of the policy the distribution of Indian land to individuals ("in severalty") and the eventual granting of U.S. citizenship to all Indians. The Dawes Act provided that excess reservation land, land not distributed to Indian families, be placed in the public domain and be opened to homesteading under existing land laws.

For the next several decades, as various Indian tribes agreed to the Dawes Act, reservations across the West containing thousands of acres of land were opened to the rush of white homesteaders and others.[3]

At the outset, the Utes refused to accept land in severalty. Many felt that their former lands along the Wasatch Front and in Colorado had been taken without cause or their consent and that now the government was doing it again. Their resistence to accepting the Dawes Act was echoed among other tribes. Negotiations with the Utes and other tribes made little progress.

The resistance by several tribes to negotiate and accept land in severalty was eventually challenged in the federal courts. In 1903 in the landmark U.S. Supreme Court case *Hitchcock v. Lone Wolf* the Court ruled that an individual Indian or tribe did not have to consent to have their lands allotted. The court further stated that although the Indians' right of occupancy prevented white trespass it did not prevent the government from acting unilaterally in the sale of the Indians' surplus reservation lands. With the Lone Wolf decision issued, the last obstacle in breaking up reservations was now in place. The federal government now could force allotment of Indian lands and open the remaining reservation lands to homesteading and mining. Thereafter, the process of distributing land in severalty to the Ute people moved quickly.

Even after land was distributed and the reservation opened to white settlement, some Ute Indians continued to resist the federal Indian program. One group of 300 White River Utes, under the leadership of Red Cap, left the Uinta Basin for South Dakota in 1906, hoping the Sioux Indians there would take them in. Many white farmers and ranchers in Utah and Wyoming were alarmed by the flight of Red Cap and his band. From time to time it was reported that a cow or two was stolen; however, on the whole, the band of Indians along with several hundred horses and a few head of cattle traveled across Wyoming peacefully and without serious incident.

Wyoming residents asked local law enforcement officials to prevent further travel of the Ute band. Fearing what might happen, two detachments of the U.S. Tenth Cavalry engaged the unhappy Utes and tried to persuade them to return to the Uinta Basin. The beleaguered Utes refused but did agree to accept an escort of soldiers to Fort Meade, South Dakota. To their dismay, the Ute band was not welcomed at the reservation in South Dakota. The Sioux had no land or supplies to share with them. For the next months, some of the Utes worked at odd jobs, but they remained dissatisfied with their conditions. In January 1908, after months of futile attempts to find a new life and place of residence for themselves, they agreed to return to the Uinta Basin. After a tragic two years they returned disillusioned and destitute; but their effort to leave was largely in protest over receiving lands in severalty.[4] Part of the resistance of Red Cap and his followers to accepting land in severalty and adopting farming as a new way of life stemmed from their traditional way of life of freely hunting and fishing. Farming simply was not something most Utes were interested in doing, despite governmental pressure to do so.

Irrigation Systems for the Utes

As early as 1899 Uintah Indian agents and Bureau of Indian Affairs officials in Washington had urged Congress to appropriate funds for an irrigation system for the Ute Indians on the Uintah Indian Reservation. Hardly any appropriations were made by Congress during the next several years for an irrigation canal system, however; and, as a result, little effort was made to construct a canal system. Similar pleas from other Indian reservations also were made and were ignored by Congress. Without water and irrigation canals farming by either whites or Indians was impossible in the Uinta Basin.

Indian agent H.P. Myton and the Ute Indian Commission understood that success of the Indian land-allotment program hinged on

Twentieth Century Pioneers, circa 1905–1910. (Uintah County Library–Regional History Center)

the Utes being able to secure water for their allotments. As part of their work, Myton and the Ute Indian Commission secured water rights from the state engineer in Salt Lake City. Myton and the commission also made preliminary plans to build an irrigation system to deliver water to the Indian farms; however, this required a great deal of money that the Utes did not have. Without irrigation canals and ditches, under state water law, the Utes would lose their rights to the water if the water wasn't used for beneficial purposes.

Indians on other reservations faced similar problems, and it soon became evident that the allotment program would fail if Congress did not provide funds to construct irrigation canals for the Indians. In 1906 Minnesota Senator Moses Edwin Clapp successfully amended the general Indian appropriations bill to add $600,000 for the construction of the Uintah Indian Irrigation Project for the Utes living in the Uinta Basin.[5] To design, construct, and operate the Uintah Indian Irrigation Project, Congress included it as part of the larger United States Indian Irrigation Service, the Indian counterpart to the Bureau of Reclamation. During the next decade, twenty-two canals stretching more than 162 miles and 635 miles of laterals and ditches were constructed, most of the work being done by Ute Indians.[6]

Homesteading the Uintah Reservation

By the summer of 1905 Indian Office and U.S. Land Office officials had completed all the necessary preparation to open the Uintah Indian Reservation to homesteading.[7] Over 111,000 acres had been allotted to Indian families. Another 282,560 acres were reserved for hunting, grazing, and other resource development for the Ute people; much of it was located in the Deep Creek area. The reserved Indian grazing ground also helped protect and guarantee water for the numerous Indian homesteads. In addition to Indian homesteads and grazing grounds, 60,160 acres were reserved for reclamation purposes.

The opening of the Uintah Indian Reservation was a welcome opportunity for Utah Valley farmers, who for some time had coveted water from the Strawberry River. They had prepared a water plan similar in nature to the earlier successful but legally questionable transmontane water diversion system built by a group of Heber Valley farmers. In 1900 Utah state senator Henry Gardner from Spanish Fork and his close friend John S. Lewis conceived of the idea to store and divert Strawberry River water to Utah Valley. The idea developed further in 1902 when the Spanish Fork East Bench Irrigation and Manufacturing Company hired an engineer to conduct a feasibility study of Gardner's plan. The engineering study provided the farmers of Utah Valley with a solid proposal to seek federal financial assistance and engineering services from the newly established United States Reclamation Service, later named the Bureau of Reclamation, for the Strawberry Valley Reclamation Project.[8]

The Utah Valley reclamation scheme called for the construction of a large storage reservoir on the upper Strawberry River, a delivery system constructed through the Wasatch Mountains to the headwaters of Sixth Water Creek, and the subsequent use of Diamond Fork Creek and the Spanish Fork River to deliver Strawberry River water to sections of Utah Valley.

The Utah Valley reclamation plan required a large financial outlay—more than the farmers of Utah Valley collectively could raise, and even more than the state of Utah could bankroll. However, financial and engineering assistance from the federal government awaited Utah Valley farmers. The Strawberry Valley reservoir and reclamation project was the first federally funded project in the state. It was made possible by the passage of the Newlands Act in 1902, which established a national revolving fund to assist in developing large reclamation projects in the West. The act also established the Bureau of Reclamation, which provided technical and economic support and direction for western reclamation projects.

Fully aware of the Utah Valley farmers' reclamation scheme to divert Uinta Basin water to Utah Valley, the *Vernal Express,* the Uinta Basin's only newspaper at the time, voiced the concerns of settlers and water users of the Uinta Basin: "We cannot help but admire the supreme effrontery with which our friends over the [Wasatch] range set about appropriating something [water] to which they have no moral right in the world."[9]

To help with the Strawberry Valley Reclamation Project and ensure a location for a reservoir, President Theodore Roosevelt issued a presidential proclamation just days before the opening of the Uintah Reservation reserving a little more than 60,100 acres specifically for the reclamation project. Six months later, in December, Secretary of the Interior Ethan A. Hitchcock authorized $150,000 for work to begin on the reclamation project.[10]

Additional former reservation land, about a million acres, was withdrawn from public entry in July and added to the Uinta National Forest by President Theodore Roosevelt. The Uinta National Forest had been created in 1897 when President William McKinley set aside 482,000 acres of forested land on the Uinta Mountains.

Other reservation land was withdrawn from homestead entry as well. Over 2,000 acres were set aside for townsites, and 2,140 acres were temporarily withdrawn from entry because of the land's potential mineral value. The balance of the reservation land, some 1,004,200 acres, was made available for homesteading.[11]

For several years prior to the opening of the Uintah Indian Reservation and the settlement of Duchesne County in 1905 much state and national political and economic intrigue and controversy swirled around the Uintah Indian Reservation. As mentioned, the

Another hopeful family of homesteaders. (Photo courtesy Uintah County Library–Regional History Center.)

virgin land and untapped water resources of the western section of the Uinta Basin were very much desired and became the source of intrigue and conflict.

At the time of statehood in 1896, Utah's population was about 250,000 people. Because of a high birthrate, the continued immigration of Mormons, and the increased immigration of non-Mormon mining and industrial workers to the new state, Utah's population continued to grow, doubling over the next two decades. The demand for arable land was already high. It was little wonder that state officials and leaders of the Mormon church looked to the Uinta Basin to help meet the state's growing land needs.

Mormon leaders were not yet accustomed to acting according to federal laws and procedures when it came to settling on new land; therefore, various church leaders in Heber City and in Salt Lake City developed their own plan to secure land for Mormon church members when the reservation opened. As a result, a political brouhaha erupted between the church hierarchy and Senator

Thomas Kearns and others over the opening of the Uintah Indian Reservation.

Part of the controversy began earlier over one of the state's two U.S. Senate seats. In the fall of 1900 Thomas Kearns, owner of the *Salt Lake Tribune* and a Catholic mining millionaire from Park City, was elected by the Utah legislature to the U.S. Senate with the support of most of the state's Republican party officials and some influential Mormon church leaders.[12] The senate term was less than the normal six-year term, however; the abbreviated term was designed to stagger the subsequent elections of Utah's U.S. Senate seats. By the fall of 1902 when elections were held again, Kearns had fallen out of political favor with the leadership of the Republican party. The result was a nasty campaign between the incumbent Kearns and his challenger Reed Smoot, who was also a member of the Council of Twelve Apostles of the Mormon church.

Smoot had organized a well-oiled political machine known as the "Federal Bunch," which gained control of the state Republican party. He won the election and joined George Sutherland, a fellow Utah Valley resident, in the U.S. Senate. Kearns was outraged by the turn of events, being denied a second term by the state Republican party. He charged the state's Republicans and certain Mormon church officials with a political double-cross for not supporting his senatorial candidacy. Kearns became politically bitter over his defeat, and he believed that Reed Smoot and Mormon church president Joseph F. Smith controlled the state Republican party and were therefore instrumental in denying him his seat in the Senate. Kearns then helped found the American party to challenge the church-dominated Republican party.

Kearns's bitterness and his fighting with the Mormon church hierarchy spread to other issues, including the opening of the Uintah Indian Reservation. Kearns learned that the Mormon church hierarchy was promoting a scheme to secure Uintah Indian Reservation lands for church members, further convincing Kearns that the church under the leadership of Smith and Smoot was working to regain political and economic control of the state—a condition similar to what Utah faced before attaining statehood.

Near the center of the Indian land scheme was William H. Smart, president of the Wasatch LDS Stake, a loyal supporter of Reed Smoot, and a member of the Republican party. With its headquarters in Heber City, Smart's ecclesiastical jurisdiction included all of the Uintah Indian Reservation.

William Smart and the Wasatch Development Company

Thomas Kearns's suspicions of a Mormon church conspiracy to gain control of the Uintah Indian Reservation were bolstered when he learned that William Smart had secretly explored the reservation prior to its planned opening to identify the best land and water sites for homesteading. Smart was convinced that certain sections of the reservation provided excellent opportunities for homesteading. As ecclesiastical leader of the area, he believed he should take the lead in helping church members homestead the reservation. He further recognized that the development of water resources was essential if Mormon homesteaders were to be successful in proving up on their homesteads.

Smart acted quickly to accomplish the land settlement scheme. Prior to the opening of the reservation, Smart organized the Wasatch Development Company, a land- and water-development company which was in effect the secular arm of the Wasatch LDS Stake. Using both his positions as president of the development company and of Wasatch Stake, Smart contacted all the LDS stake presidents in the state, informing them that his company was ready to help church members secure land on the reservation.

Thomas Kearns and the *Salt Lake Tribune,* having learned of Smart's clandestine forays to the reservation and the organization of the Wasatch Development Company, accused Smart, U.S. Senator (and Mormon Apostle) Reed Smoot, Mormon church president Joseph F. Smith, and certain land office officials in Washington, D.C., with a "hierarchic plot and conspiracy" to gain control of all of the Uintah Indian Reservation for Mormon church members. In a shrill editorial the *Salt Lake Tribune* declared:

> Besides, what mischief has the ecclesiastical jurisdiction of the stake presidency of Wasatch to do with this question of land opening by the United States? It is not in the least an ecclesiastical question, but an opportunity for American citizens to obtain a stated

William Henry Smart circa 1907. Smart was instrumental in nearly every phase of the homesteading and early history of Duchesne County. (Photo courtesy Uintah County Library–Regional History Center.)

amount of land for a homestead or other occupancy. The intrusion of the ecclesiasticism into the matter is an impertinence that deserves the sternest rebuke. It seems, however, that the beautiful and strenuous hand of President Joseph F. Smith is in this ecclesiastical move. The impudent interference assumed by the Wasatch presidency "is desired by the First Presidency," to the end that "our people" may get the land. It is the most daring encroachment upon the Government's prerogatives, the most insolent attempt to thwart by underhand means, the efforts of the Government to give every land-seeker a square deal, that has developed under the present odious presidency of Joseph F. Smith.[13]

Throughout the spring and summer of 1905 the public feud over the reservation land between Kearns and the American party and Smart and the hierarchy of the Mormon church was carried out in the two statewide daily newspapers—the *Tribune* and the *Deseret News*. The women's auxiliary of the newly established American party also took up the fray, accusing the Mormon church of a "plot [of] . . . conspiracy" to gain control of the land on the former reservation. The women's group went so far as to petition the federal government, asking for a full investigation of the Mormon church's role in controlling land and water resources on the reservation for its members. The public voice of the Mormon church responded to the women's charges.

> What can be thought by decent people of the ministerial and journalistic deceivers who, not content with making ninnies of themselves in their furious assaults upon an imaginary "hierarchy" tricked a number of ladies of this city into assuming an absurd position before the country and exposing themselves to public ridicule.[14]

Kearns and others charged the U.S. Land Office officials in Utah with being part of the conspiracy to defraud American citizens from homesteading on the Uintah Indian Reservation. W.A. Richards, U.S. Land Commissioner in Washington, D.C., took Kearns's charges seriously. Richards conducted his own investigation of the matter and found no wrongdoing by Smart, Smoot, the Mormon church hierarchy, or federal land office officials in Salt Lake City or in Washington, D.C.

Land conspiracies—some actual, some unfounded suppositions—organized to obtain vast tracts of Indian reservation lands in the West were not altogether uncommon. The alleged Mormon church conspiracy was one of many that were part of the larger endeavor by individuals and special-interest groups (including individual states) to gain control of public western land. Land speculation, land fraud, and questionable activities and improprieties by government land office officials, speculators, and homesteaders had been continuous problems since the drafting of the United States Constitution. To address these problems, Congress had passed numerous land laws during the nineteenth century.[15]

On 14 July 1905 President Theodore Roosevelt declared that on 28 August of that year the Uintah Reservation would be opened to settlement "under the general provisions of the homestead and townsite laws of the United States."[16] To ensure equal opportunity for all potential homesteaders and to prevent any possible corruption, the general land office added two special land offices at Price, Utah, and Grand Junction, Colorado, where homesteaders could register for Uintah Reservation land.[17]

A New System to Homestead Reservation Lands

At other Indian reservation openings under the Dawes Act, the U.S. Land Office encountered numerous difficulties. The rush for land often resulted in serious accidents involving overturned wagons and runaway horses. Occasionally, eager homesteaders wanting the best land engaged in fistfights and gun battles. Through accidents and fights lives were lost.

To avoid similar problems at the opening of the Uintah Indian Reservation, the United States Land Office adopted a new system to reduce the chaotic rush for land while at the same time providing a degree of fairness to all those wanting to homestead on the newly opened reservation land. New rules required would-be homesteaders to register at one of the temporary land offices at Provo, Price, or Vernal, Utah, or Grand Junction, Colorado. Each registrant received an entry permit granting permission to enter the reservation to scout possible homestead sites. The registrants' names were sent to Provo by Land Office clerks, where they were inserted in individual envelopes and placed in a large barrel. Names were then drawn and assigned numbers; those with the highest numbers had the first choice of land on the reservation.

Uinta Basin Pioneers circa 1905. Would be homesteaders came by foot with a pack on their backs and others rode horseback, but the most common was families traveling by team and wagon. (Photo courtesy Uintah County Library–Regional History Center.)

Under this procedure, during the first two weeks of August nearly 37,000 individuals from all over the country registered for former Uintah Reservation land. People who registered for the drawing of land were then given time to scout possible homesteads. During the early weeks of August, all of the roads and trails leading to the Uinta Basin were choked with wagons, horses, buggies, and homesteaders on foot.

Government land office officials believed that at least 100,000 people would register for Ute land; however, the number of registrants fell short of the anticipated number—only about a third of the anticipated number registered for the land lottery. Even with the lower number, special travel arrangements were made. The Denver and Rio Grande Railroad added several special trains to Provo to accommodate hundreds of homeseekers from Sanpete and Sevier counties. Elsewhere, the temporary land office cities were choked with people. In Grand Junction, Colorado, the city council hired special police to control the anticipated crowd of land seekers. As many as 500 single women registered for land in Grand Junction. One young single woman indicated that she was indeed interested in settling on the reservation, but she also expressed interest in a man to assist her to prove up on her land.[18] Franklin P. White, a Denver architect and leader of the Emethaehevahs, a religious sect, hoped to draw a high number, as he intended to establish a religious colony in the Uinta Basin.[19] Most of the registrants were from Utah and were members of the Mormon church, however.

In each of the land office towns, enterprising entrepreneurs vied for the homesteaders' money. In one Grand Junction newspaper appeared the following advertisement: "To get a good choice in the Uintah [Basin] you will need good eyesight. Have yours fitted with proper glasses in time by G.W. Strong, jeweler and optician."[20] In Provo, local saloons remained open all night to meet the needs of thirsty men. Due to the lack of boarding houses and hotel rooms in Provo, city officials granted temporary permits to enterprising residents to establish tent cities in several open fields. At one of the tent cities located on the west side of the courthouse as many as 150 tents, each containing from two to four cots, were hastily pitched. Cots rented out for one dollar or more per night. Members of the LDS First Ward organized a special dining room and kitchen in the basement of the old Provo LDS Tabernacle.[21]

All preparations for the land lottery in Provo were completed by the evening of 28 August. At the Proctor Academy, where the lottery took place, Land Office personnel built a temporary wooden lean-to and platform canopied with white canvas against the side of the school building. Throughout the night, men and women gathered at the school. By early the next morning the air was thick with dust from the feet of hundreds of men and women stirring up the dirt. By 9:00 A.M. the hot August sun was making the day uncomfortable. Those selling cold drinks made good money that day.

At precisely 9:00 A.M. U.S. Land Office officials John Dern and Irving Hewbert were ready to announce and record the names drawn from the barrel. Earlier, officials had chosen teenagers Lyman Noyes, Arnold Rawlings, Earl Gillespie, and Earl Dusenberry from the Parker

School in Provo and Hoyt Ray, Charles Petersen, Raymond Peterson, Walter Williams, and Arthur Goodwin from the Proctor Academy to draw the envelopes containing the names of the homesteaders from the wooden barrel.

The crowd pushed closer to the stand, and just before the first envelope was drawn an anxious homesteader shouted out: "Five hundred dollars, boy, if you draw my name first," breaking the tension of the moment.[22] The first envelope drawn from the barrel contained the name of Roy Daniels.[23] For the next several days some 5,772 names were drawn from the barrel one by one. At the end of the day, all the names drawn were reported in the state's daily newspapers. Thereafter, land office officials drew additional names from the barrels at the land office in Provo.

The drama of the opening of the reservation was centered on the securing and holding of real estate. Nearly every individual had high hopes of securing and proving up on a choice 160-acre homestead. All dreamed their name would be drawn first, giving them the first selection of unallotted reservation lands. Those who were successful in drawing high numbers immediately began moving to the Uinta Basin to claim their new homesteads. What they found was not a paradise of green meadows and sparkling streams but a dry land covered with sagebrush, cedar trees, and blown sand. Some homesteaders were successful in proving up their claims. Others, however, discouraged with the poor soil and lack of water, left the basin after a few years of struggle, hardship, and poverty.

The ultimate success of Smart's plan to secure land for Mormon church members is hard to determine. However, the proximity of the Uinta Basin to the Wasatch Front, coupled with the large number of Mormon church members who desired land, likely resulted in the fact that most of the homesteaders were members of the Church of Jesus Christ of Latter-day Saints.

At the conclusion of the homesteading period in 1912, about 450,000 acres had been homesteaded. The remaining unclaimed land was offered for sale to the highest bidder, and in 1913 another 300,000 acres were sold. The remaining land was withdrawn from sale under a temporary mineral-reserve status.[24]

The Dream of America—Land For the Taking

The drama of the Western experience is usually portrayed as gunfights, Indian battles, range wars, or other violent action. If Hollywood actually were to capture the emotional base of Western history, however, the movies would be about land issues. The "heroes" often would have been surveyors or lawyers, not gunfighters or sheriffs. Western history and the early history of Duchesne County was basically about drawing lines on maps and making borders dividing the land into manageable units of property, and then persuading people to treat those lines with respect.[25]

The settlement of Duchesne County by whites is unique in Utah history. For the most part, Utah and its counties were settled under the direction of Brigham Young and other Mormon church leaders. Frequently, calls were issued from the church pulpit and faithful members of the church accepted the calls to establish new settlements in the territory or to strengthen existing ones. This often was done under much hardship, and the stories of settlements such as San Juan's Hole-in-the-Rock expedition are forever a part of Utah's heritage.

Settlement of Duchesne County was delayed in part because of geographical barriers that isolated it and the eastern part of the state from the heartland of Utah. Discouraging reports initially postponed any church-directed settlement plans, and the establishment of the Uintah Indian Reservation delayed further the settlement of Duchesne County. As a result, Duchesne County was the last county in the state to be colonized, and it became the twenty-eighth county to be established. White settlement finally occurred under federal land laws, and it occurred as a result of a congressional solution to the national "Indian problem." One problem that wasn't solved was the continued mistreatment of the Native Americans.

ENDNOTES

1. See Helen Hunt Jackson, *Century of Dishonor,* reprint, (Boston: Roberts Brothers, 1973).

2. For a fuller discussion of the process of opening the Uintah Indian Reservation see Craig Fuller, "Land Rush in Zion: Opening of the

Uncompahgre and Uintah Indian Reservations (Ph.D. diss., Brigham Young University, 1990).

3. Richard White, *It's Your Misfortune and None of My Own* (Norman: University of Oklahoma Press, 1991), 110, 115. Before Congress passed the Dawes Act, Indians held over 155 million acres of land on ninety-nine Indian reservations and the Indian Territory (later Oklahoma). Thirteen years later, Indian reservation lands had dwindled to less than 79 million acres, almost a 50 percent reduction of land.

4. Floyd A. O'Neil, "An Anguished Odyssey: The Flight of the Utes 1906–1908" *Utah Historical Quarterly* 36 (Fall 1966): 315–27.

5. For further discussion of Ute irrigation projects see chapter 9.

6. Craig Fuller, Gregory D. Kendrick, and Robert W. Righter, "Prelude to Settlement: The Efforts of the U.S. Indian Irrigation Service in the Uinta Basin, Utah," in Gregory D. Kendrick, ed., *Beyond the Wasatch: The History of irrigation in the Uinta Basin and Upper Provo River Area of Utah* (Denver: National Park Service, n.d.), 20.

7. For a new view on the meaning of the term "opening" see Patricia Nelson Limerick, *The Legacy of Conquest: The Unbroken Past of the American West* (New York: Norton, 1987), 46. According to Limerick, opening was "a metaphor based on the assumption that the virgin West was 'closed,' locked up, held captive by the Indians." In Limerick's opinion, the entire thought process that led to reservation systems, and their failures which resulted in the "opening" of Indian lands, is based in hypocrisy and ethnocentrism.

8. Craig Fuller, "Development of Irrigation in Wasatch County" (M.S. thesis, Utah State University, 1973), 112–25. For further discussion about the diversion of water from the Uintah Basin see Thomas G. Alexander, "An Investment in Progress: Utah's First Federal Reclamation Project, The Strawberry Valley Project," *Utah Historical Quarterly* 39 (Summer 1971), 286–304; and Kathryn L. MacKay, "The Strawberry Valley Reclamation Project and the Opening of the Uintah Indian Reservation," 68–89.

9. *Vernal Express,* 5 September 1903.

10. See Alexander, "An Investment in Progress."

11. U.S. Department of the Interior, Office of Indian Affairs, *Annual Report (1905).* See also Robert Hugie, "The 1905 Opening of the Uintah Reservation," n. 41, Uintah County Library, Vernal.

12. O.N. Malmquist, *The First 100 Years: A History of the Salt Lake Tribune, 1871–1971* (Salt Lake City: Utah State Historical Society, 1971), 185–86.

13. *Salt Lake Tribune,* 2 July 1905

14. *Deseret News,* 11 July 1905.

15. There are a number of good works on the land question in American history; they include Vernon Carstensen, ed., *The Public Lands: Studies in the History of the Public Domain* (Madison: University of Wisconsin Press, 1968); Paul Wallace Gates, *History of Public Land Law Development* (Washington, D.C.: Government Printing Office, 1968); and Malcolm J. Rohrbough, *The Land Office Business: The Settlement and Administration of American Public Lands, 1789–1837* (New York: Oxford University Press, 1968). For a closer look at land policies in Utah see George W. Robbins, "Land Policies of the United States as applied to Utah to 1910," *Utah Historical Quarterly* 20 (July 1952): 239–51; Lawrence B. Lee, "Homesteading in Zion," *Utah Historical Quarterly* 28 (January 1960): 29–40; Gustive O. Larson, "Land Contest in Early Utah," *Utah Historical Quarterly* 29 (October 1961): 308–26; Carlton F. Culmsee, "Flimflam Frontier: Submarginal Land Development in Utah," *Utah Historical Quarterly* 32 (Spring 1964): 91–98; and Fuller, "Land Rush in Zion."

16. 34 U.S. Statutes 3119 (14 July 1905).

17. Detailed accounts of the controversy are found in almost every issue of the *Salt Lake Tribune* between late June and August 1905.

18. *Salt Lake Tribune,* 11 August 1905.

19. Fuller, "Land Rush in Zion," 244.

20. Ibid.

21. Ibid., 240–46.

22. *Provo Daily Enquirer,* 17 August 1905, cited in Fuller, "Land Rush in Zion," 245.

23. Daniels worked at a stone quarry east of Colton, Utah, and had come to Provo to see the circus, which was in town at the same time as the land lottery. See Fuller, "Land Rush in Zion," 244.

24. *Vernal Express,* 16 February 1912, 16 August 1912.

25. Limerick, *Legacy of Conquest,* 54.

CHAPTER 5

TWENTIETH-CENTURY HOMESTEADERS

The federal land lottery of Indian reservation land offered many twentieth century homesteaders the opportunity to acquire 160 acres of land with little cash expense. Those who settled on the reservation did so with high hopes and expectations to turn the virgin land into highly productive farmland through hard work and a desire to build a new life for themselves and their families. Many arrived with few belongings and resources. Through the sweat of their brows, the strength of their hands, and their faith and prayers some succeeded in proving up on their 160 acres, building homes, establishing communities, and creating Utah's twenty-eighth county.

It Was Less Than They Expected

Not all who filed for the right to take up land on the reservation actually took up land, and, of those who did try their hand at homesteading, perhaps more than a third left the reservation within a year of settling. These failures did not halt other families from taking up homesteads, however.

Those who stayed understood that the former reservation was

not a land of mountain meadows watered with sparkling streams and dark rich soil. Like much of the land elsewhere in Utah, they found much of the reservation full of sagebrush, cedar trees, sand, and rock. There were no ready-made irrigation canals awaiting them to irrigate their freshly plowed ground.

Charles W. Smith, an early settler in Midview, recalled his first encounter with some homesteaders, who after just a year of hard work had decided to give up on their dream:

> The second day out, we met many who were disappointed, begrimed, and weary from a hot dusty trip into the known region of the rolling, barren hills without water except that which flowed down the several rivers. To subdue the sunbaked prairie appeared to many to be an insurmountable task. Many of these discouraged victims were ready to sell their number for a song and return to their homes.[1]

Smith was one who was determined to "make a go of it" regardless of the difficulties faced. His chances to secure good land were somewhat diminished when his name was one of those drawn after the initial drawing in Provo. He later wrote, "Our numbers were so high that all of the good land had been taken before we had a chance to draw." He recalled that Provo was filled at the time with hundreds of people. "It seemed there were people from all parts of the Union: White, Black, and Yellow," he added.[2]

In the spring of 1906, after having made his selection of land, Smith proceeded at once to build a log cabin for his family. A good stand of pine was found in Strawberry Valley some distance from his homestead east of Myton. Felling the trees was easy; transporting the rough-cut logs to his homestead was difficult. Smith wrote that after having felled the trees his group traveled east: "When we reached the Strawberry and Duchesne rivers with our first load of logs, the water had risen so high that the Theodore [Duchesne] Townsite was completely under water up to our waists. There was nothing for us to do but pull back up the canyon and take the old road to Myton." Spring flooding of all the major streams in the Uinta Basin was nearly an annual occurrence. Down the road he later faced a similar situation at Myton; both the town and road were flooded.[3]

Famers in Myton circa 1915. (Utah State Historical Society)

Smith was not the only one to face the problem of high streams each spring. The families of Joseph and Zella Cowan and their young baby girl Shirley; John D. and Emma C. Wimmer; and the teenage nephew of John Wimmer, Victor Green, all had difficulties crossing the Strawberry River. Emma Wimmer wrote later of the difficulty:

> [We] reached the Strawberry river [on 14 June 1906]. . . . The Strawberry was much larger than it is now, and it being the time of year flood waters were overflowing the banks, but the river had to be crossed. The water ran over the horses backs, and almost floated the boxes off the wagons. The crossing of the cattle and all caused a little commotion.[4]

There was a steady flow of homesteaders to the west end of the Uinta Basin for several years after the opening in 1905. The third year of homesteading, 1907, brought the greatest number of settlers to the reservation. Like the hundreds who had preceded them, the later-arriving settlers traveled by every conceivable means of transportation: wagons drawn by mules and horses, surreys, and buggies.

William R. Evans, an old-time resident of the county, remembered:
"Sometimes you would see one large horse and one very small one
hitched together, some so poor and run down they could hardly
walk."[5] Some homesteaders came by horseback with pack strings or
alone with a bedroll on their saddles; others even walked with packs
on their backs.[6]

The Nine Mile Canyon road was the most popular route to the
Uinta Basin for the homesteaders. Local historian George Stewart
recalled: "My dad said he stood on a peak at the head of Gate Canyon
and from there he could trace the Stage Road all the way to Vernal
and the Land Office, by the dust churned up from the turning wheels
and pounding hoofs."[7] Less used but worthy of mention was the
Indian Canyon route. Verda Moore's extended family of twenty-two
members (including grandparents, an uncle and his family, and her
father's family) all came by train from West Virginia to Colton to live
in Zion, after having sold their farms and homes in the East. Arriving
by train at Colton when snow was still on the ground, Moore's family
group was hauled to the head of Indian Canyon by several large
sleighs. There they transferred their belongings to large wagons for
the last leg of their journey to Theodore, as Duchesne was then
called.[8]

By 1910 the 3,800 homesteaders and those who settled in the
newly surveyed towns of Myton, Theodore, and Roosevelt were a
diverse group of people. The 1910 federal census, the first census
taken after the opening of the reservation, recorded several cooks, a
servant, a jeweler, a barber, several teachers, a photographer, a ditch
rider, several druggists and merchants, an engineer, a carpenter, a
minister, laborers, and teamsters. Farmers constituted the largest
group. Years later, George Stewart recalled that many of the homesteader farmers were accompanied "with mom and the baby on the
seat [of the wagon], the older kids in the wagon box behind them,
old bossy on a lead rope and a crate of chickens tied on behind."[9]

Homesteading in the Uinta Basin was not for the faint-hearted.
The newcomers had many concerns as they moved to what seemed
to be a harsh and forbidding land. Their justified apprehensions of
settling new land were further compounded by unjustified fears of
their neighbors, the Ute Indians. The Ute farmers were friendly but

remained secluded from their white neighbors, preferring to associate among themselves. Many white settlers, having grown up hearing fearsome stories about Indians, were anxious when meeting Ute families. Friendship and trust came slowly between whites and Indians; however, the extended hand of whites was often warmly welcomed by the Indians. Harold Eldredge recalled:

> I found the Indians of the Uinta Basin very friendly and interesting. I made friends with several . . . and participated in the Bear Dance on several occasions. . . . Most of the white people would not eat Indian food. But I ate it. I wanted to show the Indians that I considered them to be my brothers and sisters. . . . I wanted their respect and got it."[10]

Swindlers and Schemers

Frequently, trouble for the white homesteaders came from other whites who endeavored to take advantage of unwary or easily fooled homesteaders. Some homesteaders came with the mistaken idea that one of the reservation's assets was a mild climate. Others were misinformed by land speculators of the land's possibilities.[11]

Land promoters used a variety of means to promote settlement on land owned by them, including the use of photographs. The photographs could be easily framed or adapted to mislead hopeful land seekers. One land company took photos of the region between Red Creek and Currant Creek which captured many cedar (juniper) trees at a distance. Using the scenes of cedar trees in the background, land promoters carefully crafted their promotional material to suggest that the region between Currant and Red creeks was suitable for fruit trees. Some eager homesteaders purchased land in the area thinking their fortune was ready to be plucked from the fruit trees which could be grown in the area. However, the hopeful fruit farmers soon realized that, with the land at nearly 7,000 feet in elevation and with an arid climate, the hope of producing fruit was fruitless, a hoax perpetrated on them by unscrupulous land schemers using misleading photographs and false promotional material. With dry humor the disappointed farmers named their community Fruitland.[12]

A few of the homesteaders were themselves guilty of defrauding the government through questionable intent and the methods they

Grain harvest in the Uinta Basin, circa 1915. (Utah State Historical Society)

used to demonstrate permanent occupancy of the land, which was one of the requirements for proving up on the 160 acres of land of the homestead claims. Shanties often were hastily built, hardly liveable dwellings; but, to demonstrate occupancy, the would-be homesteaders strung clothes from makeshift clotheslines. When federal officials inspected the homestead they would find no one at home, but they would see the supposed wash drying on the clothesline. Other similarly questionable measures were used to trick homestead inspectors.[13]

Pioneering in the Twentieth Century

A common adage told of reservation residents describes the difficult living conditions they endured: "Marry a girl from the Uinta Basin—for no matter how hard times get for you she has seen worse!"

The settlement of the reservation occurred at a time of economic and social transition in Utah and across much of the United States. As several thousand people settled on the reservation lands, their urban cousins in Salt Lake City, Provo, and elsewhere in the state were becoming recipients of modern conveniences such as indoor plumbing, telephones, sewer systems, public transportation systems, and electricity.[14] However, living conditions on the former reservation were not significantly different to those of other recently settled areas of the state.

Homesteaders of the reservation arrived late in the summer of 1905. Cabins, dugouts, and other dwellings were hastily thrown together to ward off the first winter's cold and snow. The earliest log cabins were usually one or two rooms with dirt roof and floors. Martha Giles, an early homesteader in Hanna, recalled her first years living in such a cabin:

> In March 1908 we moved to the Indian Reservation at Stockmore. Monroe [her husband] built a nice new cabin for our house. The cabin had two windows: one in the east so we could see the sunrise and one in the west so we could see the beautiful sunsets. It had a door in the south, dirt floor, dirt roof and nothing in it but chips hewed from the logs. I stood and cried while Monroe unloaded the sleigh. He asked me if I wanted to go right back home but when I thought of going over those roads again, I decided to stay until the snow was gone. Everyday I put hot water on the dirt floor to harden it. . . . It was three months before I saw another woman. . . . We lived in log cabins for twenty years.[15]

Wood floors, usually made from rough-cut boards obtained from William Jolly's and John Anderson's sawmill or some other local sawmill, were added to the cabins as soon as possible. Sawmills at various locations, including Indian Canyon, Tabiona, and John Starr Flat above Neola, were in place by 1906–07. For the first several years, glass windowpanes had to be purchased from Ashton Hardware Store in Vernal, the Wasatch Lumber Company in Heber City, or from the Price Co-operative Mercantile Institution, the J.C. Weeter Lumber Company, or the C.H. Stevenson Lumber Company in Price and shipped to the reservation. Within a year or two, windowpanes and other building products could be purchased locally from A.M. Murdock's Pioneer Supply Store in Duchesne, or from the Uinta Lumber Company or E.M. Jones's Hardware and Lumber Store, both in Myton. Rooms were added to homesteaders' cabins as time and finances allowed and as their families grew.

Arbun C. Wilkerson recalled first living in a "two-room lumber shanty." Wilkerson's father, Jennings Lachoneus "Con" Wilkerson, later bought a piece of land that already had a two-room log cabin on it. "It had," Arbun later wrote, "a dirt roof and was quite warm, but Mother had to put up a muslin ceiling to keep the dirt from leaking down into our food and into our beds."[16]

Some of the homesteaders built their first domiciles, called "soddys," using sun-baked bricks made from mud mixed with grass to give each brick strength and cohesion. Within a few years, clapboard siding milled at the several area sawmills was added to the exterior of the mud walls to protect the "soddy" from the weather. Sod homes had high insulation qualities; they were warm in the winter and cool in the summer.

Less common than log cabins or "soddys" were dugouts, which generally were temporary in nature. To make one, a homesteader would dig a four-foot-deep rectangular hole, which was eight to ten feet wide and twelve to fifteen feet long. The hard-packed dirt floor sloped upwards toward the door. Walls made from logs, sod, or field rock were added, making the inside of the dugout about eight feet high. Poles overlaid with brush and then clay dirt formed the roof. When the dugouts were abandoned for more permanent housing, many were used as root cellars. They, like soddys, possessed excellent qualities to preserve garden produce.

Some homesteaders lived in tents until they could afford to build better structures. Tents were formed with wooden frames and covered with canvas. Heavy blankets were hung on the inside of the canvas walls to help hold in the heat. Barbara May Workman Wilkerson recalled living in a tent when her father and mother first took up land on the reservation: "[Father] came to the Reservation in March [1906], and built us a one-room cabin out of cedar posts standing up with posts and dirt on the top and with a dirt floor. We had a large tent which we slept in—it was a good thing we did, for when it rained the cabin leaked everywhere."[17] Alice Firth's family moved to the reservation in the winter of 1905. For the first months, they lived in a tent lined with woven carpet and grass.[18]

Stanford Gardner, whose family settled on the North Myton Bench, recalled his first house: "We moved into our homestead into a tent. We lived in the tent through that winter and in late summer

Threshing alfalfa seed in Myton, 1915. (Uintah County Library–Regional History Center, Todd Collection)

Father built a one-room log cabin which had one bed, a stove, a table, and a few blasting powder boxes for chairs, and a stand and wash basin." With a family of several children living in it, the cabin and tent were very crowded. Gardner continued: "A clothes closet was built behind the bed, and we had to move the bed out to get into the closet. The little children slept on a straw tick which we put onto the bed through the day and pulled off onto the floor at night."[19]

Some of the original log cabins and "wooden shantys" are still in use today as farm outbuildings; a few have been incorporated into well built and fashionable houses. Still others grace the county's land-scape, a clear reminder of how recent was the homesteading experience in the county.

Hardscrabble Medical Care

Much of the doctoring performed on the reservation after its opening was administering home remedies, herbs, and salves. A favorite remedy for fevers was peppermint and yarrow tea. A sagebrush and quaking aspen bark tea was thought to purify the blood, help reduce boils, and remove the teenage problem of skin acne. Bread and milk poultices were used for infections. Lard and pepper poultices were used for sore throats. Onion or mustard poultices were applied for coughs or pneumonia, and kerosene mixed with a bit of sugar would dislodge mucous from the throat. Castor oil or turpentine would reduce inflammation of the bowels. Burnt flour was used for diaper rash, and soda relieved minor burns.

Wealthy Halliday Sheffer had a special recipe for a plaster for pneumonia that perhaps had some real medicinal value. Wealthy was educated as a nurse under Dr. Ellis Shipp in Salt Lake City before moving as a young widow to Cedarview with her sister Florence Bacon and her family. Wealthy's recipe was as follows: A pound of hog's lard mixed with four ounces of yellow bee's wax, four ounces of camphor gum, and four ounces of rosin. The mixture is heated, then cooled to a creamy stage. Four ounces of spirits of camphor is added and, if available, a few drops of whiskey. The plaster is thinly spread on several large pieces of cloth which are then placed on the upper back and the chest of the patient. The plaster was also used to treat chest colds.[20]

Midwives were essential at birthing, and volunteer nurses were essential for those bedridden illnesses. In Neola, Wilmer Burgess served as midwife and rode horseback in all weather to serve the ill and deliver babies until she was well past seventy years of age. Her regular fee for a visit was three dollars, but many of the people were too poor to pay for her services; nevertheless, she provided medical care to those in need.[21] When home remedies failed or a severe injury or illness occurred, a doctor was called.

Pharmacists and druggists were important as medical providers, dispensing favorite remedies, drugs, and offering medical advice. Before 1910 M.E. Harmston, Jim Mease, Herb Isham, James Jensen, and Robert Delaney owned drugstores in Roosevelt. Myton had several druggists—Bert Whitmore, D.M. Frost, and James Dalgleish—before 1914. According to the business gazetteer for Utah for 1912, Wilfred C. Perry was the only druggist in Theodore for several years. In addition to pulling teeth, dentist E.J. Maxwell offered other medical assistance when called upon in the Hanna area of the reservation.

Harry Walker established a small dental practice in Duchesne, where his brother Walter operated a drugstore.

Physicians located in Roosevelt, Myton, and Duchesne soon after the opening of the reservation to settlement. A Dr. Bjornson practiced in Duchesne in 1905 before moving to Myton. Five years later, Dr. W.E. Gossett filled the medical void left by Bjornson. Other dedicated doctors who practiced medicine in the county included a Dr. Thomas and a Dr. Nule, both of whom practiced in Myton; Dr. William Leonard Sutherland, who also served on the Roosevelt City Council in 1920 and 1921; Dr. L.L. Saunders, Dr. W.J. Browning, Dr. John E. Morton, Dr. C.T. Kendall, and Dr. J.W. Padget, who practiced from 1915 to 1919 in Roosevelt. Others who worked in the county were Dr. E.R. Enoch, Dr. J.D. Whitmore, and Dr. Lurrine Miles.

Of all of the physicians who practiced in the county before the 1930s, Dr. Lurrine Miles is probably the most remembered by county residents.[22] Lurrine Miles was born in 1887 in Payson and then moved to Salt Lake City, where she graduated from the University of Utah. She decided to attend medical school at Rush Medical University in Chicago and her family decided to buy a ranch in Nine Mile Canyon. She graduated in the top five of her class and was the first Utahn admitted to Alpha Omega Alpha, the National Honorary Medical Fraternity. She turned down attractive offers to practice medicine in Boston and other cities, instead returning to Utah and then going to the Uinta Basin to begin her medical practice. She felt that the Lord called her to serve the medical needs of the residents of the Uinta Basin.

Not long after arriving in the basin Dr. Miles was called to assist a woman in labor during a day of steady rain that had turned most of the roads in the county into quagmires. Arriving at the woman's cabin, Dr. Miles found the rain also had turned the packed dirt floor into a thick heavy mud, and the dirt roof leaked badly. Brown muddy water poured into the room and onto the bed of the expectant mother. A neighbor had also been called to assist and comfort in the labor. To protect the mother and baby from the badly leaking roof, pans were arranged to catch the muddy water. The leaks outnumbered the pans and buckets, however, drenching the laboring woman. Dr. Miles opened her umbrella and asked the neighbor to hold it over

Lot Powell homestead in Altonah. Log homes were common in Duchesne County through the 1930s. (Allan Kent Powell)

the birthing bed during the delivery. The birth of the baby was one of the first of an estimated 5,000 successful deliveries Dr. Miles made during her long career.[23]

Dr. Miles's fruitful career spanned nearly forty years, from 1915 to the early 1950s. She lived in good health until her death at the age of ninety-one. Her contributions to the quality and longevity of life of thousands of Duchesne County residents were numerous and legendary.[24] County residents were well served in their medical needs by the area's doctors, midwives, nurses, and others during the earliest years of settlement.

Early Life in the County

An old saying among the early homesteaders was, "The government bets the homesteader 160 acres of land at a price of $1.25 an acre that he can't live on it fourteen months without starving to death."[25] It often required fourteen months or more to clear and prepare the land before there could be a harvest of crops.

Louie Galloway settled in the Roosevelt area with his father and mother. He later recalled the long hot summers as a young teenager he and his brother spent leveling the ground on their father's farm: "I spent almost the entire summer for at least two years leveling the ground. My older brother Wesley and I took turns driving the team and loading and unloading the scraper." Working in the sun and constant winds took their toll on Louie. "It seemed the wind blew and the air was filled with dirt almost every day. My lower lip became a raw sore and never healed completely even in winter."[26] Louie Galloway's experience was typical of that of many others.

Another difficult task was clearing the land of sagebrush and cedar trees. All members of the family were expected to work at this chore. A team was hitched to a long log or, when available, an iron rail and pulled across the ground, uprooting sagebrush and other vegetation. It frequently took several passes from different directions to uproot the larger sagebrush plants. The remaining brush was cleared by hand using a grub ax.[27]

In many parts of the county, rocks were another problem. Year after year, children were put to work clearing rocks from the fields. It seemed to many farmers that they were better at producing rocks than they were at growing crops. Daniel Spencer Allen and his family had moved several times on the reservation before deciding to take up an eighty-acre homestead near Neola in 1905. He said that this homestead was rocky and hardly worth settling on: "There are so many rocks and boulders on the place, . . . there is not enough good ground in the whole eighty acres to whip a dog on."[28]

George Potts and his neighbors at Lake Fork (Upalco) were typical when it came to grubbing out a life on the reservation. A neighbor said of him, "Oh, we were poor but the Potts were rich, give George Potts a pick, shovel, crowbar, and axe and he would dig out a living anywhere."[29] Self-reliance and hard work were a way of life for the county homesteaders.

Most farm women made their own soap by rendering the lard from hogs, mixing it with wood-ash lye and then letting the mixture set up. It was then cut into bars and used for washing everything from dirty hands to clothes to the plank floors of log cabins. Clothes were washed on a scrub board in a galvanized tub. Water for the washing as well as for cooking was frequently hauled some distance by the women of the family until a well could be sunk or a canal or ditch was dug nearby. Clifford Drollinger wrote of the work to get water for the family wash and other needs: "Water for the house had to be hauled from a spring over a mile away in three wooden barrels mounted on a wagon drawn by a team of horses."[30]

Most clothes, except men's bib coveralls, were sewn at home. Dresses, shirts, coats, and boy's pants were sown; socks, mittens, and caps were knitted. Along with bib coveralls, hats and leather gloves were purchased at Myton, Roosevelt, or Duchesne.

A good share of the family income of the homesteaders in the county was derived from the labor of women on the farm. Income from the sale of cream and eggs was often the source of cash for much of the store-bought items. Eggs in particular were traded for store items. In the 1920s, eggs traded at the various stores for about twelve cents a dozen.[31] A dozen eggs traded at Murdock's store bought two yards of calico, and it took about twelve dozen eggs to buy a pair of children's shoes. Men's suits sold for $11.00 and overalls cost seventy-five cents.[32]

Periodic trips were made to town to purchase flour, salt, sugar, bacon, beans, coffee, pickles, crackers, raisins, cloth, boots, coveralls, coal oil, and other household items from A.M. Murdock's Pioneer Supply Store or Frank E. Davis's Grocery and Meats in Duchesne; or from the Roosevelt Mercantile in Roosevelt; or from Hayden Calvert's and R.E. Waugh's Mercantile or the Barry D. Mercantile Company in Myton.

Currant Canyon and Currant Creek were named because of the abundance of wild currants found at each location. Many women and children spent considerable time each late summer and early fall gathering native bullberries, elderberries, currants, and chokecherries. These delicious wild berries were transformed into jams and jellies and stocked in family pantries.

A small but important source of family income produced in part by women of the county was the cultivation of small fruits such as strawberries, raspberries, and currants. According to records, in 1919 the county produced over 10,500 quarts of small fruits. Currants remained the leading small fruit crop in 1919 accounting for about a third of the total produced in the county.[33] By 1949 the variety of small berries produced in the county for sale was reduced; however, the harvest and sale of strawberries and raspberries remained at

Homestead in Arcadia. (John D. Barton.)

about 11,000 quarts.[34] It is likely that the bulk of the harvesting and processing of the strawberries and raspberries was done by women and teenagers.

At least one woman, Mary Sulser of Midview, added to her family's income as one of a number of apiarists, or beekeepers, in the county. Honey production was an important element of the county's economy as early as 1919, when 415,000 pounds of honey valued at $84,000 was produced.[35]

Nineteen women farmers were identified by the 1920 federal agricultural census as being the head of a farm household. They constituted only 1.5 percent of county farmers, however, compared to the rest of the state in which women farmers (627 women) owned or operated 2.4 percent of all farms.[36]

Women added to the family income in other ways. Family vegetable gardens were an important source of food for the family and for market. For the year 1920 the value of vegetables raised on the 1,248 farms in the county was over $200,000, or about 3.5 percent of the total vegetable crop produced in the state.[37] Women and children cared for a large part of the 470 acres of vegetables.

Cash among farm families was a scarce commodity in the county during the first several decades of the twentieth century. Money earned went to pay for land, buy seed, purchase needed farm equipment, and pay mortgages. There was plenty of discouragement in the new county. To some early settlers, the wide-open expanses of Wyoming seemed better than parts of the reservation. Alice D. Galley recalled that the farm her father John S. Dickson bought in 1919 was "a severe disappointment. Our home in Wyoming was very pretty with a lawn and trees. And there sat this house, on a high spot of ground, surrounded by alkali. It was a very desolate-looking place."[38]

Due to the lack of ready cash, some farmers found work in the off seasons as freighters or miners. Those who had sturdy wagons and strong teams of horses hired out to haul supplies from Price and haul Gilsonite to Price. Others hired out during the winter months as Gilsonite miners. For many farmers who found work mining Gilsonite, the work was hard and conditions were difficult and unfamiliar. The separation from their families was difficult; however, the wages of four dollars a day added significantly to many incomes.[39] Some farmers found seasonal work at the various sawmills. Occasionally, housewives were hired to cook and do the laundry for the loggers and sawmill hands. Due to the combination of seasonal jobs and farming, 67 percent of the farmers in the county were mortgage free by 1920; this compared to nearly 75 percent of the farmers in the state who owned their farms free and clear.[40]

The Hope Mine

One of the largest hydrocarbon mines in Duchesne County was the Hope Elaterite Mine, located just a mile south and slightly east of the Strawberry Pinnacles. Elaterite, a hydrocarbon, is similar to Gilsonite and is sometimes identified as wurtzilite. The only known significant source of elaterite in the nation is found in the county. The Hope Mine was the home and workplace of more than a dozen families and upwards of twenty men. Complete with a pony-powered track line to haul the elaterite out of the mine and down the mountain to the road, the mine was an intricate operation. The area families lived in small log cabins, and for a time there was a short-lived school there to serve the children's educational needs.

Homespun Fun

Before the construction of Mormon meetinghouses and cultural halls and the building of schools larger than one or two rooms, community entertainment facilities in the county were limited. Community dances for the adults and older teenagers were almost everyone's favorite entertainment. For most older single people, Friday night community dances were the only occasions to meet and socialize. Friday and then Saturday night dances were very popular among the single men and women of the communities. Woodrow Wilkerson recalled a story about his father, Con Wilkerson, and several other young men, who, after working twelve- to fourteen-hour days for several weeks at the sawmill on Johnny Starr Flat, decided to walk the twenty miles to Neola to a Saturday night dance. Following the dance, they walked back in time to report to work the following Monday morning.[41]

In the town of Duchesne, for the first several years the only building large enough for more than a few couples to dance at the same time was the Murdock store, and it soon became too small. According to Bernice Peterson Mecham, a "40 x 50 [foot] amusement hall" was built to accommodate the growing numbers of dancers.[42] Mecham added that most community dances were held on Friday evenings, with music generally provided by a fiddle player supplemented by a whole array of instruments ranging from a harmonica to piano to guitars. For the first few years in Roosevelt Peter Peterson played his fiddle for square dances. By 1915 James Barnes built an amusement hall in Roosevelt, where, in addition to dances, motion pictures were shown to audiences of settlers and Utes.[43] Occasionally, phonographs with large horns were used to provide music for dances. They played cylindrical records of "In the Shade of the Old Apple Tree" and other favorites.

The Friday night community dances in Duchesne and elsewhere in the county were family affairs. When the hour got late, small children were bedded down along the walls where they could be easily checked. The adults and teens danced waltzes, the popular two-step, and quadrilles. During holidays locals sometimes danced two or

Myton baseball team 1912. (Uintah County Library–Regional History Center)

three nights in a row. Ute Indian families often came to watch and were amused by the dancing of their white neighbors.[44]

The first local orchestra in the Roosevelt area consisted of German Workman, Pearletta Taylor, Janez Taylor, Richard Beeler, and Sadie Burgess. A brass band was organized in 1916 in Roosevelt and entertained throughout the area for years.[45] Myton also had a town band, with Fritz Schleinitz as director. The *Duchesne Record* boastfully claimed that the Myton town band was "one of the best local bands in eastern Utah."[46]

Skits and plays were often practiced and performed in the communities. Also, professional theater productions visited the county from time to time. In July 1914, for instance, the Ralph Collings Theatre Company gave three performances in the Myton Opera House.

Nearly every community in the Uinta Basin—Craig, Colorado, Vernal, Watson, Myton, Roosevelt, Fruitland, Lakefork, Cedarview, Altonah, Bennett, Neola, and Boneta—had baseball teams, and

Moffat boasted an Indian team. Games were frequently played on Sundays until June 1914, at which time Myton and Roosevelt, the two dominant teams in the county, made an informal pact that no Sunday games would be played thereafter.

Baseball games were played for prizes or to raise money for worthy causes. In the summer of 1914, for example, the residents of Myton were building a new church and needed financial help. After a hotly contested game between Myton and Roosevelt that Myton won, the proceeds of the game, some eighteen dollars, went to the building fund to purchase lumber. Frequently the Myton Hotel hosted dinners for visiting teams when they played Myton, often termed the "perennial" champion.

Baseball games, dances, parades, speeches, roping contests, and other activities were at the core of many communities' celebrations of July Fourth and Utah Pioneer Day on 24 July. For Altonah's July Fourth celebration for 1914, the *Duchesne Record* proclaimed, "We have no autos yet, but have some mighty fine saddle horses on which the young folks [will] enjoy themselves."[47] The Altonah celebration began with the firing of guns at sunrise; guns were shot off again at noon, and a final volley was fired at sunset. In between all of the gunfire, a parade was held which included portrayals of the Goddess of Liberty, the Queen of Utah (with twenty-four little girls as maids of honor), and numerous floats. Not to be outdone, Lakefork also held a July Fourth parade which included three floats representing the Reservation Past, the Reservation Present, and the Reservation Future. Following the parade, a sham battle with Indians was held. In the afternoon, a baseball game was played against the Ioka team. Following a community dinner, dances for both children and adults were held.

A baseball tournament was the center of Roosevelt's celebration of Pioneer Day in 1914. In a six-team, three-game tournament, Roosevelt upset Myton 10 to 7 in the first game and then proceeded to beat Vernal 9 to 5 in the second game to win the tournament.[48]

Travel in the County

After the reservation was opened to settlement, the responsibility for area roads fell to Wasatch County, of which the land was a part at the time. The earliest roads were constructed to serve the military at Fort Duchesne and the Indian agency. The best of the early roads, discussed earlier, was the Price to Myton road. The Indian Canyon Road, the Strawberry Valley Road to Heber City, and the road over Wolf Creek Pass to Park City were rough roads, used primarily by homesteaders, livestockmen, and freighters.

The "roads" between the several towns and villages on the reservation were little more than ruts. Few dollars were budgeted for roads in the county, and what little was budgeted generally went for improvements of the roads in Heber Valley. Roads and bridges were high on the agenda of the reservation settlers, however. It was difficult to travel to the county seat at Heber City to conduct important legal business. It often took several days to travel to Heber City or Vernal, and in bad weather travel to Heber City was nearly impossible.

Elden Wilkens told of a time he and his family went from Hanna to Provo to visit relatives.[49] Traveling by wagon, they crossed Wolf Creek Pass into Heber and then proceeded down Provo Canyon. The trip, including the four-day visit, took nearly two weeks. Peter Duncan remembered it taking him all day to travel between Roosevelt and Neola, a distance of ten miles.[50]

Roads on the former reservation began to be improved after the state legislature established the state road commission and created a state road system in 1909. Designation of state roads was limited. No more than one road in the same general direction in each county was declared a state road, and the authority to designate which county roads became part of the state road system fell to the county commissions. In 1910 the Wasatch County Commission designated the roads from Duchesne to Heber City, from Duchesne to Roosevelt, and from Duchesne to Colton as state roads.

Funding for road construction and maintenance remained scarce. The state bonded itself to raise money to build and improve roads that had been designated part of the state road system in each of the counties. Wasatch County and the other counties in the state were also hard-pressed for funds to make road improvements. Federal funds of $7,000 were made available for an upgrade of the road from Stockmore to Kamas through the Uintah National Forest.[51]

Coyotes were the most hated and hunted of all predatory animals in early Duchesne County history. These early Basin residents show their trapping success cira 1925. (Uintah County Library–Regional History Center)

Highway maps were distributed in Utah and Colorado promoting travel by automobile between Denver and Salt Lake City. The Myton Commercial Club, with its membership of D.J. Pierce, H.G. Clarke, and D.M. Frost, joined with the Roosevelt and Duchesne commercial clubs to encourage the development of the Uinta Basin, including its use for automobile tourism, fishing, and hunting.

The *Duchesne Record* wrote in June 1914 that the state should pay more attention to the road needs of the Uinta Basin:

> The first proposition for the coming year—the building of a road into the Uintah Basin. Salt Lake must surely be awakening to the real value of this basin! We may criticize Zion's Capital for her long slumber as to our wonderful empire, yet we must admit that she has been working for her own advancement.[52]

The newspaper's call for better roads, the work of the commercial clubs, increased commercial activities, improved mail service, and a national "Good Roads" campaign all placed pressure on county officials to make road improvements. The lack of funds for roads from the Wasatch County Commission continued, however, and the lack of road improvements was one reason that the residents of the former reservation voted to establish their own county in 1914. By 1915 at least twenty miles of roads in the county were graded and another 1.5 miles were surfaced with either clay or gravel. Road improvements continued; by 1918 over 100 miles of road had been graded in the county.[53]

Increased travel by gasoline-powered cars and trucks in the county made local services for the machines necessary. The Odekirk and Company Mercantile in Duchesne, for example, installed some of the county's first gasoline tanks in 1915. By the early 1920s the Hotel Grant Garage and Grocery Company and the Victory Service Station had been established in Duchesne. In Myton similar companies were established, including Bridge Garage, operated by H.O. Tuttle, and the Tourist Service Station. Myton Motor Inn sold Dodge and Ford trucks and cars. Roosevelt had Basin Service Garage and M & L Auto Wreckage and Repair.

Funding for road improvements in the county remained a problem. Federal funds did come to the county in 1916 from the Federal Aid Act to help with road construction; the Castle Gate to Duchesne road was one of several roads to which the state assigned federal money. The state also provided some labor for several years for road improvements in the county. For example, Governor Simon Bamberger assigned convicts from the state prison in Salt Lake City to make improvements on the Indian Canyon road.

Ownership of automobiles remained limited in the county. Horses and wagons were the standard method to travel into the 1920s and remained common with many of the farming families until the 1940s. Jack Barton remembered his and many other families in Boneta driving teams and wagons to church as late as the World War II years.

Wild Animal Predation

The early settlers not only fought the harsh mountain desert terrain to wrest a farming livelihood but also contended with wild animals. Grazing on ranges alongside domestic stock were thousands of wild horses that roamed at will. At the turn of the century, the homesteaders fought wolves with a vengeance. Bears, cougars, and coyotes also were hard on early livestock, especially sheep. It was not uncommon for coyotes to scatter and kill dozens of sheep in a single night. It was estimated that at the turn of the century Utah farmers lost over $1 million a year to predation, and early Duchesne County residents shared in that loss. Coyotes were so hated that a bounty was offered on them that continued until World War II.[54] Mountain lions also killed sheep, but their special prey was colts and yearling horses. Homesteaders' chickens and turkeys were threatened by skunks, weasels, foxes, and coyotes.

To combat predators every stockman relied on the keen ears and noses of his dogs to warn him when sheep and cattle were in danger. Guns were always at hand when out herding. Poison and trapping were heavily used at the turn of the century. From 20 March 1915 to 20 March 1916 bounty was paid by Duchesne County on eighteen bears killed.[55] The federal government also employed professional trappers at this time to curb predation. Within a few years after settlement the wolves were gone and the bears and mountain lions for the most part had retreated into the higher mountains. Coyotes continue to plague sheepmen even to this date. Present-day sheepmen rely on trained dogs or even llamas to ward off or kill coyotes that come near their herds.

The early residents saw few deer and elk. Natural predation coupled with intense hunting by the Utes for several years of reservation life had greatly thinned the herds. The successful hunting that frequently supplemented homesteaders' diets in other places rarely happened in early Duchesne County. Homesteaders' stories of Mountain Home told of a time a doe came down a wash and was shot by a resident. It was such an uncommon incident that the neighbors were invited to barbecue and eat the animal.[56]

Cattle Drives

Without a railroad in the region, cattle and sheep were driven to Heber or Colton for shipment.[57] These drives, although much shorter, were similar to the cattle drives of earlier generations. George Fisher,

Sheep grazing in the high Uintas. (Utah State Historical Society)

Sr., a prominent early cattleman of Altonah, related that the cattle were rounded up and then the men and boys would start them overland to Heber by way of Strawberry and Daniel's canyons. The trip usually took just over a week. The cattle were sold upon arrival to a buyer and loaded on railcars for transport. The cattlemen would then would purchase supplies for their families and load them on the well-trained pack horses. These horses, most having made the trip many times, were turned loose to go home. The cowboys usually stayed in town for a day or so to reward their hard work.[58]

Sheep Country

County sheepmen would rely on traveling shearing companies to clip the wool from their sheep in the spring. In 1915 the average price for wool was twenty-two cents a pound, and sheepmen did well that year. When the forests of the high Uintas were opened to grazing, many herds were brought in. The U.S. Forest Service would only issue a limited number of permits, which were usually renewed each year. These high-country grazing permits drew sheepmen from the north slope of the Uintas in Wyoming; some came west from Colorado, and other flocks of sheep were brought in from many other parts of the state. There was a down side to the grazing of sheep in the high Uintas: some depletion of the range occurred, and the sheep herds brought diseases that infected the few remaining bighorn sheep that lived in the region. It is estimated that the last native bighorn sheep in the region were gone by the early 1930s. (Bighorn sheep have been reintroduced into the Uinta Mountains by the Division of Wildlife Resources and limited numbers are found there presently.)

Some cattlemen also were granted forest grazing permits, usually for the lower elevations rather than the high basins where sheep ranged. This limited conflict between cattlemen and sheepmen in the Uintas, unlike areas in southeastern Utah and western Colorado where range wars went on at that time. There is no mention in the county papers of politicking to restrict the grazing permits to only local stock growers. The grazing permits issued by the Forest Service were granted on a first-come, first-served basis. Once obtained, they would usually remain in the family for many years; some of the cattle grazing permits still in use today were originally obtained two or three generations ago. The permits were issued for specific areas of the Uintas, and this kept competition and conflicts over grazing to a minimum between all stockmen.

Stephan and Edward Barton moved into the Uinta Basin in the early 1920s when they obtained a grazing permit for Ottoson and Cleveland basins on the Rock Creek and Lake Fork drainages in the high Uintas. It took over one month for Edward (Ted) Barton to trail his herd of sheep from Manti to Boneta. He did moderately well for the next several years before the Great Depression and a drought hit. One cold winter a large band of coyotes attacked Barton's sheep on Blue Bench. Barton spent the whole winter riding the country from Rock Creek to Duchesne looking for what was left of his scattered and slaughtered herd. He lost two-thirds of his flock that winter. Barton's experience was not unlike that of many other sheepmen in Duchesne County's early era. The 1920s saw the high point in sheep raising for the period.

Some of the stockmen were successful. With the reservation

opening in 1905 an individual could only obtain 160 acres of land to homestead. As some settlers left the Uinta Basin due to poor crops, droughts from 1918 through 1922, poor soil on many of the homesteads, or many other problems, stockmen were able to purchase or lease land from homesteaders who had stayed long enough to obtain title to their lands. Purchasing and leasing land at reasonable prices enabled stockmen to control many acres and graze larger herds. Starting in 1912 larger blocks of land were put up for sale, and from time to time over the next three decades the government occasionally sold large pieces of land on a sealed-bid basis. This also added to the acreage available to stockmen. Presently the descendants of early stockmen each utilize ranges of several thousand acres. Most descendants of pioneering stockmen have continued to add to the land their fathers and grandfathers left them. Some of the notable names of stockmen in Duchesne County who have been ranching for two or more generations include the Moon, Jessen, Brotherson, Peatross, Fisher, Hartman, Horrocks, and Bastian families.

Grazing Public Lands

Around the turn of the century most stockmen in the West worried little about overgrazing public lands. In Utah most of the early Mormon settlers had only a few cattle, which they grazed in cooperative herds that shared the pasture lands. As people and livestock increased, however, over the decades throughout the state rangelands became overgrazed. By the 1920s most of the Uinta Basin range was overgrazed as well. In fact, the most notable grazing legislation, the Taylor Grazing Act of 1934, was passed due to problems brought into national focus because of overgrazing throughout the West. U.S. Representative Don B. Colton from Vernal, concerned about overgrazing on Taylor Mountain, began work on the bill that gave more control to government agencies to manage the rangelands. The intent of the Taylor Grazing Act was to "stop degradation of public grazing lands through improper usage, stabilize the range livestock industries, classify lands in order to assure proper use, . . . establish grazing districts and permits to graze, and facilitate the charging of a reasonable fee for use of grazing lands."[59]

Overgrazing, unfortunately, was a problem in early Duchesne

County. Much of the land that had been unclaimed by homesteaders as worthless did provide grazing areas to stockmen. The mostly unregulated grazing on the Tavaputs Plateau region attracted many ranchers to bring their cattle, horses, and sheep there. This region was both legally and illegally grazed by local and outside stockmen. The competition for free grass and the fact that the ranchers were not overly concerned by range conditions on land that was not theirs led to overgrazing in parts of the region. Early settlers told of the "belly high to a horse" grass on many of the benches. The open range country between Myton and Gate Canyon, for example, was lush gamma grass mixed with crested wheat; both grow well with little water but do not tolerate overgrazing. Today, most of the grasses are gone and the area is bleak, with stunted sage and brittlebush as its primary vegetation.[60] In other places in the county overgrazing caused severe damage to riparian lands, which led to erosion that formed deep gullies and washes, such as one in Indian Canyon.

It took some residents many years to realize that regulation of the land, though unwelcome, was necessary to help preserve the resources that remained. It is hoped that concerted efforts to better care for the land will help lead to the restoration of some valuable plants and animals. County stockmen presently are very conscientious about the land they graze; however, they face accusations and accept responsibility for damage caused by three and four generations of past cattlemen. All grazing on public lands in Duchesne County is controlled by either the Bureau of Land Management or the U.S. Forest Service.

The creation of Duchesne County in 1914 closed the brief "pioneer" period in the county's settlement history. The nearly 4,000 new residents of the county worked hard to create homes and farms. They shared tasks, struggled against difficult weather conditions, and were isolated from each other and from the rest of the state. They helped bear each others' burdens when there was illness and they created their own fun. In many ways the land was less than many hoped for, and some left in discouragement; but most stayed and built communities that are testaments to their industry.

ENDNOTES

1. Emily Wilkerson, compiler, *From Then Until Now,* (Roosevelt, UT: n.p., n.d.), 795–96.

2. Ibid.

3. Ibid. The old road to Myton that Smith mentioned goes from about two miles from the mouth of Indian Canyon eastward through the hills and comes out at Antelope Creek; a dirt road presently follows that route.

4. Quoted in Mildred Miles Dillman, comp. *Early History of Duchesne County* (Springville: Art City Publishing Company, 1948), 223.

5. William R. Evans, *Homesteads and Indian Leases on the Lake Fork* (Provo: Stevens Genealogical Center, 1983), 1–4, 11.

6. See George Stewart, "Roosevelt's Yesterdays," copy in Uintah County Library and also in the Utah State Historical Society Library.

7. Ibid., 4.

8. Verda Moore, interview with J.P. Tanner, May 1991, Duchesne, Utah, copy held by the author.

9. Stewart, "Roosevelt's Yesterdays," 4.

10. Pearce, *O My Father,* 74–75, 81–82.

11. Wilkerson, *From Then Until Now,* 991–92.

12. Another commonly told story on the name of Fruitland is that an early fruit trader's wagon overturned there, prompting the name.

13. Wilkerson, *From Then Until Now,* 991–92.

14. In several oral interviews in the past few years with surviving settlers, most of whom were children when they came with their families into the Uinta Basin to homestead, all remember coming in by teams and wagons, none came by automobile. See Donna Barton, "Pioneer Medical Practices in the Uintah Basin—1905–1945," (Master's thesis, Utah State University, 1991), 4. See also Wilkerson, *From Then Until Now.*

15. Martha B. Giles, *Footprints in a Beautiful Valley: A History of Tabiona-Hanna* (Tabiona and Hanna, UT: n.p., 1908), 308.

16. Quoted in Wilkerson, *From Then Until Now,* 926.

17. Ibid., 930.

18. Stories told the author by Barbara Wilkerson. See also Alice Firth, interview with J.P. Tanner, July 1991, Duchesne, Utah, transcript held by the author, original in the possession of J.P. Tanner, Duchesne, Utah.

19. Wilkerson, *From Then Until Now,* 289.

20. Ibid., 781.

21. Dillman, *Early History of Duchesne County,* 320. In spite of her will-

ingness to treat the sick and leave her own home's warmth, "Grandma" Burgess, as she was called, lived to be ninety-two years old.

22. Barton, "Pioneer Medical Practices," 21.

23. Ibid., 6, 21.

24. Donna Barton, "Dr. Lurrine Miles, A Cultured Lady in a Frontier Land," *Outlaw Trail Journal* 2 (Winter/Spring 1992): 3–11. A newspaper reporter interviewed Dr. Miles shortly before her death and asked her if she had delivered 5,000 babies in the area. She did not know precisely but conceded that she must have delivered four-fifths of those in the Uinta Basin. See "Uintah Doctor's Career Proves 'Involvement,'" *Salt Lake Tribune,* 3 October 1977.

25. Dillman, *Early History of Duchesne County,* 97.

26. Wilkerson, *From Then Until Now,* 280.

27. Vera Hinckley Mayhew, "Of Our Family Life," 1965, 66, manuscript copy in possession of the author.

28. Quoted in Wilkerson, *From Then Until Now,*14.

29. Percy Potts, "History of Percy Potts," in *A Harvest of Memories, 1905 to 1988; Histories of Upalco, Altonah, Mt. Emmons, Altamont,* (n.p.: History Preservation Committee, 1988), 135.

30. Wilkerson, *From Then Until Now,* 229.

31. Potts, "History," 133–34.

32. Dillman, *Early History of Duchesne County,* 207.

33. Bureau of the Census, *Fourteenth Census of the United States: Utah* (Washington, D.C.: Government Printing Office, 1924), 60–61.

34. Bureau of the Census, *United States Census of Agriculture: 1950: Utah and Nevada,* Part 31 (Washington, D.C.: Government Printing Office, 1952), 66.

35. Ibid., 58.

36. Ibid., 54.

37. *Fourteenth Census of the United States: Utah,* 60.

38. Wilkerson, *From Then Until Now,* 218.

39. Ibid., 796.

40. *Fourteenth Census of the United States: Utah,* 54.

41. Stories told to the author by Woodrow Wilkerson.

42. Dillman, *Early History of Duchesne County,* 206.

43. Ibid., 318.

44. Ibid., 206.

45. Ibid., 320.

46. *Duchesne Record* (Myton), 17 July 1914.

47. *Duchesne Record,* 12 June 1914.

48. The *Duchesne Record,* published in Myton, periodically provided readers with box scores of games between Myton and its opponents. For a county newspaper to provide such detailed information about baseball games before the 1930s was unusual and demonstrates the tremendous pride the community had in its hometown team.

49. Elden Wilken, interview with John Barton, 14 May 1991, Duchesne, Utah, copy in author's possession.

50. Dillman, *Early History of Duchesne County,* 321.

51. *Vernal Express,* 21 February 1913, 26 April 1915.

52. *Duchesne Record,* 5 June 1914.

53. Utah Secretary of State Biennial Reports, 1917–1918, copy at Utah State Historical Society Library.

54. *Vernal Express,* 21 February 1913.

55. *Roosevelt Standard,* 13 September 1916.

56. Stories told by Jack D. Barton, Altamont, Utah. The few numbers of deer in the Uinta Basin is confirmed in the *Vernal Express* of 16 October 1914. Only about 1,000 deer were killed in Utah during 1914, yet there was a concern that if this number was not reduced the herds would be exterminated. At this writing the Division of Wildlife Resources is again concerned about the number of deer in the Utah herds. A 16 April 1994 *Vernal Express* article reported the 1993 hunt had only an 18 percent success ratio. This was the poorest hunt since 1936 when 13,800 deer were killed. The number of Uinta Basin elk in the early 1940s were so depleted that the Division of Wildlife Resources purchased elk for seed herds from Jackson, Wyoming, and trucked then into the Uinta Mountains.

57. The old train stop at Colton is presently found along the highway between Price and Soldier Summit. There is a small store there called Hill Top. Colton in its heyday had cattle pens, a store, loading docks, and even a roundhouse.

58. Stories told to the author by George Fisher, Jr.

59. Cited in Jerry Spangler, *Paradigms and Perspectives,* 832.

60. Information from H. Bert Jenson, based on stories told him by his grandmother, Gladys Stewart Dennis. Jenson's grandfather, Wallace Dennis, was a farmer who hauled freight between Fort Duchesne and Price on the Nine Mile Road to augment family income.

CHAPTER 6

DUCHESNE COUNTY COMMUNITIES AND THE MAKING OF UTAH'S TWENTY-EIGHTH COUNTY

The establishment of towns and villages on the reservation and the eventual creation of Duchesne County in 1914 followed a different settlement pattern than that of much of the state. Some 2,100 acres were reserved by presidential proclamation for new towns on the Uintah Indian Reservation. State law carefully outlined how counties could be created. Since statehood in 1896, only two counties, Duchesne and Daggett, have been organized.[1]

In addition to the allotment of land to Indian families and the withdrawal of land for town sites, there were other developments that took place prior to the opening of the reservation and impacted the settlement of towns on the reservation and the organization of the county. In 1897, as part of a national effort to preserve precious watersheds in the West, the Uinta National Forest Reserve of about 482,000 acres was established by presidential proclamation. In the summer of 1905 an additional 1.4 million acres, much of it located on the Uintah Indian Reservation, was withdrawn from public entry and added to the Uinta National Forest Reserve. The 1905 withdrawal was a result of an earlier survey of forested lands in Utah conducted by Albert Potter, chief grazing officer for the Department of the Interior.[2] Additional land, about 200,000 acres, was withdrawn from public entry by President Theodore Roosevelt for agricultural and reclamation purposes in the summer of 1905.

Creating a New County

As early as 1909 the residents of the reservation portion of Wasatch County began the effort for home rule and the establishment of their own county. The desire was precipitated in part by the reservation's isolation from Heber City, the Wasatch County seat. Travel between the Uinta Basin and Heber City was particularly difficult from late fall to early spring of each year. Conducting legal and county business was costly to residents in terms of money and time because of their distance from county offices.

The issues of home rule and schools were closely linked. By 1908 there were over a dozen school districts in the eastern half of Wasatch County, all accountable to the county school superintendent in Heber City. With the large number of school districts came an effort by the state legislature to consolidate districts, thus reducing costs while improving the quality of education. The remoteness and isolation of the Uinta Basin portion of the resulting Wasatch School District further promoted the will of those residents to divide Wasatch County. To have their own county would mean having a school superintendent who understood the particulars of providing educational facilities and opportunities to the newly settled and developing area.

There was at least one other significant driving force for home rule. In 1910 the Duchesne LDS Stake was organized, and it established local ecclesiastical leadership apart from the Wasatch LDS Stake in Heber City and the Uintah LDS Stake in Vernal. The resulting ecclesiastical independence of local Mormons thus supported the drive for a new county on the reservation.

The first effort to achieve home rule came in 1909 when the residents of the reservation portion of Wasatch County petitioned the county commission to separate themselves from the rest of the county. This petition for home rule failed in part because county commissions lacked legal authority to divide and make new counties.

Old wooden bridge spanning the Duchesne River at Bridge (Myton) 1907. (Uintah County Library–Regional History Center)

In January 1911 Don B. Colton of Vernal and William Smart of Roosevelt were appointed to work with the state legislature to change the law and give county commissions the authority to divide and create new counties. A second effort subsequently was organized to change the law. The Roosevelt Commercial Club under the leadership of Reuben S. Collett and Harden Bennion petitioned the state legislature for a change in the law. The Commercial Club's stated reason for a change in the law and the creation of a new county was that Wasatch County was too large to effectively govern and that additional counties would be required as the Uinta Basin developed. The *Vernal Express* reported: "This large territory, now so much in need of the benefits of county government, will in all probability yet require to again at some time in the future, be segregated into additional counties."[3]

The work of both committees ultimately paid off. In 1913 William L. Van Wagoner from Midway introduced the "Van Wagoner Amendment" in the state legislature, which provided for the creation of new counties. The new law stipulated that qualified voters from both the new and old counties must approve the division by a majority of each section and agree to the new county lines.

The first hurdle for home rule had been crossed; however, a second, more difficult, hurdle now faced the residents of the reservation—to secure a majority consensus. A county boundary line committee of forty people was organized with H.C. Means as chair to decide where the new county should be located. According to the newspaper, Means and the others were very much concerned with questions of fairness in locating the new county line: "The question is fair dealing with the people of the western portion of the county was not lost sight of and all present agreed that the division ought to be made with that in view."[4]

The proposed location of the county line was hotly contested by the residents from the rest of Wasatch County. At the heart of the issue was the control of the natural resources, particularly timber, water, summer grazing ground, and coal found in abundance in the west end of the Uinta Basin. The 1913 measure was also vigorously opposed by several of the leading businessmen in Heber City but was supported by leaders of the Mormon church.

Satisfied with what they believed was a fair county line, 926 residents of the reservation petitioned the Wasatch County Commission to hold a special election for the purpose of organizing a new county. More than 800 residents from the west end of Wasatch County added their names to the petition. In July 1913 a special election was held and voters from the west end of the county turned down the division by a two-to-one margin. In the east end, an "overwhelming" majority voted in favor of creating a new county. The majority of opposition votes from the east side of the county were cast in Myton.[5]

Disappointed with the results, voters on the reservation soon set about again to win home rule for themselves. The major sticking point was the location of the county line. According to the *Vernal Express*:

> The west end people have insisted upon a line that will include most of the grazing land in the Fruitland District as well as the coal lands of that section, while the reservation people have stood with

Myton in 1905. (Utah State Historical Society)

Fruitland who desired to cast their lot with the proposed new county.[6]

Working with west end voters, east end voters proposed a new county line in 1914 which seemed to satisfy the concerns of many voters from Wasatch County's west end. The county commissioners also supported dividing the county. Their reasons included the inconvenience in managing such a large county, the lack of represen-tation from the Duchesne side of the county, and the fact that law enforcement officers needed to travel from Heber over poor roads. In short, most of the reasons had to do with geographical considera-tions. Both roads from Wasatch County to Duchesne—Daniels Canyon through Strawberry and over Wolf Creek—were often com-pletely blocked by winter snows and spring mud, making travel impossible for several months each year. Even with the commission's support for the division, however, the first election held in 1914 failed.[7] In July 1914 a second election was held. This time, east end voters voted 675 to 65 to create Duchesne County, approving the

Wasatch-Duchesne county line. Wasatch County's west end voters voted 833 in favor and 409 against. Home rule for Duchesne was obtained. On 13 August 1914, Governor William Spry, as stipulated in the Van Wagoner law, issued a proclamation establishing Duchesne County, which had a population of nearly 9,000 people.[8] Duchesne County became Utah's twenty-eighth county. The newly elected officials included County Clerk and Recorder Edward Mackey; Treasurer Lula Hood; Assessor C.W. Smith; County Attorney Ray E. Dillman; and County Commissioners J.E.L. Carey, George Lindsay, and S.A. Russell.

A number of issues faced the new county. One was the lack of a tax base to build roads and other infrastructure. Nearly 80 percent of the new county's budget was dedicated to education. The *Duchesne Record,* which moved from Myton to Duchesne in 1915, published an open letter to the state legislature, asking it for financial help:

> We don't ask you to build a railroad, the prime requisite, but we do ask for help that we may grow quickly to that point that a road shall be built. Wagon roads always precede the railroad. We have not yet a good wagon road in any direction, either in the basin, or leading out of the basin. All that we have we have built ourselves, without taxes, without aid from the State worth mentioning. What do we want? We want the great State of Utah to either loan us about $500,000, or arrange for our securing such an amount, for completing our irrigation projects. This is not all: We ask help to build a western gateway so that we may go to Salt Lake, or Utah county—to the old settled part of Utah, with a load, so that autos may go east and west during the major part of the year. Is it possible for Utah to do this? Yes, it is not only possible but it is morally obligatory that the state does this. . . . We think it is about time that the legislature awaken to your plain duty. Incidently, we trust that you have seated Duchesne county's representative. A little more cold-hearted treatment of this section, will turn us all toward Denver and we shall likely get some help.[9]

The county's first representative to the state legislature was William O'Neil of Roosevelt. At his first session as a member of the state legislature, O'Neil introduced a bill to appropriate $10,000 to build a new bridge over the Duchesne River near Utahn. The repre-

Main Street Myton 1912. (Uintah County Library–Regional History Center, Todd Collection)

sentative from Uintah County introduced a bill to appropriate $25,000 for a highway to be constructed from Vernal to Heber City. Both bills passed both houses of the state legislature. However, O'Neil's supplication and that of his constituents for help in building better wagon roads did not meet with Governor William Spry's approval. Neither did a dozen or more other road construction bills; Spry did not want to expend money for road improvements.[10]

The Fight to Locate the County Seat

The struggle to establish a county seat presents a study of early rural politics. The law stipulated that a majority of voters of a new

This building housed the Myton Bank, Opera House and Myton Free Press, circa 1920. (Uintah County Library–Regional History Center, Todd Collection)

county were to select their new county seat. The drive for the county seat triggered a hotly contested race among the communities of Myton, Roosevelt, Duchesne, and Lakefork. As the various town promoters campaigned, it soon became apparent that the three largest towns—Myton, Roosevelt, and Duchesne—were the prime contenders.

Myton was the principal community of the non-Mormon population and Roosevelt was the county's center for Mormon homesteaders and the Mormon church. The people of Roosevelt campaigned hard, and the hometown *Roosevelt Standard* urged its readers to place their mark for Roosevelt. The *Standard* of 12 October 1914 had as its front-page headline the prediction, "Roosevelt, as largest and best town in the basin will be the choice for county seat." A week before the election, the newspaper's headline was "If you Think, Your Choice Is Roosevelt!"[11] When the vote was taken, however, Duchesne was selected by a majority of county voters.

There were several reasons Duchesne was able to edge out the other towns for the county seat. Although a larger portion of the population was concentrated in the east end of the county, Duchesne and Roosevelt residents voted almost as a block for their own towns, as was to be expected, as did the citizens of Myton. However, the town of Roosevelt failed to win the surrounding votes. Altonah, with 146 voters (the fourth-largest town), split its vote, with 54 for Duchesne and 48 for Roosevelt. The remaining votes from Altonah were divided between Lakefork and Myton. The deciding votes for Duchesne came from Boneta and Stockmore, with 384 votes for Duchesne and only 53 for Roosevelt.

The voting figures also help reveal the number of people in the towns of the county. There were 2,378 votes cast in this election among adults over twenty-one years of age. Voting for the county seat is seen in the accompanying chart.

Duchesne County Seat Vote by Precinct:

	Duchesne	Myton	Lakefork	Roosevelt
Duchesne	412	3	1	3
Roosevelt	3	4	1	485
Boneta	244	2	0	40
Altonah	54	12	32	48
Utahn	48	1	0	6
Midview	31	17	0	0
Antelope	18	13	0	0
Lakefork	17	8	64	7
Packard	5	1	0	78
Stockmore1	40	2	0	13
Cedarview	5	7	0	13
Myton	4	211	58	21
Fruitland	86	0	0	0
Totals	1,067	331	163	817[12]

Having achieved the victory for county seat, the town of Duchesne was assured growth, with new jobs created for the various county officers, school district office, and the county court. Presently the county government still constitutes a significant portion of employment in Duchesne City.

Myton Main Street, circa 1922. Notice the change in just a few short years between the traffic of horse and wagon to automobiles. (Uintah County Library–Regional History Center, Todd Collection)

Duchesne-Uintah County Line

In creating Duchesne County there was one final issue to be resolved—the Uintah-Duchesne county line. During the campaign to select the county seat, a rumor circulated in the new county that Roosevelt was not really in Duchesne County. "Malicious persons, thinking, to check the people from voting for Roosevelt for the County Seat of the new county, are actively circulating the story that Roosevelt is not in Wasatch County and therefore cannot be the county seat of Duchesne County," wrote the *Roosevelt Standard*.[13] The disputation was more than rumor, however. A close reading of the original Wasatch-Uintah county line description revealed a serious difference between the earliest survey and the more recent survey, which was done after the election for the county seat and the approving of the new Duchesne County. The results were confusing, and the possibility existed that all previous elections associated with the establishment of Duchesne County and the county seat would be nullified. For several months the controversy occupied the front pages in the *Roosevelt Standard*. To the supporters of Myton, this was an opportunity to hold new elections and win the campaign for the county seat.

At the core of the controversy was the Interior Department's survey of the Great Basin and eastern Utah in 1876. Problems were compounded when the territorial legislature created Uintah County using the inaccurate 1876 survey. At the time of Utah statehood in 1896, the legislature reaffirmed that the Uintah-Wasatch county line was the 110th meridian, used earlier by the territorial legislature. A new survey was conducted following statehood, however, which determined the 110th meridian to be one and three-eighths miles farther west than the older survey had it. The new survey running the entire length of Duchesne County's eastern boundary placed more than 130 square miles, including some of the best reservation land, in Uintah County.

The potential loss of revenue from property taxes was serious. All land deeds which had been recorded in Wasatch County and later filed in Duchesne County would need to be refiled in Uintah County.[14] Some of the newly elected county officials, including County Attorney Ray Dillman, County Surveyor Craig Harmston, and County Sheriff Roy Wilkins, all lived east of the disputed line. Equally troubling was the fact that the newly completed Duchesne County high school, paid for by Duchesne County citizens, was located east of the new survey line.

Bitter feelings were felt throughout the county over the county-seat election, and many Roosevelt citizens felt that the rest of the county did not want them in Duchesne County. Lines from a letter published in the *Roosevelt Standard* summed up many people's feelings: "Roosevelt is still on the map but we hardly know what map. Are we in Uintah or Duchesne County? . . . Don't [sic] Duchesne County want us?[15]

For a short time there was a move, led mostly by Roosevelt citizens who were disgruntled over losing the county seat, to create their own county, with Lake Fork and the Sand Ridge as the west and east boundaries, respectively. The proposed new county also would have included Altonah, Fort Duchesne, and Myton. As the controversy continued, Uintah County even considered giving a five-mile strip on the west end of its county to Duchesne County. This would have placed Fort Duchesne and Whiterocks in Duchesne County.[16]

Several paths were taken to resolve the county-line question. The state attorney general, after an investigation by the state engineer in October 1914, decided that Roosevelt was in fact in Duchesne County. Based upon this decision, the Utah Supreme Court ruled on the county line and established it at the present location.[17] Some residents of Roosevelt asked Utah Attorney General A.R. Barnes if the question over the disputed county line could not be resolved by holding an election. Barnes responded that such elections were illegal. To end the dispute, William O'Neil from Duchesne County introduced a bill in the state legislature in 1915 clarifying the county line. Two years later, the state legislature passed such a bill and the issues were finally resolved.[18]

Myton

Sometime in the mid-1880s, William Henderson of Vernal was granted a license from Indian officials to establish a trading post on the Uintah Indian Reservation. Henderson's trading post was located near one of several natural fords of the Duchesne River and initially consisted of a single building of rough-cut pine. The trading post served a small segment of the Indian population until 1886, when the army, as part of building the road between Price and the newly established Fort Duchesne, built a bridge over the treacherous Duchesne River. To defray construction costs, a toll was charged for use of the bridge for the next few years.

The trading post's importance increased with the completion of the bridge and the Nine Mile Road. Henderson's trading post soon became an important way-station on the Nine Mile Road as well as the less-traveled road to Heber City through Strawberry Valley. It was the first watering place between Smith Wells and Fort Duchesne. The trading post was quickly identified as "The Bridge" or "Bridges." Several additional wooden buildings were added to accommodate the dozens of teamsters hauling freight between Price and Fort Duchesne and Vernal, and returning with Gilsonite to the railroad at Price. In 1888 a stage stopped twice weekly at The Bridge, and a year later daily stage service was established, which added to the business and other activities at The Bridge.

Myton Baseball Team. (Uintah County Library–Regional History Center, Todd Collection)

Sometime near the turn of the century, Owen Smith, after selling out his business to I.W. "Ike" Odekirk at Smith Wells, moved to The Bridge and opened a store to serve a growing clientele of Indians and travelers on the two roads.[19] Sometime prior to the opening of the reservation in 1905, William Henderson sold out to H.C. Clark who in turn sold the trading post to Hayden Calvert. Calvert was already familiar with the Uinta Basin and the Uintah Indian Reservation, having been employed in the Indian Service at White Rocks since the mid-1880s.

Prior to the opening of the Uintah Indian Reservation, The Bridge bustled with federal government surveyors and members of the Uintah Indian Commission, which was making allotments to some of the Uintah and White River Ute Indian families. Major Howell Plummer Myton, Indian agent for the combined Uintah and Ouray Indian Agency, spent considerable time at The Bridge making preparations for the opening of the reservation in 1905.

The Bridge quickly changed from a small but bustling way-station and Indian trading post to a town of tents and a few wooden buildings in September 1905. The Calvert family and others at The Bridge naturally wanted to establish their community as a full fledged town, and William H. Smart, promoter of settlement of the reservation and stake president of Wasatch LDS Stake, encouraged the establishment of The Bridge as the reservation's first town.[20]

Myton, Calvert, and others took immediate steps to secure a post office for their community. A petition was submitted to Joseph Briston, a friend of Myton and a U.S. Post Office official in Washington, D.C., requesting that a post office be established at The Bridge. The petitioners suggested the name of Briston for their new post office and, hence, for their community. Joseph Briston, however, changed the name to Myton. Years later, Howell Myton, in an autobiographical sketch, recalled the community's effort to secure a post office and the changing of the name from The Bridge to Myton.

> I was U. S. Indian agent and the settlers handed me a petition for a Post Office there. Joseph Briston a friend of mine from Kansas was 4th assistant Post Master General and I sent the petition to him and named the Post Office "Briston." He scratched the word "Briston," and named the office "Myton," that is the way the town got its name."[21]

Myton attracted people from various parts of the world. Settlers from Denmark, England, Switzerland, Sweden, Wales, and Germany, as well as many states of the Union were found on the dirt streets of Myton. Myton and the reservation offered settlers fresh opportunities to secure land cheaply or to establish new businesses.[22]

The young town of Myton faced numerous challenges, not the least of which was spring flooding. The winter of 1908–09 was particularly harsh, with more than average snowfall in the Uinta Basin and deep snow on the Uinta and Wasatch mountains. The spring of 1909 was late in arriving, and its arrival then caused the Duchesne River to run extremely high, with a great deal of flooding as a result. At Myton the forceful floodwaters of the Duchesne River carved a new channel, leaving the bridge built by the army spanning a dry gulch. A bridge across the Duchesne River was critical for the existence of the new town of Myton as well as the economic vitality of

Myton baseball field with game in progress, circa 1920s. Note the extensive stands which evidence large attendance. (Uintah County Library–Regional History Center, Todd Collection.)

much of the Uinta Basin. Transportation was seriously hampered, stage travel was disrupted, and freight wagons had to be transported across the river by raft.

The citizens of Myton and the entire Uinta Basin appealed for a new bridge. Senator Reed Smoot responded and secured a $25,000 appropriation from Congress for a new bridge at Myton.[23] A year later, in September 1910, the new "government" bridge was completed at Myton. In addition, part of the Duchesne River channel was straightened near Myton, reducing the threat of flooding from the Duchesne River. The people of Myton and the reservation portion of Wasatch County organized a two-day celebration to officially open the new bridge. Governor William Spry, Senator Reed Smoot, and a host of state officials and LDS church leaders were invited to participate. The *Vernal Express* wrote of the event that the state officials from Salt Lake City were met at Colton and transported by carriage to the outskirts of Myton, where the distinguished guests were met by a "bevy of young girls dressed in white." The company proceeded to the government bridge between two lines of the country's finest young women and girls and were welcomed with a "bomb blast of dynamite."

At the bridge speeches were made, and cheers from 3,000 people in attendance followed each speech. At the conclusion of the speeches, the master of ceremonies asked who should unlock the large padlock. The key was offered to Senator Smoot, who acknowledged the honor but told the master of ceremonies to give the honor "To the Governor of the greatest state of the greatest country in the world." Governor Spry then did the honors of unlocking the padlock to the bridge.[24]

The rapid construction of the new bridge with federal dollars and the support of the state reflected the importance of good transportation facilities and the increasing interstate commerce to the Uinta Basin including the town of Myton. The construction of the government bridge was one of several important building projects in Myton. Later that year, the Myton Opera House Company was organized. Investors elected Joseph M. Bryant as president, and H.C. Means, J.M. Coltharp, J.L. Ewing, and I.W. Odekirk as directors of the company. The construction of a 40-by-80-foot building was begun. It was later used as a dance hall, theater, and a conference center. At least a dozen homes were built in Myton in 1910, along with an eight-room lodging house and the Calvert and Waugh general store.[25] A year earlier, the Myton State Bank was organized and a bank building was planned.

Life was less than the homesteaders expected not only because of the bleak landscape but also due to the lawlessness of the first years of the homesteading era. Joseph Harold Eldredge, who settled in Myton in 1913, said of the frontier town:

> The saloons had all the rough elements which could be attracted to a frontier town. There were shooting scrapes. One man was shot down in the street as he ran from the marshal. . . . They eventually got another marshal in office. However, he worried so much about the fighting and rough stuff that went on in the saloons that he eventually became mentally disturbed and tried to

Roosevelt Main Street 1907, two years after its founding.(Utah State Historical Society)

blow up the saloons with explosives. . . . I had not been in town many months until I heard two shots which killed two people.[26]

The rough elements of frontier life were short-lived and mostly confined to Myton and the west end of Uintah County, especially The Strip, but they were distressing to those who came to the area from well-established regions that had passed their frontier times a full generation before.

The building boom and the establishment of new business continued for the next several years, and by 1912 Myton's business district included the Barry D. Mercantile Company, a general merchandise and agricultural implement store; Calvert and Waugh General Store; the Myton Hotel, operated by Mrs. E. McGuire; Ike Odekirk's general store; the Myton Trading Company, a general merchandise store owned by A.F. Maxwell; the Uinta Lumber Company, a hardware and lumber store owned by E.M. Jones; Abraham Liddell's livery; a construction and carpentry business owned by J.O. Hahn; the opera house, and a school.[27]

Fred Watrous published the weekly *Uintah Record* newspaper. The *Uintah Record* was the successor to the *Uintah Chieftan* and the

Uinta Standard, both of which had been published in Roosevelt and owned by Watrous. The *Uintah Record* changed publishers in 1913 when William H. Smart took over the newspaper. A year later the newspaper changed publishers again; J.P. May became the new publisher and moved the paper to Duchesne, where he changed its name to the *Duchesne Record.*[28]

The *Reservation News* was published in Altonah in 1913 by Morton Alexander. This newspaper's masthead championed the cause of the common man: "Always fighting for the Plain People and the Under Dog."[29] Myton was not left without a newspaper when the *Uintah Record* was moved to Duchesne. In 1915 C.B. Cook, who was associated earlier with the *Vernal Express,* began the *Myton Free Press.*

Myton's business district attracted homesteaders from a wide area of the reservation. Harold Eldredge recalled trips that people from outlying communities made to Myton.

> When I first came to Myton, the people came from Altonah, Mountain Home, and all of that high country and outlying areas to do their shopping and business in Myton. They came in wagons, and it was a long day's trip to town. Many of the people would stay for two or three days doing their buying and other business when they came to town. Then they had the long trip back to their farms and ranches again.[30]

At the very outset of the opening of the reservation, the citizens of Myton aspired to make their town the governmental, social, and economic center of the reservation. With its opera house and other facilities, Myton leaders encouraged the LDS church to hold its quarterly regional conferences in Myton. For a short time both Mormon and Presbyterian church services were held at the opera house. Frequently, in fact, they met at the same hour, and a sheet was hung to separate the congregations. Following their respective Sunday services they combined to enjoy a pot-luck dinner together.[31] By 1915 sufficient funds had been raised that the congregants under the ministry of George Sloan built themselves a new church in Myton.[32]

Myton civic leaders promoted a fair for the reservation, and for a few years following the establishment of Duchesne County annual county fairs were held in Myton. However, despite all of its promo-

Roosevelt Main Street 1917. (Uintah County Library–Regional History Center)

tional efforts, its strong economic role, and its location, Myton failed to win the position of primary city for the reservation and later county seat for Duchesne County. A local story tells of a LDS committee, headed by stake president William Smart, that came to Myton to meet with the non-Mormon town council to ask that certain Mormon interests have the opportunity to buy into one of the banks in town as well as several of the businesses. The town council and business owners emphatically declined the request. At this point, according to the story, Smart uttered what has afterward been called the "Mormon Curse." He reportedly said: "If you do not allow us to buy into your town, you will see the day when only jackrabbits and tumbleweeds will inhabit your main street."[33]

Another version of the Mormon curse relates that when President Smart came to a church stake conference in Myton he was dismayed at the attitude and actions of many of the local church members. Especially detrimental to spiritual growth in Smart's opinion was the support church members living around Myton were giving to the saloons of the town. He warned the members that if such action were not immediately stopped Myton would fail and weeds would grow in the sidewalks.

A third version of the curse deals with the building of a Mormon chapel. Bill Peatross, old-time resident of the county and the son of William Stuart Peatross, who was involved with the *Myton Free Press* newspaper in 1915, related the following:

> In September of 1910 during a meeting held to discuss the pro-
> posal of a new Mormon Stake Center to be built in Myton, oppos-
> ing non-Mormons fiercely shouted the Mormon leader down
> telling him that if he even tried it they would tar and feather him
> and ride him out of town on a rail. The Mormon leader, President
> William H. Smart, told the fierce crowd that the stake center would
> be built in Roosevelt . . . and from that day forward Myton would
> go down hill until the day would come when they would see weeds
> growing in the cracks of the side walks, rabbits would play in the
> streets, and many of their busy streets would turn into swamps.[34]

Whatever the true story, many county residents believe in the Mormon curse.

Several historical developments help explain the declining position of Myton. Fred Todd, long-time resident of Myton, claimed that the founding of a local Masonic lodge in Myton contributed to the town's decline. It was chartered on 19 January 1916, and members met in the Myton State Bank, owned by Ralph Dart.[35] Todd maintained that Mormon homesteaders feared, unreasonably, that the Masons were conspiring against them in business and banking; this resulted in the Mormons pulling their support from the Myton business district.[36] Financial difficulties of the Myton State Bank in August 1922 forced suspension of banking activities until the bank could be reorganized. The bank problems severely disrupted financial activities in Myton and placed a dark shadow over the bank following its reorganization.

The viability of Myton as a town of commerce and trade was severely affected during the early morning hours of 19 June 1915 when a fire razed virtually the entire business district of Myton. The fire began about 2:00 A.M. at the back of J.D. Beaver's saloon, pool hall, and rooming house. The townspeople tried valiantly to put out the inferno, but Myton was without a water system. Ironically, the citizens of Myton days earlier had voted by a wide margin (49 to 3) to bond themselves for a new town water system. High winds fanned

Duchesne County High School, built in Roosevelt 1919–20. (Uintah County Library–Regional History Center, Snow Collection)

the flames, and the heat from the fire forced the bucket line of fire-fighters to retreat across the street. Without a water system in town, the fire raged for four hours and was only halted when the Airdome Theater, which had been vacant for several years, was hurriedly torn down and the combustible materials removed from the fire's path.

Estimated value of the losses varied; according to one newspaper report, the loss was placed at $30,000. Beaver's establishment was totally destroyed, as was the *Myton Free Press* facilities. However, the day before the fire, the newspaper had moved most of the printing equipment and paper supply to another building, and therefore the loss to the newspaper company was minimal. E.J. Marchant's barber shop, Reservation Realty, the office of the mayor, Wells's butcher shop, the law offices of R.B. Croix, the office of the Pleasant Valley Irrigation Company, a dental office, and other offices were totally destroyed.[37]

Fires struck Myton in 1925 and again in 1930. The 1930 fire turned much of the business district into ashes and rubble. The 1930 fire, coupled with the onset of the national Depression, made it impossible for most businesses in Myton to fully recover.[38] Today the community is bravely struggling to reinstate a viable business district and attract new construction and families to the area.

Other challenges to Myton's efforts to become the preeminent city on the reservation came from the communities of Duchesne and Roosevelt. In 1910 Myton's population was 350; Duchesne's population was 150 people less than Myton's; and Roosevelt topped Myton, with a population of 563. Geographically, Duchesne was more centrally located in the county and was situated on the increasingly more-traveled Strawberry Valley road to Heber City.

Myton also faced stiff competition from the community of Roosevelt. Earlier, before the opening of the reservation, William Smart had made it known that he wanted to prevent any land-grabbing on the reservation, meaning that he wanted the reservation reserved for Mormon homesteaders.[39] This had irritated many non-Mormons in the state and the few residents already living in Myton. This irritation was further provoked by Stake President Smart when in 1910 he wanted to build a "theological seminary" in Myton and wanted the building financed with public bonds. Smart even wanted to change the town's name to "please the Lord."[40] The residents of Myton objected, and Smart turned to Roosevelt to develop his plans to establish the ecclesiastical center of the Mormon church on the reservation.

Despite these challenges, the citizens of Myton continued to promote the town and the surrounding area as the best town and the choicest land to farm. Earlier, in 1894, through a bill sponsored by Wyoming Senator Joseph M. Carey which bears his name, Congress granted up to 1 million acres of additional federal land to each of ten semiarid western states and territories, with the provision that the state make efforts to reclaim the land and make it available to actual settlers in tracts not exceeding 160 acres. In 1910, Public Law 114 was passed; it extended the provisions of the Carey Act to include land that was once Indian reservation land.

Frank Lott of Denver, Colorado, using the provisions of the Carey Act, applied to the state of Utah for permission to develop and irrigate over 30,900 acres of land southeast of Myton. Financing the

Theodore (Duchesne) 1910. (Uintah County Library–Regional History Center. Snow Collection)

large South Duchesne Irrigation Project (also known as the South Myton Carey Project) was estimated to cost $500,000—well beyond the collective means of the homesteaders. J.P. Smith and George C. Jones, both from Oklahoma, Isaac Odikirk of Myton, and William Smart, LDS stake president and president of the Wasatch Development Company, lent their financial support to the South Duchesne Irrigation Project.

The combination of homesteaders and investors applied for financial assistance and leeway under the federal Carey Act. It was hoped that much of the money could be raised through selling the 30,900 acres as well as selling water shares. The homesteaders already on the Myton Bench joined Lott's scheme and in a cooperative effort planned to help dig a canal from the Duchesne River to their homesteads. The plan called for the start of the canal thirty miles upstream. This long distance was needed to provide sufficient grade to successfully lift the water to the land on the south Myton Bench.

The announcement of Lott's plan in the summer of 1909 created great expectancy, even an atmosphere of economic boom and land rush, which would bring some 600 families and upwards of 3,000 additional people to the immediate vicinity around Myton. Headlines such as "Myton on the Eve of Great Boom" and "Magic Myton Destined to Become the Commercial Metropolis of the Rich Duchesne Valley" appeared frequently in the weekly *Uintah Chieftain* and lent encouragement to the boosters and backers of the land and water project.[41] The scheme received a hopeful boost when word circulated throughout eastern Utah that the new Moffat Railroad Company was planning to construct a rail line through the Uinta Basin to connect Denver with Salt Lake City. Other railroad companies, including the Grand River and the Meeker and Salt Lake railroads, indicated strong interest in building a rail line through the reservation.[42]

However, both the railroad and Lott's land and reclamation scheme went bust. Lott's filing for nearly 500 second-feet of Duchesne River water lapsed in November 1916 and was never renewed.[43] A significant problem for Lott and the others was that the financing for the scheme never was met. The railroad plan, one of several proposals rumored from time to time in the Uinta Basin, also failed to materialize because of the lack of financial backing, the limited transportation market, a small population base in the Uinta Basin, and the presence of the Denver and Rio Grande Railroad to the south of the Uinta Basin.

For those homesteaders who managed to stay on the south Myton Bench, it took nearly sixty years for the South Duchesne Irrigation Project canal to be completed. The canal from the Duchesne River to the south Myton Bench finally was dug after Starvation Dam was completed. For many anxious homesteaders this was much too late. The disappointment of both the failed railroad and the delayed irrigation project stunted Myton's commercial development.

Newspapers of the Uinta Basin were full of the spirit of promotion and boosterism. Local business organizations and chambers of commerce, and even state and national organizations, promoted the Uinta Basin and the newly formed Duchesne County towns as places to prosper in. Newly established county extension agents from the state agricultural college in Logan frequently reported on the agricultural possibilities of the basin. Newspaper headlines and stories

Theodore (Duchesne) 1910. (Uintah County Library–Regional History Center, Todd Collection)

such as "Peaches and Pea-nuts and many, many varieties of other farm and garden products proclaim the great fertility of the reservation," "Lakefork Prospering," and "Altonah is the Place to Settle" appeared often in local and state newspapers. The hope was that others would come and settle and thus share in the great amount of work that needed to be done for all to prosper; and the tone of these articles boosted the morale of some of those already in the Uinta Basin.[44]

Poor crops, early or late frosts, the lack of transportation facilities and infrastructure, problems of insect infestations, and even the failure of the Duchesne Irrigation Project did not halt the continued promotion of the region. There were other possibilities to promote. The *Uintah Chieftain* ran one headline that read, "Great Hydro-Carbon Wealth," and continued, "new discoveries throughout the Uinta Basin is a sure indication that with the advent of the railroad this part of Northeast Utah will become world famous."[45] At the opening of the reservation and for years after, the promise of one or more railroads loomed on the horizon of promoters and settlers alike. Politicians and businessmen courted officials from the Union

Pacific, Denver & Rio Grande, and other companies, hoping a railroad would be built.

Newspaper headlines varied from hope to despair to virtual certainty about the prospects of the railroad coming. As late as the 1940s there was still hope and talk of a railroad and how it would raise the Uinta Basin's fortunes to new heights. But the railroad never did come to the county. However, the narrow-gauge Uintah Railway was built from Mack, Colorado, to Dragon in southeastern Uintah County in 1904.[46]

Roosevelt

The area of Roosevelt was homesteaded by Ed F. Harmston, Frank Orser, Henry Guckert, J. Garnet Holmes, Elroy Wilkins, Dan Llyberts, A. Birch, and George M. Pickup in September 1905.[47] Their homesteads along with others were located in the heart of William Smart's Wasatch Development Company's land plans and those of the newly formed Dry Gulch Irrigation Company. As early as December 1906 the Dry Gulch Irrigation Company and its assignee, the Wasatch Development Company, were making plans to make water rights applications with the state engineer.[48]

Much too busy to prove up on his homestead himself, Harmston had two of his sons, A.C. and Floyd, live there in a boarded tent. To demonstrate that improvements were being made on the land they piled up rocks and dug a well. The following spring Harmston turned his homestead claim into a townsite.[49] While men were surveying and laying out the townsite, a curious Ute Indian asked what they were doing. When told they were laying out a city, his incredulous reply was that they were crazy.[50]

Harmston planned to call the new town Dry Gulch City, thinking it had a western ring to it. His wife, Mary, was dismayed with the name. "Imagine naming a town after a dry gulcher who shoots a man in the back from ambush. This will be a respectable town. Its got to have a respectable name," she said.[51] She promptly named the new town in honor of President of the United States Theodore Roosevelt, whom she greatly admired.

Roosevelt's beginnings were unique. Most towns in Utah were located near a dependable water source; not Roosevelt. One water

Abe Murdock's Store in Duchesne circa 1915. (Utah State Historical Society)

source, from Dry Gulch, was frequently roily and sometimes dry. The other source was some distance from the townsite. Some early residents of Roosevelt were forced to haul their water in barrels from the Duchesne River; others obtained water from the closer but smaller stream.

Clearing the water of silt was done by placing small chunks of prickly pear cacti in the barrels of water and letting the water stand for a few days. The cacti drew the silt and other sediments to the bottom of the barrel, leaving the top clear and ready to be boiled and used. During windy days this method was hampered when blowing dust was deposited in the barrels of water. Also, during the winter water in the nearby stream and in the water barrels frequently froze.[52] By 1914 the citizens of Roosevelt in their need had developed a municipal water system, months before the older community of Myton bonded itself to build a similar water system.[53]

The promise of an irrigation system from the Dry Gulch Irrigation Company was an encouragement for homesteaders and townfolks alike. In spite of the water concerns, the town grew rapidly. By 1910, according to the federal census, the precinct of Roosevelt numbered 688, Myton's population was 1,048, and the Theodore precinct was second largest on the reservation, with 939 people.[54] Seven years later, the estimated populations of the three towns were: Roosevelt, 1,000; Myton, 700; and Duchesne (Theodore), 650.[55]

Roosevelt quickly became a commercial center for the eastern end of the former reservation. Closer to Fort Duchesne than was Myton, Roosevelt soon eclipsed Myton in providing commerce, trade, and other services to the soldiers and Indians at the fort. In 1911 a post office was established, which added stature to Roosevelt; and by 1914 Roosevelt became a town of the third class, being so designated by the state legislature.

The *Roosevelt Standard* on 18 January 1915, in a booster effort for the community, listed the businesses and institutions located in Roosevelt. The article said that the town had a population of 563 and had waterworks, electric lights, a telephone exchange, and a school system with Duchesne High School. Businesses included the newspaper, three general stores, a meat market, two drug stores, two carriage repositories, one implement store, two hardware stores, a furniture store, a harness shop, two barber shops, a bank, a bakery, a photograph studio, two blacksmith shops, a hotel, three lawyers, two civil engineers, two doctors, two livery stables, one hospital, seven real estate offices, one ice cream factory, three planing mills, a flour mill, a millinery shop, a brickyard, and the Dry Gulch office. There was also an Odd Fellow Lodge, a Presbyterian church, and a LDS church.

C.C. Larson epitomized the can-do spirit of early Roosevelt settlers and businessmen. This hardy Danish immigrant did everything from pulling teeth to selling almost everything settlers needed. A widower with several children, Larson remarried a widow who also had several children. Two years after their marriage Larson moved his family to the new town of Roosevelt and lived there in a tent for three years before building a twenty-one-room house.[56]

Numerous other entrepreneurs chanced the opportunity to settle in the new town. In addition to the Larsons and Harmstons, others included R.S. Collett and family, the O.H. Bracken family, the Owen Bennion family, Clarence I. Johnson and family, Ernest H. Burgess and family, and dozens of others.[57]

By 1909 the Mormon population was sufficiently large that Roosevelt LDS Stake was created, and William Smart chose Roosevelt

Duchesne circa 1920. (Uintah County Library–Regional History Center, Todd Collection)

as the ecclesiastical headquarters for the reservation area. Smart believed that towns and those who controlled them were important to building the "Utah empire"—meaning the Mormon church kingdom.[58] The designation of Roosevelt as the stake center and other business activities of William Smart, such as locating the Dry Gulch Irrigation Company offices in town, provided an economic boon to Harmston and the other early town settlers, many of whom were not members of the Mormon church but seemed to be more accommodating to the faith than were the people of Myton. Roosevelt's growth was also facilitated by its location on the roads to Price and Heber City.

A community's economic development and stability usually depends on diversity, and, as the county's communities grew, so did the local economy. Roosevelt soon became more diversified, having more services than did Myton. The Roosevelt Mercantile Company, organized by J.G. Holmes, William Smart, H.J. Harding, and Ward Pack, offered a wide variety of dry goods, groceries, and farm implements. Beginning in 1907, Robert Marshall and Caleb Sprouse operated a meat market. Other commercial establishments included the J.M. Russell Investment Company, the Motter-Bracken Realty Company, Roosevelt Drug, the Birch Furniture Store, and the Roosevelt Brick Company. In 1907 Smart established the Uintah Telephone Company, which brought telephone service to the Uinta Basin.[59] Smart added to his economic empire by acquiring several newspapers in the Uinta Basin, including the *Vernal Express,* the *Duchesne Standard,* and the *Duchesne Messenger,* among others.

Another important factor that brought Roosevelt into early prominence over Myton, Cedarview, and Ioka, which all were aggressively seeking settlers and promoting themselves, was its accessibility to roads. Roosevelt businessmen took advantage of the town's location on the important road between Price, Heber City, and Vernal. They promoted a stage line stop in Roosevelt and offered a wide variety of services for stage-line passengers as well as freighters.

Equally important to the growing importance and dominance of Roosevelt as the area's ecclesiastical and commercial center was the establishment there of an educational system. While other communities on the reservation worked to establish school districts and build schools, the citizens of Roosevelt possessed the resources to move quickly to establish their own school district and to build schools. In 1907 the Harmston family donated two acres of land for a school. The first class included about fifteen pupils of mixed ages. These early students brought whatever books were available at their homes to study from.

Plans soon were made for a high school. State law required that each county establish a separate high school district. The high school building for Wasatch County was located in Heber City, an impossible distance to travel for high-school-age students on the reservation. Also, it was too expensive for families to board their children with families in Heber City. People of the reservation voted to create a second high school district in the eastern end of Wasatch County. In February 1914 the taxpayers of Wasatch High School District Number 2 voted to issue $39,000 worth of bonds to build a high school building in Roosevelt.[60]

The residents of Myton, Duchesne, and Boneta all wanted the

Main Street Altonah circa 1915. Altonah became, for a short time, the largest community in the upper country. (Uintah County Library–Regional History Center, Neal Collection)

new high school to be located in their communities. The larger population in and around Roosevelt and an offer made by William Smart to sell more than twenty-one acres at seventy-five dollars per acre made Roosevelt the logical site, however. In the fall of 1914 the new high school building was started; it was dedicated on 17 February 1915. The building cost came to $36,817.[61] The school had nearly fifty students initially, and Principal J.F. Hoyt expected the number to be 150 students within a few weeks as people sent their children to the school.[62] The first fifteen graduates graduated in the spring of 1915. Later, after Duchesne County was established, the high school was renamed Duchesne High School Number One. The high school later was renamed Roosevelt High School, and it served the east end of the county until 1952 when the new Union High School was completed and dedicated.

The funding, management, and location of the new Union High School were unusual. In the early 1950s the federal government was in the midst of changing its Indian programs, including the schooling of Indian children. Beginning in the 1920s Indian boarding schools were deemphasized and the Bureau of Indian Affairs placed emphasis on the states educating Indian children. The education of Indian children in day schools and in public schools was underscored by the legislation and policies of the New Deal of the 1930s. Following World War II Congress enacted a policy of "termination," which attempted to end all federal programs and responsibilities for Indian peoples and tribes. Although short-lived, the termination policy further encouraged the enrollment of Indian children in public schools and in high schools. The federal government wanted to integrate Indian students into local schools and society, and it encouraged states to take more responsibility for educating their Indian students.

Following World War II, Roosevelt's population grew, placing stress on the existing high school building. (The population census indicated a shift of population within the county from 1930 to 1950. The more rural areas of the county lost population while Roosevelt grew steadily—from 1,051 in 1930 to 1,628 in 1950.)[63] The Uintah County School District was also of a mind to improve Alteria High School, located in the west end of that county. A union of interests approved a joint project to build a high school to serve the various needs. The federal government made a special grant of $250,000 toward the building of a new high school, and the two county school districts agreed to appropriate $150,000 each.[64] Union High School is located on the county line, with the main hallway positioned so that each county physically contains part of the school. At the present time in Roosevelt, in addition to Union High School, there is East Roosevelt Elementary, Roosevelt Middle School, and Roosevelt Junior High School.

One important economic element that was missing in Roosevelt was a bank. William Smart joined with W.A. Miles and several other citizens of Roosevelt and, with additional financial backing from the Merchants Bank of Salt Lake City, incorporated the Roosevelt Banking Company in 1914. Miles was elected president of the new bank. Before organizing the Roosevelt Banking Company, Smart had founded the Heber City Bank and helped to establish the Uintah Stake Bank in Vernal.[65]

Lake Fork (Upalco) flour mill, circa 1925. (Uintah County Library–Regional History Center, Todd Collection)

The establishment of the Roosevelt Banking Company came on the heels of a financial crisis for many farmers in the county. In 1909, after a poor harvest the previous year, many farmers faced financial ruin and loss of their farms. Rock M. Pope, state legislator from Wasatch County, made an appeal for state relief for "the destitute settlers on the reservation."[66] The legislature then appropriated $7,500 for the relief of the homesteaders. Governor William Spry established a relief committee that consisted of R.S. Collett of Roosevelt, Reverend Hershey of Randlett, and George Cluff of Duchesne to distribute relief funds used to purchase feed for livestock and seed for the 1909 growing season.

By 1920 the new Roosevelt Bank, like other small banks in the state, faced financial difficulties. World War I had stimulated the agricultural sector of the national economy, and this encouraged excessive capitalization and expansion by farmers. After the war, however, agricultural markets changed and many farmers who had gambled on a continued strong agricultural market found those markets no longer as strong and were caught with excessive loans.

William Smart, as one of the bank's founders, attempted to secure additional financial support for the young financial institution. Concerning the bank's problems and those of its depositors, Smart wrote:

> I am compelled to leave my duties to answer the cry of my helpless people to help save them from financial drowning in the waters of this bank. Regardless of their mistakes, what can one do before the cries of a helpless and dependent child but make an effort to respond.[67]

The Roosevelt Bank weathered the financial crisis successfully and continued strong through the country's Great Depression of the 1930s. The other two area banks, Myton State Bank and the Bank of Duchesne, were unable to meet the financial crisis of the early 1920s, and both failed—the Bank of Duchesne closed its doors in March 1921; Myton State Bank followed in July 1922.

The settlement of large numbers of Mormon church members on former reservation land promoted Wasatch LDS Stake officials in Heber City to organize the Theodore Branch of the church in Duchesne in November 1905. A year later, the Duchesne LDS Branch was formed into the Duchesne Ward, and in 1907 the Duchesne Ward was divided into the Roosevelt, Indian, and Hayden branches. Bishop Ephraim Lambert of the newly organized Duchesne Ward was given jurisdiction over the Roosevelt Branch. In August 1908 the

Roosevelt Ward was formed from the Roosevelt Branch and Daniel Lambert was called to serve as bishop.

In 1910 the reservation portion of the Wasatch LDS Stake became the Duchesne Stake.[68] William Smart was called to serve as the first stake president of the Duchesne Stake. Smart served as stake president until 1920. In 1920 the Duchesne Stake was split and a second stake, the Roosevelt Stake, was organized. William Smart was appointed president of the new stake; Owen Bennion was sustained as president of the Duchesne Stake.[69] There are presently (1998) three LDS stakes in the county, with ten wards in Roosevelt and several wards in outlying areas.

The Episcopal church has had a long presence in the county and in the Uinta Basin. Under a program initiated by President Ulysses S. Grant in the 1870s, religious groups were assigned to administer various Indian reservations, and the Uintah Indian Reservation was assigned to the Episcopal church. In addition to other services, members of the church were sent to the reservation to teach school and otherwise improve the lot of the Ute Indians.

After Grant's Indian reservation policy was changed, a number of church members remained to work on the reservation as employees of the Office of Indian Affairs or as Indian traders. The Roosevelt mission of the Episcopal church was established in 1914, and a year later twenty-eight communicants and some forty-five church attendees built a red-brick church in Roosevelt. Elsewhere, there were more than fifty church members in Duchesne attending St. Paul's Church in Vernal, more than twenty-five members of the St. Thomas Church in Myton, and other church members at Whiterocks and at Fort Duchesne in Uintah County. The Trinity Church House, as the Roosevelt structure was called, did not have an assigned minister for the first few years; but Miss Florence Circle officiated as Sunday School superintendent. The Episcopal bishop's annual report for 1916 indicates that Roosevelt's Episcopal church had "a thriving Sunday School and Guild." Lay leaders of the church in Roosevelt included Charles F. Huntley and Harry F. Keller. Mrs. J.R. Lewis was the lay leader in Duchesne, according to the proceedings of the ninth annual convocation of the Protestant Episcopal Church, which was held in Vernal.[70] Other officials of the Episcopal church in Roosevelt in the 1910s were Albin Berch, Edward Harmston, Axel V. Johnson, W.H. Doggett, and W.S. Nicholson. The Trinity Chapel is no longer standing, and membership in the Episcopal church in Roosevelt and in the county has remained relatively small.[71]

As discussed, the first Christian presence in the county was that of the Roman Catholic church; but Fathers Domínguez and Escalante did not tarry long in the county. During the years of the reservation, Bishop Lawrence Scanlan of Salt Lake City and priests from Fruita and Grand Junction, Colorado, occasionally visited Fort Duchesne and the Indians on the reservation. With the conversion of Indian families and the presence of some Italian homesteading families in the upper Duchesne River Valley, more frequent visits were made by priests from various parishes. By the early 1920s Roosevelt and Duchesne County were attended by priests from Vernal and Price. In 1922 Bishop Joseph S. Glass sent Father Duane G. Hunt to Vernal to establish St. James Parish to serve the Uinta Basin.[72] In 1938 Roosevelt was made a mission to the Vernal Parish. In 1940 a rectory hall was built and Father Maurice Fitzgerald was appointed to preside over the new St. Helen's Church. During the 1930s frequent visits were made by priests from Notre Dame de Lourdes in Price to say Mass, hear confessions, baptize, and bury the dead of church members.[73] The number of area church members had increased to about 200 by 1971.[74]

On 2 July 1944 the Roosevelt Baptist Church was organized with eight members, and for the next three years the members met in the rented Episcopal church. In 1947 members of the Roosevelt Baptist Church built their own place of worship on First East Street. Membership in the Southern Baptist Convention has grown, and in 1971 there were more than 225 members in the county, most living in the Roosevelt area.[75]

Other churches represented in the county include the Christian Assembly of God, Jehovah's Witnesses, the Lutheran church, Harvest Fellowship church, and the Presbyterian church, among other denominations. With the exception of the Presbyterian church, the denominations listed above are quite recent in the county, most established in Roosevelt after the 1960s. All have been accepted into the society, which remains predominantly Mormon.

After a generation of grubbing out sagebrush and developing irrigation canals and laterals, the upper county of Mountain Home became lush and fertile. (John D. Barton)

Many Ute tribal members living in the county belong to the Native American church. In addition to this more "formal" spiritual practice, some tribal members continue to maintain strong ties to ceremonies and traditions which provide them strong spiritual and healing relationships.

In the mid-1990s Roosevelt is home to 4,500 people and serves as the commercial and educational center of the area. Educational opportunities include classes at the Uintah Basin Area Technology Center and Utah State University's Uintah Basin Branch Campus, which are discussed in more detail in a later chapter. Roosevelt is also home of the only hospital in the county—the Uintah Basin Medical Center—which is also examined in more detail later.

Duchesne

The community of Duchesne is located just above the junction of the Strawberry and Duchesne rivers in the central part of the county. The city of Duchesne's geographical location is also at the mouth of Indian Canyon and on present-day U.S. Highway 191, which passes through the Tavaputs Plateau from Castle Gate a few miles northwest of Helper in Carbon County. This road and U.S. Highway 40, which connects Salt Lake City with Denver and is Duchesne's Main Street, provide good access to Duchesne as well as the western half of the Duchesne Basin.

The locale was recognized as a potential townsite by Father Escalante when he and other members of the Domínguez-Escalante expedition camped near the present-day town on 18 September 1776. Escalante noted, "There is good land . . . that we crossed today, and plenty of it for farming with the aid of irrigation—beautiful popular groves, fine pastures, timber and firewood not too far away."[76]

A.M. (Al) Murdock was the first settler in Duchesne. Several years before the opening of the Uintah Indian Reservation, Murdock secured a concession from the U.S. Indian Office to establish a small trading post to serve the Indians in the area. Murdock earlier had experience as an Indian trader when he was involved with the Indian trading post at Whiterocks.

Murdock and several others took advantage of their location and situation when the reservation was opened to homesteading in 1905. In June 1905 Murdock made ready for the anticipated large numbers of homesteaders by enlarging his business, pitching a large circus tent and stocking it with hay, grain, hardware, and food supplies. Later that summer he and others claimed the area as a government town-site and set about organizing themselves into a town. Government surveyors laid out the streets, and the survey was accepted by the federal government on 18 October 1905. The new town was named Dora for Murdock's young daughter.[77]

Others joined Murdock in making Dora a center of commerce and trade. Tents were commonly used as places of business for the first year. In 1906 Murdock built a wood-frame store to replace the large tent store. The building quickly became the community center. Nearby homesteaders talked over news when they came to purchase goods, and on special occasions community dances were held in the store.

Early Mormon church services were held in Murdock's tent and later in his store, which was sometimes called the "ward house." Others rented Murdock's building for various activities—town meet-

The Calder Brothers of Vernal established a creamery in Altonah. (Uintah County Library–Regional History Center)

ings were held regularly in the building, and the building was used for youth have activities including basketball, dances, and other socials. Murdock later sold it to the Mormon church to be used as a meeting hall.[78] By the fall of 1906 the residents of community had constructed a city hall, which measured 35 feet by 50 feet.

In September 1906 the Duchesne Branch of the LDS church was organized with Ephraim Lambert as branch president. A year later, the Duchesne Ward replaced the branch and A.M. Murdock was made bishop. Murdock not only was Duchesne's first LDS bishop but also became mayor before the community was incorporated in 1917. As bishop and mayor he worked many years for the good of the community. Murdock also served as the unofficial banker for the area for several years. Many stories are told of his generosity and kindness to those who had financial difficulties during the earliest years of homesteading. It is estimated that he held as much as $125,000 in debts owed him. His clerks, having better financial sense, sometimes refused to give further credit. Confident in Murdock's generosity, however, the supplicants would appeal directly to Murdock, who literally would steal his own merchandise and give it to them. "He would write it down in a little book and . . . when it would get filled he would throw it away and get another one." Murdock eventually went bankrupt, yet he gained the love and admiration of many of the struggling homesteaders.[79]

Social life in Duchesne's early years was community and family centered. Children played games and swam in the river during the summer. One of the men in town had a bugle that he would blow every night so that all the children in town, his own included, would know it was time to go home to prepare for bed. In the winter people would play games in their homes and have such events as taffy-pulls.[80] Bernice Peterson was the first schoolteacher in Duchesne; she and her students met in a tent. After its construction, Murdock's hall was used for a school.

Town lore suggests that the name Dora stuck with the community for several years before the citizens changed the name to Theodore in honor of President Theodore Roosevelt. However, the town was commonly known as Theodore as early as the fall of 1906.[81]

Theodore underwent another name change. When the community applied for a post office, it offered the name of Theodore. However, the U.S. postal service thought that the new town names of Theodore and Roosevelt were too closely related and insisted that the town of Theodore should have another name. Theodore was changed to Duchesne in September 1911 to comply with these wishes.

By 1913 Duchesne and Myton were chartered as towns. Duchesne's unofficial population was 500 and Myton's population was 350. Roosevelt was the largest of the three at 650 and was designated as a third-class city. A year later, after having been selected county seat by the voters of the new county of Duchesne, 115 property owners petitioned the new county commission that the town be incorporated as a city. On 20 March 1917, by a vote of 124 for and 12 against, local citizens voted for incorporation and elected city officials, with R.M. Pope replacing Murdock as mayor. Three years later the population of Duchesne reached 700.[82] The *Vernal Express* in 1906 indicated that the bulk of the population of Duchesne had called Colorado home before settling in Duchesne, and there also were a few people originally from Missouri.[83]

Significant to the growth of Duchesne City was the nearby mining activity of the Raven Mining Company. The company's mining of Gilsonite offered employment during the winter months for local homesteaders of the area and it added to the population of Duchesne with a small number of permanent miners and mine officials who did much of their business in Duchesne.

The town of Duchesne challenged Myton and Roosevelt for commercial and trade supremacy. Like the other two towns on the reservation, its location along established roads promoted business and trade. The Hotel Grant was founded by James Grant and his wife Susan as a tent hotel in 1907. The Grants for many years were affectionately known to the community as "Daddy" and "Mother" Grant. They built a brick hotel which claimed to be the "most up-to date hotel in the Basin." Nightly rates were fifty cents and one dollar per night; meals were fifty cents and baths were free.[84] The first telephone in Duchesne was installed in the Hotel Grant, and Susan Grant was hired as the telephone operator. Charles Odekirk built the Odekirk Hotel in 1914; however, five years later, the new wooden structure burnt to the ground. Other overnight lodgings followed the Grant and Odekirk hotels; they included the Plaza and Cottage hotels, and Margaret "Grandma" Odekirk also ran a boarding house for a number of years.[85]

Kohl's General Store and Hardware, the oldest continuous business in Duchesne, was started by George Kohl and Tom Firth as a meat market in 1916. Over the years it has changed ownership and added groceries, notions, dry goods, and sporting goods to its line of products and goods sold.[86] John Lewis established a blacksmith shop soon after the opening of the reservation. James Hair, Fred Davis, Steve Shelton, Lucy Crites, Louella Washburn, Ernest W. Schonian, and others established a variety of commercial establishments including millinery, grocery, dry goods, feed, livery, and furniture stores, saloons, a barber shop, two cafes, and real estate and abstract companies.

Significant to the commercial community of Duchesne was the establishment of the Bank of Duchesne, founded by Laird Dean, Fern

Gray, and others from Kansas. It failed in 1921, however. During the 1920s the value of agricultural land declined while the costs for agricultural machinery, fencing material, and other farming expenses continued upward. The economic strain on farmers who had borrowed heavily from the Bank of Duchesne to develop land, buy seed and livestock, and build irrigation canals finally stretched the financial assets of the bank beyond their limit.

Presently Duchesne is a town of approximately 1,200 people and serves as a commercial and religious center for the nearby smaller unincorporated areas of Fruitland, Antelope, Bridgeland, Utahn, Bluebench, and Arcadia. There are four religious denomination structures in Duchesne including the LDS church, with four wards and two buildings, a Baptist church, and St. Helen's Catholic Church (presently not in use). There are two schools, Duchesne Elementary and Duchesne Junior/Senior High School, several businesses, and county offices.

For several years workers on the Central Utah Project, employees of the Bureau of Reclamation, boosted the community's population and economy, and the Bureau even built a park and a bowling alley to make the city more attractive for its employees. However, in the mid-1980s the area's dam projects were completed and Duchesne's population declined by several hundred people. The economic base of the community is presently centered in farming, oil production, and the county and school district offices. As county seat, Duchesne's major celebration is the annual county fair held in August. Events include stock judging and auctions, a two-day rodeo; 4-H and other exhibits, canning and produce judging and exhibits, arts and crafts entries, a demolition derby, dances, and an outdoor concert by professional entertainers.

Other Communities

Other towns were organized in the immediate years after the opening of the reservation. Neola is located ten miles north of Roosevelt and south of Uinta Canyon. This small hamlet is beautifully situated among green fields. When homesteaders settled the Neola area, they discovered it to be the home of hundreds of wild horses that hampered the raising of crops until fences could be built and other preventive measures taken. Isaac Nathaniel Workman, Benjamin Wilkerson, and George Averett were among the early settlers in the Neola area. Other early Neola settlers included James Woodward, William Greenhall, Joseph Peterson, Peter Duncan, John Houston, and Joseph Horrocks.

In 1908 the area's first townsite, called Packer and located about two miles east of the present town, was established. Three years later, in the spring of 1911, the settlers of the area held a meeting to locate a more desirable townsite. Forty acres of land was purchased from Sam Ponowitz, a Ute Indian, and Nile Hugel, a civil engineer from Vernal, was hired to survey the new townsite. The settlers named their new community Neola, which is thought to have been derived from a Ute word meaning "the last move" or "move no more."[87]

People moved to the new town quickly, and by 1915 there were thirty-eight families and a total population of some 200 people calling Neola home. William A. Wilkerson worked a blacksmith shop for years, making and sharpening plow shears and shoeing horses, a much-needed service for the area. For the first several years farmers in the Neola area traveled either to Roosevelt or to the trading post at Whiterocks to conduct their business. In 1915 Leslie Allen and T.T. Wilkerson each started stores in Neola; for a brief period Wilkerson operated his store out of a tent. Ten years later, the Allen and Wilkerson enterprises were purchased and combined by Lionel Jensen and L.D. Gardner, who named their new company the Neola Trading Company.[88]

The town lacked an indoor recreational facility until James Barnes, postmaster at Neola, built an amusement hall in 1925.[89] The amusement hall provided welcome relief on the weekends from the daily farming activities. Barnes organized community dances as well as booking silent movies to show in his hall. Lumber for the amusement hall as well as for most of the buildings in Neola came primarily from two sawmills—one located on the north part of Johnny Starr Flat, fifteen miles north of Neola in the foothills of the Uinta Mountains, the other, LeGrande Gardner's sawmill on Pole Creek Mountain.

Neola truly coalesced into a community with the establishment of a school and the Neola LDS Ward. In the summer of 1915 the

Packer log schoolhouse was moved to Neola, and that fall Miss Alice Clark and Mrs. Charles Bennett were hired as teachers for the Neola school. For three years the small school served students through the eighth grade. In 1918 a two-classroom brick school was completed at a cost of $4,000.

The need for a larger school was evident in the 1920s due to an increased school population. A four-room schoolhouse was completed at a cost of $19,000 in 1927. A decade later, during the Depression in 1936 and 1937, a gymnasium, stage, lunchroom, and indoor restrooms costing $10,000 were added as part of a federally funded Public Works Administration project.[90] The building was abandoned in 1979 when the new elementary school that presently serves the community was completed.

Beginning in the early 1920s, due to improved roads and the use of school buses, students of the higher grades were transported to the high school in Roosevelt.

The LDS Neola Branch (first called the Packer Branch) of the Hayden Ward was established with John A. Olsen as presiding elder in July 1915. A year later, the Neola Ward was organized and Olsen was sustained as bishop. Without a building to call their own, the Neola Ward purchased Barnes's amusement hall and for several years held Sunday services and weekday evening activities in the former amusement hall. Eventually sufficient local funds were raised that ward members were able to build a new wardhouse.

The creamery built by C.J. Nelson in 1921 was important to the economic development of Neola and the surrounding area. For the first time, local farmers had a place to sell their milk for hard cash. Dairying became the most important agricultural activity in the Neola area for the next several decades.

Scattered elsewhere throughout the county, a number of areas were settled and various people worked to establish them as towns or cities. Some developed a separate identity. In addition to the six incorporated communities in the county, there are several areas that have a local store and/or post office.

At the extreme west end of the county is Fruitland. A small combination general store-gas station-post office is located there, and there is also a small LDS chapel where the Fruitland Branch meets.

A small post office and a LDS chapel in Bridgeland serve Bridgeland and Arcadia residents. Bluebell has a combination store and post office along with a small city park; but Bluebell residents now go to church in Altamont. There is a store and LDS chapel in Mountain Home.

Going into the county's small rural stores is like taking a trip back in time. The Fruitland Store, for example, sells convenience goods, sporting goods, limited groceries, hardware, and tack; it also has a couple of tables with chairs for people to sit at and converse. The store serves as the community center. To keep up with changing times, videos now can be rented. The post boxes are made of antique brass and have been there for decades.

The once growing and hopeful towns of Altonah, Ioka, Midview, Cedarview, Monarch, Cresent, Upalco, Boneta, Utahn, and Stockmore no longer have stores or post offices. They are served on rural postal routes, and residents drive into larger towns for church and shopping. The would-be towns of Basin, Palmer, Hartford, Lakefork, McAffee, Blumasa, Meadowdell, Woodbine, and Falls all have disappeared from modern maps and are, for the most part, unknown even to most county residents.

Upper Country

Sandwiched by the U-shaped Uintah and Ouray Indian Reservation and located on the south slope of the Uinta Mountains in the county is the area known locally as "Upper Country." More specifically, Upper Country is identified with the Rock Creek drainage, extending south of the Uintah and Ouray Indian Reservation, east of Rock Creek, north of Blue Bench, and west of Monarch Ridge.

Several communities are located in the Upper Country including Mt. Emmons—known for a short time as Banner (settled in 1906); Boneta (1906); Clay Basin (Alexander and later Altonah), Bluebell, and Lake Fork, later renamed Upalco (1907); Mountain Home (1908); and Talmage (1909). Altonah was settled in 1912, and the town of Altamont was established in the 1930s.

Talmage initially was settled by Joseph Draper and H.P. Ottosen. A post office was established in 1911 and was known as Winn. The community's name was later changed to Talmage in honor of Mormon church official Dr. James E. Talmage. Education was important to the families of Talmage; in 1912, with only twelve pupils, the farmers of Talmage along with those of Mountain Home and Boneta formed the Winn School District. LDS settlers organized a branch of the Boneta Ward in September 1913, and Lewis E. Allred was named presiding elder. The Talmage LDS Ward was established three years later, and Austin G. Burton was called as bishop.[91]

Upalco, first called Lake Fork, was settled by the Ephraim Marret, Ted Howell, and John Horton families, among others. T.B. Hallet established a small store there in a tent in 1907, and in 1909 a school was built to educate twenty-one local children. Electricity was introduced in the county shortly before World War I, and a suitable location was needed to generate electricity. Lake Fork was considered to be an ideal stream to build a hydroelectric plant. In about 1913, not far from the community of Lake Fork, the newly organized Uintah Power and Light Company built its plant to generate electricity for the communities of Roosevelt and Myton. A post office soon was established and adopted the name of Upalco, a contraction of Uintah Power and Light Company. Soon thereafter the community's name of Lake Fork was changed to Upalco.

In January 1915 the Lake Fork Branch of the Murial LDS Ward was organized. Two years later the branch was organized into the Upalco LDS Ward. The ward was discontinued in November 1957 and its members combined with those of the Mt. Emmons Ward.

Clay Basin, later called Alexander and still later renamed Altonah, was settled by a handful of families from Vernal in 1905. Some of the early settler families included those of John Glenn, James B. Murray, William Ashby, William Bowden, and J.B. Payne. In 1906, farmers of the area organized the Farmers Irrigation Company (formally incorporated in June 1910) and commenced work on the Payne Canal.[92] The farmers of Clay Basin united with the Dry Gulch Irrigation Company and in cooperation with the Indian Irrigation Service helped construct the Lake Fork Canal.[93] Non-Indian farmers, individual Indian landowners, and Bureau of Indian Affairs local officials all worked very closely together to develop the water resources of the Upper Country.

Unlike some of the other communities in the county, the driving force behind the establishment of Altamont was its suitable location for a high school to serve the surrounding communities of Altonah, Mt. Emmons, Mountain Home, Boneta, Bluebell, and Talmage. In 1911 the state legislature had authorized each county to create its own high school district. People in the communities of Altonah and Mt. Emmons were not satisfied with having to send their children to the high school in Roosevelt. Leaders of the two towns invited other neighboring communities in the Upper Country to join with them to build a high school at a convenient location. In a spirit of cooperation, the surrounding communities agreed.

From Talmage, Mountain Home, Boneta, and Bluebell came additional students and support for the high school. The school was completed in 1935 but was without a suitable name. Tenth-grade student Clarence Snyder coined "Altamont" for the new high school, combining "Alt" from Altonah and "mont" from Mt. Emmons.[94] A small LDS seminary building was built nearby shortly after the completion of the high school.

The growth of Altmont's business district near the new high school occurred slowly. The only business for a number of years was LaForges cafe and filling station. In 1951 Glen and Florence Mohlman built a store to serve the area, having previously owned stores in Altonah and Tabiona. They ran the store until 1966, at which time they sold out to Dee and Lou Roberts, who sold it to Douglas and Sandra Swasey in 1989. An elementary school was built in Altamont, as was the LDS Altamont chapel and stake center in 1966. Earlier, in November 1957, the LDS wards of Altonah and Boneta were combined into the new Altamont Ward.

In January 1953 the U.S. Postal Service opened a post office in Altamont. That same month a majority of the thirty-four qualified voters of Altamont petitioned the Duchesne County Commission to incorporate as a town. In May the county commission approved the petition for Altamont to incorporate. Ferrell Mohlman was chosen town president, and Leland Stevenson, Waldo Hansen, Jewell Kolb, Lindon K. Farnsworth, and Flora Dastrup were appointed to the town council to serve until an election in November. Town council member Flora Dastrup later observed: "I have particularly observed a more sincere and courteous attitude toward each other and to our community as a whole, since we became a town.[95] In 1974 a branch of First Security Bank was added to the Altamont business district.

Education and the location of high schools have continued to be matters of occasional and sometimes heated discussion in the county. Unlike earlier amiable discussions and agreement among the Upper Country communities to build a high school, discussions held in 1992 by the Duchesne County School Board to consolidate the high schools in Tabiona, Duchesne, and Altamont were heated. Altamont community leaders considered forming a new school district encompassing the Upper Country if the high schools were to be combined. Citizens there believed they had a sufficiently sizeable and stable tax base—including the Bluebell Oil Field, which represents a large portion of the county's property tax base used for school funding—to fund and manage their own school district. After the school board understood this possibility, consolidation talks ended quickly.

Altamont is close-knit rural community. Many of the people who live in Altamont have been there for several generations, and it is likely that over half the residents have at least one line of ancestors who came as homesteaders into the Upper Country. The town of Altamont has grown steadily since its incorporation. In 1960 its population was 102; two decades later, the population reached 247. By 1990 the town's population had slipped to 167, but it had grown slightly to 179 in 1994.[96]

The primary winter entertainment events in Altamont are the school sports programs, especially basketball. School sports are discussed early each winter as readily as the weather or the crops. A significant portion of the citizenry also comes out for the homecoming queen contest and other school functions. Altamont High School has produced some very competitive athletic teams, and, more recently, students in a wide variety of school activities have risen to high achievements in track-and-field events, wrestling, forensics, and drama.[97] The community's big summer celebration centers on the 24 July rodeo, complete with a parade down Main Street in the morning and a barbecue in the evening at the town park.

Altonah is located in northern Duchesne County on the upper Lake Fork Bench at approximately 6,000 feet in elevation. The Lake

Fork River forms the border of Altonah on the west, separating the community from Mountain Home. The families of Robert Milton, Bird Alexander, Lott Powell, and Raymond Burgess were among the earliest homesteaders in the area. The early residents boastfully labeled their community "Queen City of the Reservation."

The town was initially called Alexander, but LDS stake president William Smart changed the name to Altonah when a branch of the Church of Jesus Christ of Latter-day Saints was organized there soon after its settlement. Heber Bowden was called as the first branch president. In 1915 the Altonah and West Bluebell branches combined to form the Altonah LDS Ward; sustained as bishop was Owen Bennion.[98]

Shortly after taking up homesteads, farmers of the Upper Country turned to developing several irrigation canals, diverting water from the Lake Fork River. The first school in the area was taught by James Bird Alexander in a small log cabin with dirt floors. There were thirteen students initially. The one-room schoolhouse was one of twenty-two one-room and one-teacher schoolhouses on the reservation in 1916.

The first store in Altonah was established in 1912 by J.M. Mallard; within a short time other businesses included Maxwell's Store, Fowler's Store, a post office, a butcher shop, a barber shop, a blacksmith shop, a planing mill, and a commercial club. The first phone in Altonah was in Maxwell's Store. When calls came in runners were dispatched to inform residents of their phone call. Residents close to the store paid runners twenty-five cents for the message; if messages had to be delivered by horse or auto the cost increased.[99]

Altonah claimed the distinction of having the only newspaper in the Upper Country. In 1915 and 1916 the weekly newspaper's masthead read *Reservation News,* and it was published by Harold and Cook Dubondroff. The newspaper's publishers apparently held strong socialist leanings, which were clearly presented in the newspaper. Financially unsuccessful, the Dubondroffs sold their newspaper to Aaron Johnson in 1916 or 1917. Johnson renamed the newspaper the *Intermountain News;* however, it survived for only a short time.

No known copies of the *Reservation News* exist today. A monthly socialist newspaper, the *Dawn,* was published in Myton in 1915.

Early cash crops grown by the farmers around Altonah were potatoes, wheat, and other grains. Dairying, however, proved to be the most profitable activity for area farmers. For a number of years, dairy farmers marketed only cream. Using hand-cranked separators, farmers hauled their cream weekly to the Mutual Creamery or Nelson's Creamery, receiving twenty-seven to thirty-one cents a pound.[100] In the fall of 1933 James and John Calder of Vernal built a creamery and cheese factory. For some time area farmers had been increasing their dairy herds, and with the construction of the creamery dairy farmers in the Upper Country had a local creamery and cheese factor to process their milk. Soon after its completion, the creamery produced 700 pounds of cheese per day. The Calders' dairy and the increased production of milk from larger dairy herds created a very strong local dairy market that lasted until the end of World War II.

Located about four miles south of Altonah and Altamont is the Mt. Emmons Bench. Most of the bench was allotted to the Ute Indians, except for a section of land along the west side of Sand Wash. In 1906 this land was claimed by James H. Evans, Simeon E. Atwood, and Chester H. Hartman.[101] During the next two years additional farmers located on the bench. By 1913 there was sufficient Mormon church membership in the area that local stake president William Smart organized the West Branch of the Bluebell Ward, with Fred Case as branch president. On 17 September 1916 Owen Bennion was sustained as bishop of the Emmons Ward. Eight years later, in June 1924, the Mt. Emmons chapel was dedicated, with over 500 people in attendance.

As with other communities in the county, education was an important focus of the families living on the Mt. Emmons bench, and in 1913 logs were hauled to Mt. Emmons from the Uinta Mountains to build the Cataract School. On 20 June 1915 farmers gathered at the school to discuss a name for their small community, with various names suggested including Yellowstone, Clearwater, Superior, Banner, and Mt. Emmons, which was selected.

The name of the town of Boneta is derived from a Spanish word meaning beautiful or pretty. The area was settled primarily by a group of families from Sanpete County in 1906. In addition, two families from Carbon County settled on Boneta Flat. The families from Sanpete County were those of Edward E. Cox, Peter O. Madsen, John W. Moffit, Fred Bench, Andrew Madsen, Taylor Tidwell, and Thomas Merriweather. William Jessen and Edward Reynolds moved from Carbon County and Maroni Fisher came Vernal.[102] A small store operated by James Mickelson opened in 1907 and a one-room school was opened in the Wallace Moffitt home the same year.

In December 1910 there was a sufficient number of LDS church members that the Boneta Ward was created from the Theodore and Roosevelt wards. Oscar Wilkins was sustained as bishop.[103] It appears that the population of the Boneta area grew steadily until 1930, when it reached 240. During the following two decades the population dropped, and in 1950 Boneta precinct's population was only about half (134) that of the population in 1930.[104] With the decline in population, the Boneta Ward disbanded in 1957 and local Mormon church members joined the new Altamont Ward of the Moon Lake Stake.

Mountain Home is located directly west of Altonah and between Lake Fork River and Pigeon Water Creek. In 1908 the Joseph D. West family was among the early families to settle in the area. In September 1913 Mormon church officials separated the north side of the Boneta Ward to form the Mountain Home Ward; Oscar Wilkins was sustained as bishop. The population of the Mountain Home precinct remained stable through 1950.[105] A new Mormon church building was dedicated in Mountain Home in April 1957.

Tabiona/Hanna

Tabiona is situated in the beautiful upper Duchesne River Valley. The Duchesne River meanders along the valley floor, creating a well-watered pasture land for livestock, the primary agricultural product. The narrow upper Duchesne River Valley, oriented in a northwest-southeast direction, is abutted on either side by the Uinta Mountains. Imposing Tabby Mountain at over 10,000 feet in elevation looms over the west side of the valley.

Tabiona was named after the respected and peaceful Ute chief

Tabby, who had lived in the valley prior to the Ute agency's being moved to Whiterocks. Tabby died in 1903, reportedly at the age of 104 years, just prior to the arrival of homesteaders in the Uinta Basin. The name Tabiona is a composite of two Indian names—those of Tabby and his daughter Ona.[106] For many years the upper valley was a favorite hunting spot for Ute Indians.

Geographical isolation and the fact of the Uintah Indian Reservation being located directly east of Tabiona and Hanna have helped foster a strong spirit of community in the two communities. Marriage among the various families has been common, which adds significantly to the area's sense of community, although, over time, new blood also has been infused into the two isolated communities. For example, Etta Fuller was hired to teach school at the one-room schoolhouse at Farm Creek in 1927.[107] Soon she and Nephi Moon were married. Floyd Allen came to the area during the Great Depression as a member of the Civilian Conservation Corps and soon made the area his new home. Jack Young, from Pike County, Kentucky, joined the Civilian Conservation Corps at the age of eighteen and was soon at work at Ouray, Utah. He met Bernice Collett and the couple were married in Hanna in 1937. They decided to stay and make the upper Duchesne River Valley their home.[108] Several Indian families, including those of Jesse and Ishabroom Codge Copperfield, Ephraim and Susan Theresa Panowitz, and Nephi Winchester, among others, had homesteads in the Tabiona and Hanna area.

Shortly before the opening of the Uintah Indian Reservation in 1905, several land developers promised the establishment of a town they called Stockmore.[109] Even before the reservation had been opened, they persuaded some homeseekers to take up land in the new community. However, Stockmore was not much more than a town on paper soon after the opening the reservation. It was during the years between 1905 and 1909 that most of the Duchesne River Valley was homesteaded. A number of the earliest families to settle in the Tabiona and Hanna area came from Summit County and Heber Valley. Several single Italian men and Italian families including Charley Bertola, John Barbieri, Felix Chiarelli, and Francesco De Fabrizio (later changed to Frank Defa), among others found the upper Duchesne River Valley to their liking and made the decision to take up land in the area.[110]

On 24 July 1910 the Tabbyville LDS Branch was established and Thomas A. White was called as the presiding elder. A year later, the branch was renamed Tabiona and was organized as a ward.

In 1915 a school was built to serve the educational needs of the students living in the upper valley. Prior to 1915, both church services and school classes were held in various homes in Tabiona and Hanna. With a population of 277 in 1939 in the Tabiona precinct, the community decided to build a new school for grades from kindergarten to twelfth. When completed, the school served about 200 students. In 1982 this structure was torn down and a new school was completed that currently serves the upper Duchesne River Valley. A great portion of Tabiona's identity comes from the school. In 1969 and again in 1991 the boys' basketball team took consolation honors in the state tournament, and these events are sources of pride for the community.

There have been efforts on the part of the school district and state school board to consolidate Tabiona High School with Duchesne High School for years. Perhaps the most serious attempt was in the 1969–70 school year when the state superintendent of schools tried to consolidate smaller schools throughout the state. Acting on that directive, the state school board ordered Tabiona High School to close and merge with Duchesne High. Tabiona residents and school officials appealed that ruling, arguing that Duchesne was too far away and that daily bus travel of such a distance would create a hardship on students. State officials traveled to Tabiona to ride a school bus into Duchesne to see if such transportation of students was feasible. That day there were herds of cattle and sheep in the road and traffic was busier and slower than normal, all of which delayed the arrival of the bus in Duchesne to the point that the state officials made no further mention of busing students to Duchesne.[111]

Business in the Tabiona region is centered in ranching and farming, along with some timbering. The business district of Tabiona and Hanna combined presently includes two small general stores, two cafes, a bar, a sawmill, and a dude ranch. At present the formerly rough road over Wolf Creek Pass linking Hanna with Kamas is being paved. What used to be a 2.5-hour trip from Salt Lake City to Tabiona will be shortened by a full hour. In anticipation of this, property values throughout the valley are rising rapidly. It well may be that Tabiona will lose some of its isolation and become a resort getaway for the Wasatch Front.

The Uintah Basin Industrial Celebration

In the years that followed the opening of the Uintah Indian Reservation, various non-Indian communities of the county held occasional celebrations, the largest most often held on or near the Fourth of July or Utah Pioneer Day on 24 July. Dances were frequently held as part of the festivities, and parades, although short in duration, were sometimes held, as were community games and activities such as community baseball teams challenging other teams. The Ute community also held several celebrations, including the Bear Dance, which celebrates the coming of spring, and the Sun Dance, more of a spiritual occasion.

The town of Roosevelt in 1911 put on one of the area's biggest and most successful Fourth of July celebrations. Among the activities was a sham battle between men of the community and Ute Indians. Much effort was made to make the skirmish more "real." The "settlers" even circled their covered wagons for the fight. Heber Timothy painted his bald head red before putting on a wig, which was "scalped" during the battle. Several women screamed and one fainted at the realism. The next year, county citizens built a large hay palace using baled hay to form the walls and canvas tenting for the roof. Each town in the county was represented with booths and displays inside.[112]

These community celebrations recalled the past or celebrated the present, and for the first dozen years there was great excitement among many about the prospects the area would provide them. However, there was much that was needed for those prospects to be fulfilled, both for individual families and collectively for the county. There was always the need to improve farming techniques and understanding. To build a strong economy, individuals in the county asked for improved transportation. A railroad besides the short Gilsonite railroad in southeastern Uintah County was hoped for. And

Uintah Basin Industrial Convention 1925. (Uintah County Library–
Regional History Center)

there was a need for an improved marketing system for the county's
agricultural goods.

Following World War I in the county and across the country
there were darkening economic clouds lingering on the horizon,
especially for farmers. World War I had seriously affected the agricultural sector of the national economy, with prices generally high
and farmers aggresively expanding their acreage. This was to some
extent also true of Duchesne County farmers. After the war, however,
agricultural prices dropped as worldwide demand decreased due to
European farmers again growing crops and a surplus on U.S. markets
due to the expanded production. Farmers began to fall into increasing debt, many losing their farms. In addition, there was growing
anxiety among farmers in the county and nationwide over a loss of
control of their lives. Larger operations farming specialized crops
were now beginning to become extablished at the expense of smaller
farmers with limited acreage.

As early as 1909, area newspapers discouraged local farmers from

Parade during the Uintah Basin Industrial Convention in 1925. (Uintah County Library–Regional History Center)

starting commercial orchards and encouraged them to plant alfalfa and sugar beets. By the 1920s alfalfa had become the county's main crop; however, in 1923 the alfalfa crop failed for the second year in a row and many farmers were desperate. Some abandoned their farms and left the Uinta Basin. In order to slow the migration of farmers, Hylas Smith conceived of the idea of a gathering that became known as the Uintah Basin Industrial Convention. He believed that if county inhabitants got together and talked over their problems, offering mutual support, they could overcome their feelings of hopelessness and be able to ride out the hard times. To make the convention more attractive and help farmers forget their despairing concerns recreational activities were held in conjunction with lectures and demonstrations of new farming techniques, methods, crops, and implements.

World War I had encouraged many farmers in various counties of the state to organize themselves into farm bureaus. In February 1923 the Duchesne County Farm Bureau was organized.[113] The call for cooperation continued. On the front page of the *Duchesne Courier* for 23 February 1923 was the headline, "Co-Operation is

Necessary to Solve Basin Problems." The front-page editorial urged those in the Uinta Basin to move forward and shun the passive spirit in the county. Newspaper publisher J.P. May, among others, urged county cooperation and a spirit of "We can do it." Other ardent supporters of the county and region included Hylas Smith, Indian farm agent; Erastus Peterson, Uintah County farm agent; William Wolfe; and Albert H. Kneale, Indian agent.[114]

In March 1923, representatives from several commercial clubs, the newly established county farm bureau, the churches in the county, the Indian community, and others met to form the Uintah Basin Industrial Corporation. Various names were suggested for the basinwide organization, including Uintah Basin Jubilee, Uintah Basin Farmers' Institute, Basin Farmers Round-Up, Uintah Basin Educational Convention, and others. The name adopted was the Uintah Basin Industrial Convention (UBIC).[115]

The purpose of the UBIC has evolved over time. According to J.P. May, publisher of the *Duchesne Courier,* the UBIC was organized to promote the building of "canals, reservoirs, to buy and sell land and water rights, to promote, own and operate sugar factories, railroads, hydro-carbon veins, including oil, to own and operate saw-mills and do any and all work relating to these activities." It was to be a vast "power, political as well as economical."[116] The new organization was to be a mutual corporation directed by a majority of stockholders. Its organizers challenged individuals in both Uintah and Duchesne counties to participate in the new organization.

More than 3,500 people attended the first convention. Families came in covered wagons and automobiles from all corners of the Uinta Basin. Each family made camp and provided its own meals for the several-day affair. A military band from Fort Douglas provided musical entertainment for the first gathering.

During the next decade, the UBIC evolved into an event much broader in purpose and scope than the founders had first envisioned. By the mid-1930s the UBIC was a multi-day event, with people from the Colorado part of the Uinta Basin as well as residents of the two Utah counties involved in the activities. In 1938, for example, the three-day event held in late August at Fort Duchesne was a combined chautauqua, fair, recreational outing, and family camping program.

A wide variety of formal classes was held and numerous speeches given. Speakers included J. Reuben Clark, Jr., former ambassador to Mexico and member of the First Presidency of the LDS church; Dr. Adam S. Bennion, noted educator; Governor Henry H. Blood; Dr. H.T. Plumb of the General Electric Company, who spoke on the "House of Magic"—miraculous uses of electricity; Dr. Franklin F. Harris, president of Brigham Young University; E.G. Peterson, president of Utah State Agricultural College; and George P. LaVatta, field agent for Indian services.

Classes for men, women, and children were held during the three days. Information on raising children and control of communicable diseases was popular among the women. Other popular classes included reading of dramatic plays, modern music, flower arranging, home management, soil conservation, caring for sheep and cattle, and methods for eradicating pests and vermin. Teenage boys participated in various scouting activities. The Indian population was involved in exhibits of Indian handicrafts and dances. There also were art and photographic exhibits on the beauties of the Uinta Basin. The 1938 UBIC also included numerous contests: horseshoe pitching, baseball games, a tennis tournament, and horse pulls.[117]

At least one year barnstormers in biplanes were present to give rides for $1.50. This was the first time many of the Basin residents had seen airplanes. For the first several years the convention was held in Fort Duchesne on grounds provided by Ute Indian Agent Albert H. Kneale, with the support and sanction for the project by the federal government and the Bureau of Indian Affairs. When the convention opened, thousands of people from throughout both Duchesne and western Uintah counties converged on Fort Duchesne to visit with old friends, learn new farming methods, and escape, even if only for a day or two, the routine of their work-filled lives on lonely farms.[118]

Except for the years of World War II when the UBIC was not held, the convention has remained a tradition for Duchesne County. After the war the convention tradition was renewed and the event was moved to Roosevelt, where it remains the community's yearly gala celebration. The focus has shifted from farming techniques and education to entertainment and cultural enhancement. Instead of lectures and demonstrations on farming and canning techniques, there currently is a three-day showcase for the talents of local youth and adults.

The name was also changed from Uintah Basin Industrial Convention to Uintah Basin Industrial Celebration. A parade down Roosevelt's Main Street, quilt and art shows, baby contests, a mini-marathon, a pet show, an archery shoot, a horseshoe throwing contest, clogging, singing, children's games, softball and tennis tournaments, free swimming at the city pool, special performances by Ute Indians and professional entertainers, and public dances now make up the Uintah Basin Industrial Celebration.

ENDNOTES

1. Daggett County on the north slopes of the Uinta Mountains was the last county created in the state, in 1917. For further discussion of the creation of Utah counties see James B. Allen, "The Evolution of County Boundaries," *Utah Historical Quarterly* 23:261–78.

2. See Charles S. Peterson, "Albert F. Potter's Wasatch Survey, 1902: A Beginning for Public Management of Natural Resources in Utah," *Utah Historical Quarterly* 39 (Summer 1971): 238–53; and Thomas G. Alexander, *The Rise of Multiple-Use Management in the Mountain West: A History of Region 4 of the Forest Service* (Washington, D.C.: U.S. Forest Service, 1987).

3. *Vernal Express,* 28 March 1913.

4. Ibid.

5. *Vernal Express,* 11 July 1913.

6. *Vernal Express,* 15 May 1914.

7. Jessie L. Embry, *A History of Wasatch County* (Salt Lake City: Utah State Historical Society/Wasatch County Commission, 1996), 99–100.

8. Bureau of the Census, *Fifteenth Census of the United States: 1930, Volume I Population* (Washington, D.C.: U.S. Department of Commerce, 1931,), 1, 100.

9. *Duchesne Record,* 16 January 1915.

10. *Duchesne Record,* 27 March 1915.

11. *Roosevelt Standard,* 2 November 1914.

12. *Vernal Express,* 6 November 1914.

13. *Roosevelt Standard,* 19 October 1914.

14. *Uintah Basin Standard,* 6 February 1996.

15. *Roosevelt Standard,* 8 September 1915.

16. *Vernal Express,* 11 September 1914; *Roosevelt Standard,* 21 December 1914.

17. The *Roosevelt Standard,* 19 October 1914 through spring 1915, contains many stories on this issue. Note that the dates of the controversy, the investigation by the state engineer,and the final Utah Supreme Court deliberations were all going on at the same time.

18. The 1917 legal description of the county reads: "Beginning at a point on the summit of the Uintah Mountains two and one-fifth miles west of the point where the Uintah Special Meridian intersects the summit of said Uintah Mountains, thence southwesterly along the summit of said mountains to a point due north of the center line between the east and west range lines of Range 9 West of the Uintah Special Meridian; thence south intersecting and thence following the said center line of said Range 9 West of the Uintah Special Meridian to a point where it intersects with the Second Standard Parallel South, Salt Lake Base and Meridian (which point is also an extension east from the Salt Lake Meridan); thence east to the line between Ranges 9 and 10 east of Salt Lake Meridian; thence south to the township line between Townships 11 and 12 South of the Salt Lake Meridian; thence east along said township line to a point due south of the point of beginning; thence due north to point of beginning." *Laws of Utah, 1917,* 103–4.

19. H. Bert Jenson, "Smith Wells, Stagecoach Inn on the Nine Mile Road," *Utah Historical Quarterly* 61 (Spring 1993): 187–91.

20. *Roosevelt Standard,* 8 December 1938.

21. "Letter of H.P. Myton" (undated), Works Progress Administration Collection, Utah State Historical Society Library.

22. Alexia (Ludy) Cooper, "Myton History," copy in possession of the author, 3, 5. Ludy Cooper served as the mayor of Myton for several terms in the 1980s and early 1990s.

23. *Uintah Basin Standard,* 30 April 1996.

24. *Vernal Express,* 23 September 1910.

25. *Vernal Express,* 30 September 1910.

26. Finley C. Pearce, *O My Father: A Biography of Joseph Harold Eldredge,* (Yorba Linda, CA.: Pierce, 1980), 82–84.

27. Mildred Miles Dillman, comp., *Early History of Duchesne County,* 291–93, R. L. Polk, *Utah State Gazetteer & Business Directory, 1912–1913* (Salt Lake City: Polk, 1913), 295–98.

28. J. Cecil Alter, *Early Utah Journalism* (Salt Lake City: Utah State Historical Society, 1938), 131–35.

29. Ibid., 135.

30. Pearce, *O My Father,* 74.

31. Cooper, "Myton History," 7.

32. *Vernal Express,* 3 July 1914, 20 January 1915.

33. Cooper, "Myton History," 6, 7.

34. William Padres, "The Mormon Curse," *Uintah Basin Standard,* 30 April 1996.

35. "Proceedings," M W Grand Lodge of Free and Accepted Masons of Utah Forty-Fifth Annual Communication, Salt Lake City, 18 and 19 January 1916, 86, Utah State Historical Society Library.

36. Fred Todd, stories told to H. Bert Jenson and retold to author.

37. *Vernal Express,* 25 June 1915; *Salt Lake Tribune,* 19 June 1915.

38. *Uintah Basin Standard,* 30 April 1996.

39. Kristen Smart Rogers, "William Henry Smart: Uinta Basin Pioneer Leader," *Utah Historical Quarterly* 45 (Winter 1977): 64.

40. Ibid., 67–69.

41. See *Uintah Chieftain,* August 1909, headlines and stories through-out that month, microfilm copies at Uintah County Library, Vernal, Utah.

42. *Vernal Express,* 3 February 1911.

43. Dillman, *Early History of Duchesne County,*300.

44. See headlines and articles in the *Roosevelt Standard, Myton Free Press, Uintah Chieftain,* and *Vernal Express* from 1906 to 1920.

45. *Uintah Chieftain,* 14 October 1909.

46. Stephen L. Carr and Robert W. Edwards, *Utah Ghost Rails* (Salt Lake City: Western Epics, 1989), 196–99. See also Henry E. Bender, Jr., *Uintah Railway: The Gilsonite Route* (Berkeley, CA: Howell-North Books, 1970).

47. Dillman, *Early History of Duchesne County,*335.

48. See Dry Gulch Irrigation Company Record Book A, Dry Gulch Irrigation Company Files, Roosevelt, Utah.

49. Ed F. Harmston later served as president of the town board of Roosevelt and was elected to the local school board. He worked as a real estate agent and for many years as a surveyor. He did many surveys in the Vernal region including surveying a route for the Uinta Railroad.

50. George Stewart, "Roosevelt's Yesterdays," 8.

51. Ibid., 9.

52. Louise Larsen Fisher, *Family Courageous* (Salt Lake City: Deseret Book Company, 1957), 17.

53. *Vernal Express,* 16 February 1914.

54. Bureau of the Census, *Thirteenth Census of the United States,*

Supplement for Utah (Washington, D.C.: Government Printing Office, 1913), 576.

55. See *Third Report of the State Bureau of Immigration, Labor, and Statistics, 1915–1916* (Salt Lake City: State of Utah, 1917).

56. Fisher, *Family Courageous.*

57. For a more complete list of early families of Roosevelt and the nearby area see Dillman, *Early History of Duchesne County,* 340–45.

58. Rogers, "William Henry Smart," 67–69.

59. Ibid., 68. Between 1910 and 1913 William Smart served as a LDS mission president in Germany. During his absence, much of the economic leadership in Roosevelt and elsewhere on the reservation rested with other churchmen, including R.S. Collett.

60. *Vernal Express,* 13 February 1914.

61. Dillman, *Early History of Duchesne County,* 387.

62. *Roosevelt Standard,* 21 September 1914.

63. Bureau of the Census, *Seventeenth Census of the United States, 1950, Part 44, Utah* (Washington, D.C.: Government Printing Office, 1952), 10.

64. Kim M. Gruenwald, "American Indians and the Public School System: A Case Study of the Northern Utes," *Utah Historical Quarterly* 64 (Summer 1996): 246–63.

65. Doris Burton, *A History of Uintah County* (Salt Lake City: Utah State Historical Society/Uintah County Commission, 1996), 156.

66. *Deseret News,* 7 May 1909.

67. Quoted from William H. Smart diaries in Rogers, "William Henry Smart," 72.

68. Andrew Jenson, *Encyclopedic History of the Church of Jesus Christ of Latter-day Saints* (Salt Lake City: Deseret News Publishing Company, 1941), 199–201, 718.

69. Ibid., 199–200, 718.

70. "Journal of the Proceedings of the Ninth Annual Convocation of the Protestant Episcopal Church in the Missionary District of Utah," years 1915 and 1916, copies at the Utah State Historical Society Library.

71. *Atlas of Utah* (Provo: Brigham Young University Press, 1981), 140, indicates there were only fourteen members of the Episcopal Church in the county in 1971.

72. See Bernice Maher Mooney, *Salt of the Earth: The History of the Catholic Diocese of Salt Lake City, 1776–1987* (Salt Lake City: Catholic Diocese of Salt Lake City, 1987).

73. *Footprints in a Beautiful Valley: A History of Tabiona-Hanna* (Springville: Art City Publishing Company, n.d.), 91.

74. Milford Randall Rathjen, "The Distribution of Major Non-Mormon Denominations in Utah" (M.S. thesis, University of Utah, 1966), 117; *Atlas of Utah,* 140–41.

75. *Atlas of Utah,* 140–41.

76. *Domínguez-Escalante Journals,* 48.

77. Dillman, *Early History of Duchesne County,* 190–91. The Works Progress Administration conducted a statewide survey and study of geographic place-names, history, and government records in the mid-1930s that indicates that the townsite was called Theodore and was later changed to Duchesne in 1911; see WPA Manuscript Collection, Utah State Historical Society. A third study suggests that the town was first called Dora after Murdock's young daughter and was changed to Theodore in honor of President Theodore Roosevelt. When Roosevelt was officially named in 1915, "the original request for Duchesne was finally accepted"; see John W. Van Cott, *Utah Place Names* (Salt Lake City: University of Utah Press, 1990), 117.

78. See Abe W. Turner, "A Tribute to Uncle Al Murdock," copy held by the author. According to one story, Murdock's asking price was more than church officials thought the property was worth. With some hurt feelings, Murdock then gave them the deed without charge.

79. Ibid.; William Murdock interview, with J.P. Tanner, Roosevelt, Utah, transcript in possession of the author, original held by J.P. Tanner of Duchesne, Utah.

80. Verda Moore, interview.

81. *Vernal Express,* 15 September 1906.

82. *Fifteenth Census of the United States: 1930,* 100.

83. *Vernal Express,* 15 September 1906. In addition, the newspaper mentioned that there "are a few Missourians" who called Duchesne home. One of the early area Gilsonite mining companies was headquartered in St. Louis, Missouri.

84. Dillman, *Early History of Duchesne County,* 193.

85. Ibid., 198.

86. Deon Brown, interview with John D. Barton, 1 June 1994, Duchesne, Utah, transcript in possession of author.

87. Dillman, *Early History of Duchesne County,* 317. However, Van Cott in *Utah Place Names* suggests that Neola is a Greek work of an unspecified meaning.

88. Dillman, *Early History of Duchesne County,* 322.

89. Ibid., 318.

90. Ibid., 325.

91. Jenson, *Encyclopedic History,* 861. According to LDS church records, Talmage Ward was discontinued in November 1957 and members of the Talmage Ward combined with the Mountain Home Ward to form the Moon Lake Ward.

92. Farmers Irrigation Company Minutes, microfilm copy at Utah State Historical Society Library.

93. Ibid., and Dry Gulch Irrigation Company, Record Book "A."

94. Clarence L. Snyder, *A Harvest of Memories,* 392.

95. *Uintah Basin Record,* 5 November 1953. Altamont was incorporated as a town on 8 June 1953. The other incorporated town in the county was Tabiona, and the three incorporated cities were Roosevelt, Duchesne, and Myton.

96. *Statistical Abstract of Utah, 1996.* (Salt Lake City: Bureau of Economic and Business Research, 1996), table 22.

97. According to the *Utah High School Activities Association Handbook, 1997–1998,* in 1976 Altamont High School took first place in men's volleyball for 1A schools. In 1994 Altamont won the 1A state wrestling championship. In 1997–98 Duchesne placed first in drama competition. Many individual competitors in various sports and events are also listed for their accomplishments over the years.

98. Jenson, *Encyclopedic History,* 18.

99. Burr Eldredge, interview with John D. Barton, Roosevelt, Utah, 8 June 1997, transcript in possession of author.

100. Dillman, *Early History of Duchesne County,* 140–52; also see *A Harvest of Memories,* 167.

101. Dillman, *Early History of Duchesne County,* 270.

102. Ibid., 163.

103. Index to the Journal History of the LDS Church, microfilm copy, Utah State Historical Society Library.

104. *Seventeenth Census of the United States, Utah,* 44:10.

105. The *Seventeenth Census* indicates that the population of the Mountain Home precinct was 326 in 1950, page 44:10.

106. *Footprints in a Beautiful Valley,* 3. Van Cott, *Utah Place Names,* 363, suggests that the name was a merging of the names of the Ute Chiefs Tava (Tabby) and Tayneena.

107. *Footprints In a Beautiful Valley,* 458.

108. Ibid., 163.

109. Details of the Ute Agency and the Stockmore land swindle are outlined in chapter two.

110. For brief histories of the Italian families see *Footprints in a Beautiful Valley*.

111. Robert L. Park, interview by John D. Barton, 8 December 1995, transcript in author's possession.

112. Dillman, *Early History of Duchesne County*, 397.

113. *Duchesne Courier*, 16 February 1923.

114. *Vernal Express-Roosevelt Standard*, UBIC-Indian Affairs Scenic Edition, 18 August 1938.

115. *Duchesne Courier*, 14 September 1923.

116. *Duchesne Courier*, 23 March 1923.

117. *Vernal Express-Roosevelt Standard*, UBIC-Indian Affairs Scenic Edition, 18 August 1938.

118. Dillman, *Early History of Duchesne County*, 128–32. See also Daniel S. Dennis, *Horizons Beyond the Rim* (Roosevelt, UT: Daniel Dennis, 1991), 7.

CHAPTER 7

FROM SETTLEMENT TO THE GREAT DEPRESSION— IN ONE GENERATION

Duchesne County residents faced numerous challenges following the creation of their county and the establishment of the county seat in 1914. Better roads were high on the list. Many county roads turned to quagmires each spring, making travel by car, truck, or horse team nearly impossible. Irrigation improvements also continued during the 1920s and 1930s, although there was a serious setback of the Blue Bench irrigation scheme. Many farm families struggled financially. Between 1920 and 1940 the number of farms in the county decreased by 11.5 percent—from 1,248 to 1,104 farms. The number of farms in the state also decreased during the same period; however, the percentage of decrease statewide was much smaller, less than 1 percent.[1]

Even as individual farmers struggled financially during the economic difficulties of the 1930s, important irrigation improvements and additions were made in the county that increased the production of county farms significantly. There were other water users along the Wasatch Front, however, who made plans to divert and use water from the county and the Uinta Basin.

IT TAKES OUR BOYS TO CAN THE KAISER

Patriotic parade during World War I, Myton 1917. (Uintah County Library–Regional History Center, Todd Collection)

World War I and its aftermath impacted the county, as did the terrible worldwide influenza epidemic of 1918–19. The political panorama changed from government taking a much less active role in the 1920s to returning to a more active position during the Great Depression. The nation and the state struggled over the question of alcohol and in 1920 prohibited its manufacture and sale. There were some in the county, the state, and across the nation who viewed prohibition as a troublesome inconvenience and spawned a new occupation—bootlegging.

The Rural Electrification Administration, part of the Roosevelt administration's New Deal of the 1930s, linked most farms and ranches to electricity by the outbreak of World War II. Electricity dramatically changed the lives of county residents, particularly women. Much of the heavy work done by women in their homes was lightened considerably when their homes were wired with electricity. Electric ranges, washing machines, irons, and refrigerators liberated many county women. Family activities during the evening hours were also changed significantly, with music, drama, and news brought into homes by the radio.

World War I

Like the rest of the state and the nation, the majority of county voters in the 1916 presidential election voted for Woodrow Wilson. Wilson gained more than a two-to-one popular vote advantage in the county—1,443 for Wilson and 687 for his Republican challenger Charles Evans Hughes. The margin of victory for Wilson was not as large in the state, however; Wilson received 84,145 Utah votes and Hughes received 54,137 votes.

County voters marked their ballots for other Democratic party candidates as well. For the U.S. Senate seat, William H. King received 1,378 to 754 for Republican nominee George Sutherland. County voters supported Simon Bamberger (1,305) for governor over his Republican challenger Nephi L. Morris (843). Democrat G. Victor Billings was elected to the state House of Representatives; Don B. Colton, favorite son of Uinta Basin voters, was the only Republican to win a major office in the county.[2]

Notable in the voting behavior of county voters was the number of votes Socialist party candidates received. Between 1912 and 1920, the Socialist party formed a strong third party in the county. In 1912 nearly 21 percent of the votes cast in the county for president of the United States went to Eugene V. Debs candidate of the Socialist Party of America. Debs garnished 8 percent of the vote in Utah. Four years later, the Socialist party candidate for president received 16 percent of the popular vote. In 1920 the combined popular vote for the Socialist and the Farm-Labor parties dropped to about 4.9 percent in the county.[3] Strong personalities of party representatives as well as the promptings of the county newspaper the *Reservation News* seemed to have swayed some in the county to favor the Socialist party's political platform.

Financial difficulties of some farm families also may have influenced their political behavior. Charles S. Rice, a home missionary of the Presbyterian church who served for a few years in the early 1910s in the county, years later wrote of the hard conditions he saw in the county:

> To file on a "piece of dry land" which, without irrigation water, can raise little save sagebrush and grease wood, to build a cabin on

Parade and return of troops at the end of World War I, Myton. (Uintah County Library–Regional History Center, Todd Collection)

it, and then to plan and to work for water, eking out an existence in some way while you maintain residence upon the land, requires genuine fortitude and physical strength. Possessed of some financial resources the way was not too rough. Without money, the struggle became near martyrdom, wives and children suffering terribly. Yet out of such stern environments some of the greatest Americans have come.[4]

One of the major political issues that confronted voters in the county and across the country in 1916 was the darkening clouds of war in Europe. Prior to the active participation of the United States in the war, patriotism throughout the nation and state was vigorously promoted. As the country inched closer to war, many national leaders urged the country to prepare itself for conflict. War was declared in April 1917 when President Woodrow Wilson signed the war resolution passed by Congress. Americans quickly were urged to do their duty to the nation by enlisting in the military, buying Liberty Bonds, or joining the "Industrial Army."

Part of the national government's efforts to move the nation towards new levels of patriotism included the "four minute men" program. Some 75,000 men of unquestioned loyalty and good speaking ability were sent throughout the country to buoy up the nation's patriotism and to promote the administration's war programs of newly raised taxes to pay for U.S. participation in the war and the compulsory draft of military-age men.

Reuben S. Collett, city councilman and prominent civic leader in Roosevelt, was the "four minute man" for Duchesne County. He delivered speeches in schools and church buildings and wrote articles for the newspaper urging county residents to purchase Liberty Bonds and conserve food and natural resources. He also encouraged the young men of the county to register with the newly enacted Selective Service.

Each of the counties and cities in the United States was given quotas to meet for the purchase of Liberty Bonds to assist the government in financing the war. Bonds could be purchased for as little as fifty dollars and bought through monthly installments; they also were exempt from the newly passed federal income tax. Throughout the war, Duchesne County met or exceeded its bond-drive quotas; for example, the county's 1918 fall quota of bond sales was $72,000, yet county residents purchased more than $86,300 in bonds.[5]

Duchesne County newspapers urged young male county residents to do their patriotic duty and enlist. A 17 April 1917 article in the *Roosevelt Standard* also stated, "Attention Citizens We are at war! Every patriot should enlist. Citizens of the Basin can not well enlist to carry arms but every citizen can enlist in the "Industrial Army of Uncle Sam."[6] Fred L. Watrous, editor of the *Duchesne Record,* urged the young men of the county to heed the president's appeal and take up arms against the Kaiser:

> Are you going to stand supinely by and later see the fighting forces
> of Kaiser Wilhelm . . . land on your shores and take terrible toll of
> the nation and its manhood and womanhood? . . . Go to the
> recruiting office today. Take up arms in defense of your family and
> country, and never have it said by others . . . that you had to be
> forced to respond to your country's call.[7]

Bamberger Monument at the entry of the Bamberger Road built in 1918 to assist Duchesne County farmers get their grain to the railhead at Colton. (John D. Barton)

Some young men of the county did not wait for the encouragement from Collett and the newspapers. Several months earlier, P.W. Billings and Otto Buys set about to encourage young men of the county to join a battery of the Utah National Guard. Billings was already serving as a second lieutenant in the Utah National Guard, and Buys had recently returned from the Mexican-U.S. border, where he had served in a Utah battery that recently had been mustered out of active service.[8]

In early June 1917, to encourage eligible age men to register for the draft, Collett along with community leaders organized special days to promote the war effort. In Roosevelt, for example, Collett organized an enlistment drive at the town's library. The registration effort turned into a patriotic rally, all local businesses closed for the occasion. Young women gave out punch, cookies, occasional kisses, and pinned colored ribbons on those who registered. A band played and Collett and others gave speeches. A free dance was held in the evening. That night, 110 young men registered for the draft.[9]

Community leaders in Boneta declared 5 June a "holiday" in support of the nation's war effort. W.R. Rust encouraged the young men of Boneta to enlist, William C. Crook delivered a patriotic speech, and Oneta Moffitt led a chorus in singing patriotic songs.[10]

By the middle of July men throughout the nation who had registered for the draft began to be called to active duty. This first selective service draft call included forty-six young men from Duchesne County. To add incentive to young homesteaders to join the military, Congress enacted the Homestead Military Act of 1917. It provided that homesteaders who entered the military and spent time away from their homesteads could return after the war and without penalty resume the process of proving up their land claims.

According to one Utah historian of World War I, three men from the county were inducted into the marines; sixteen enlisted in the navy; and 218 young men either enlisted or were inducted into the army. Of those who served during World War I, four died either from disease or wounds.[11] One of those drafted from Duchesne County was Orson Mott of Duchesne, who for a time deferred his draft notice to run his father's homestead. He trained at Fort Lewis, Washington, before he left for Europe, where he fought in both

France and Belgium. Mott's experience was representative of that of those who went from the county.[12]

President Woodrow Wilson urged the nation towards intense patriotism and conservative policies. The Espionage Act was passed on 5 June 1917; it provided hefty fines and even prison terms for anyone "obstructing military operations in wartime." This was interpreted to mean speaking out against the war, failing to register for the Selective Service, or any similar anti-war activity. The act also provided severe penalties for anyone using the postal system to mail anything that was termed "anti-patriotic." Fines up to $5,000 were levied against anyone who used the postal system to mail "treasonable" material. The act dampened the political activities of socialist parties and newspapers. The county's socialist newspaper, the *Reservation News*, published in Altonah, was discontinued.

The threat of sabotage was on the minds of many local law enforcement officials in the state. Increased vigilance of "suspicious" people was undertaken. On 16 June 1917, for instance, the *Duchesne Record* reported that the county sheriff's deputy apprehended a person believed to be German in Daniels Canyon while the stranger was apparently on his way to blow up the Strawberry Dam. The suspect was carrying a small suitcase containing a quantity of dynamite. The *Record* reporter wondered how the suspect believed he could damage the large earthen dam with so little dynamite.

A number of civilian war-related efforts were organized to raise money, provide services, conserve food and goods, and make items for the military hospitals and soldiers. Mrs. Flora E. Collett and Homer P. Edwards were selected to direct the county's Liberty Loan drives. R.D. Collett headed up the War Savings Thrift Campaign, R.S. Collett was the county's chair for the Committee on Food Supply and Conservation; and Mrs. Flora E. Collett also headed the local Women Members of County Councils of Defense. The latter organization promoted food production and home economics, encouraged child welfare, and supported women in industry.

It was declared that "the nation which can best preserve and conserve its resources, both temporal and spiritual, is the one sure to win eventually." The *Roosevelt Standard* urged citizens of the county to support the war by being frugal in the consumption of food, fuel, and

Duchesne County Fair Display by the Peppard Seed Company, circa 1920.
(Uintah County Library–Regional History Center)

especially dairy products and red meat. To emphasize this point, the
newspaper reported:

> If every one of our 20,000,000 American families wastes one
> oz. of edible meat or fat, it wastes 1,250,000 lbs. of animal food—
> 456,000,000 pounds of valuable animal food a year. This is equal
> to 875,000 steers or 3,000,000 hogs counting bones and all.
>
> If everyone of our 20,000,000 American families wastes 1/2
> cup of milk, 2,500,000 qts. daily, 912,500,000 qts. a year—the total
> product of more than 400,000 cows.[13]

The first week of June 1917 the county joined with the rest of the
state in holding a Liberty Loan Sabbath, Farmers' Day, Women's Day,
and Children's Day to promote the purchase of Liberty Bonds. By the
end of the war, county residents had subscribed $80,900 in Liberty
loans, surpassing the county's quota of $72,850. Over 1,180 residents
of the county purchased Liberty Bonds.[14]

County defense councils were established throughout the state as umbrella organizations for local civilian war efforts. Homer P. Edwards served as secretary of the Duchesne County Defense Council. Fred L. Watrous was placed in charge of publicity, C.L. Ashton handled legal matters, Reuben S. Collett supervised food supply and conservation efforts, M.P. Pope was selected as vice-chair of the industrial survey committee, Thomas Rhodes directed the labor committee, R.M. Pope headed military affairs, William O'Neil was the county's chair for the state protection committee, and Flora E. Collett was treasurer for the women's work committee.[15]

The airplane, the tank, chemical warfare, and other instruments of killing were used for the first time in World War I. However, during much of the conflict and the training of American soldiers, horses were used for a variety of transportation needs. At the outbreak of the war, British purchasing agents came to the Uinta Basin to buy horses for England's cavalry.[16] Basin farmers and ranchers quickly gained a reputation for raising quality horses, and farmers and ranchers were urged to raise more. To assist farmers in raising quality horses, the government established remount stations and provided purebred stallions to breed with local farmers' mares for a fee of fifteen dollars. The stallions, usually either thoroughbreds or Morgans, were changed periodically to avoid inbreeding. At least two remount stations located in the county, in Altonah and Neola, continued operating for the next twenty years.[17]

The war's impact on Duchesne County was much greater in the economic and political arenas than it was in the number of soldiers from the county who were drafted to fight. The national move to increase agricultural production proved costly for Duchesne County farmers in the long term, however. Farmers were encouraged to increase the production of agricultural commodities. New loan policies and practices made qualifications for loans easier, and many county farmers borrowed heavily at local banks at attractive interest rates to expand their operations. The War Finance Corporation of the Treasury Department advertised loans directly to livestock raisers and farmers, since it was deemed necessary to the war effort. Other support came from the U.S. Food Administration, which guaranteed base prices for agricultural goods. Headlines in the county newspapers urged, "Farmers Get Busy!" German Workman, a local high

The many alfalfa fields under production for seed and hay gave rise to bee-keeping. (Utah State Historical Society)

school teacher, thought he could better serve his country and show his patriotism working behind the plow than teaching in the class-room at Duchesne High School, so he quit his job and took up farm-ing full time.[18]

The armistice signed at the eleventh hour on the eleventh day of the eleventh month of 1918 brought an end to war and the return of normal economic activities in Europe and around the world. When word was received in Duchesne County there were celebrations in many of the communities. Speeches were made, bands played, and other gala activities were held. People rode in their cars and on horses up and down the streets of the county firing guns and shouting for joy.

Although the fighting ended in 1918, federal support for agricul-tural production continued for the next few years. Many agricultural experts believed that agricultural prices would remain high and over-seas markets strong. Peace brought turmoil to the domestic agriculture and to the farmers in Duchesne County, however, as agricultural prices fell. A bushel of wheat sold for between $3.35 and $3.50 in 1917; two years later, the price of a bushel of wheat dropped to ninety-eight cents.[19]

The lack of export markets resulted in an abundance of domestic agricultural commodities, which drove down prices. The loss to county wheat producers was enormous. For example, in 1919, county farmers produced 40,875 bushels of wheat; with low prices of ninety-eight cents a bushel, county farmers experienced a loss of between $92,800 and $103,000. Near the end of the war, a permit system was adopted to sell grain. These permits were issued on a statewide basis and were given out on a first-come, first-served basis. Counties with early harvests received the majority of grain permits, which placed limits of grain sales on county wheat producers.[20] Prices for wool, lamb, barley, eggs, and other farm products also dropped dramatically or were extremely unstable. Bank loans remained due, however, causing serious financial problems for county farmers. Farm foreclosure notices in county newspapers escalated sharply in late 1919 and early 1920.[21] Banks too experienced difficulties as their loans went bad and property values dropped; the Bank of Duchesne and the Myton State Bank closed their doors in March 1921 and July 1922, respectively.

The hoped-for farming fortunes that had been anticipated during the war generally only brought new failures and overexpansion without the expected financial rewards. Many farmers, broke and in debt, left the Uinta Basin and their farms. The migration of Duchesne County farmers to urban areas for employment was part of a nationwide change in demographics during the late 1910s and early 1920s. In the early 1920s some 6 million people across the country left their farms for cities.[22]

Transportation

The war effort blocked the purchase of many goods, and one consumer item in demand in the county was the automobile. However, with the need for war materials and a significant increase in steel prices of about 30 percent, few automobiles were purchased in the county during the war years. People of the county who could

Midview Reservoir was built during the depression as a CCC project. (John D. Barton)

afford cars were often required to wait months for delivery.[23] The primary means of transportation locally during the war remained the horse and wagon.

In 1917 an automobile was driven to Lake Fork (Upalco). It was the first car many residents had ever seen. The people were dazzled with its wonderful speed, which reached about fifteen miles per hour, and all were thrilled with the possibility of riding in this new "contraption." Eva Meldrum, then a young girl, recalled her ride: "Everyone held on to his hat and the car lurched forward. We bounced from rock to rock and rut to rut but it was wonderful. I could hardly count the fence posts as the car sped along."[24]

The Model-T Ford was the most popular make in the county and the state in the early 1920s. They were relatively inexpensive and light enough to lift out of mud and ruts. Other popular makes were Buick, Chevrolet, Oakland, and Studebaker. There were not nearly as many cars as teams and wagons, since cars were beyond most peoples' ability to purchase. In 1917 Verd Washburn opened a mechanic shop in Duchesne to provide a service business for automobile owners. In

1921 county residents owned 236 automobiles; seven other Utah counties had fewer cars, with Daggett County residents owning only two; Uintah County residents owned 347.[25]

A stage line ran from Salt Lake to Duchesne beginning in 1912; the old stage route through Nine Mile Canyon was discontinued when Fort Duchesne closed that year. Stage service was extended to Roosevelt in September 1916.[26] Within just a few months, however, this service was discontinued and trucks carried the mail to Duchesne County. People traveling there had to make their own way.

Roads remained a problem in the county during and after the war. Some effort was made during World War I to improve roads in the county, primarily the roads between Vernal and Heber City and between Duchesne and Castle Gate in Carbon County. Nearly all county roads lacked gravel or treated surfaces. The road to Heber City through Strawberry Valley generally was not opened before March, and horse-drawn graders often spent time regrading and leveling the road to make it useable.

The road through Indian Canyon to the railroad at Castle Gate was important to the early economic vitality and growth of the county. During the war, state and local funds for road construction and improvements were scarce. To make needed improvements to the Indian Canyon road, Governor Simon Bamberger authorized the use of prisoners. For the better part of two summers prisoners from the state penitentiary in Salt Lake City worked on the road. The improvements shaved off several miles and eliminated a treacherous section of the Price Canyon road, especially beneficial for those hauling produce to the railhead at Colton in Utah County.[27]

The anticipated improvements in the road were not totally completed by the fall of 1918, forcing many farmers to store a bumper harvest of grain until the next year, when the road would be completed. In the meantime, farmers of the county faced a severe shortage of storage facilities. Not a single grain silo existed in the county. Ben Eldredge, U.S. Department of Agriculture agent, reported that the county needed thirty silos built to meet the farm expansion requirements outlined by the state Council of Defense.[28] County production of grain had outpaced local storage and transportation capabilities, with the result that much of the 1918 grain harvest spoiled.

When the Indian Canyon road was finally completed in 1919, it proved to be a vital link to regional and national rail transportation.

Following the war, county officials and Uinta Basin leaders called for the development of a railroad through the Uinta Basin to link Denver with Salt Lake City. For years there had been rumors of just such a railroad being constructed through the Uinta Basin. In 1924, following the annual UBIC meetings, county residents asked why there was no railroad:

> The war is now over, has been over for six years but where, oh where is our railroad? Is it wise for us to continue to sleep soundly with Salt Lake year after year—follow the same old rut decade after decade, or should we turn to other sources for relief? Think it over and let us turn to our neighbors on the east and find what they have done to give us rail transportation to the east.[29]

Little indication was shown by financial interests in Salt Lake City or Denver to build a railroad through the county, however. County residents for their part called for improved transportation in and out of the county and the Uinta Basin. The Salt Lake City Chamber of Commerce did become interested in developing a link between Salt Lake City and Denver. In the mid-1920s federal funds, through a 7 percent highway funding scheme, were made more available to the state for highway development, including snow removal. The state then agreed to undertake the expensive effort of snow removal from state highways; however, the state highway department had to make choices which roads were eligible for the federal funds.

For nearly a decade, county residents had used the roads from Duchesne to Helper, Colton, and Castle Gate, as well as the road to Heber City. The latter road provided a more direct route to the Wasatch Front and Salt Lake City, and the Salt Lake City Chamber of Commerce showed interest in it as a segment of a larger road scheme more directly linking Salt Lake City and Denver.

To meet the stipulations of the federal Bureau of Public Roads, state highway officials asked the county to select which road it wanted designated as the primary state highway in the county. Important in the decision of the county commission was the federal funds for snow removal on the designated road. In 1924 and 1925 the

Moon Lake Dam and overflow. (John D. Barton)

Duchesne County Commission conducted an extensive snow study of the various roads from Duchesne to the railroad in Carbon County and the Strawberry Valley road and held meetings with county residents to determine which road was best for their needs. In 1926 the county commission selected the Duchesne-Heber City road as the county's primary state road.

The Fruitland section of the road was then made eligible for the 7 percent federal funding program, and other parts of the road became eligible for funds from the United States Forest Service road building and maintenance program. This decision and the use of federal and state funds paved the way for the development of the Duchesne-Heber City road as a twelve-month highway.

Funding for road construction and maintenance in the county remained an issue throughout the 1920s. In 1923 the state legislature passed the first gasoline tax, 2.5 cents per gallon, which provided money to make improvements on roads in the counties of the state. Bridges in the county were built and improved during the 1920s, and, beginning in 1927, oil and gravel were used for improved road surfaces.

Influenza Epidemic of 1918–19

In the weekly *Duchesne Record* during November 1918 welcome news was reported of the end of World War I and of political victory for most Democratic party candidates in the county. Milton H. Welling was victorious over his Republican challenger Henry H. Wattis, and William O'Neil beat R.S. Collett for the county's representative to the state House of Representatives by a 135-vote margin. Other victories for county Democrats included J. Austin Pack over Dan E. Lybbert for four-year county commissioner, Joseph Timothy over Charles Wall for sheriff, A.M. Todd over J.C. Jacobs for county surveyor, and George Bowers over C.W. Smith for county assessor. Republicans did win several county races including Earnest H. Burgess for county attorney, Afton Pope Ring for county recorder, C.I. Dickerson for county treasurer, and Owen Bennion for two-year county commissioner.[30]

But there was bad news also reported in November. The headline for the *Duchesne Record* for 23 November 1915 read, "Influenza and Its Symptoms." The newspaper also carried a story from Washington declaring, "Influenza is More Deadly than Big War."

The worldwide Spanish influenza epidemic of 1918–19 derived its name because of the terrible toll it had on the people of Spain; according to some historians, 8 million Spaniards were afflicted with the flu. The Spanish flu was particularly deadly, killing about 21 million people worldwide in a span of just four months. In the United States about 675,000 people died from the flu.[31] The epidemic was the world's worst since the bubonic plague of the fourteenth century.

Utah and Duchesne County were not immune from the dreadful flu. By early October the first cases of the flu were reported in Salt Lake City, Provo, and Ogden. Schools were soon closed, emergency hospitals were established, and large public gatherings were prohibited or severely restricted in Ogden, Provo, and Salt Lake City. No public funeral was held for LDS church president Joseph F. Smith, who died during the period. In Salt Lake City health officials reported 117 deaths from the flu.[32]

Symptoms of the flu included both chills and high fevers, severe backache, and headache. The stricken person was both restless and

CCC Camp at Yellowstone. (John D. Barton)

sleepy, and sometimes delirious. The flu often affected the lungs, kidneys, heart, and nervous systems in a manner similar to the symptoms of meningitis. Flu symptoms hit with little warning and set in very rapidly. Relapse among those affected was common.[33]

Duchesne County was not immune from this terrible epidemic; however, attempts were made by some county leaders to prevent the spread of stories of the disease in the county. Robert S. Collett requested that the "rumors about the heavy fatality of the influenza should be squelched because people are afraid to help those in need or to do the work that needs to be done." He added that evidence showed that older people were not susceptible to this particular flu.[34] Statements like that were irresponsible and added to the confusion about the flu; the elderly were among the most severely impacted.

The first county deaths credited to the flu were reported in Roosevelt in late October 1918, and Roosevelt Mayor George Bracken ordered all schools, churches, and other public gatherings closed.[35] The *Roosevelt Standard* complained a few weeks later,

> It seems strange for Roosevelt to have no schools, picture shows, Sunday Schools or churches, and no public gatherings. No, not

even Red Cross meetings. How much longer will this last before the ban is lifted. The young fellows are complaining that they are not allowed to call on their best girls.[36]

The disease was not confined to the communities in the county. Brothers J.W. and W.A. Alexander, a pair of cowboys driving a herd of cattle from Duchesne to Price, were late delivering the cattle. A search was conducted and the missing cowboys were found dead from the influenza in their tent. The cattle they had been driving had strayed but their faithful dog was still standing guard over the bodies.[37] William Alexander, another brother, also contracted the flu and in a matter of days was dead. Their sister's house at Hancock Cove was turned into a makeshift hospital to care for influenza patients.[38]

Many able-bodied people took care of those who were ill. For example, Brigham and Hannah Timothy came from Altonah to Hancock Cove to care for victims of the Spanish flu. Family history indicates that Brigham and Hannah didn't contract the flu because each night "they had a hot toddy" before going to bed.[39]

Elsewhere in the county, the flu hit some with severity and speed. "In one week," the *Roosevelt Standard* reported, "LaPoint had 90 cases. Mt. Home had 30 cases, and Duchesne had over 100 cases."[40] One of the communities hardest hit was Altonah, where as many as thirteen died in a very short time. Survivors were unable to properly prepare the dead for burial quickly enough, so the thirteen bodies were stored in Heber Carrol's otherwise unoccupied house until they could be prepared and graves dug.

The winter of 1918–19 was severe; the ground was often frozen, making it difficult for the few able-bodied men of the community to dig graves. Those with sufficient strength worked in shifts to dig the graves in the frozen ground. On at least one occasion the gravediggers found it easier to dig through the frozen hardpan and rocky ground of the Altonah cemetery at one spot and then tunnel sideways for adjacent graves. Through one grave opening, the dead were buried in hastily constructed wooden coffins.[41]

During the height of the flu epidemic there were too few able-bodied men in Altonah to dig the graves. "One night in Altonah," Harold Eldredge recalled, "there were nine corpses awaiting burial

R.E.A. Dam on the Yellowstone River. (John D. Barton)

and no one well enough to dig a grave." The people of Altonah had to send to Roosevelt and Myton to get help to bury their dead.[42] The volunteer gravediggers from Roosevelt and Myton were careful not to get too close to the residents of Altonah, fearing that they might contract the flu. The Altonah men respectfully withdrew, not wanting to infect those who came to help.

Some families were so sick and bedridden by the illness that there were none well enough in the family to care for the sick. The Burgess family lost three members in less than one week: the father, Raymond; his adult son, Laverne; and a daughter, Thelma.[43] Kindhearted and brave neighbors helped when they could. Emily Wall, a neighbor of the Burgess family and sick herself, provided them with homemade soup.

Many times infected families left kettles outside their doors for neighbors to fill with soup, thereby avoiding unnecessary contact and exposure. In a few instances, neighbors and friends perhaps failed to take necessary precautions when they tried to help and they too became ill and some died. Many people of the county were so afraid of contracting the flu from sick neighbors that some stricken families were left to struggle on their own. Fear frequently prevented the healthy from providing aid and comfort to those afflicted. For example, a girl in Bridgeland died and all the townspeople were too frightened to help. Victor Billings from Duchesne finally went without any assistance from the townspeople. Finding the family too ill to help, he "built a coffin, layed the girl out, dressed her, and provided all the means possible."[44]

Many men and women worked on homemade caskets to bury their dead. Public funerals were rare, but the graves were dedicated and small graveside services held. Much sacrifice and effort was rendered by religious leaders in the county and others to comfort the grieving and conduct religious funerals.

Of the several doctors in the county only Dr. E.R. Enoch of Myton was unaffected by the illness. He grew so weary trying to care for the many sick that men were hired to drive his car while he slept. It was written that he would do what he could, but far too often it was not enough: "When his friends lay dying he whispered, 'There is nothing more that I can do.' Then the tears came into his eyes and he wept, having nothing more that he could give to his dear friends."[45] Nurses and doctors at the Uintah Basin Hospital that had been established on 30 June 1914 in Roosevelt did what they could with the twelve-bed facility. Dr. J.E. Morton was superintendent and Sarah Pumphries and Isobelle Dillman Harmston were among the nurses serving the sick during the influenza epidemic.

In Duchesne the flu struck with a fury, but only one death occurred in the community. According to John Madsen, who lived through the epidemic in Duchesne, out of a population of 700 only seven were not stricken. Madsen, who was one of those seven, recalled:

> the seven of us had to take care of the ones that were ill. We had a quack doctor here that didn't know too much about medicine or flu or anything else. Her orders were to stay in bed and we tried to keep the people in bed which meant we had to chop wood, carry water, carry food, take care of the sick, and it required a lot of effort to do that. However, the Master was kind enough to us so that we were able to get through without any loss.[46]

Moon Lake Electric Building in Roosevelt. (John D. Barton)

Isolation, quarantine, and fumigation were the major means of combating the influenza. Some merchants in the county would not allow anyone in their stores; they filled orders and delivered the merchandise to the people, who were standing outside the stores. Clerks and others wore face masks and gloves. In Altonah, shopping lists were left on fence posts or hung on the door of the Altonah store. Orders then were filled and the goods left in front of the store. In Roosevelt a notice from the city board of health was posted that ordered no loafing or gathering allowed in any place of business; any person who was sick was required to report their condition to the board of health.

As was the case in many other communities in the state, schools were closed in Altonah from October 1918 to early February 1919. Churches also closed in the county during the winter of 1918–19. In Roosevelt the churches and schools were opened on 8 January 1919, but they closed again on 29 January due to a new flu outbreak.[47] In Roosevelt vaccinations were given free of charge at the drug stores.

County board of health inspectors posted signs on front doors or gates of houses of the sick warning people away. Following a period of usually six weeks, by which time the influenza usually had run its course, quarantines of individual houses was lifted. Homes were fumigated using either formaldehyde or sulphur, and clothing and bedding were boiled several times in heavy lye soap when individual quarantines were lifted. Family members bathed using borax. All these efforts were performed in the hope that the people would not be reinfected.[48]

The Spanish influenza did not discriminate, and the Ute Indian population of the county also was hit hard. Historian Leonard J. Arrington reported that sixty-two Ute Indians died, including Chief Atchee, and that twenty Uncompahgre Utes also died from the flu by the end of 1918.[49]

In the county and throughout the state the Spanish influenza epidemic ended for the most part by the spring of 1919, but not before leaving dozens of newly filled graves in the county.

Prohibition

One of the great national controversies of the late nineteenth and the early twentieth centuries was over the use of liquor. National temperance societies demanded that prohibition laws be passed and enforced. The debate in Utah was equally heated and was often one of the period's major political issues. Existing state and federal prohibition laws had limited impact on Duchesne County; federal law had prohibited the sale or distribution of liquor to Indians for decades. When the reservation was opened in 1905 liquor was made more easily available to this segment of the county's adult population.

The national and statewide effort to legislate against alcoholic drinks had existed for several decades, and some Duchesne County communities had unsuccessfully tried to curb the unregulated manufacture and sale of liquor. In 1909 a real political fight broke out in the Utah legislature over the issue of prohibition—the question of "wet" versus "dry." Two prohibition bills were debated in the state legislature and one was passed; however, Governor William Spry promptly vetoed it. Only Wasatch, Morgan, and Sevier counties remained totally dry, those citizens having earlier voted to that effect.

In 1911 the state legislature enacted a local option law. Some communities voted to be wet while others, even in the same county, voted to be dry, leaving a patchwork of wet and dry communities in the state. In June 1916 the city council voted to make Myton dry. The ordinance was implemented on Saturday night, 4 October 1916. Those who wanted to drink legally had to travel to Price or Heber, both seventy miles away. None of the other communities in the county had bars or saloons operating at the time.

For the next several years, prohibitionists campaigned hard to rid the state totally of hard liquor. Both major political parties included a prohibition plank in their platforms. Other planks in the county Democratic platform included support of a nine-month grade-school year, a four-year high school, and a state legislator from Duchesne County. Citizens of the new county felt that they had not been represented adequately.[50] Fred Watrous, editor of the *Duchesne Record*, editorialized strongly for prohibition. He wrote that it appeared that both the Republican and Democratic parties were united on this issue and that it was very likely that either or both parties would submit a constitutional amendment calling for total prohibition in the state, "thereby having the effect of putting Utah in the high and dry class forever and anon."[51]

It was not until a year later, however, that the county joined with the rest of the state and elected Simon Bamberger, a Democrat and Jewish German immigrant. The 1917 election brought a significant change in the political makeup of the state legislature, with the Democrats controlling both houses. Duchesne County elected Democrat G. Victor Billings to the Utah House of Representatives.

The change of ruling political parties and the growing mood in the state provided sufficient support for the passage of a state constitutional amendment prohibiting the trafficking and sale of alcoholic beverages in the state. Some 835 county residents voted for the amendment and 139 voted against it.[52] Utah later ratified the Eighteenth Amendment to the U.S. Constitution, joining forty-five other states in the grand social experiment.

The county did not become completely dry, however; illegal alcohol was occasionally sold in the county. Unable to legally purchase alcohol, those who were determined to drink took to making their own liquor or purchasing it from bootleggers. Homemade recipes and stills were found in Duchesne County. "Corn Squeezins," "Raisin

Toyack Building, constructed in 1933–34 by the Toyack Chapter of the Future Farmers of America. (John D. Barton)

Jack," "Peach Brandy," "Apricot Wine," and other liquor recipes were brewed in the county. The illegal manufacture of alcoholic beverages ranged from those who had large stills secreted away in remote areas in the county to those who simply let their apple cider ferment.

Charley Potter, a known bootlegger and moonshiner during prohibition years, operated several stills near Mountain Home and Boneta. Potter was careful to hide his stills in places where ordinary travelers would not find them. On one occasion Potter was caught and charged with illegal production of liquor. With insufficient money to pay the fine and bail, he begged the judge to let him have three days to get his farm in order before serving his sentence. The judge agreed. Potter then hurried to another of his stills, drained the liquor, and went to Heber City to sell it. He made enough money in Heber to pay his fine and bail.[53]

Bootleggers used various means to transport the alcohol. One bootlegger was caught in Roosevelt with a false gas tank full of booze; investigating lawmen found 175 pints and 40 half pints in the car's false tank. The bootlegger was arrested and then let out on bail; he promptly left town.[54]

For the most part, county residents obeyed the prohibition laws.[55] However, the grand national prohibition crusade was a social failure. Many in Utah and across the nation soon came to believe that the social and economic costs were too large to continue prohibition. In the fall of 1933 debate on prohibition appeared in the local papers. A significant majority of the articles in the *Uintah Basin Record* called for the repeal of prohibition but not of temperance. For example, L.A. Hollenbeck wrote:

> Repeal would give the government 1.5 billion dollars in taxes. Besides the states and the municipalities would get tax aid. Statistics as well as our personal observation shows that prohibition has caused a lawlessness that never existed before prohibition—even under the salon. . . . We have learned something. We believe in liquor control, and proper regulation. We want something that will have public sentiment behind it. Public sentiment is against prohibition, and you can't enforce anything without public sentiment.[56]

In November 1933, voters in Utah went to the polls to decide whether they should continue with prohibition or repeal the national constitutional amendment. Also on the ballot was the repeal of Utah's constitutional amendment relating to intoxicating liquors. County voters voted by a margin of only thirty votes (1,175 for and 1,145 against) to repeal federal prohibition. By a slightly larger margin, county voters also voted to repeal Utah's prohibition law.[57]

A closer look at the election returns reveals that voters in the voting precincts of Altonah, Bluebell, Boneta, Cedarview, Hanna, Hayden, Ioka, Monarch, Mt. Emmons, Neola, Strawberry, Talmage, and Tabiona voted against repeal of federal prohibition; the voters in the precincts of Antelope, Duchesne, Fruitland, Harper, Lake Fork, Myton, Midview, Mountain Home, Roosevelt, Red Cap, and Utahn favored repeal. The above pattern was followed to repeal the state prohibition law, with the exception of the voters in Hanna and Strawberry—they reversed their vote when it came to repealing the state prohibition law.[58]

Utahns voted by a margin of three to two for the Twenty-first Amendment repealing the Eighteenth Amendment and by a two to one ratio to repeal the state's prohibition law. Most rural Utah counties voted against the Twenty-first Amendment, but Duchesne was joined by the majority of counties in voting to repeal the state's prohibition law.[59]

Agriculture

An important cash crop for county farmers was the growing of alfalfa and other cultivated grasses. In 1919, for example, county farmers produced nearly 60,000 tons of cultivated grasses.

Another important cash crop for county farmers in the 1920s was the growing of alfalfa seed, which did especially well in the Myton, Roosevelt, and Fort Duchesne areas. In 1916 county alfalfa-seed producers received slightly more than ten dollars per bushel for their seed.[60] Two years later, Utah produced one-fifth of the entire alfalfa seed crop in the United States, and the state's two major alfalfa-seed-producing areas were western Millard County and the Uinta Basin.[61] Alfalfa-seed production continued to be an important export crop in the state, and by 1925 Utah produced nearly 40 percent of all the alfalfa seed in the United States. The Uinta Basin alfalfa-seed producers produced 147,000 bushels of alfalfa seed, or about one-third of the total state production that year.[62]

The success of the county alfalfa-seed producers was attributed to the generally dry climate that featured light summer rainfalls which fostered the production of alfalfa blossoms. This also tied in with the growing production of honey in the Uinta Basin; and for part of the 1920s apiculturists and alfalfa seed producers were a significant part of the county's agricultural economy.

Many farmers kept bee colonies in their alfalfa and clover fields, which greatly aided in the production of blossoms and seed. Much of the top-grade honey produced in the county was purchased by the Los Angeles Honey Company at the price of two dollars per sixty pounds, which was the top price paid in the nation for honey in the early 1920s. The 1923 honey crop yielded about $100,000 for local farmers.[63]

The early success of the alfalfa-seed producers was fostered by a cooperative marketing effort. N.L. Peterson and George H. Tingley were two leaders who worked to form the Uintah Basin Seed Growers

Association, located in Myton. The association marketed the county's alfalfa seed through the Western Seed and Marketing Company to all parts of the country.[64]

Leading businessmen from Roosevelt and Myton invited the J.G. Peppard Seed Company of Kansas City, Missouri, to establish alfalfa-seed processing plants in the county.[65] The high prices and the connection with two national seed companies encouraged more area farmers to raise alfalfa seed, and by 1923 county seed producers sold 5 million pounds of seed at an average of fifteen cents per pound. By 1924 there were 1,211 seed growers in Duchesne and western Uintah counties planting 39,000 acres of alfalfa seed.[66]

The zenith of alfalfa-seed production in the county occurred in 1925. That year the Uintah Basin Alfalfa Experimental Farm was established at Fort Duchesne to study alfalfa-seed pollination and commercial production, develop new and improved strains of seed, and find effective ways to combat the lygus bugs that were destructive to the high-quality alfalfa seed yield.

During the 1920s the county was also plagued by grasshoppers, which created serious problems for the seed farmers as well as for other farmers in the county. In 1923 the grasshopper problem was so serious that a county bounty of one cent per pound was paid for grasshoppers.[67] Poisoning was a common method used to rid the fields of the hoppers; however, according to local farmer Fred Dickerson, "every time [I] poison a hopper, ten million come to the funeral."[68]

Between 1925 and 1930 alfalfa-seed production in the county and in the state dropped precipitously. The Peppard Seed Company kept its doors open until 1936, when it closed its activities in the county. In 1930 Utah produced less than 3.8 percent of the alfalfa seed in the United States.[69] In Duchesne County several of the alfalfa-seed processing and marketing companies closed their doors. In 1934 the agricultural college's alfalfa experiment farm at Fort Duchesne closed as well. The downturn in the production of alfalfa seed was devastating to the county's economy, especially as the nation entered the most serious economic crisis in its history.[70]

There were other factors involved in the downturn in the alfalfa seed market nationally and locally: drought, competition from abroad and from midwestern growers, overall degradation of the quality of seed in the county caused by weeds and parasites, and the Depression itself.[71] As a result, most seed producers in the county turned to growing other crops or raising livestock or poultry.

An important market for alfalfa and hay grasses grown in the county was the growth in dairy farming. The region was touted in newspapers as "Favored by Nature's Smiles"—having feed and climate to "guarantee prosperity" to those who started milking cows.[72] Creameries were started in Duchesne, Altonah, Neola, and Roosevelt to accommodate the increased milk production, as many area farmers installed dairy barns and started milking cows. In 1919 there was more than 4,900 dairy cows in the county; sixteen years later the number had increased to more than 6,260 cows.[73] Hog raising on a commercial scale was also encouraged, but it did not flourish.[74]

During the 1920s, while much of the nation was engaged in stock speculation and purchasing newly invented ringer washers, radios, vacuum cleaners, and other electrical items, many Duchesne County residents went without. It was not until the 1930s that the New Deal Rural Electric Administration brought electrical power to most county farms. Until that time, wash was still done on a washboard, floors were swept, and cows were milked by hand.

In 1918 the first tractor was brought into the county by A.T. Thompson, who drove it all the way from Price. When a new car was shipped to the C.W.&M. Company in Roosevelt for sale, it made the news.[75] Most farmers still relied on horses for farm work and transportation in the early 1920s; however, by the end of the decade cars and trucks were more common. Jack Barton remembered that the first rubber-wheeled tractor in Boneta was purchased by Sherman Swasey in the early 1940s. Swasey was so proud of it that he hooked a wagon to it and drove his family to church.

The Great Depression

When the stock market crashed on 29 October 1929, it signaled the beginning of this nation's worst financial depression. With the homesteading era shortly behind them, coupled with the setbacks of agricultural overproduction and the drought years the 1920s, county residents faced a difficult decade. Between 1929 and 1933 twenty-five banks failed in the state. Early in the 1920s two local banks—one in Myton and one in Duchesne—failed; only the Roosevelt State Bank survived the economic turmoil of the 1920s and 1930s.

Newly elected Governor Henry Blood at his inaugural ceremony in 1933 spoke grimly of the economic situation in the state:

> Agriculture is in helpless and almost hopeless distress. Basic farm commodity prices in recent weeks have receded to levels never before reached in modern times. Shrinkage of values is rendering private and public income uncertain. Unemployment stalks the city streets, and reflects its shadow on rural life.[76]

When Blood spoke, between 25 and 33 percent of Utah's labor force was unemployed. A year earlier Utah's unemployment rate had peaked at nearly 36 percent.[77]

Across the country prices dropped to new lows, and farmers who normally played a significant role in the county's economy had less and less cash to spend. The state's second-leading export commodity for the years from 1900 to 1920 was livestock; however, by 1930 the exporting of livestock dropped out of the top four economic categories.[78] The changing economic structure of the state placed county farmers and ranchers in a precarious economic situation. Local farmers received less income as farm prices fell due to the nationwide overproduction of farm produce. Three years before the stock market crash of 1929 prices received by farmers for their agricultural commodities fell by a whopping 54 percent. Goods purchased by farmers during the same period dropped by 32 percent and wholesale prices dropped by 31 percent, leaving farmers facing a deficit between their incomes and expenditures.[79]

As the Depression progressed, local businesses in the county worked together to remain open. Most businesses offered credit to their customers, who were, for the most part, careful to pay as soon as they could. According to Verda Moore in Duchesne, "There was not a door on main street that closed."[80]

Most Duchesne County voters reacted to the Depression like those in the rest of the state and the nation, voting for Democratic party candidates. In 1932, voters in the county gave Franklin Delano Roosevelt 1,348 votes compared to Republican incumbent Herbert

Hoover's 1,117 votes. Reed Smoot lost his long-held U.S. Senate seat to his Democratic challenger, university professor Elbert D. Thomas—1,202 votes to 1,289 votes, respectively. Republican and Uinta Basin favorite son Don B. Colton received 1,484 votes from county voters to his rival Abe Murdock's 1,004 for the seat in the United States Congress; however, Murdock statewide bested Colton by nearly 3,000 votes—47,148 to 44,284.[81] Only four of the voting precincts—Antelope, Fruitland, Strawberry, and Red Cap—voted a straight Democratic majority for the presidential, U.S. Senate, and U.S. Congress races; the majority of voters of Neola, Bluebell, Boneta, Hanna, Talmage, Ioka, and Mt. Emmons precincts voted straight Republican for the above seats. The other voting precincts split their votes.

During the Depression much of the nation experienced the worst drought in history, and parts of Utah, including the Uinta Basin, also experienced severe drought. Some old-timers have indicated that if it were not for the drought most area farmers would not have known the Depression was any different than life had been prior to it.[82]

The drought that brought on the dust-bowl conditions of the Midwest also affected Duchesne County. Beginning in the late 1920s and continuing for the next few years there was just too little rainfall for most crops to grow well, if at all. From 1925 through 1936, the three-year average of annual precipitation was less than 5.5 inches, except for the years of 1930, 1931, and 1936, when the average precipitation exceeded that amount. In 1934 the annual precipitation recorded at Fort Duchesne was only 3.67 inches—the third-driest year since 1888.[83]

The drought was the worst ever recorded in the country's history. It extended over 75 percent of the country and severely affected twenty-seven states, including Utah and the Uinta Basin. Crops of all types were severely impacted and summer grazing ground for livestock was virtually nonexistent. In the fall of 1934 cattle and sheep came off the Uinta and Wasatch mountains thin and very weak.

Most of the agricultural industries begun in the 1920s, including the alfalfa-seed industry, were defunct by the middle of the 1930s. Water shortages prevented farms from being completely irrigated, and summer grazing on nearby forest lands was less than adequate.

Livestock raisers were hit particularly hard in the 1930s, especially sheepmen and wool producers. Coupled with a general overgrazing on many parts of the Uinta Mountains, there were few good summer grazing areas for their livestock in the early 1930s.[84] In part due to the depletion of summer grazing, Don B. Colton drafted a new grazing law that he hoped would solve the overgrazing problem. Before the law was passed, however, Colton was defeated in the Democratic sweep of 1932. Two years later Congress passed Colton's proposal, which is better known as the Taylor Grazing Act, named for Representative Edward T. Taylor of Colorado.[85]

Many farmers in the county were unable to grow sufficient forage crops to feed their cattle. In desperation, some harvested tumbleweeds to feed their hungry cows. Other farmers tried other possibilities to secure cattle feed. When rumors reached Talmage that there was hay available in Nine Mile Canyon, a group of Talmage farmers pooled their resources and drove their wagons the seventy miles to purchase the much-needed hay. On the return trip home a blizzard hit, however, and their travel was so slow that by the time they got home they had fed all the hay to their teams and had nothing left to feed their cattle.[86]

Some farmers resorted to slaughtering some of their cattle, hoping for a better hay and pasture crop in the future. Others merely turned their cattle loose to forage for themselves, especially on the southern end of the county on the Tavaputs Plateau. John Wills remembered going with his father on horses with a few bales of hay into the Nine Mile country and finding abandoned cattle that were snowed in. They broke a trail to the starving cattle with their horses and scattered a little hay along the trail to entice the cattle to follow them, but most of the animals were so weak they did not survive the trip out of the hills.[87]

The most seriously hurt economically were local wool producers. There were other factors besides the drought that contributed to the decline of wool production and sheep, including imports, changing fabric needs, overgrazing, and overproduction. In 1930 there were over 101,800 sheep and lambs in Duchesne County, producing 721,724 pounds of wool. Five years later, there were slightly more than 61,900 sheep, producing 570,800 pounds of wool; by 1940 the number of sheep and lambs in the county had slipped to 35,400 sheep and lambs and 314,600 pounds of wool.[88]

Some county farmers turned to raising turkeys, which did well in the late 1920s. By the fall of 1927, county turkey farmers shipped 40,000 pounds of dressed turkey from Roosevelt to the Fulton and Armour meat-packing companies. Three years later, the Uinta Basin producers shipped 195,000 pounds of turkey.[89] However, beginning in the mid-1930s, fewer county farmers raised turkeys; as a result, there was a decline in the number of turkeys raised. By 1939, 14,131 turkeys were raised in the county; the number declined to 8,328 in 1944. The decline continued in 1949, when 1,286 birds were raised; there were 1,276 in 1959.[90] Toward the end of the Depression, in 1941, the Lee Brown Poultry Company built a small processing plant near Roosevelt and encouraged farmers to raise turkeys; but the enterprise did not trigger much interest in raising turkeys in the Uinta Basin.[91] Competition from elsewhere in the state had forced many county turkey growers to abandon this once profitable agricultural activity.

Even the most economically successful segment of the county's agricultural industry, dairying, struggled to survive during the Depression. Milk prices fell from 20 to 40 percent, and county milk production dropped by over 20 percent. In 1929 county milk producers produced 3,187,990 gallons; in 1935 county production had dropped to 2,424,471 gallons.[92]

Some federal programs were initiated immediately prior to the general election of 1932 and more were started during the New Deal to correct the marketing and production structure of the nation's agriculture, to improve the lives of rural Americans and others, and to enact widespread conservation and natural resource management programs. Under President Franklin D. Roosevelt's administration's Agricultural Adjustment and Federal Emergency Relief programs a plan was outlined to provide feed for livestock or purchase emaciated livestock and slaughter them, with the meat going to individual farmers and their neighbors. Under this program, during the summer, fall, and winter of 1934 the federal government purchased 128,000 cattle in Utah.[93]

The Surplus Relief Cattle Program was the first federal drought-relief program to impact Uinta Basin residents, and William K. Dye of Neola was put in charge of the program in the county. Funds for the program came from the Federal Surplus Relief Corporation, administered locally by G.V. Billings. In early June, Dye outlined the government's plan to more than 270 farmers from Duchesne and Uintah counties who qualified for the emergency relief program.[94] All cattle from the cooperating farmers and ranches had to be inspected to determine the health and overall condition of the animals. If the cattle were found to be too thin, they were purchased at fifteen dollars a head and slaughtered. In some instances, some of the more vigorous cattle were purchased by the government and shipped out of the Uinta Basin to be butchered.[95] Dairymen faced similar difficulties, and the federal government paid farmers twenty dollars for each milk cow and five dollars a head for each calf.

Emergency feed was also made available through the Federal Emergency Relief Administration and the county's manager of the program, William H. Case. One thousand tons of hay was made available to county farmers at $13 per ton, including shipping charges. The catch for many farmers was that the purchase had to be made with cash.[96]

During the summer of 1934, 590 farmers in the county participated in the emergency drought-relief program; 2,997 cattle were killed; 3,274 cattle were shipped out of the county for slaughter; and 9,663 cattle remained on county farms to be fed with feed assistance from the federal government.[97] The cattle buy-out program continued into the next year, when the period of severe drought ended. Proof of slaughter was the submission of pairs of ears. Individual farmers were allowed to keep all meat from their slaughtered livestock, and for many months bottled meat was plentiful in many pantries in the county.[98]

For many years following the drought of 1934 numerous stories were told of earless cattle running wild on the foothills of the Uintas, in Nine Mile Canyon, and along the Green River.[99] One drought story is told of a Neola farmer who milked his small herd of earless cows until he was eventually caught by a county livestock inspector.[100] Louwana Timothy remembered as a child seeing her grandfather and uncles driving their fine herd of Hereford cattle to Sand Wash, where the animals were shot and then pushed over the rim into the wash. There was simply nothing to feed the animals due to the drought. "It was just like a funeral. Several of the ladies were crying. . . . We didn't know what would happen to us. Hopelessness and desperation was what I remember," she recalled.[101]

Several Altonah ranchers, not wanting to kill their herds but lacking forage, sought other sources of feed. They approached other farmers in the area, offering to work for them in exchange for the straw used as roofing material on sheds and stables. The aging straw provided enough nutrition to keep some of the cattle alive.[102]

Through the remainder of the 1930s, cattle prices remained low across the country, and obtaining winter feed locally was often doubtful. By 1940 cattle prices in Duchesne County reached $9.10 per hundredweight, a significant gain from the fifteen dollars a head paid by the government six years earlier in its buy-out program. But even with these prices cattlemen in the county were hard-pressed to make a living.[103]

The drought of 1934 compounded the economic difficulties of some cattlemen in Altonah. Four years earlier an unscrupulous cattle buyer had offered unusually high prices for cattle, and the cattlemen from Altonah made a verbal agreement. Having dealt with cattle buyers in the past, the ranchers saw no reason not to trust the individual. The buyer was to trail the cattle to Heber City, where they were to be purchased and shipped. Payment for the cattle was to be made following the sale and shipment. No checks were ever received, however. The buyer, having swindled the twenty ranchers of their money, fled to Canada. The loss of money and cattle was compounded several years later with the drought. The 1930 sale of cattle had been the last opportunity for the cattlemen of Altonah to receive a good price for their cattle.

County livestock producers and others sought other forms of relief during the Depression. One was to petition the county commission for an extension on the payment of taxes due. In December 1934, when taxes were due, roughly 500 property owners in the county were listed in the newspapers as being delinquent in the payment of their taxes. In one instance, the property-tax delinquency was for as little twenty-two cents for a town lot in Duchesne.[104] A group of displeased taxpayers, the Duchesne Taxpayers Association, a year earlier had petitioned the Utah Board of Education, the Utah Tax Commission, and the Duchesne County Commission demanding tax reductions and a 30 percent reduction in property valuation. The county taxpayers association stated, "We declare dissatisfaction with our county school board in holding the [tax] rate so high, that the taxpayers cannot pay."[105] The tax rates were lowered.

A number of New Deal programs were implemented in the county to help alleviate the economic ills found in the county, provide work, make civic and road improvements, implement conservation programs, and do numerous other projects and programs needed in the county. And yet, although there were many local and federal relief programs at work, some county men were still so desperately in need of employment that they left the county to work in the mines of Carbon County or walk the tracks to pick up coal fallen from coal trains.[106]

At the beginning of the summer of 1934, the National Reemployment Service program placed fifty-three unemployed men on work projects in the county; by July, an additional 168 men were employed by the program.[107] When men were hired to work for the county or other government entities, the local government was required to provide 25 percent of the earned wages, and the balance came from the Civil Works Administration. A number of men worked on county road projects earning fifty cents an hour for a six-hour work day and a thirty-hour work week. Throughout the Depression, many miles of county roads were improved, primarily from the farm-to-market road program of the Works Progress Administration (WPA). In December 1937, for example, the county received $33,000 from the WPA to employ sixty men and to purchase construction materials. Roads improved included the roads from Bluebell to Mt. Emmons, from Altonah to Mountain Home, and from Altamont to Boneta. Streets in Myton were graveled, and hundreds of feet of concrete sidewalks were laid in Duchesne and Roosevelt by WPA workers.

Women in the county were also employed—many at home, others working at several emergency relief canning projects scattered throughout the county. Some attended Red Cross family health classes and in turn taught family health and home sanitation techniques to their neighbors. Mrs. Lettie Brown was hired to be the Duchesne County supervisor for the county's sewing and canning projects. Brown reported that through the emergency relief projects some 200 county families received clothing and bottled and canned food. In 1934, county women repaired 232 quilts, 36 slips, 89 shirts, 105 sleeping garments, 27 bloomers, and 33 pairs of stockings, and they made 65 infant garments, two rugs from rags, and other clothing items. Under Brown's supervision, women of the county canned more than 20,000 cans of vegetables at Neola, Myton, Roosevelt, Duchesne, and Altonah canneries and distributed the canned food items to 600 needy families in the county. There also were other commodities distributed to families in need.[108]

A major project undertaken in the county in 1935 was the construction of fifteen sewage septic tanks and 130 privies. Labor was provided under the auspices of the Sanitation Project headed by Ernest W. Crocker of Duchesne. Homeowners and businesses that benefited were required to provide the material.[109]

In addition to road construction and repair and sanitation projects, various other civic improvements were made throughout the county. For example, the town of Duchesne received funds from the Federal Emergency Relief Administration to hire twenty men and five teams of horses to make improvements at the town park, construct a horse racetrack, level the baseball field, complete the city's swimming pool, and drain several sloughs along the Duchesne River.[110]

A significant improvement was made to the culinary water supply for the town of Duchesne. Federal Emergency Relief Administration engineer W.R. Weyman worked with the town leaders to construct new eight-inch and six-inch water mains to the city at a cost of $40,000.[111] Elsewhere in the county, cisterns were built to improve rural culinary water needs, and WPA workers drained swampy areas and worked to reduce the spread of weeds by digging thistles and other weeds from fields and roadsides.

Federal funds were made available for school construction and improvements as well as for assisting high school students. For example, forty-one needy high school students were given six dollars a month for nine months by the National Youth Administration to attend school during the 1935–36 school year. In return for the financial aid, the recipients worked as school custodians or in the school library.[112]

Important in meeting the needs of hungry schoolchildren and providing a market for excess agricultural commodities was the government's school lunch program. Students bought school lunches for three cents. If the families lacked money, they could exchange home-grown produce for school lunches.

Over $100,000 was budgeted by the county school district for school remodeling and construction, with most of the money coming from various federal relief programs. A new elementary school costing $41,000 was built in Myton in 1936. In Duchesne, five classrooms, a library, gymnasium, and auditorium were built for the high school. The county received $31,000 from the Public Works Administration to support the Indian education program in the county.[113]

Through various commodity, tax, and financial programs, county farmers were provided financial relief. For example, the Farm Credit Administration provided $244,000 to 130 farm families in the county at an interest rate of 7.3 percent to help refinance their farm debts.[114]

By fall of 1936, 37 percent of the county's unemployed were at work on various federal projects. Three years later, the federal government pumped $307,329.51 into the county in the form of wages and spent $137,572.13 on materials for road projects, school building repairs and construction, job training programs, construction of new culinary water and sewer systems, and many other projects.[115]

Despite the aid, the demands for relief assistance remained large in the county. With a population of 8,263, which accounted for only 1.63 percent of the state population, Duchesne County was one of the highest-assisted counties per capita in the state—with 3,356, or slightly more than 40 percent of the county, receiving some form of public assistance.[116] In October 1935 the *Uintah Basin Record* stated that statewide Duchesne County carried the highest percentage of its population on government relief rolls.[117]

Federal assistance programs, the rebounding of normal annual precipitation amounts, and slight improvements in the national economy reduced the number on direct assistance to 682 people by December 1938. However, despite the drop in direct relief assistance, federal relief programs continued in the county until the outbreak of World War II.[118]

The Moon Lake Project

One of the largest emergency relief and reclamation programs in the county in which various local, state, and federal agencies were involved was the construction of the Moon Lake Dam and the associated Midview reclamation project. Construction plans and funding proposals for a dam at Moon Lake to store spring snowmelt for summer irrigation had been a major county concern for several years. The earlier Strawberry Valley Reservoir project clearly demonstrated that mountain reservoirs were feasible, but such large reclamation projects required large sums of money, something that was not plentiful in the county or in the state.

County irrigators had first turned to the Hoover administration to fund the project. President Herbert Hoover was a mining engineer by training and was familiar with such construction schemes. Hoover was defeated, however, in the election of 1932 before any construction began on the project. The new president, Franklin Delano Roosevelt, and his agricultural secretary, Henry Agard Wallace, a former Iowa farmer and experimenter in corn genetics, opposed placing more land into production. There already existed a nationwide surplus of many agricultural commodities, and to help farmers secure a higher return from their produce farmers were encouraged through various programs to produce less. The county's Moon Lake reclamation project flew in the face of Wallace's concerns.

The *Uintah Basin Record* was one of several county and state voices that still argued for the Moon Lake project. "We need this project," stated an editorial in the *Record*, "but it looks like we will have to do a lot of 'Hollering' if we [want to] get it."[119] All of the hollering seemed to have paid off, however; in December 1933 government officials agreed to provide more than a million dollars for the project.

The Moon Lake project proved not only to be an important reclamation project but also an important project to provide jobs for those unemployed locally as well as providing the Civilian

Conservation Corps (CCC) with a significant reclamation project. The Moon Lake project also primed the economic pump in the county through the purchase of building materials, equipment, and supplies.

Approximately half of the more than $1 million project was awarded to the T.E. Connelly Construction Company of San Francisco. According to the Bureau of Reclamation contract, Connelly hired a number of local men to work on the project. More than 130 men were hired to work on the dam. Nearly half of the million dollar price tag was given to the Public Works Administration, which in turn purchased materials for the dam locally and supplied much of the equipment for its construction.

The completion of the Moon Lake project came too late to help alleviate the severe drought of 1934. However, local irrigators fully understood that when the dam was completed and its reservoir filled from winter snow there would be water for irrigation during the summer months and they never again would face the severe shortage of water they experienced during the 1934 drought.[120]

Headlines and stories in the local newspapers captured the enthusiasm for the project and the good news of its approval. One read:

> Cheer Up, Basin Folks! We should consider ourselves among the more fortunate ones in the entire U.S. . . . . Last week was the breaking point of the depression in the Uintah Basin. When the news broke telling us that the state and government had decided to construct the Moon Lake water storage project, which will cost . . . about $1,200,000. It will give hundreds of jobs, bring more land under cultivation, create a chance for a sugar factory with plenty of water.[121]

Everything associated with the reclamation project was not joyous, however. Several serious accidents and two deaths resulted from construction of the reclamation project. Howard Mitchell, a nineteen-year-old truck driver, spent several weeks in the hospital with a severe skull fracture caused when his truck rolled on the Moon Lake road; Howard Wardle was electrocuted while he was working on a 440-volt power line at the Moon Lake dam site; and Charles F.

Boreham, a CCC enrollee from Salt Lake City, died from a construction accident at the associated Midview Reservoir being constructed in Arcadia.[122]

Work progressed rapidly on the Midview Reservoir. It was dedicated on 10 September 1937 with much celebration and community activities. Mrs. Charles Boreham, the widowed mother of killed CCC enrollee Charles Boreham, was honored, as was the work of the CCC. Congressman Abe Murdock delivered the main address; it was followed with a large community lunch, boxing and wrestling matches, a baseball game, and a dance in the evening.[123]

Work on the Moon Lake Dam progressed more slowly. Severe winter weather closed the project down, and for a time the contractor lacked workers. The dam was sufficiently completed in June 1938 that storage of water from the spring snowmelt began. Within weeks the new reservoir was filled to capacity, and later in the summer water was released to farmers downstream.

The Civilian Conservation Corps

In addition to the many conservation and other much-needed projects supported or funded in the county by the Public Works Administration (PWA) and the Works Projects Administration (WPA), the Civilian Conservation Corps (CCC) accomplished a great deal in the county improving roads, building reclamation projects, and helping rehabilitate forest grazing land and recreational sites. Corpsmen also were involved in many other community activities.

Run much like the army, the CCC was perhaps the most popular of Roosevelt's New Deal programs. The CCC program operated from 1933 through 1942. Roosevelt hoped that the program would assist two of the nation's best resources—its natural resources and its youth. The president hoped that by providing jobs for young men protecting the natural resources in the nation all would be beneficiaries.

Young men signed up for periods of six months, with the opportunity to reenlist for a maximum period of three years. Pay was thirty dollars a month, of which twenty-five dollars was sent to the youth's family; the remainder was kept as spending money. Many of the young men received training in heavy-equipment operation, as mechanics, and in other skilled areas which served them the rest of their lives.

The CCC program got underway in Utah in the spring of 1933 when it was decided in Washington that conservation work was urgently required in the various national forests in the state. With Utah's high unemployment, local young men with experience working with horses and with outdoor skills were encouraged to sign up in the CCC program.[124] Duchesne County's share of the earliest CCC allotment was forty young men.

In addition to the acceptance of local men with experience to work on the national forests, another special CCC program under the direction of the Bureau of Indian Affairs rather than the army was organized for unemployed Indians. Nationwide, more than 14,000 CCC positions for Indians were established; Utah's quota was 200 Indians, most from the Uinta Basin.[125] The Indian CCC program in the Uinta Basin worked primarily in the field of conservation.

During the nine years of the CCC there were over 100 camps established in the state. The first CCC camp in the Uinta Basin was established near Vernal in May 1933 to work on the Ashley National Forest. The company consisted of twenty-five men from Virginia. Men in Company 2910 performed conservation work on the national forest and men of Company 1968 worked on the Midview reclamation project. A year later, in October 1934, two CCC companies were established in the county at Moon Lake and at Bridgeland, with four additional temporary or seasonal camps located in Yellowstone Canyon, near Altonah, at Myton, and in Uinta Canyon.

The CCC men at the Yellowstone camp worked on mountain trails and other forest projects; men of the Altonah camp built the twenty-mile, cement-lined Highline Canal, which diverts water from the Lake Fork River to the farmland around Neola. The Bridgeland CCC group worked on a canal from the Duchesne River to Arcadia and construction of the Boreham (Midview) Reservoir, the largest of the CCC projects in the county. The first task of the CCC at the Midview Storage Project was to help relocate several families who lived at the reservoir site. Once the families were relocated, work at the Midview Dam progressed rapidly. The CCC also built several feeder canals to supply the new reservoir with water and then built distribution canals from the reservoir to the fields in the Red Cap area.

The Myton CCC men did road work, graveled Myton and Roosevelt streets, and worked on weed and rodent control. The Uinta Canyon CCC camp worked on bridges, fish dams, and camp-grounds.[126]

In addition to providing employment, men of the CCC program were active in the county, participating in various sporting events, writing a weekly column for the *Uintah Basin Record,* organizing special activities, and participating in numerous community socials and other activities. Some CCC young men became romantically involved with local girls. Curtis Robertson recalled:

> I was in the CCC camp when I met my wife. She lived in Roosevelt. I was standing inside the dance hall and she came in with the fellow that she was engaged to. They had been for a ride, and her hair was all messed up. She asked him if he had a comb, and he said that he didn't. I was standing there and I said, "Well, I have one. Do you want to use mine?" So she borrowed my comb. Then I asked her for a dance. And that was the beginning of our little affair. We have been married thirty-five years.[127]

Jack Young from Kentucky joined the CCC at the age of eighteen and soon found himself working on various projects in the Uinta Basin. He met and married Bernice Collett in 1937 and settled in Hanna where he went to work at the Fabrizio sawmill.

County residents were profoundly appreciative of work done by the CCC program, and when state and federal officials wanted to move the Bridgeland CCC camp to another reclamation project, the county put up a strong argument for the Bridgeland and Myton camps to remain in the county. The Moon Lake CCC camp remained in the county until spring 1935, when it was reassigned elsewhere. The Bridgeland camp stayed in the county until the spring of 1939.

Rural Electrification Association And Moon Lake Electric

For many isolated farm families in the county, electricity remained a wonder only to be witnessed in the larger communities in the county or on those farms located near transmission lines. Of all the New Deal programs in Duchesne County, perhaps none had more impact and a longer-lasting effect than the Rural Electrification Administration (REA). The REA was created in 1935 to connect the thousands of isolated farmsteads across America with electric services. The REA worked closely with the Work Projects Administration to secure manpower to string electrical wire and place thousands of poles, and it worked with the Reconstruction Finance Corporation to provide loans and grants to newly established rural electricity cooperatives. Walter LeFevre, who had settled in Tabiona in 1915, was hired in 1939 by the Moon Lake Electric Association with funds from the WPA to install electricity in Tabiona. Private electric power companies attempted to limit the activities of the REA; however, public opinion was strongly in favor of the New Deal program, and in 1939 the REA was made a permanent agency within the Department of Agriculture. The REA proved to be very successful in providing inexpensive electricity to rural Americans, including isolated farmers and their families in Duchesne County. Today, even the most remote farmstead in the county has electricity.

Prior to the formation of the REA, there was, of course, electric service in many parts of the county. The Uintah Power and Light Company had been started in 1918 and a power plant was built on the Lake Fork River at what was then called Lake Fork. After completion of the power plant, the area was renamed Upalco, a contraction of the company name. This private power company provided the first electric service in Duchesne County, supplying Roosevelt, Myton, Duchesne, and Upalco.

In 1937 Shirley K. Daniels of Mt. Emmons, having heard of the new federal program, wrote to the Rural Electrification Association offices in Washington, D.C., to find out how he and his neighbors could get electricity. Daniels, along with Chester Hartman, Edward Holder, and Edward Conklin, formulated a plan to organize an electrical cooperative. With the assistance of George Stewart, a young attorney from Roosevelt, and Zella Rust (Bennion), who later worked as bookkeeper for the cooperative, the small group organized a meeting in January 1938 to incorporate the Altonah-Bluebell-Mt. Emmons Rural Electrification Association. They worked for the next several months inviting others to join the cooperative for a five-dollar fee. Many who paid the fee did so with money they could ill afford, but they realized the difference that electricity would make in their lives and on their farms.

In September 1938 the REA approved a project for Altonah, Mt. Emmons, and Bluebell; $74,000 was allocated to build sixty-five miles of power lines to 233 homes. Lines needed to be strung, rights-of-way obtained, homes wired, and contracts signed, and a multitude of other tasks needed to be completed for electric service to be possible. The following March another $10,000 was approved to wire each of the homes with electricity. At the suggestion of Zelda Rust, the Altonah-Bluebell-Mt. Emmons Rural Electrification Association changed its name in June 1939 to the simpler Moon Lake Electric Association.

Following the example of Altonah, Bluebell, and Mt. Emmons, the residents of Mountain Home, Boneta, Tabiona, Ioka, Hancock Cove, Cedarview, Montwell, Neola, and LaPoint applied to REA officials asking permission to form a similar cooperative electrical association. Instead, they were encouraged to join the Moon Lake Electric Association, and, as a result, $285,000 was granted to the Moon Lake Association to expand its services.

During the next several years Moon Lake Electric expanded to Dry Fork, northwest of Vernal, buying electricity wholesale from Uintah Power and Light Company. As a small, privately owned company, the Uintah Power and Light Company had neither sufficient power nor the reliability of service to meet the high standards expected by the Moon Lake Electric board of directors. To better service Moon Lake Electric Association, Uintah Power and Light Company applied for a grant from the REA to construct a dam to generate more electricity. Several hydroelectric sites in the Uinta Mountains were considered, and, in 1940, a place was chosen on the Yellowstone River in Yellowstone Canyon, north of Altonah. Two years later, $200,000 was approved by the REA for the construction of a power plant on the Yellowstone River. A dam with three turbines of 300-kilowatt capacity each was built to augment the power needs of the rapidly growing cooperative. The power plant began generating electricity in September 1941 to meet the needs of 700 new consumers and was expanded with an additional unit in 1946 to serve 1,250 consumers.

In 1949 a diesel generating plant was built in Leeton and later moved to Altamont as the cooperative grew. More electric power was needed, and in 1951 Moon Lake Electric Association purchased Rangley Power and Light Company. Nine years later, Moon Lake Electric Association was granted permission from the REA to purchase stock in Uintah Power and Light Company.

In 1958 Moon Lake contracted with the Flaming Gorge Dam project for additional power. Four years later, a forty-mile transmission line from Meeker, Colorado, to the substation in Rangely was completed to transport power purchased from a Colorado company. In 1975 a contract was signed between Utah Power and Light and Moon Lake Electric to purchase additional power from the Hunter II plant. In 1980 Moon Lake Electric purchased a portion of the Hunter II plant at Bonanza. Presently this plant supplies some 70 percent of Moon Lake's power.[128]

When Moon Lake Electric began service, its minimum bill was $3.25 a month for 40 kilowatt hours of power. This was thought to be sufficient for all the new modern conveniences. Bringing power to rural Duchesne County radically and permanently changed the lives of those farmers and their families. Dairymen were able to cool their milk, making it more marketable. Electricity greatly eased the labors of women. Heated running water and indoor plumbing were made possible. Electric wringer washers replaced scrub boards. Radios brought the news of the world and entertainment into rural homes. Electric fans cooled hot kitchens during the late summer canning season.

Electric service will be the predominant factor in building up the area, excited county residents proclaimed.[129] And, in fact, electricity did bring about more and faster changes than any other single development in rural Duchesne County. By 1961 Moon Lake Electric had purchased all the Uintah Power and Light Company shares and in 1971 had incorporated the service areas. Moon Lake Electric Association presently serves the region from the Strawberry Valley to Rangely, Colorado, making it the tenth-largest REA cooperative in the nation.

The Toyackers

One of the success stories in the county during the Depression was the county's Future Farmers of America (FFA) chapter. Chapter members adopted the name Toyack, a Ute word meaning "good enough or okay."[130] The Toyack chapter was organized in the late 1920s by Walter E. Atwood, who taught at the Roosevelt High School. Under Atwood's leadership, dozens of boys in grades 7 through 12 were encouraged to take agricultural classes to become better future farmers. Many out-of-school projects were undertaken by the young boys. One of the significant activities was the construction of a chapter house in Roosevelt; another was a trip to the Chicago World's Fair in 1933.

To lift the spirits of many of the boys during the Depression, Harold Behunin, president of the Toyack chapter in 1932, suggested to Walter Atwood, that he would like to do something big for the chapter, and the trip to the world's fair was planned.[131] In December 1932 eighty-seven Duchesne County residents made plans to attend the 1933 Chicago World's Fair, whose theme was a "Century of Progress." For some of the boys, the economic difficulties they and their parents were experiencing was something less than "progress"; nevertheless, the chapter agreed to raise money for the long trip.

Most Toyackers had never traveled out of the Uinta Basin. Their dream trip was to be the longest journey and largest project any chapter of the Future Farmers of America had undertaken. "I was a well-traveled man. I had been to Vernal, Salt Lake City, and the high Uintah Mountains," Walt Redmond, a 1933 Toyack member, recalled. "Most of the kids going on the trip had only been to Vernal, if that far from home."[132]

Money was needed for the dream trip. "On to Chicago" fund-raisers were held. Dances and boxing matches between the boys were among the many activities organized to raise money. Walt Redmond remembered the group made most of their money by boxing each other and charging admission: "The room would always be filled and it cost twenty-five cents to watch."[133]

The group fund-raising was the easy part; each boy also had to raise $12.50 on his own. Walt Redmond raised two calves as a FFA project and sold one for the trip. His profit from the sale of the one calf was enough to pay his $12.50, buy clothing for the trip, and have $10.00 for spending money. Victor Brown remembered earning his money by harvesting hay during the summer for his father along with four other Toyackers.[134]

The $12.50 went for "transportation and grub." Often the meals were meager. Wrote Redmond: "I am so hungry and gaunt that my pants are wearing blisters on my hips from rubbing . . . all Oral and I got for supper was bread and butter. . . . We got 2 oranges for supper. It was just enough to torment us."[135] Each Toyack member was required to buy a "ten gallon" hat as a means of group identification and a symbol of coming from the West. The hats were purchased from the J.C. Penney store in Roosevelt for a reduced price of five dollars. Each boy also had to provide a blanket, a pillow, and a tarp to provide shelter at night.

The twenty-one-day journey began on 11 August 1933. The group traveled in two buses and a flatbed truck, which carried their gear and served as a chuck wagon. Albert LaRose and Dwight Copperfield were invited to go on the trip to represent the Ute Indian community. Shortly after leaving Roosevelt for Chicago, Albert LaRose got homesick and returned home. Advisor Walter Atwood was a World War I veteran and ran everything in a military manner. Fred Gagon sounded his bugle every morning at 5:00 A.M. He reportedly only missed one day because "of a fat lip someone gave him."[136] Accompanying the boys was Martha Shanks, an army nurse during World War I. Her only medical "emergencies" on the trip were treating sore feet and homesickness.

The novelty of a large group of boys and their three-vehicle caravan grew each day as they traveled farther east. In many of the towns where the American Legion hosted them the seventy-five boys— dressed in overalls, flannel shirts and ten-gallon hats—performed a special march to the sound of the bugle. Walt Redmond noted in his diary, "Boy are we attracting attention. I guess they shore think we are hayseeds."[137]

During their travel east, the Toyackers visited two state fairs and a rodeo. They were awed by the fat cattle, the likes of which they had not seen in the drought-stricken Uinta Basin. Redmond particularly noted the farms he saw:

> There were rolling fields of corn . . . as far as you can see; not five or ten acres, but five or six miles. It makes one wonder how they ever get it cultivated. . . . Saw some queer sights today; ten or fifteen stacks of hay in each field with not more than 5 tons in the stack. They put rubber tires on mower machines and truck wheels on rakes.[138]

Frequently the boys spent the night sleeping in a stockyard filled with the smell of cattle. Advisor Raymond Wiscombe recalled "sleeping on soft horse manure at the various fair grounds along the way to and from Chicago."[139] The nights were often uncomfortable and cold. Accommodations did get better when the caravan reached Chicago. At one camp the Toyackers stayed at Maple Lake, a beautiful resort area twenty-seven miles out of Chicago and formerly owned by the notorious Al Capone. Before being incarcerated for his crimes, Capone gave the lake resort to the American Legion. Walter Atwood, himself a Legionnaire, made arrangements for the hospitality. The boys were able to sleep under a roof for three nights at that camp.

Several days were spent at the world's fair. Coming from farms, many of the boys were surprised that the fair did not have much in the way of livestock exhibits, although they were impressed by its size. "It would take at least two weeks to cover everything," one Toyacker wrote. [140] They marveled at seeing a Chinese temple and Admiral Richard Byrd's airplane. Lights at the world's fair were turned by the illumination of a distant star, a wonder sponsored by an electric company. The Toyackers witnessed an automobile being assembled in the Chrysler exhibit building and saw wonders of the world that were out of reach of their family and friends in Duchesne County.

Their journey home was also filled with sights not found in their isolated county. Wrote one:

> The country over which we traveled was much different that the west. The corn fields of Iowa were a sight to behold. Then there was Kansas with wheat stubble or plowed ground as far as the eye could see. I recall fertile valleys, wooded areas with many trees,

huge rivers, but nothing looked as great as the Rocky Mountains as they appeared on the journey homeward.[141]

A parade was organized upon their arrival home. Their 3,400-mile journey was over, but a new project—the building of a chapter house—was to involve their youthful energies for the next several years. Atwood had dreamed of the FFA chapter in Roosevelt having its own building; however, the problem was money and commitment. Both were solved at the last breakfast before the boys reached Roosevelt. In Craig, Colorado, the boys and their advisors decided to do something special to commemorate their journey—they would build their own chapter house in Roosevelt—the first FFA chapter house in the country. Nearly $300 was saved from the Chicago trip, and, with a similar amount provided by the local American Legion post, sufficient funds were on hand to begin the construction of the chapter house later in the summer of 1933.[142]

Most of the construction material was collected by FFA club members from different parts of the county. One group cut and hauled 35,000 board feet of timber from the Ashley National Forest, paying for the timber permit and milling of the lumber used in their house. Another group of boys with their fathers gathered stone from Pleasant Valley for the building's foundation; ninety-one loads of rock were hauled to Roosevelt. A third group of boys made 10,000 adobe bricks at an abandoned brickyard to line the interior walls of their building.[143]

The most outstanding architectural feature of the Toyack House (as the building was known) is its fireplace, in which over forty special bricks or stones from different FFA chapters were used. Alabama's contribution to the fireplace, for example, was a stone of polished white marble with the state's name carved in it.[144]

Along with donations from the American Legion and the savings and work done by the boys themselves, aid and labor also came from the CCC and WPA programs. In 1936 the house was completed. Walter E. Atwood said, "Every community and town in the Basin were concerned or involved in the completion of the Toyack Chapter House."[145] The construction of the house was a physical symbol of hope in the community. Atwood summed it up well:

The Depression and drought had found many people leaving the Uintah Basin and many of those who stayed were dismayed and discouraged. The trip to the World Fair attracted a great deal of attention and gave the Basin a hope, an interest, and a belief that conditions would improve.[146]

The Toyack Chapter House was used by the FFA until 1952, when a new high school was built at the east end of town. The old facilities, including the Toyack House, were taken over by the junior high school. The house served for many years as a classroom for the junior high. The "Century of Progress" trip and the Toyack House were a community's way of showing its American spirit and not giving up to despair when confronted with adverse conditions.

Depression But Not Depressed

Duchesne County residents, like most of the nation, took the hardship of the Great Depression with stoic determination and dry humor. Woodrow Wilkerson of Neola, a teenager during the time, summed it up: "We didn't miss any meals during the depression—but we sure postponed a lot of them!"[147] Meals were sometimes meager; Olive Miles, a mother of several young children during the Depression, recalled, "I can remember when I could have bought a sack of flour for 11 cents—but I didn't have 11 cents."[148] Poaching of deer and other wild game occurred occasionally to supplement the diets of county residents.

The difficult economic conditions were magnified due to the recent settlement of the county—many residents were deeply in debt. The county's geographical isolation also added to its economic woes. National government programs and the determination of most county residents carried them through the difficult economic conditions. Numerous county building projects were started and others were accelerated during the Depression. Schools were improved, roads were graded and graveled, and many miles of asphalt and oil and rock mix were laid and reclamation projects built. The electric-power service area was greatly expanded, reaching virtually every farm and ranch in the county, radically changing the lives of hundreds of county families. A group of young men witnessed the marvels of the outside world for the first time. A new, modern hospital was built at Fort Duchesne to serve the Indian population of the Uinta Basin. The Great Depression also changed the political behavior of county voters as it did in the state and the nation.

The county's population changed during the Depression. The population of the county had dropped by more than 800 in the decade of the 1920s, from 9,093 in 1920 to 8,263 in 1930; but by the end of the 1930s it had increased to 8,958, an 8.41 percent increase, which was slightly larger than the state's increase of 8.36 percent. The communities of Duchesne, Myton, and Roosevelt experienced significant growth during the Depression decade as well. Myton's population grew by slightly more than 10 percent, a significant reversal from the previous decade, during which the town dropped in population from 479 in 1920 to 395 in 1930. The population of the town of Duchesne grew from 590 people in 1930 to more than 900 by 1940. Duchesne's population had declined by 110 people during the previous decade.[149]

The number of farms declined during the decade of the 1930s—from over 1,200 to less than 1,050. The decline in the number of farms also was true for the state and the nation. County livestockmen raised fewer sheep and there was a smaller wool clip during the decade. In 1930 there were more than 101,000 sheep in the county and the wool clip for 1929 was some 721,700 pounds. Ten years later there were fewer than 35,500 head of sheep in the county and the wool clip was 314,600 pounds. Many stockmen shifted from raising sheep to raising cattle, and others took up dairying during the decade. In 1930 there were 9,616 head of cattle in the county; by 1940 there were more than 13,000 cattle. For the same period, the number of milch cows increased from 5,419 to 6,356. However, milk production decreased from 3,187,000 gallons in 1929 to 2,939,000 gallons in 1940.[150]

ENDNOTES

1. Bureau of the Census, *Fourteenth Census of the United States: Utah* (Washington, D.C.: Government Printing Office, 1924), 54; Bureau of the Census, *United States Census of Agriculture: 1945, Utah and Nevada*, Part 31 (Washington, D.C.: Government Printing Office, 1946), 19.

2. See *Report of the Secretary of State* (Salt Lake City: State of Utah), var-

ious years, copies at the Utah State Historical Society; and Wayne Stout, *History of Utah, 1896–1929* (Salt Lake City: n.p., 1968) 2:345–46, 367–68, 376, 397–98, 406, 419–20.

3. See *Report of the Secretary of State* for the years 1911–12, 1913–14, 1915–16, 1917–18, and 1919–20, copies at the Utah State Historical Society Library.

4. Clayton S. Rice, *Ambassador to the Saints* (Boston: Christopher Publishing House, 1967), 133.

5. *Roosevelt Standard,* 23 October 1918.

6. *Roosevelt Standard,* 18 April 1917.

7. *Duchesne Record,* 16 June 1917.

8. *Duchesne Record,* 14 April 1917. A week later the newspaper reported that a dozen of the county's young men had enlisted.

9. *Roosevelt Standard,* 6 June 1917.

10. *Duchesne Record,* 9 June 1917.

11. See Noble Warrum, *Utah in the World War: The Men behind the Guns and the Men and Women Behind the Men behind the Guns* (n.p., 1924), Utah State Historical Society Library.

12. *Roosevelt Standard,* 29 August 1917, Dillman, *Early History of Duchesne County,* 485. See also Orson Mott, interview with J.P. Tanner, February 1989, Duchesne, Utah, copy in the possession of the author.

13. *Roosevelt Standard,* 9 May 1917.

14. Andrew L. Neff, World War I Papers, Utah State Historical Society Library.

15. Warrum, *Utah in the World War,* 99.

16. *Vernal Express,* 20 November 1914.

17. Max Hartman, interview with John D. Barton, Altamont, Utah, 4 November 1994, transcript in possession of the author.

18. *Roosevelt Standard,* 18 April 1917.

19. Thomas G. Alexander, "The Economic Consequences of the War: Utah and the Depression of the Early 1920s," in *A Dependent Commonwealth: Utah's Economy from Statehood to the Great Depression,* ed. by Dean L. May, Charles Redd Monographs in Western History No. 4 (Provo: Brigham Young University Press, 1974), 63.

20. *Roosevelt Standard,* 9 October 1918, 25 November 1918.

21. *Roosevelt Standard,* 25 November 1918. See also foreclosure notices posted weekly from November 1919 to February 1920.

22. Mary Beth Norton et al., *A People and a Nation: A History of the United States* (Boston: Houghton Mifflin, 1991), 417, 418.

23. *Roosevelt Standard,* 6 September 1916.

24. Eva LaMar Meldrum, *The Girl On The Milk-White Horse* (New York: Vintage Press, 1975), 26–27.

25. *Utah Farmer,* 11 February 1922. See also Jesse Washburn, "History of Jesse Washburn," 17, copy in possession of the author.

26. *Roosevelt Standard,* 13 September 1916. For more on the closing of Fort Duchesne see Thomas Alexander and Leonard Arrington, "The Utah Military Frontier 1872–1912: Forts Cameron, Thornburg, and Duchesne," *The Utah Historical Quarterly* 32 (Fall 1964): 330–54.

27. *Roosevelt Standard,* 25 April 1917. The Bamberger Road is still in use today. It is a paved road linking the Indian Canyon Highway with the Price to Spanish Fork Highway; however, it is only open for summer months and is not plowed when winter snows make it impassable. A monument to Governor Bamberger on the east end of the road is still standing.

28. *Roosevelt Standard,* 2 October 1918.

29. *Duchesne Courier,* 22 August 1924.

30. *Duchesne Record,* 16 November 1918.

31. Leonard J. Arrington, "The Influenza Epidemic of 1918–19 in Utah," *Utah Historical Quarterly* 58 (Spring 1990): 165–66.

32. Ibid., 167.

33. *Roosevelt Standard,* 16 October 1918.

34. *Roosevelt Standard,* 13 November 1918.

35. *Roosevelt Standard,* 23 October 1918.

36. *Roosevelt Standard,* 24 November 1918.

37. *Roosevelt Standard,* 31 October 1918.

38. Emily T. Wilkerson and Lester Bartlett, comp., *From Then Until Now: 75 Years in Central Uintah Basin, 1905–1980* (Roosevelt, UT: Ink Spot, 1987), 11.

39. Ibid.

40. *Roosevelt Standard,* 4 December 1918.

41. Altonah Ward Record Book, 1918–1919, microfilm copy, Church of Jesus Christ of Latter-day Saints Archives, Salt Lake City, Utah.

42. Finley C. Pearce, *O My Father,* 108. See also Donna Barton, "Pioneer Medical Practices in the Uintah Basin—1905–1945," copy in possession of author.

43. *A Harvest of Memories,* 365.

44. John Madsen, "History of John Madsen," (1965), copy in possession of the author.

45. Pearce, *Oh My Father,* 106.

46. Madsen, "History of John Madsen," 5.

47. *Roosevelt Standard,* 8 January 1919, 29 January 1919.

48. Barton, "Pioneer Medical Practices," 16, 17. See also *A Harvest of Memories,* 169.

49. Arrington, "Influenza Epidemic," 176.

50. *Roosevelt Standard,* 4 October 1916.

51. *Duchesne Record,* 23 February 1916.

52. "Eleventh Biennial Report of the Secretary of State, 1917–1918," in *Utah State Public Documents, 1917–1918,* vol. 3, 18–19.

53. Stories told the author by Alfred Potter. The author has heard stories of stills in all parts of the county, including Myton, Tabiona, Fruitland, Hanna, Big Hollow in Boneta, and Hancock Cove.

54. *Roosevelt Standard,* 18 October 1918.

55. In the struggle of Utahns to obtain statehood and avoid national political quarrels in the early part of the century, the Mormon church did not actively support prohibition, although many of its leading apostles and members did. When prohibition was passed, most of the Mormon population was pleased. See Larry E. Nelson, "Utah Goes Dry," *Utah Historical Quarterly* 41 (Fall 1973): 341–57.

56. *Uintah Basin Record,* 20 October 1933.

57. *Uintah Basin Record,* 10 November 1933.

58. Ibid.

59. *Salt Lake Tribune,* 8 November 1933.

60. J. Cecil Alter, "Alfalfa Seed Supremacy in Utah," *Improvement Era* 22 (November 1918): 58.

61. Ibid., 56.

62. L.J. Sorenson, "Lygus Bugs in Relation to Alfalfa Seed Production," *Utah Agricultural Experiment Station Bulletin* 284 (1939), 1; John W. Carlson, "Alfalfa-Seed Investigations in Utah," *Utah Agricultural Experiment Station Bulletin* 258 (1935), 1.

63. "Honey Industry in Uintah Basin," *The Happy Homeland,* compiled for distribution at the 1924 Uintah Basin Industrial Convention, Fort Duchesne, Utah, copy in possession of author.

64. Dillman, *Early History of Duchesne County,* 308.

65. *Roosevelt Standard,* 12 April 1922; Dr. Daniel Dennis, interview with John D. Barton, 12 January 1996, transcript in possession of the author.

66. "J.G. Peppard Seed Company," *The Happy Homeland,* pages not numbered.

67. *Duchesne Courier,* 15 June 1923.

68. *Duchesne Courier,* 13 July 1923.

69. Sorenson, "Lygus Bugs," 1.

70. The census of 1920 indicates that Duchesne County produced "other grains and seed" valued at $187,383; the federal agricultural census for 1940 reported the value of alfalfa and red clover seed harvested in the county to be only $16,625. However, five years later, the value of both seeds harvested topped $72,600. See *Fourteenth Census of the United States: Utah,* and *United States Census of Agriculture, 1945: Utah and Nevada,* Part 31 (Washington, D.C.: Government Printing Office, 1946).

71. Dennis, interview.

72. *Roosevelt Standard,* 10 March 1926.

73. *Fourteenth Census of the United States, Utah,*57; *United States Census of Agriculture: 1935* (Washington, D.C.: Government Printing Office, 1936), 2:891.

74. *Roosevelt Standard,* 17 July 1930.

75. *Roosevelt Standard,* 31 October 1918.

76. Quoted in R. Thomas Quinn, "Out of the Depression's Depths: Henry H. Blood's First Year as Governor," *Utah Historical Quarterly* 54 (Summer 1986): 217.

77. Thomas G. Alexander, *Utah: The Right Place* (Salt Lake City: Gibbs Smith, 1995), 323; Miriam Murphy, "Henry H. Blood," in *Utah History Encyclopedia,* ed. Allan Kent Powell, 46; Wayne K. Hinton, "The Economics of Ambivalence: Utah's Depression Experience," *Utah Historical Quarterly* 54 (Summer 1986): 271.

78. Leonard J. Arrington, "The Changing Economic Structure of the Mountain West, 1850–1950," *Utah State University Monograph Series* 10 (June 1963): 54–59.

79. Stout, *History of Utah,* 3:97.

80. Verda Moore, interview with J.P. Tanner, February 1991, Duchesne, Utah, copy in possession of the author.

81. *Uintah Basin Record,* 11 November 1932. The majority of county voters cast their votes for all Democratic candidates except for Arthur V. Watkins (district court judge) and Merrill H. Larsen (county attorney).

82. Arthur Timothy, interview with John D. Barton, 30 September 1994, Altonah, Utah, transcript in possession of author.

83. L.A. Stoddart et al., "Range Conditions in the Uinta Basin Utah," *Utah State Agricultural College Agricultural Experiment Station Bulletin* 283 (October 1938): 13.

84. Ibid., 19.

85. Robert Parson, "Prelude to the Taylor Grazing Act: Don B. Colton

and the Utah Public Domian Committee, 1927–1933," *Encyclia* 68 (1991): 209–32.

86. Stories told the author by Jack D. Barton.

87. Stories told the author by John Wills of Roosevelt, Utah.

88. *United States Census of Agriculture: 1935*, 891; *United States Census of Agriculture: 1945; Utah and Nevada*, 48–49.

89. *Roosevelt Standard*, 17 November 1927, 20 November 1930.

90. *Utah Agricultural Statistics, 1920–1962*, (Logan: Utah State University, 1963), table 132.

91. See *Roosevelt Standard*, 20 February to 20 March 1941.

92. *U.S. Census of Agriculture*, 1936, 891; U. S. Department of Commerce, Bureau of the Census, *United States Census of Agriculture, 1945, Utah and Nevada*, 48–49.

93. *Eighth Biennial Report of the Utah State Board of Agriculture, 1934–1936*, in *Utah Public Documents, 1934–1936* 1:77, Utah State Historical Society Library.

94. *Roosevelt Standard*, 28 June 1934.

95. *Roosevelt Standard*, 12 July 1934, 9 August 1934, 20 September 1934, 18 October 1934, 28 March 1935.

96. *Uintah Basin Record*, 30 November 1934.

97. *Roosevelt Standard*, 9 August 1934.

98. Arthur Timothy, interview.

99. Vera Miles Hansen, interview by John Barton, 3 October 1994, Roosevelt, Utah, transcript in the possession of the author.

100. Arthur Timothy, interview.

101. Louwana Timothy, interview by John Barton, 30 September 1994, Altonah, Utah, transcript in possession of author.

102. Vera Hansen, interview.

103. *Roosevelt Standard*, 30 May 1940.

104. *Uintah Basin Record*, 14 December 1934.

105. *Uintah Basin Record*, 27 January 1933.

106. Vera Hansen, interview.

107. *Uintah Basin Record*, 26 October 1934.

108. *Uintah Basin Record*, 1 February 1935, 24 July 1936; *Roosevelt Standard*, 25 January 1934; Arthur Timothy, interview.

109. *Roosevelt Standard*, 1 March 1935.

110. *Roosevelt Standard*, 8 March 1935.

111. *Roosevelt Standard*, 17 May 1935.

112. *Roosevelt Standard,* 20 September 1935.

113. *Roosevelt Standard,* 6 March 1936, 1 May 1936.

114. *Roosevelt Standard,* 24 April 1936.

115. *Roosevelt Standard,* 8 October 1936.

116. "Statistical Summary of Expenditures and Accomplishments" Utah Emergency Relief Program, 1 October 1935–15 February 1936, Utah State Historical Society Library.

117. *Uintah Basin Record,* 18 October 1935.

118. Utah Department of Public Welfare, "First Biennial Report," (Salt Lake City: State of Utah, 1 July 1936–30 June 1938), 148, Table A-10. The only counties that had a greater number of persons on some type of assistance were counties with significantly greater population, such as Davis, Box Elder, and Cache.

119. *Uintah Basin Record,* 6 October 1933.

120. See, for example, the *Roosevelt Standard,* 27 October 1926. There were several such articles during the next few years.

121. *Roosevelt Standard,* 2 July 1931.

122. *Roosevelt Standard,* 13 February 1936, 16 September 1937.

123. *Uintah Basin Record,* 17 September 1937.

124. See Kenneth W. Baldridge, "Nine Years of Achievement: The Civilian Conservation Corps in Utah," (Ph.D. diss., Brigham Young University, 1971).

125. Ibid., 30.

126. Arthur Timothy, interview. See also Beth R. Olsen, "Utah's CCCs: The Conservators' Medium For Young Men, Nature, Economy, and Freedom," *Utah Historical Quarterly,* 62 (Summer 1994): 261–74.

127. Curtis Robertson, interview with Kim Stewart, Southeastern Utah Project, Utah State Historical Society and California State University, Fullerton, 1971, copy at the Utah State Historical Society Library.

128. *Roosevelt Standard,* 29 September 1938, 23 March 1939, 22 June 1939, and 23 January 1941. See also Moon Lake Electric Association Minutes from 27 September 1938 to present.

129. F.J. Faherty to Moon Lake Electric Association, 25 September 1945, original in possession of Moon Lake Electric Association. Also see letters from Clair Haslem, 14 December 1944; Frank G. Shelley, 26 April 1946; Erna Anderton, 26 May 1941, Files A-32 and A-17 Moon Lake Electric Association offices.

130. Walter E. Atwood, to Duchesne County School District, 10 November 1983.

131. This section on the Toyackers is based on research and writing of

Michelle Miles of Mountain Home, Utah, and is used with her permission. See also the *Roosevelt Standard,* 11 January 1984.

132. Walt Mason Redmond, interview with Michelle Miles, 19 May 1987.

133. Ibid.

134. The total cost of the trip was significant when one considers that the average rural American farmer during the Depression made less than $200 a year. See Carl N Degler, *The New Deal* (New York: New York Times, 1937), 171–79.

135. Walter Mason Redmond, Journal, 15, 19, 27 August 1933.

136. Raymond Wiscombe, Journal, 25 July 1984.

137. Redmond, Journal, 18 August 1933.

138. Ibid., 11 August 1933.

139. Wiscombe, Journal, 25 July 1984.

140. Leon Jorgensen, Journal, August 1933.

141. James F. Secome, to Duchesne County School District, 30 July 1984.

142. United States Department of the Interior Heritage Conservation and Recreation Service, National Register of Historic Places Inventory— Nomination Form, Toyack F.F.A. Chapter House, 2, Utah Historical Records Survey, Works Progress Administration Collection, Utah State Historical Society.

143. Ibid. The Toyack House is listed on the National Register of Historic Places.

144. Atwood, 10 November 1983.

145. Ibid.

146. Ibid. For approximately the last twenty years, the building has been vacant. Roosevelt City and the Duchesne Historical Society are currently involved in trying to raise funds to restore the building as a local museum.

147. Stories told the author by Woodrow Wilkerson, Neola, Utah.

148. See *A Harvest of Memories,* 597.

149. Powell, *Utah History Encyclopedia,* 432–38.

150. *United States Census of Agriculture: 1935,* 891; *United States Census of Agriculture: 1945, Utah & Nevada,* 48–49.

CHAPTER 8

SOCIAL LIFE IN DUCHESNE COUNTY FROM WORLD WAR II TO THE PRESENT

In late September 1940, Myton town baseball team members Frank Adams, Leon Olsen, John Murdock, DeVere Dennis, Alma Murdock, William Sutter, Howard Bingham, Lowell Bingham, Acel Bingham, Clyde Bingham, and Owen Bingham returned from Levan, where the state baseball championship series was played, without having won a game. Although the team was disappointed with the outcome, the *Uintah Basin Record* of 27 September 1940 reported that Alma Murdock was awarded a special prize for striking out fifteen batters in their only game played in Levan.

On the front page of the same issue of the *Uintah Basin Record* was another news item, which was smaller than the baseball team's results but of much more importance. The story was about the appointment of county commissioner Lyle Young and county clerk G.A. Goodrich to the newly established county Selective Service board. Two weeks earlier, Congress had passed the Selective Training and Service Act, which required all men in the country to register with their local Selective Service, or military draft, board. The schools in the county were selected as registration locations, and registration was to begin on 16 October. By the end of the month, 972 Duchesne County men had registered with the county draft board.[1]

The registration of young men older than eighteen was yet another sign of the nation and the county drawing closer to war. (As the nation became more involved in the war, the selective service age was lowered to eighteen.) For several previous years bloody wars had been fought in China, elsewhere in Asia, and in Europe. Many Americans and most county residents paid little attention to the overseas conflicts, however; people throughout the nation and the county were still very concerned about solving the decade-long economic problems.

During the ensuing months, as the European war expanded, more residents of the county became increasingly concerned about the war overseas. Throughout 1941, as conflict overseas became more widespread, a number of young men from the county volunteered for military duty; others were drafted into the armed forces. By December 1941, after Pearl Harbor was attacked by Japan and war was formally declared against the Axis powers, draft quotas were established for each state and county in the nation.

World War II

During the course of World War II, all men in the county eligible for military service were either drafted or given deferments from serving. In Duchesne County deferments were awarded because of physical conditions or the critical need of that person to raise food for the war effort. Of the 972 men in the county that were registered for the draft, only about fifty were deferred.[2]

All who served in World War II from the county were war heroes to their grateful contrymen, and some were so honored by receiving medals for their valor. The most-decorated war hero from the county was Harvey Natches, a Ute Indian son of Edward and Vera Loney Natches and a graduate of Roosevelt High School. In 1942, twenty-two-year-old Natches enlisted in the army and was sent to France, where he served in the European theater as a member of the famous U.S. Second Army armored "Hell on Wheels" division. Later, Pfc. Natches was one of the first American soldiers to enter the Russian-held sector of the German capital, where he and other Americans

Union High School was completed in 1951 and the new sign was added in 1997. (John D. Barton)

were warmly greeted by many Berlin residents. Natches drove in the American convoy of jeeps, trucks, and tanks and was accompanied by Associated Press correspondent Daniel De Luce. Natches was given a set of postcards of Berlin by a street vendor who commented, "It is good to see the Americans again." De Luce wrote that Natches, from "the Ute Indian reservation, who wears a silver star, a bronze star and purple heart with oak leaf cluster, was the first American soldier to enter the center of the capital."[3] Weeks later, Natches was in Potsdam, Germany, when President Harry Truman ordered the use of the atomic bomb against Japan.

Men from Duchesne County were not the only ones to serve their country; eighteen women from the county served in the different branches of the armed forces. For them, it was a bold move to join the military. Like their male counterparts, military service provided many new opportunities to experience life beyond their communities and the Uinta Basin. Some served as nurses; others served in other important positions. Women who served in World War II from Duchesne County included Betty Jo Morrison, Amelia Munz, Thelma De Stephano, Kathleen Jensen, Orba M. Eldredge, Emily

Madsen, Myra A. Iorg, Maxine Fairbanks, Ruby Jenkins, Alice Eggleston, Helen Huish, Vera Johnson, Boneta LeBean, Marlyn Whitmore, Norma Hancock, Ruth Burgess, Audrey Gardner, and Betty Wimmer.

Myra Iorg (Mitchell), for example, volunteered to serve her country in the Marine Corps. When asked why she joined, Myra answered: "All the boys were going off to war and I'd had some training as a welder and women were needed in defense at the time. I didn't want to weld and wanted something more adventuresome so I joined the marines."[4] She trained as an electrician in New York City at Hunter College, a womens' college converted during the war to a training facility. In addition to Myra, her family from Upalco provided four sons to the war effort.

The War at Home

Patriotism characterized life on the home front during World War II. On 2 January 1942, a large front-page headline in the *Roosevelt Standard* read:

FOR A HAPPIER NEW YEAR RESOLUTION

I Resolve To Give *First* Consideration During
1942 To The Defense Effort Of My Country!

Five days after Pearl Harbor, the *Uintah Basin Record* reflected on the feelings and the commitment of the county towards the war:

We are at War. It gives us a feeling of sorrow and apprehension indeed, to realize that this, our Christmas edition, must carry on its first page, mingled with news of the approaching Holiday season, the stirring accounts of the entrance of the United States into the war. . . .

Of this we can feel sure though; whatever the cost, however long the time, America, united, can and will pay the price and give the time to win. . . . We here in the Basin will probably see no great change; we should not be in danger of air raids or other form of attack, we have no air fields, army posts or munitions factories to take on an increased tempo. But we will be affected just the same. Many of our young men are right now in the thick of the conflict either as fighters or civilian workers; we will be called on without delay to start bearing an increased proportion of the costs, we will have to give up many of the things we would like to have, we must begin to produce and conserve far out of proportion to our own requirements. . . . [W]e will do all this cheerfully and freely, secure in the belief that America is great enough and right enough to win what her people will.[5]

During the war, at least half the space of every issue of the local newspapers included coverage of the war, keeping county residents abreast of the conditions at home and overseas. War pictures, stories, reports on progress, and even propaganda were commonplace in the *Roosevelt Standard*. Photos and drawings caricaturing Hitler, Hirohito, and Nazi and Japanese soldiers appeared frequently.

Even before Pearl Harbor, farmers and ranchers of the county were asked to become involved in producing more food. J. Edgar Holder, chairman of the county's agricultural defense board, directed the county's agricultural production effort. In the fall of 1941 Holder urged all farmers to put forth great effort. He conducted a county-wide agricultural survey in which he asked each farmer to prepare a food defense plan, "giving the extent to which his farm can contribute to the county 'Food for Freedom' production goals." In addition, each farmer was asked the number of cows milked the previous year, the number of hogs marketed and slaughtered, the number of cattle marketed, and the number of eggs produced. Holder then asked what each farmer could do "to help meet the [production] goals for these commodities in 1942."[6]

County farmers and ranchers responded to the call to produce more food and fiber for the war effort. For example, on fewer farms (from 1,104 farms in 1940 to 1,044 farms in 1945) more acres were farmed (from some 300,300 acres to over 536,900 acres). Area farmers produced more small grains (oats, winter wheat, and spring wheat)—from a total yield of 30,400 bushels in 1940 to more than 44,600 bushels in 1945. Similarly, there was a sizeable increase in the number of cattle raised during the period—from 23,449 to more than 33,000 head of cattle. Sheep producers increased the number of sheep from 35,400 to over 53,300. The number of milk cows increased by over 600, from 5,695 in 1940 to 6,356 in 1945, and county milk production increased from 2.9 million gallons to 3.7

million gallons. There was an increase in the number of chickens and eggs produced as well.[7]

Throughout the war farmers were continually encouraged to produce more. Local newspaper headlines such as "Farmers Stay On the Farm" and "Fight On The Farm" were common.[8] Even with an increase in agricultural production, however, all Americans were required to accept rations of food, fiber, and energy.

Women of the county took up the slack on the farms. Working side-by-side with their husbands or fathers and with young children of the family, women milked cows, branded and castrated cattle, and planted, irrigated, and harvested crops. All families were encouraged to plant large gardens for their own use. Like their mothers or older sisters during the Depression years, county women of the 1940s were asked to make continued sacrifices, including making their own clothes.

Marvella Bowden Wilkerson recalled living with a small child and without her husband for most of the war. In September 1941, before Pearl Harbor was attacked, she married Woodrow Wilkerson of Neola. Wilkerson provided for his new bride that fall and winter by working at a variety of odd jobs, including topping beets in Axtell, Sanpete County, and hauling coal from Price to the Uinta Basin. The following summer the couple moved to Ogden where he took a job at the newly constructed Hill Field (later renamed Hill Air Force Base). The job only lasted only a few months before he was drafted in December 1942. The next month, while Woodrow was at boot camp, Marvella delivered their first baby.

In August 1943 Woodrow was sent to Europe; he served there until November 1945 when he returned to the Uinta Basin. He and his small family then took up residence in a two-room log cabin on a forty-acre homestead in Neola he had purchased from his parents. Their new house was without electricity or running water. Water came from a cement cistern in front of the cabin that was filled with irrigation water from a nearby ditch.[9] They raised hay and milked a few cows on their forty-acre farm, just one of the many families of the area who struggled through the war years and their immediate aftermath.

Duchesne County Hospital changed its name to Uintah Basin Medical Center in 1984. (John D. Barton)

Rationing and Other War Measures

To control prices, President Roosevelt established the Office of Price Administration in April 1941. After war was declared prices were frozen and various goods were allocated through a system of rationing. County rationing boards were organized to establish and monitor the numerous commodities rationed for agriculture and consumer consumption. For instance, Joseph Moysh, chairman of the Council of Defense for Duchesne County, appointed Lotus Fischer, Tennis Poulson, Hildur W. Johnstun, Ted R. Harmston, Marden Broadbent, Mrs. Letta Robbins, Shirley K. Daniels, Howard Dunn, and Mrs. Joseph Young to the tire-rationing board in January 1942.[10]

As the war progressed, additional commodities and consumer goods of all kinds were added to the rationing system—gas, meat, sugar, cheese, and nylon hosiery, to mention a few. Ammunition was also rationed; purchasing bullets for hunting required a coupon. Everyone was encouraged to conserve, and rationing stamps were common.

Duchesne County farmers and ranchers received proportionally more coupons for gasoline and for rubber tires than did their city cousins. It was critical for the war effort that farmers and ranchers across the county continued to be productive. A small black market in ration coupons and stamps emerged in the county, although the vast majority of residents endeavored to contribute to the war effort by their careful and proper use of stamps and coupons.[11]

Along with rationing came various salvage and recycling efforts. People were encouraged to save grease, rubber, tin, metals, and paper. Labrum's gas station in Roosevelt was the collection center for used tires and other rubber items. In one salvage project the county collected twelve tons of paper.[12] Children in the county participated in saving and collecting scraps of tinfoil. Emptied tin tubes of toothpaste had to be exchanged at stores before a new tube could be purchased. Salvage bins for small items were found in all stores of the county.

Families in the county were encouraged at school and in church to plant "victory gardens" to supplement their food supply and make them less dependant upon national food supplies. Families living in Roosevelt, Myton, and Duchesne were asked to convert some of their lawns to gardens. Articles in the *Roosevelt Standard* encouraged and informed people how to best utilize some of their yard in gardening. The county Future Farmers of America (FFA) assisted people in the tasks of getting started.[13]

Young children, Boy Scout troops, 4-H clubs, and others were asked to collect milkweed pods. Fiber from the milkweed pods was used to fill lifejackets of marines and navy personnel. The *Roosevelt Standard* reminded the children that by collecting the milkweed pods they might be saving the life of their father, older brother, uncle, or friend.[14]

The government asked a great deal of its citizens, and Duchesne County, for the most part, responded with patriotism and sacrifice both at the battlefront and on the home front. Financing the war in part came from the sale of war bonds, and during the course of the war seven bond drives were held. Quotas were set to encourage the purchase of war bonds. Several of the bond quotas rivaled the annual budget of the county; for instance, the county budget for 1942 was $77,091 and the war-bond quota for the year 1944 was $96,100.[15] The county met or exceeded every bond quota except for the last one, which ended after victory was achieved.

One of the important domestic concerns of many Americans following the attack on Pearl Harbor was the prejudice against Americans of Japanese ancestry. A vast majority of these people resided on the Pacific coast, and many government officials saw them as a security risk. As a result, President Roosevelt issued Executive Order 9066, which set in motion the forced removal of more than 125,000 Japanese-Americans from the west coast. The Topaz Relocation Camp, located in western Millard County a few miles northwest from Delta, was created in the summer of 1942, and by September the first of its 8,232 internees began arriving in the bleak environment. At first, Governor Herbert Maw was opposed to housing the Japanese people in the state, but he soon agreed. In March 1942, Duchesne County officials contacted Governor Maw to offer 2,000 acres south of Myton as a work camp for the evacuees.[16] The offer was never accepted by the governor, but work camps located elsewhere in the state were established by the spring of the following year.

Work in the City

As a growing number of the county's young men and women went off to war, an increasing number of other county residents began to leave the county for defense work along the Wasatch Front or elsewhere in the West. Several defense installations and defense industries were begun prior to December 1941 or were greatly enlarged shortly thereafter including Lehi Refactory and U.S. Steel Geneva Works in Utah County; Fort Douglas, Eitel McCullough Radio Tube Plant, Remington Small Arms Plant, and Utah Oil Refinery in Salt Lake County; Clearfield Naval Supply Depot, Hill Field, Ogden Arsenal, and Utah General Depot in Weber County; and Wendover Air Field, Tooele Army Depot, Dugway Proving Grounds, and Deseret Chemical Depot in Tooele County. All needed workers, both men and women, and all paid good wages.

Edward and Opal Barton, for example, moved from their farm in Boneta to Salt Lake City for the winter of 1943. Edward Barton worked in a meat plant and his wife found employment at the Remington Arms plant. Wilma Iorg (Noakes) left Upalco and became a journeyman welder at Hill Air Field.[17] For some county residents, the move to the Wasatch Front was a permanent relocation; many found permanent wages and regular work shifts more attractive than the long hours and uncertainty of making a living on a farm in Duchesne County. During the decade of the 1940s, the county's population decreased by slightly more than 800—which was about a 9 percent decline—from 8,958 to 8,134. Of all the communities in the county with recorded population figures, only Roosevelt showed an increase of population during the war—from 1,264 in 1940 to 1,628 in 1950, a healthy 28.8 percent increase. Other community population figures showed Tabiona with a 24.2 percent decrease, Mt. Emmons down by 24.7 percent, and Arcadia with a 31.7 percent decrease.[18]

Victory and the War's Ending

The continental United States, for the most part, escaped the bombings that devastated Europe and Japan. One of the few bombs to land in the United States is believed to have done so on Blue Bench north of Duchesne. Near the end of the war, the Japanese launched many balloon bombs, hoping the winds would carry them over the United States, where they would land and detonate, creating fear and havoc in America. Only a few made it to land, however; most fell harmlessly into the ocean. The bomb at Blue Bench hit but did not explode. Several local residents called the sheriff's department to investigate the matter; it in turn called on military experts to remove the unexploded bomb.[19]

As victory drew closer for the Allies, the several local newspapers provided their readers with personal accounts of the war through letters received from the war fronts in Europe and the Pacific. More often than not, good news was reported. In May 1945, a month before victory in Europe, Mr. and Mrs. Eugene Harmston of Roosevelt received the good news that their son, Lt. Howard L. Harmston, had been liberated from a prisoner-of-war camp. In February 1944 his B-17 had been shot down over Germany and he had been captured.[20] In June 1945 the *Uintah Basin Record* was pleased to print that Pfc. Alva Defa, son of Mr. and Mrs. Andrew Defa, was also liberated from a German prison camp. He had been missing since December 1944.[21]

Roosevelt City and Duchesne County Library. (John D. Barton)

Pvt. Carl Rhoades of Hanna provided his parents with a report of crops being grown in Italy and Germany: "The days are getting awfully warm now. Some of the grain looks almost ready to cut." Ending on a positive note, he penned, "I hope you have the crops in at home. Don't forget to plant an extra potato, as I may be there to help eat one or two this fall."[22]

A few months later, in August, after Japan surrendered, the county along with the whole nation wildly celebrated. A number of wartime bans were lifted. Joyous songs like "When The Lights Go On Again All Over The World" were heard on the radio. County residents were glad that blackouts and the time of extreme caution for the use of electricity had ended.[23] Those who remained at home also felt a sense of shared victory because of their efforts and sacrifices for the war effort. The return to the county for most soldiers and sailors was still several months off. Sadly, some never returned.

The Post-War Period—1945 to 1960

Peace brought new employment and educational opportunities for returning soldiers and their families. The nation showed its gratitude by providing financial support to veterans who wished to

attend college, and the government also helped finance home building and strengthened health and hospital benefits for veterans and
their wives. Returning soldiers hoped to live the American dream of a
family, education, home, and a good job. However, to attend college
meant leaving Duchesne County. Also, good-paying employment
opportunities were generally only found outside the county and the
Uinta Basin.

For those who remained in the county after the war, the employment opportunities changed, particularly in the county's main economic sector of agriculture. There were fewer farms, but the average
size of farms grew. In 1940, for instance, there were 1,104 farms in
the county, with 300,321 total acres being farmed, for an average of
272 acres per farm. Nineteen years later there were only 743 county
farms, but they had an average size of 754 acres, for well over 500,000
acres total.[24]

War and peace greatly changed the way farmers did their work as
well. In 1940 there were only eighty-four tractors in the county; during the next five years the number increased to 237 tractors. Farm
trucks also increased during the same period, from 137 to 344.[25]
Mechanization of the farm dramatically increased agricultural production in the county, and it also reduced the need for as much extra
labor. According to the U.S. census, in 1950 there were 1,280 agricultural jobs in the county. A decade later, the number had shrunk to
967 agricultural jobs.[26]

As discussed earlier, during the war and for the next several
decades there was a decline in the county's population. The trend was
reversed beginning in the 1970s; by 1980 the population of the
county reached 12,565.[27]

Agriculture production was mixed during the remainder of the
1940s and 1950s. The average hay yield per acre in the county was
near the bottom of the state, only Daggett County's average was
smaller. In 1944 county farmers raised 1.6 tons to the acre; that figure increased slightly fifteen years later to 1.95 tons per acre.[28] The
number of cattle raised in the county continued to increase after
World War II, however. During the Depression, after the government
cattle buy-out in 1934, there were only 9,663 cattle in the county. By
April 1940 there were 23,449, and five years later the number of cattle

had increased to 33,037 head. By 1959 there was a total of 35,034 head of cattle in the county.[29]

Duchesne County dairy farmers ranked sixth in the state in the number of dairy cows—6,356 in 1944; only Cache, Box Elder, Salt Lake, Weber, and Utah counties had more dairy cows. The number of dairy cows had decreased to 5,764 by 1959; however, the total production of whole milk sold increased from 2,229,000 gallons in 1944 to 4,376,000 gallons in 1959, or about 759 gallons per year per cow.[30]

Water was critical to the agricultural production of the county. The construction of the Moon Lake reclamation project during the Depression greatly augmented the irrigation water available; however, with more land being farmed, more irrigation water was needed, as will be discussed later.

New Business and Economic Trends

Thirty-three new businesses opened in Roosevelt alone between 1945 and 1949, including a Sprouse Reitz variety store, the first national-chain store in the county. Perhaps the most important new business was oil. On 12 July 1951 the *Uintah Basin Record* proudly proclaimed the first oil strike in the county: "Duchesne County's First Oil Well 'Blew in' Last Sunday." Located on Ute tribal land, the Duchesne Ute Tribal No. 1 Well was the fourth oil strike made in the Uinta Basin and the sixth strike in Utah since 1948, when oil was struck in Ashley Valley. The well, a small producer of about 240 barrels a day, did not immediately create an oil boom in the county; but it did clearly demonstrate that beneath the surface in the Green River Formation "black gold" was waiting to be tapped. Other oil fields were opened in the Uinta Basin at Red Wash in 1951, Walker Hollow in 1953, and Bluebell in 1955. The discovery also provided new employment for county residents as riggers, roustabouts, truck drivers, and welders, among others.

The real oil boom in the county occurred in part because of overseas events in the mid-1970s. In 1973 the United States supplied massive aid to Israel during the Yom Kippur War. The Organization of Petroleum Exporting Countries (OPEC)—principally composed of Middle East countries—countered, using oil as a political and economic weapon against countries, including the United States, that supported Israel. The price per barrel of Middle East oil increased by more than 400 percent. Coupled with an oil embargo, American oil producers returned to the United States and locations like Duchesne County and the Uinta Basin in search of domestic oil.

The county experienced new construction and expansion of business from 1948 to 1955. The county courthouse in Duchesne was completed in 1953. Union High School was finished in 1951 at a construction cost of $515,500, providing improved educational opportunities for 500 students in grades ten through twelve. The new Altamont High School was completed in 1955, and Duchesne High School was added onto and remodeled in 1958. Each of those schools served about 200 students in grades seven through twelve.[31]

A new state road through Indian Canyon was built and another to Talmage over Blue Bench was paved. The proposal to complete the new road through Indian Canyon was hotly debated. Many in the eastern end of the county wanted the road, linking U.S. Highway 40 with Carbon County, to follow the Nine Mile Route that had been heavily used for over fifty years. After a show of strength by Duchesne City, however, the Indian Canyon route won and the road was completed. Both routes in the late 1950s were passable by truck or a determined auto driver, but not until the work was done on the Indian Canyon route was it considered a good road.

Many county residents recalled frightening drives over the Indian Canyon Road, especially during the winters when deep snows made the road nearly impassable and often stranded travelers before the road was improved. In the early 1970s the Indian Canyon road was completely reworked, widened, and at places the old route was abandoned in favor of better grades and less turns. The Nine Mile Road, although graded and widened, remains unpaved.[32]

By the early 1960s, of $4,215,295 disbursed in wages and salaries in Duchesne County, $2,992,929 was farm income—about half of the wages and salaries in the county. Most of the farm income came from farmers who were sole proprietors; only about $280,000 was paid in wages to farm laborers. Government employment—at the county, state, and federal levels—made great gains in the county, accounting for the second-highest employment sector, with an average of $1,439,037 paid in wages from 1962 to 1966. Salaries and wages

Roosevelt City Building. (John D. Barton)

earned from the wholesale and retail trades followed, with $816,720 for the same period. Contract construction followed with $410,880. Services ranging from hotels to professionals such as physicians and lawyers accounted for $310,417. Communications and public utilities amounted to $192,987, and transportation came to $107,647.[33] Even with the decrease in population in the county, the job market adapted to fit the times.

The Ute Tribe versus the Federal Government

Several other significant events took place in the Uinta Basin which affected a large segment of the county's population. In 1934 Congress passed the Wheeler-Howard (Indian Reorganization) Act, which reversed much of the earlier Dawes General Allotment Act of 1887. The Wheeler-Howard Act provided for the reestablishment of Indian tribes and also provided for Indian self-government. Members of the Ute Tribe in both Duchesne and Uintah counties organized a tribal business committee to govern the affairs of the tribe.

Following World War II, however, there was once again renewed interest in the condition of Indians generally. From this concern Congress formulated a new Indian policy, commonly called "termination." The new arrangement was to end the special Indian-federal relationship that had been reinstated under the Wheeler-Howard Act a decade earlier. Those supporting termination believed that the Indian population would be better served and more quickly integrated into society if special federal government treatment of Indians and tribes was removed and state and local governments provided health, educational, legal, and other public services similar to the those provided non-Indian citizens.

Two congressional advocates for termination were Democrat Reva Beck Bosone, elected to the House of Representatives in 1948, where she served for four years, and Republican Arthur V. Watkins in the U.S. Senate, where he served for twelve years beginning in 1953. In addition, both were strong advocates for reclamation projects in the West. Senator Watkins also served as chair of the Senate select committee that recommended the censure of Wisconsin senator Joseph McCarthy.

Watkins was educated in Uintah County and later attended law school at New York University. After he graduated from NYU, he returned to establish his legal practice in Vernal before moving to the Wasatch Front. Watkins said of the new Indian program of termination:

> Unfortunately, the major and continuing congressional movement towards full freedom was delayed for a time by the Indian Reorganization Act of 1934. . . . Amid the deep social concern of the depression years, Congress diverted from its accustomed policy under the concept of promoting the general Indian welfare. In the post depression years Congress—realizing this change of policy— sought to return to the historic principles of much earlier decades.[34]

Termination proceedings began immediately for a group of mixed-blood Ute Indians after a House of Representatives' resolution was passed in 1953. In 1961 the federal government terminated federal supervision of nearly 500 mixed-blood Indians, most living in the Uinta Basin. However, the pace of termination proceedings slowed beginning in 1960. The pattern then shifted to a new policy of self-determination, with Indian tribes receiving assistance and aid from various federal programs, including the Rural Electrification Administration.

President Richard Nixon moved the Indian program further away from termination to tribal self-determination and direction. In a campaign speech in 1968 Nixon said,

American society can allow many different cultures to flourish in harmony [including Indians who wish] to lead a useful and prosperous life in an Indian environment. . . . Indian future is determined by Indian acts and Indian decisions.[35]

Since the 1970s, Ute Indians collectively have taken a stronger hand in directing their own affairs and managing their collective assets—including more than 1 million acres in Duchesne and Uintah counties, fish and game, and water—through their elected Ute Business Committee.

A second significant event was the creation of an Indian Claims Commission (ICC) by Congress in 1946. The purpose of the ICC was to hear and settle the numerous tribal claims against the United States. Utah attorney Ernest L. Wilkinson represented the Ute people in one case and won a judgement totaling $1.678 million for the loss of nearly 1 million acres of their former lands that were added to the national forests located in Duchesne, Uintah, and Wasatch counties.[36] The dispersal of the judgement was made to the Ute Tribe in three payments over the next few years. In a second judgement, the Uintah and Whiteriver bands were awarded $3.25 million in January 1958. This judgement was for the loss of land taken through the allotment process back to 1903 without the consent of members of the Ute Tribe.[37] Ernest Wilkinson later was appointed president of Brigham Young University and in 1964 ran for the United States senate.

The court's judgements provided a boost to the county's economy over the next several decades. County businessmen were pleased to have additional business when Ute tribal members purchased goods and services locally.

The relationship between the Indian and non-Indian community in Uintah and Duchesne counties was amicable for several decades. But beginning in the 1980s there developed serious differences of opinion over legal jurisdiction and management of fish and game laws, land use, water rights, and the enforcement of laws. Hard feelings were generated, with many county residents expressing anger towards their Indian neighbors. According to some, the Utes had been paid several times for the land, and they asked why the courts should give them jurisdiction of the land now. In addition, the Utes were paid $1,100 each by the federal government in payment of lands taken as Uintah National Forest. A government report adds: "With the aid of this money, some Indians were able to seek out a living on the farm while others spent the money unwisely and received no permanent benefit therefrom."[38] In a law case filed 14 September 1962, The Confederated Bands of Ute Indians v. The United States of America, the Interlocutory Order explains why the Utes filed several suits against the government, even after they had been paid in earlier judgements: "The consideration of $507,662.84 paid to the petitioner for a cession of its lands having a fair market value of $8,500,000.00 was so grossly inadequate as to make the consideration unconscionable." This particular suit was for Uncompahgre Park in Colorado, but the wording sums up the feeling of the Ute people for their loss of lands and the payment they had received for them.

Many members of the tribe retaliated for white opposition by economically boycotting their neighbors, refusing to spend their money in Roosevelt. Legal jurisdictional issues, specifically what constitutes the Uintah-Ouray Indian Reservation, have gone before the courts. The land jurisdiction issues led to the courts ruling in favor of the Indians and establishing the reservation at some 4.1 million acres in three Utah counties. A similar boycott of Roosevelt merchants by Indians in the late 1990s has been centered on jurisdiction for the prosecution of misdemeanors committed by Indians in Roosevelt.

Polio

Between 1948 and 1953 a serious health crisis—poliomyelitis, or infantile paralysis—swept the nation and the state, crippling and killing young and old alike. In 1951 there were more than 455 cases reported in the state, most victims living in the counties along the Wasatch Front. Dr. George A. Spendlove, state health director, characterized the polio outbreak as a "borderline epidemic."[39] Warnings about the disease's early symptoms and talk of hoped-for cures for the dreaded virus were common topics of discussion among citizens and in the local newspapers.

Dorothy Stevenson (Hicken) of Mountain Home contracted one of the few cases of polio in the county when she was two years old. After several visits to doctors in Vernal, Price, and Salt Lake City, she was admitted to the Shriners Crippled Childrens Hospital in Salt Lake City. She was isolated for over three months in a polio ward for recovery and when she was finally allowed to return home had to wear braces and do exercises to strengthen her legs. Dorothy recalled that she did not like to do the exercises or wear the leg braces. Her family bribed her to wear them. She said: "I was very lucky. I remember kids in iron lungs in the hospital. When kids died they never told us. They just said they had been moved."[40]

Periodic March of Dimes campaigns were held in the county to raise money for research and to aid those afflicted. Hope through vaccination came in 1953 when a vaccine developed by Dr. Jonas Salk proved to be effective. The county along with the whole nation was hopeful that the disease could be controlled and perhaps eliminated.[41] For the next several years immunization clinics located in the county were advertised in the local newspapers. The local public campaign was successful. There were few cases of polio in the county in the 1950s.

Duchesne County Hospitals

The first hospital in the county was located in Roosevelt and was run by Drs. J.E. Morton and W.J. Browning. Established in June 1914, the hospital's capacity was twelve beds.[42] However, the Roosevelt hospital, like many others in the state, was private. The activities of the Roosevelt hospital are sketchy over the next several decades. In March 1937 a group of citizens organized themselves to secure funds to build and equip a new hospital. W. Russell Todd was appointed to head the building committee. Unable to raise funds locally, Todd and the others turned to the LDS church, which agreed to fund 60 percent of the new hospital and equipment; the community agreed to raise the remaining 40 percent.

Construction for the new hospital began in April 1939, and in

December 1941 the hospital was completed. With war breaking out, it was difficult to secure the necessary medical equipment for the hospital until April 1944, at which time it was officially opened. The community raised in cash and labor contributions more than $16,400 for the twenty-one-bed hospital with one operating room.

The new hospital was incorporated in April 1944 as a non-profit corporation. Ray E. Dillman, William H. Rupple, Ernest Morrison, Leandrew J. Gilbert, and Edwin L. Murphy were selected as the hospital's first board of directors. Mrs. Martha Shanks, formerly the county nurse, was hired as superintendent of the hospital.[43]

A quarter-century later the Mormon church wanted to divest itself of all its hospitals. At about the same time, the Roosevelt Hospital's board of directors believed it was necessary to build a newer and larger hospital. Alva Snow, newly called stake president of the Roosevelt LDS Stake in 1966, met with county and city officials as well as with LDS church authorities from Salt Lake City to begin talks on a new hospital. LDS stake leaders over the previous twenty years had also served on the hospital board of directors. The doctors in the area were hopeful that a new facility could be built to improve the region's medical care.

The Roosevelt LDS Stake owned property on Third West and Third North that all agreed would be an excellent location for a new hospital. With Snow's recommendation, the church-owned land was pledged if the county agreed to raise the necessary funds to build the new hospital. The county held a special bond election held in October 1966, and voters approved a bond for $500,000. In addition to issuing bonds, $350,000 for construction purposes came from the hospital cash reserves and accounts receivable. To save some costs, some of the equipment from the old hospital was moved to the new hospital after it was completed. The planned hospital also qualified for $308,000 in federal assistance. For many years the old Roosevelt hospital had provided 50 percent of the outpatient medical care for Ute people living in Duchesne and Uintah counties.[44] Another $100,000 was promised by the federal Public Health Service for construction of a wing of the new hospital to serve as an Indian outpatient clinic. With the funding flowing in at a rate that surprised and pleased those working on the new hospital project, the dream became a reality and the new thirty-one-bed hospital was completed in 1969.[45]

In 1984 the Duchesne County Hospital was remodeled and enlarged, bringing it to a forty-two-bed capacity. The name also was changed at that time to the Uintah Basin Medical Center (UBMC). It currently hosts fourteen physicians, up from the three physicians who served the community in the early 1960s. For a rural county hospital, it offers an outstanding record of service.

The west end of the county became concerned with the lack of medical care in the area following World War II. Appeals went out for doctors to establish their medical practice in the west end of the county; when this was unsuccessful, it was recognized that a medical facility was needed to attract doctors and provide medical care. In 1951 a group of citizens headed by the Duchesne Lion's Club decided to build a hospital. Financial help was asked from the LDS church as well as from other institutions and organizations. A problem in many people's minds, however, was there were too few residents to support a hospital. Not to be deterred, the citizens of the west end agreed that they would build their own hospital.

For the next three years numerous organizations held banquets, organized community fund-raisers, and pitched in to pour concrete, hammer nails, and paint. In 1955, for example, over $1,300 was raised for the community hospital by the Presbyterian church of Myton, the Duchesne Mothers Club, the Duchesne Lions Club, Salt Lake Pipeline Company, Duchesne County Business and Professional Women's Club, the Duchesne American Legion, the Duchesne American Legion Auxiliary, and Hi-Land Dairy.

The Duchesne Health Center opened its doors in early January 1956 with much fanfare. "There is nothing but the highest kind of praise due to the men and women of Duchesne and immediate vicinity, who have sweat and worked together over the years . . . to keep their project moving," reported the *Uintah Basin Record* at the time of the hospital's opening. The first officials of the new medical facilities included George C. Kohl, president; Vernal Bromley, vice-president; Clifton C. Mickelson, secretary-treasurer; and B.A. Jacoby, Walter Nelson, John Munz, and Chester Lyman, directors.[46] As part of the grand opening of the much-needed hospital, numerous gifts were donated to the first baby born in the facility. Gifts for the new-born, its parents, and its grandparents included a theatre pass, cash, baby supplies; an oil change, car wash and lubricant job, and twenty-five gallons of gasoline, a steak dinner, a hair cut and shave to the father, and a pair of nylon hose to the mother. A few weeks later Mrs. Jean Saddreth of Mountain Home gave birth to the first baby born in the new hospital; days later, twins were born at the medical facility.

Shortly after the hospital opened it became a participant hospital in the statewide Blue Cross hospital plan. However, like other small community hospitals in the state, the Duchesne City hospital fell on hard financial times and by the early 1960s had closed its doors.

Life in Duchesne County

In the latter part of the 1950s television entered the homes of millions of Americans. In 1957 test signals were conducted for television reception in Duchesne County. The signals were sufficiently strong that some homes were able to receive programs from one of the channels in Salt Lake City. Four years later a new tower was installed at LaPoint Hill that improved reception and provided for a broader coverage of all three major network television stations in Salt Lake City.[47] Now county residents could watch the evening news and such programs as Lawrence Welk, Ed Sullivan, and Bonanza. County teens danced to American Bandstand, and the residents of the county became more integrated with the rest of the nation.

With nightly television viewing taking place in many homes in the county, many residents of the area took pride in the fact that one of their own had invented television. Philo T. Farnsworth was a leader in conceiving the idea of transmitting moving pictures on air waves. Born in a hamlet in Beaver County, Farnsworth lived in Mountain Home during part of his youth before has family moved to Idaho, where he graduated from high school. Many residents of Mountain Home are related to Farnsworth.

The hard times of the Great Depression and World War II encouraged the organization of civic organizations, social clubs, and professional groups in the county, many of which promoted and encouraged new developments and county improvements. The

Duchesne County Jaycees and the Lady Jaycees, for example, were important supporters of the annual Duchesne County Stampede and accompanying parade. The Duchesne County Lions Club joined with the business organization the Duchesne Gateway Club to promote tourism and summer recreation in the county, including fishing, hiking, and hunting. The Gateway Club in 1937 worked hard but unsuccessfully to have the Utah State Prison relocated to the county. The Duchesne County Business and Professional Women's Club promoted women's business and professional activities. These and other organizations carried their activities into the 1950s and the decades that have followed.

One of the most unusual local promotional activities was the horse versus man race held in October 1957 and organized by the Bullberry Boys Booster Club of Duchesne County. The local chapter of the club was organized to bring positive attention to the county and to work with local business and commercial interests to encourage and build morale and community pride.

The planned 157-mile race soon caught the attention of local, state, and national media. Two county residents—seventy-one-year-old rancher Roy Hatch and eighteen-year-old oil-field worker DeRay Hall—were pitted against two Brigham Young University track stars—Shim Bok Suk from Korea and Albert Gray from New York. Suk later was replaced by eighteen-year-old Terry Jensen from Idaho Falls. Hatch rode a thoroughbred quarterhorse and Hall rode a mustang that had been caught two years earlier in Wild Horse Canyon. The race began at the Brigham Young Monument in downtown Salt Lake City and went south to Orem, where runners and horsemen turned east through Provo and Daniels canyons and then through Strawberry Valley. The race ended in Roosevelt, where Duchesne County Sheriff Lorin Stevenson and Roosevelt Mayor Paul Murphy judged the winner of the race.

Riding and running day and night through rain and some snow, Roy Hatch and DeRay Hall completed the race in 57 hours, 9 minutes. They were greeted in Roosevelt by a crowd of over 6,000 people. Neither of the long-distance runners finished the race; Al Gray dropped out at Deer Creek and Terry Jensen stopped at Current Creek. Hatch said of the race: "I never had such a thrill as when someone from Salt Lake City called me Roy Rogers." Hatch praised his horse by adding: "The only thing is, I don't think Trigger [Roy Rogers's horse] could have made the run."[48]

Hearing of the race, other runners of national standing challenged the horsemen to a similar race in 1958. The results were the same—the horses finished with ease and none of the runners completed the course. Steward Paulick, winner of the race, covered the distance in 29 hours and 20 minutes. A third race was organized in 1959; this time the race was between men and women horse riders. Dorothy Luck of Neola won the race and a $3,000 cash prize. She covered the 157 miles in just over sixteen hours on a thoroughbred horse.

County Political Concerns

Between the end of World War II and the 1960s, the majority of voters in the county shifted their political allegiance from the Democratic party to the Republican party. In the presidential election of 1952, for example, most county voters placed their mark next to World War II general and hero Dwight D. Eisenhower. Eisenhower received 1,969 votes and his Democratic challenge Adlai Stevenson received 1,242 votes. Four years earlier, the county and the state had voted to return President Harry Truman to the White House.[49] The 1952 election was the first county Republican victory in a national race since Herbert Hoover was elected in 1928.

County voters deviated from voting for the Republican party's presidential candidate in 1964 when the majority of them, like most other voters of the state, voted for President Lyndon B. Johnson. Johnson garnered 1,320 votes from county voters to Republican presidential candidate Barry Goldwater's 1,251 votes. Democratic candidate for governor Calvin Rampton and Democratic candidate for the U.S. Senate Frank Moss both won a majority of the votes in the county as well as receiving a majority of votes from the rest of the state.

Elections for local offices generally favored the candidates with the most common-sense answers to the county's problems. The candidate's integrity and personality counted for much more than party affiliation.[50]

Numerous articles and political cartoons in the county newspapers spoke out strongly against communism and socialism during the Cold War, reflecting the political views of the residents of the county, which echoed national sentiment. This was particularly the case during the McCarthy era of the early 1950s, but even after the McCarthy era ended in the mid-1950s, these articles continued well into the 1960s. Throughout the nation and in the county there was much concern about the Cold War, which pitted the United States and its allies against the Soviet Union and other communist countries in political battles for global control that often threatened to erupt into full-scale war, which could mean mutual nuclear annihilation. During the early months of 1956, for example, there was much activity in the county related to civilian defense. In March the *Uintah Basin Record* happily reported that the "Sky Watchers" in Myton had just completed building a civilian defense watchtower on top of the fire station "so they can better carry out" their duties watching the skies for airplanes.[51]

Concerned because members of the Duchesne City Ground Observation Corps lacked such an observation tower, the newspaper in an editorial urged the community of Duchesne to build such a structure and also issued a plea for volunteers to serve a few hours a week.[52] Weeks later, the *Uintah Basin Record* was pleased to announce that the first all-Indian ground observation corps in the United States had been organized at Whiterocks by T.H. York, Baptist minister at Gusher. Wilson Taveapont was chief observer, with fourteen volunteers including women and children involved in watching for airplanes.[53]

The earliest years of the Cold War prompted extensive prospecting and mining of uranium in the county. In the spring of 1954 the national Sandia Mining and Development Company reported opening the Canary Bird, Eagle's Nest, and Eureka uranium mining claims in the area and was working on fifteen other claims located on the South Myton Bench. The mining company reported that one of the claims contained a vein thirty-four inches thick, although it thinned considerably. Larger discoveries of uranium ore elsewhere in the state and in the West, however, diverted national attention from the promised uranium mining boom in the county.

While the rest of the nation moved toward the turbulent decade of the 1960s, marked with rock and roll music, youth protest, and radical hair and clothing styles, Duchesne County remained in the backwaters. News of the race riots in Cleveland, Detroit, Chicago, and Newark, the growing protest and drug culture of hippies and flower children, and the civil rights protests on the Mall in the nation's capital, in Birmingham, Alabama, and elsewhere came each evening on the nightly television news programs. The music many teenagers listened to gave their parents and church leaders concern, but most local youth continued to embrace the social values of their parents and community. On at least one occasion when a male student's hair was considered too long, several of his peers at Altamont High School gave him a forced haircut.

Many in the county grew increasingly concerned with the perceived menace of communism in Southeast Asia, Cuba, and elsewhere. Particularly distressing was the increasing conflict in Vietnam. The more conservative residents of the county believed it was better to fight and stop communism in Southeast Asia than to eventually have to fight communists on the beaches of California.

Young men of the country were once again called upon to fight a war overseas. Unlike some of their counterparts elsewhere who resisted the draft by burning their draft cards or fleeing to Canada, most male high school graduates of the county served willingly. Some county residents of draft age received deferments to attend college or to serve LDS missions. Bruce Peatross, a Vietnam veteran from Duchesne who was drafted in 1968, reflected on the local attitude towards the war and the draft: "There were no draft dodgers or real complaints from those who were drafted. It was something we had to do for our country and we went and did it."[54]

While many were drafted, others like Ronny Dean Roberts from Roosevelt enlisted; Roberts joined the Marine Corps in July 1966. In November 1967 Roberts was sent to Vietnam, where he became the first casualty from the county, killed Thanksgiving Day 1967, when his floating, tracked vehicle used to transport troops from ship to land was sunk. Roberts was credited with saving eighteen of his buddies' lives before he drowned. It was later determined that the vehicle had been sabotaged. He was posthumously awarded the Purple Heart and Medal of Valor. His father and uncles had fought in World War II, and he felt that fighting in Vietnam was necessary for freedom's cause.[55] The Roberts family, like most county residents during the Vietnam War, supported the government and the war.

The counterculture that sprang up in many parts of the nation during the 1960s had little impact on Duchesne County. The county school district undertook an active prevention program against drug use. Movies and documentaries were shown in health classes, and the program was bolstered by local ecclesiastical leaders and established family standards. Those few teenagers who did use drugs smoked marijuana or popped various pills; hard-core drug use was virtually unknown in the county.

Teens who wanted to kick up their heels usually did so by consuming beer or occasionally hard liquor. Alcohol was difficult to purchase by underage consumers, however. Most residents in the small tight-knit communities of Duchesne County felt a shared responsibility for the youth of their communities; not only did local storeowners refuse to sell beer to teenagers, there also were few stores in the county or in the Uinta Basin that sold beer. Only state-owned liquor stores in Roosevelt and Duchesne sold packaged beverages. In 1980 there were two state-owned liquor stores and one restaurant licenced to sell alcohol in the county. The annual per capita alcohol sales for 1979 was between twenty and thirty dollars.[56]

In 1957 the county commission had debated whether they should grant a beer license to a store in Neola. A decade later the same question was raised when a store in Altamont applied for a license to sell beer.[57] The rapid increase of population in the late 1970s and the growth of convenience stores in the county later in the decade has made it easier for residents and tourists to purchase beer.

Growing Pains

In October 1973 the Organization of Petroleum Exporting Countries (OPEC) declared an embargo on the shipment of crude oil to those countries who had been supporting Israel in its conflict with Egypt. The Arab oil embargo triggered a renewed search for oil in the United States.

Late in 1940s the Upper Colorado River Compact was approved

and Congress approved the Colorado River Storage Project, which authorized the construction of massive reclamation projects on the upper Colorado River. In the mid-1960s project design and engineering work was well underway and would be followed with construction of elements of the Central Utah Project, Utah's segment of the Colorado River Storage Project.

These two events resulted in a rapid increase in population in the county, matched only by the opening of the Uintah Reservation in 1905. In both instances, large numbers of families—not just single men—immigrated into the county. The population of the city of Duchesne, for example, increased 42 percent during the 1960s; it increased even more—53 percent—during the decade of the 1970s.[58]

The county's experience with the exploding population was mixed. Many LDS churches were remodeled and new ones were built. This was also true of the schools at the onset of the county's increase of population. In Roosevelt, the water and sewer systems were modernized and expanded, new wells dug, and additional water added. New sewage treatment ponds were built south of Roosevelt that more than doubled the city's sewer capacity.

Other public services such as law enforcement and health departments scrambled to meet the bulging population needs. Contractors built housing. Total housing units in the county in 1970 numbered 2,348; a decade later the number of housing units jumped by nearly 91 percent to 4,478 units. During the decade of the 1980s total housing units in the county continued to grow—this time to 5,860, an increase of nearly 31 percent over the preceding decade.[59]

The percentage rate of growth of new housing units placed the county sixth in the state in the decade of the 1970s, exceeded only by Daggett County (140.8 percent), Washington County (121.6 percent), Kane County (113.1 percent), Emery County (109.7 percent), and Summit County (103.9 percent). The overall rate of housing growth for the state for the decade was 55.2 percent. The county ranked seventh in the rate of change (30.9 percent) for total housing units during the decade of the 1980s. The average percentage of change for the state for the decade was slightly more than 24 percent.

Oil exploration and production figures are hard to determine before the 1980s; but, with the boom, seemingly overnight hundreds of rigs were drilling around the clock, each with a crew of several men, support crews, and services. Motels and restaurants could barely meet customer needs; often they were crowded to capacity and beyond. Traffic reached record volume as hundreds of new residents and oil-related businesses used the roads and highways. When the oil boom began there was not a single traffic light in the county; however, the Utah Department of Transportation soon added stoplights at Roosevelt's main intersections.

Enrollment in the schools of the county nearly doubled. Each of the grades in the schools in Altamont and Duchesne, for example, rose from an average of twenty-five students per grade to nearly twice that number. The schools in Roosevelt experienced similar increases in student enrollments. In desperation, the school district bought trailer houses and remodeled them into classrooms to augment the number of available classrooms. The average daily enrollment in the school district for 1959 was 2,140; during the 1972–73 school year the average daily enrollment jumped to 3,124 students. Daily enrollment for all grades continued upward, reaching a peak of 4,132 students during the 1983–84 school year. During the 1990–91 school year the average daily enrollment was 3,865 students.[60]

For the first time in the county's history, jobs were plentiful and wages were good. New graduates from high school could double their former teachers' salaries by going to work on oil rigs. Support businesses for the oil industry, including construction companies, roustabouts, tool companies, pipeline companies, oil hauling companies, and several others, added jobs to the region. The boom times brought sudden and new prosperity along with the growth.

In 1962 there were sixty-nine people employed in the mining sector, which also included oil and natural-gas production. Thirteen years later, the number of people employed in mining had increased fifteenfold to 1,059—the peak figure for the period from 1959 to 1990. Reflecting the increases in population and the work being done by the Bureau of Reclamation, government employment in the county jumped from 541 in 1962 to 1,402 in 1985.[61] Energy and water-reclamation projects enabled many of the Uinta Basin's high school graduates to remain in the county and find employment; also, many former residents returned to reestablish their homes in the county.

Many local businesses including grocers, builders, auto dealers, retail stores, movie theaters, and drug stores expanded and hired additional help. New stores and businesses sprang up; they included repair shops, tire stores, gas stations, and convenience stores.

The explosive population growth in the county as a result of energy exploration and development and the construction and management of reclamation projects brought some change to the county, although many newcomers were from Utah. By 1971 county membership in the LDS church reached more than 6,600.[62] Membership in several of the other denominations also grew, and several new congregations were formed. Growth continued in the 1980s, and by 1990 there were more than 9,600 local LDS church members.[63]

The Salt Lake Diocese of the Roman Catholic church sent Bishop Duane Hunt to Vernal to preside over St. John's Parish in 1922. In 1938 Roosevelt was made a mission to the Vernal parish, and in 1940 a rectory hall was built and Father Maurice Fitzgerald was appointed to preside over the new St. Helen's Church. In 1990 there were three Roman Catholic churches in the county and the total number of adherents was 250.[64]

The Episcopal church has had a long-established presence in the county, although church membership had declined to fourteen by 1971. On 2 July 1944 the Roosevelt Baptist Church was organized with eight members. The group rented the Episcopal church for their Sunday services. They completed their own church in 1947. In 1971 membership in the Southern Baptist Convention numbered 237; in 1990 there were 159 members. Other faiths represented in the county include the Christian Assembly of God, Jehovah's Witnesses, Lutheran, Presbyterian, and Harvest Fellowship churches, among others.[65] The Indian population have joined various faiths, with many choosing to follow their Native American Religion. The several faiths have for the most part lived harmoniously in the communities of the county.

The economic forces driving the growth of population in the county during the last quarter of the twentieth century have been the development of water, energy, and land. Political issues of ownership and management of these resources are sometimes hotly contested. These natural resources not only are important to the county's economic vitality but are increasingly part of the larger state and national economic pictures.

Other important developments have occurred that also have helped break the county's geographical isolation. These have included improved and new roads, access to information and entertainment, and the development of post-high school educational opportunities. These developments have brought more economic diversity and have generally improved the living conditions of residents of the county.

ENDNOTES

1. *Roosevelt Standard,* 17 October 1940.

2. See Dillman, *Early History of Duchesne County,* 486–547.

3. Quoted in *Salt Lake Tribune,* 7 July 1945. See also *Roosevelt Standard,* 5 July 1945, and *Beehive History* 17 (1991): 23. Following the war, Natches returned to Duchesne County and became a cattle rancher. He later served on the Ute Tribal Business Committee and was superintendent of the tribe's water department. He died in 1980 and was buried with full military honors at the Fort Duchesne Cemetery.

4. Myra Iorg Mitchell, interview with John Barton, 3 December 1996, Upalco, Utah, transcript in possession of the author. See *Early History of Duchesne County,* 486 - 547.

5. *Uintah Basin Record,* 12 December 1941.

6. *Uintah Basin Record,* 24 October 1941.

7. See *United States Census of Agriculture, 1945, Utah and Nevada.*

8. *Roosevelt Standard,* 12 February 1942, 31 December 1942.

9. Marvella Wilkerson, interview with John Barton, 12 November 1994, Duchesne, Utah, transcript in possession of the author. In all the interviews the author has done with women who were on farms during the war years, they share their experiences as commonplace for everyone they knew.

10. *Uintah Basin Record,* 2 January 1942.

11. *Roosevelt Standard,* 30 April 1942, 3 December 1942, 18 March 1943, 19 October 1944. Hunters were warned of bullet scalpers who charged excessive prices for hunting ammunition. A price list of what ammunition should cost was printed to protect those who might otherwise be taken advantage of.

12. *Roosevelt Standard,* 8 March 1945.

13. See *Roosevelt Standard,* 19 March 1942 and 29 April 1943 for two of many such articles.

14. *Roosevelt Standard,* 16 November 1944.

15. *Roosevelt Standard,* 1 January 1942, 27 January 1944.

16. *Roosevelt Standard,* 26 March 1942.

17. Allan Kent Powell, *Utah Remembers World War II* (Logan: Utah State University Press 1991), 138–39.

18. See 1940 and 1950 United States census records,various pages.

19. Jack D. Barton, interview with John Barton, 9 December 1994, Altonah, Utah, transcript in possession of author. Mention of this bomb is conspicuously absent from the local paper. The authorities likely did not want to create local fear.

20. *Uintah Basin Record,* 25 May 1945.

21. *Uintah Basin Record,* 1 June 1945.

22. Ibid.

23. Wilkerson, interview.

24. *Utah Agricultural Statistics,* (Salt Lake City: Utah Department of Agriculture/U.S. Department of Agriculture, 1971), tables 21, 14, 15.

25. *United States Census of Agriculture: 1945, Utah and Nevada,* 25.

26. *Utah Agricultural Statistics,* table 36.

27. Allan Kent Powell, ed., *Utah History Encyclopedia,* 433.

28. *Utah Agricultural Statistics,* table 83.

29. *Roosevelt Standard,* 9 August 1934; *Utah Agricultural Statistics,* table 126.

30. *Utah Agricultural Statistics,* table 127.

31. Duchesne County School Board, Minutes, 1951–1958, Duchesne County School District Offices, Duchesne, Utah. Union High School is one of the few schools in the state that serves more than one county. It was built by agreement between Uintah and Duchesne County School Districts to serve eastern Uintah and western Duchesne County residents.

32. *Roosevelt Standard,* 11 August 1949, 1 September 1949, 11 December 1949, 12 July 1951, 13 September 1951, 30 April 1953, 4 February 1954, 10 June 1954, 27 June 1957.

33. J. Whitney Hanks, "Personal Income In Utah Counties: 1962–1966," University of Utah Bureau of Economic and Business Research, 22.

34. Quoted in Lyman Tyler, *A History of Indian Policy* (Washington, D.C.: U.S. Department of Interior, 1973), 152.

35. Ibid., 217–18.

36. *Roosevelt Standard,* 25 October 1951.

37. The Uintah Ute Indians of Utah v. The United States of America, 14 May 1954. Also see *Uintah Basin Standard,* 10 January 1958. Note that the *Roosevelt Standard* changed its name to the *Uintah Basin Standard* with the first edition of the paper in 1957.

38. See *Three Year Report To The Commissioner Of Indian Affairs, Bureau Of Indian Affairs, U.S. Department Of Interior, By The Ute Indian Tribe Of The Uintah And Ouray Reservation, Utah* (21 August 1951–21 August 1954), 5.

39. *Salt Lake Tribune,* 19 July 1951.

40. Dorothy Stevenson Hicken, interview with John Barton, Roosevelt, Utah, 9 June 1997, transcript in possession of the author.

41. For just a few of many mentions of polio in the local paper see *Roosevelt Standard,* 18 January 1951, 12 January 1953, 8 October 1953, 31 December 1953.

42. Dillman, *Early History of Duchesne County,* 369.

43. Ibid., 377–81; *Uintah Basin Standard,* 25 August 1944; Tom Vitelli, *The Story of Intermountain Health Care* (Salt Lake City: Intermountain Health Care, 1995), 53–54.

44. *Uintah Basin Standard,* 6 October 1966; Alva Snow, interview with John Barton, 11 November 1994, Roosevelt, Utah, transcript in possession of author. Congress had approved a grant for an Indian clinic in Alaska that could not meet the construction deadline within the fiscal year, so the $308,000 approved funds were given to Duchesne County if they could start soon enough to meet the time conditions for the year.

45. *Uintah Basin Standard,* 2 January 1969; Snow, interview. Snow played a major role in many areas of the county's development including the Duchesne County Hospital, Utah State University Uintah Basin Campus, Zion's Bank, the Moon Lake Electric building in Roosevelt, and the development and expansion of LDS church facilities in the area. Under his direction, at a time when LDS church members had to put up approximately 40 percent of the funds, three new chapels were built, and every existing church building in the stake was added onto or remodeled.

46. *Uintah Basin Record,* 19 January 1956, 9 February 1956, 19 April 1956, 17 May 1956.

47. *Uintah Basin Standard,* 14 February 1957, 28 February 1957, 15 June 1961.

48. *Uintah Basin Standard,* 21 November 1957; *Salt Lake Tribune,* 18 November 1957.

49. The county election results for president in 1948 included 1,588 votes for Truman and 1,266 for Dewey. The state voters voted in like man-

ner—Truman received 149,151 votes to Dewey's 124,402 votes. See Wayne Stout, *History of Utah, 1930–1970* (Salt Lake City: n.p., 1971), 3:423.

50. *Uintah Basin Standard,* 9 November 1950, 6 November 1952.

51. *Uintah Basin Record,* 29 March 1956.

52. *Uintah Basin Record,* 26 April 1956.

53. *Uintah Basin Record,* 10 May 1956.

54. Bruce Peatross, interview with John Barton, 25 January 1996, transcript in possession of the author. Peatross was wounded in the legs while in Vietnam and sent back to the states to recover; he was released from the service in 1970. He was the only one from the area he knew of who was wounded.

55. Terry Roberts, interview with John Barton, 17 December 1996, Roosevelt, Utah, transcript in possession of the author.

56. *Atlas of Utah,* 234–35.

57. *Uintah Basin Standard,* 7 February 1957. Despite protest from local residents, the stores were granted beer licenses.

58. Powell, *Utah History Encyclopedia,* 434–35.

59. *Statistical Abstract of Utah, 1993* (Salt Lake City: University of Utah Bureau of Economic and Business Research, 1993), 346.

60. See *Statistical Abstract of Utah,* various years.

61. Ibid.

62. *Atlas of Utah,* 140.

63. Martin B. Bradley et al., *Churches and Church Membership in the United States, 1990* (Atlanta: Glenmary Research Center, 1992), 393.

64. Ibid.

65. Ibid.

CHAPTER 9

WATER: LIFEBLOOD OF THE COUNTY

One of the most significant factors of Western history is the general aridity of the West and the struggle of westerners to make the dry lands productive and life-sustaining.[1] As it has been in the twentieth century, water will likely prove to be the most contested Western resource of the twenty-first century. In the West more court battles between regions and states, and even more fights between neighbors, have occurred over water than over any other issue. The effort expended to create the water system now in use in Duchesne County is beyond doubt the largest expenditure of time, work, and money that has gone into building up of the region. When one includes the construction of early canals and ditches, use of the high mountain lakes, the building of massive tunnels and reservoirs, the service roads built to these projects, and the construction of buildings to house those who came to the area as workers, only the highway system and the development of the oil fields can begin to rival the impact of water development in the county.

Following the great model of California's Imperial Valley and its agricultural value with a reliable source of water, elsewhere in the

301

West economic development and agricultural growth grew increasingly dependent upon finding and developing reliable sources of water. National and regional political and economic forces began to coalesce over the development of water resources at the turn of the twentieth century. Annual irrigation conferences strongly supported by Utah and other western states urged national attention to the development of water in the West. In 1902 Congress responded with the passage of the Newlands Act, which created a revolving fund for the development of reclamation projects and the establishment of what soon became known as the Bureau of Reclamation.

The unbridled Colorado River created problems for Imperial Valley farmers of southern California at the turn of the century. Farmers and land promoters began preparing plans and schemes to protect the fertile farmland of the Colorado River delta and at the same time divert more water to more undeveloped land. California water users pressed their claims of prior rights to nearly all of the Colorado River water. Others, including the Mexican government, also made claims to the river, however. The claims to the water were partially resolved in the courts, and federal court cases and further developments of the Colorado River brought the management and use of the river into the national political arena.

In 1922 the Fall-Davis Report, considered by many as the "Bible of the Colorado River," prepared the agenda for later conferences and multistate and international water agreements.[2] At a conference held in Santa Fe, New Mexico, representatives from the states of the Colorado River Basin—Wyoming, Colorado, Utah, Arizona, New Mexico, Nevada, and California—gathered to hammer out an agreement to water claims and management of the Colorado River. What emerged was the Colorado River Compact, an agreement among all of the states associated with the Colorado River to divide its waters between "upper" and "lower" basin states and Mexico.

Utahns were quick to point out the state's need for upper Colorado River water. In 1925, at hearings before the United States Senate Committee on Irrigation and Reclamation, Governor George Dern emphasized the importance of the Uinta Basin in the larger programs of the development of the Colorado River and the economic development of Utah. "The most important part of the

Rock Creek below Upper Still-Water Reservoir. (John D. Barton)

Colorado drainage in Utah is what we know as the Uintah Basin. This basin is a potential empire in itself," he stated.[3] Governor Dern explained further that the Uinta Basin including Duchesne County contained untapped hydrocarbon resources, vast timber reserves, and vast tracts of agricultural land that were central to the economic development of the state.

For more than 150 years, the development of the Uinta Basin had been neglected or overlooked. Catholic friars Domínguez and Escalante recognized the agricultural potential of large areas of the basin, but the Spanish failed to return to colonize the basin. Brigham Young overlooked the possibilities of the Uinta Basin in the 1860s following an unfavorable report. He and Indian agents deemed the Uinta Basin a perfect location for an Indian reservation. However, by the turn of the twentieth century, the Uinta Basin (and future Duchesne County) was very much a desired region, largely because of its water resources.

Settlement by whites in the county represented a planned and pragmatic effort to develop the water resources of the region. Homesteaders were determined to make the Uinta Basin "blossom as a rose," similar to the earlier work of colonizers of the Great Basin. Today, an extensive network of 1,400 miles of canals, laterals, and ditches provides irrigation water to more than 117,000 acres of farmland in Duchesne County.[4]

The earliest developer of the water resources in the county was the federal government through the United States Indian Irrigation Service with the Ute Indians. This was followed by the Dry Gulch Irrigation Company, which was largely a tool of the Mormon colonizing effort. Two other very large water projects have impacted water development in the county: the Strawberry Valley Project, developed by the Strawberry River Water Users Association of Utah County (discussed in chapter 4), and the more recent and much larger multicounty Central Utah Project.

Uintah Indian Irrigation Project

As early as the 1870s Indian agents assigned to the Uintah Indian Reservation recognized the need for irrigation canals if the land of the reservation was to be transformed into productive agricultural land. Little by little they and other Indian agents in the West secured small appropriations to construct irrigation canals on Indian reservations. By the 1890s more than a dozen small irrigation canals of various lengths and capacities had been built on the Uintah Indian Reservation. These canals included Number One, Bench, Henry Jim, Ouray School, Gray Mountain, U.S. Dry Gulch, Ouray Park, North Myton Bench, Lake Fork Ditch, Red Gap, and South Myton Bench canals. These canals watered about 3,000 acres of lands from Tabiona to Ouray, with the possibility of irrigating many hundreds of acres more.[5]

In 1891 Uintah-Ouray Indian Agent Robert Waugh urged that a more comprehensive and systematic approach be taken in the construction of Indian irrigation canals. In part because of his suggestions, the Uintah Indian Irrigation project was established and Congress agreed to appropriate $600,000 for the project. The federal government was to be reimbursed for the irrigation project from the sale of reservation land.[6]

The bulk of the work to construct the project was done by local farmers. By 1913 the Uintah Indian Irrigation project provided water to 85,800 acres, of which 13,000 acres were irrigated. As a result, irrigation on the Indian land reached new levels. Most of these projects took place in what is now Uintah County and therefore are not detailed.[7]

Non-Indian farmers also faced the difficult chore of building canals to deliver water to their farms. The Dry Gulch Irrigation Company was organized to build and manage an irrigation system for non-Indian farmers. It soon became clear that there was much duplication of the two irrigation networks. Out of necessity, the Ute farmers and the white farmers of the county agreed in theory that a cooperative approach be made to the use of existing canals and that further cooperation be promoted in the construction of future canals. As a result of this cooperative effort, much of the water used by Indians and white farmers alike is "mingled" and moved through both Indian and non-Indian canals.

The mingling of "Indian water" and "white water" and the fair and equitable distribution of that water has caused no small amount of concern and some hard feelings between the Indian and non-Indian irrigators, and it has been a headache for the ditch riders and managers of the two irrigation systems.[8]

There is an additional water problem in Duchesne and Uintah counties—the conflicting claims and uses of water. For white farmers of the county and the state, the distribution and use of water in Utah is based on custom, law, and a philosophy centering on "beneficial use." Part of the legal basis for Utah and arid West water law is rooted in a Spanish concept of "Doctrine of Prior Appropriation." First users of water generally had first claim to the water as long as the well-being of other water users was not neglected.[9] The Ute people claim simply that they have always used the water, so it is theirs by right of prior possession. Under Utah water law, water is distributed to those who demonstrate a "beneficial use" of it over a given period of time. Once beneficial use has been demonstrated, the individual water applicant may be granted perpetual right to the water by the state engineer, acting on behalf of the collective societal interest.

In the summer of 1905, Indian agent H.P. Myton, on behalf of hundreds of Indian allottees, filed on hundreds of second-feet of

Hundreds of high mountain lakes are found in the Uinta Mountains of Duchesne County. Many were dammed to store run-off water for irrigation later in the summer. Note the dam at the far end of this lake. (Utah State Historical Society)

water with the state engineer. These water filings were then distributed to the Indian allottees, who were responsible for demonstrating beneficial use. This burden to prove beneficial use was more than many Indian farmers could manage, and, as a result, many later faced the loss of water claims and the depreciation of the value of their land.

To gain something from their allotments, some Indian allottees sold their land along with the water filings to their white neighbors for prices ranging up to twenty dollars an acre. In other cases, Indian allottees and the tribe chose to lease their land to whites. In 1915 the *Roosevelt Standard* reminded white farmers of the opportunities in leasing Indian land:

> Under the laws of the State of Utah beneficial use must be made before summer of 1919 of water that irrigates 65,000 acres of land belonging to Uintah and Ouray Reservation. In order to develop

this land 1,000 white lessees will be offered excellent opportunities
to lease the greater part of this land ranging from 40 to 540 acres
for a term of 5 years.[10]

Between 1915 and 1919, the leasing or selling of Indian allotments was common. By 1920 more than 18,000 acres of Indian land
had been sold to white homesteaders and thousands more acres were
leased. The *Roosevelt Standard* of 19 May 1915 mentioned that the
land sold for ten to forty-five dollars an acre depending on the quality of the land. The leased and sold allotments carried the nearly
priceless bonus of a water claim.

Today, the fair and equitable distribution of water and the right
to the water between Indian and non-Indian water users remains a
problem. Each group of water users remains suspicious of the other.
However, these suspicions and concerns are not unique to the county,
and all water users of the county are continuously maintaining a
watchful eye on water developments and needs of the Wasatch Front.
Further, all Utahns remained concerned with the unquenchable thirst
of downstream water users in other states.

Dry Gulch Irrigation Company

As mentioned, William Smart, president of the Wasatch LDS
Stake in Heber City, formed the Wasatch Development Company
several months before the opening of the Uintah Reservation in
1905.[11] Smart recognized that the land on the reservation was of little
value without water. To ensure that irrigation water was available to
homesteaders, Smart and the Wasatch Stake presidency organized the
Dry Gulch Irrigation Company in early August 1905.

Four months later, on 1 December 1905, the company was incorporated under the laws of the state and a board of directors elected.
The Dry Gulch Irrigation Company became an important driving
force for water development and its management in the county. For a
number of years, the Dry Gulch Irrigation Company maintained an
extraordinary close association with William Smart and other local
Mormon church officials.

Because of the close association of the Dry Gulch Irrigation
Company with the Wasatch Development Company, non-Mormon
homesteaders found it difficult to be a part of the Mormon con-

trolled irrigation company.[12] Consequently, the Dry Gulch Homesteaders Irrigation and Improvement Association of Denver was organized along with several other land associations and water development organizations. Known locally as the "Denver Company," the Dry Gulch Homesteaders Irrigation and Improvement Association's objective was to ensure water for "every homesteader on equal terms. . . . [with] No Cliques, No Special Privileges." All of the smaller canal and land-promotion companies, including the Denver Company, were limited financially, and many either folded or were absorbed into the Dry Gulch Irrigation Company within a few years after the opening of the reservation. Some of the other irrigation companies that were formed soon after the opening of the reservation included the Cedarview Irrigation Company, the Lake Fork Irrigation Company, the Uteland Ditch Company, the Lake Fork Western Irrigation Company, the Purdy Ditch Company, the New Hope Irrigation Company, the Anderson Ditch Company, the Good Luck Ditch Company, the Hartzell-O'Hagen Company, the Mines Ditch Company, the Knutson Company, the McPhee Company, the Uintah Independent Ditch Company, the Pioneer Canal Company, the T.N. Dodd Irrigation Company, the Blue Bench Irrigation Company, the Boneta Irrigation Company, the Myton Irrigation Company (later called the Uintah Irrigation Company), the Duchesne Irrigation Company, the Rhodes Ditch Company, and the Rocky-Point Ditch Company.[13]

To ensure the availability of water for its members, the Dry Gulch Irrigation Company undertook an extensive canal-building project, built mainly by assessed labor. The irrigation company also entered into agreements with the Indian Irrigation Service and the Department of the Interior to utilize some of the existing Indian canals to deliver "white" water to its members. In one of its first agreements with the Indians, the Dry Gulch Irrigation Company agreed to pay $10,000 for some of the unused Indian water rights and to maintain, repair, and enlarge sections of the Uintah Indian Irrigation Service canal system.[14]

This and later agreements between the Indian Irrigation Service and the Dry Gulch Irrigation Company proved to be very beneficial for white farmers. In addition to the initial appropriation of

$600,000, Congress later appropriated an additional $400,000 to the Uintah Indian Irrigation project to make canal improvements, and the Uintah Indian Irrigation project proved to be an indirect federal subsidy to the white farmers of the county.

By 1992, over 117,000 acres of land in the county were being irrigated, with a vast majority being served by canals of the Dry Gulch Irrigation Company or the United States Indian Irrigation Service.

High Uinta Mountain Reservoirs

Even though the Dry Gulch Irrigation Company was marshaling its resources to develop an impressive network of irrigation canals, local farmers still believed they needed more water, particularly later in the growing season. Farmers turned their attention to the Uinta Mountains and the many natural lakes, which were seen as an important source of water that was as yet untapped. The general plan of local irrigation companies was to secure approval from the United States Forest Service to transform many of the lakes into reservoirs for agricultural purposes.[15] This philosophy also was in basic accord with policies of the U.S. Forest Service. Gifford Pinchot, the nation's first professional forester, reflected on the philosophy of full public use of natural resources. It is a fundamental principle of the forest service, Pinchot wrote, "to take every part of the land and its resources and put it to the use which will serve the most people."[16]

In July 1915 the Farnsworth Canal and Reservoir Company applied for permits to build several dams at Brown Duck, Island, and Kidney lakes in the Brown Duck Basin part of the Lake Fork River drainage. Work began with the hauling of construction material and supplies to the area during the winter of 1916–17 when packed snow made an easier passage for horse-drawn sleighs. The following spring the actual work of excavating, moving, and grading dirt was fully underway. All the heavy work was done using horse-drawn plows, rollers, graders, and scrapers. In addition to increasing the capacity of these and other Uinta lakes, outlet gates were installed to regulate the flow of water.

After the drought of 1918–19, and with more land coming under the plow, farmers turned once again to the Uinta Mountains for more water. The Farnsworth Canal and Reservoir Company's stockholders agreed that more storage was needed, and plans were formed to make a reservoir at Twin Potts, a large grassy bowl located a few miles south of Moon Lake. With much energy and determination, farmers set to work to build a dirt-and-rock dam at Twin Potts. The newly built dam was ready to store water by the spring of 1921. Twin Potts became one of a dozen or more lakes converted to storage reservoirs in the 1920s. Often, however, many of the reservoirs were built as cheaply as possible and without careful design or sound construction techniques. For several, the threat of disaster was real.

For the next six summers water stored in the Twin Potts Reservoir provided much-needed water for area farmers. However, on Thanksgiving Day 1927 disaster struck the dam. Seepage had undermined the dam and it failed. The failure of the Twin Potts Dam has remained the most significant dam failure in the history of the county. In the fall of 1930 the reservoir company secured a loan to reconstruct the dam. This was completed in 1931 at a cost of $40,000. The dependency of many on the dam was significant; when it failed it forced many farmers in Mountain Home to sell out and leave the county.[17]

Another company that filed for and was granted storage rights in the Uintas was the Farmers Irrigation Company. Its first project was at Water Lily Lake on the drainage of the Yellowstone River. In addition, the Farmers Irrigation Company added Farmers Lake, Deer Lake, and White Miller Lake to its Uinta Mountains water-storage projects. The company later built additional dams at Bluebell Lake in 1928 and at Drift Lake in 1930. The company's most ambitious projects were the dams constructed at Five Point and Superior Lakes, completed between 1927 and 1929. Superior Lake, the largest on the Yellowstone drainage, was doubled in size with the addition of a dam, making a reservoir of about eighty-two surface acres.[18]

Not wanting to be left out, the Dry Gulch Irrigation Company hurried to complete similar projects. Its first project, however, met with failure. The Dry Gulch Irrigation Company faced the drought of 1919 with more enthusiasm than wisdom. It decided to build a less than substantial dam at Moon Lake to store water for use later in the fall. Without consulting a professional engineer, about fifty men and teams went to work making an earth-and-log dam at the lake. A critical element in their design of the dam was their failure to include an overflow outlet. As a result, the hastily constructed dam failed.

Before construction began company officials were warned of a possible disaster by their own hired engineer. William Woolf quickly recognized the faulty plans, the lack of an overflow outlet, the overall poor design, and the poor building material used at the dam when he was sent by the company to oversee and complete the project after it was well underway. It was felt that work on the dam had progressed too far to begin again. The dam was completed by late summer; within a few days of its completion it failed.

According to Woolf, he was placed in an impossible situation. On the one hand he was employed full time by the company and was directed to finish the project. On the other hand, his professional evaluation of the dam indicated that a dam failure was likely. Woolf insisted that a letter he wrote expressing his concerns about the dam be placed in his file at the Dry Gulch Irrigation Company in Roosevelt. When the dam failed, members of the irrigation company looked to lay the blame on Woolf; however, the reading of his letter cleared Woolf of any responsibility for the dam's failure.[19]

Not to be deterred from the Moon Lake failure, the Dry Gulch Irrigation Company during the next several years constructed other irrigation dams on the Uinta River drainage, including dams at Chain Lakes, at Atwood Lake, and at Fox Lake.

By 1931 there were twenty-four lakes located in the south drainages of the Uinta Mountains that had been dammed for water storage. Six were on the Uinta drainage and operated by Dry Gulch Company; four were on the Whiterocks drainage in Uintah County, and fourteen were on the Lake Fork drainage managed by the Farnsworth, Dry Gulch, and Farmers irrigation companies. Two of the lakes were transformed into regulated storage facilities by Brigham Timothy and Chester Hartman.

The Knight Canal

On 14 June 1909 a group of forty homesteaders who had taken up land on Blue Bench north of Duchesne met to develop an irrigation plan to divert water from Rock Creek. A month later they formally incorporated themselves into a mutual irrigation district and elected Joseph S. Birch, George Hemphill, and B.V. Barlow as the first trustees.[20] In the weeks that followed, several plans were discussed to build a canal from Rock Creek onto the bench. The head of the canal had to be built three miles upstream in order to provide the necessary fall to freely lift the water onto the bench. The route of the canal hugged the northwest rim of the bench and crossed several small ravines and some rugged gullies and washes.

The 100-second-feet-capacity canal presented a number of engineering and design problems far beyond the capabilities of any of the farmers of the Blue Bench District. The district hired Albert Halan, a licensed engineer, to design the diversion canal. Along several sections of the face of Blue Bench wooden flumes had to be built. At several locations wooden trestles were needed to span the dry gullies, and at one location Halan designed a special wooden siphon to carry the water across one of the wider ravines.

Financing the project was equally difficult. A large sum of money was needed, more than the Blue Bench Irrigation District could raise by its annual fees. Several years earlier the state legislature had passed a law authorizing incorporated irrigation districts to raise money through the selling of bonds. The Blue Bench Irrigation District issued bonds to finance the project, and the Knight Trust and Savings Bank owned by mining entrepreneur Jesse Knight of Provo purchased over $100,000 of Blue Bench Canal bonds.

Knight also owned the Provo Construction Company, which was awarded the contract to build the Blue Bench Canal. In March 1913 work on the canal began in earnest, and for two years construction crews worked feverishly on the canal. Douglas fir was cut from the nearby Uinta Mountains to provide the thousands of board feet for the miles of wooden flumes and siphons. After nearly three miles of fluming, the canal reached the top of Blue Bench, and an earthen canal was constructed to complete the water's journey. The canal was completed in time for the 1915 farming season.

The wooden flumes and trestles were vulnerable to the vicissitudes of natural forces, however. Hopes ran high for the canal's success, but trouble soon followed. Within weeks, sections of the wooden flume began to leak. Falling rocks crashed into sections of the flume, calling for immediate repair. Elsewhere, the wooden slates of the

The Knight Canal carried water from Rock Creek to the Blue Bench by a
wooden flume that was several miles in length. (John D. Barton)

flume did not fit snugly, resulting in the loss of water and in some
cases eroding the footing of the canal. When the water flow was
halted to repair the flume, the hot summer sun dried and warped the
lumber, which caused further leaks. Repair crews worked practically
non-stop repairing sections of the canal.

Spring runoffs caused serious damage to sections of the flume.
At other locations, water that had leaked during the late growing season froze and then thawed, creating serious instability of the flume.
The disruption in the flow of water presented a serious hardship for
farmers who depended on a steady flow of water.

The expense of maintaining the newly constructed canal was
exceedingly high and added to the large debt in the form of the irrigation company bonds. Many of the Blue Bench farmers were forced
to abandon their farms by the end of World War I; however, Jesse
Knight, the financial backer and contractor of the scheme, remained
hopeful.[21] He had to be optimistic, his bank held many of the construction bonds; to abandon what became known as the Knight
Canal would mean serious financial problems for Knight.

Jesse Knight, born in the Mormon community of Nauvoo, Illinois, in 1845, first came to Utah in 1850 at the age of five with his pioneer parents. He saw his talent for making money as a calling from the Lord to assist others in need. His personal thoughts on the subject coincided with those of LDS church president Lorenzo Snow, who in 1901 asked "men and women of wealth" to use their riches "to give employment to the laborer. . . . Unloose your purses, and embark in enterprises that will give work to the unemployed, and relieve the wretchedness that leads to . . . vice and crime."[22] Knight had embarked on several projects to create jobs. In some he made money, in others he did not.

Jesse Knight was affectionately called by many "Uncle" Jesse. In addition to his involvement in Duchesne County, Knight invested heavily in agricultural enterprises in western Juab County and in Canada. He made his fortune in the Tintic Mining District in Juab and Utah counties. There Knight established his own mining town, where it said that he forbade the establishment of any saloons, a rarity for any mining town in the West.

Within a very short time, Knight became a major landowner on the Blue Bench. As farmers quit the bench, he bought many of the abandoned homesteads. It was his plan to develop a large farming operation utilizing dozens of hired farm workers to run the farm. He hoped it would become what in today's agriculture is termed a corporate farm. The land was fertile and there was plenty of irrigation water. The troublesome problem for Knight and the other farmers who remained was to make the canal work. In 1918 Knight hired engineer William Woolf to survey the mountains above Rock Creek for potential dam sites and to measure stream flows. On one of his visits Woolf commented:

> I found the Knight farm a beehive of activity. They had nearly a hundred men at work. There was a neatly kept tent city where the men slept. . . . The men worked at removing sagebrush from new land, plowing with gasoline driven engines, and leveling for irrigation.[23]

By 1920 Knight had hired a ten-man crew to patrol the canal for leaks and do the needed repairs to keep water flowing. When water flowed through the canal, Knight was successful in raising crops. As a

Upper Stillwater Reservoir was the last major CUP project completed in Duchesne County. (John D. Barton)

young man, Ray Oman of Boneta recalled to Jack D. Barton working one summer in the alfalfa fields, where an excellent crop was raised. However, the few good crops did not offset the many problems of the canal. The success of Blue Bench as a significant agricultural area in the county rested on Jesse Knight and his commitment to the enterprise. That commitment dwindled in 1921 when Knight died.

The Knight Investment Company, still in control of the canal and owner of much of the benchland, continued to try and wrest a profit from Blue Bench. The odds against the reclamation and farm project mounted, however, with the Great Depression and World War II. Labor shortages, lack of finances, and continued canal problems moved the project from bad to worse, and in 1949 the company folded. It sold its water rights to the county for $621.30.[24] Thus ended one of the most ambitious water projects of early Duchesne County. Difficult canal construction, marginal farming land, and national economic problems proved more than could be overcome by hard work and dreams. The Knight Canal project on Blue Bench was called the basin's "most spectacular [reclamation] failure."[25]

Moon Lake Dam Project and the Bureau of Reclamation

The transformation of many of the lakes into regulated reservoirs troubled some Indian irrigators. Increasingly, they experienced diminished stream flows and availability of water to their own farms. In 1930 Uintah Irrigation Project Supervising Engineer L.M. Holt assigned assistant engineer W.F. Gettleman to conduct an extensive and comprehensive investigation of the streams, lakes, and dams of the Uinta Mountains. Following a careful measurement of stream flow from the several new reservoirs during the summer and fall of 1930, Gettleman concluded that the dams built by white irrigators likely reduced stream flows, particularly during the summer irrigation season.[26]

The Gettleman survey touched off a water skirmish between white irrigation companies and the Bureau of Indian Affairs (BIA) that lasted for the next several years. The BIA insisted that the water companies either release enough water to raise the rivers' levels to where they had been prior to construction of the dams or that they allow some of the stored water to be dedicated to Indian use.

As a compensation to meet Indian concerns and to augment their existing storage projects, white irrigation companies along with the Bureau of Reclamation proposed to build Moon Lake Dam, the largest dam in the county to date. Moon Lake had been first considered as a possible reservoir in 1905 when William Smart scouted the lands that were soon going to be opened for homesteading.[27] But costs and other factors prohibited Smart from pursuing the lake's development as a storage reservoir.

Moon Lake, located on the drainage of the Lake Fork River, is the largest natural lake at the south end of the Uinta Mountains. The lake is wedged between two steep mountains and is shaped like a crescent moon. By building a dam south of the lake's natural shoreline, the surface size of the lake would be nearly doubled.

Years before the controversy over the shortage of water arose between white and Indian water users, the *Roosevelt Standard* had urged farmers of the Upper Country to consider transforming Moon Lake into a regulated irrigation reservoir. The Dry Gulch Irrigation Company and the Utah Water Storage Commission each put up

$2,500 to conduct a preliminary survey, which revealed that a reservoir could be built but that it would take more capital than the individual irrigation companies could finance.

The water shortage problem of the early 1930s and the continued disputation over water revived interest in the Moon Lake project. Because of the involvement of the Bureau of Indian Affairs, another federal agency under the administration of the Department of the Interior, the Moon Lake Project was proposed as a federal reclamation project. The non-Indian water users could hardly complain, however, since their continued farming success was largely connected to completion of a large-scale project such as the Moon Lake Dam, which was beyond their ability to complete with their horse-drawn machinery.

The Bureau of Reclamation required all of the canal and irrigation companies to work collectively. This was accomplished by means of the organization of the Moon Lake Water Users Association, which included primarily the Dry Gulch Irrigation, Farnsworth Canal, Farmers Irrigation, and Lake Fork Irrigation companies. It was estimated that the project would cost $1,200,000; and, to make it cost-effective, the association had to subscribe to 44,880 acre-feet of stored water.

With the support of the Bureau of Reclamation hopes for the project to be completed quickly ran high. A front-page article in the *Roosevelt Standard* summed up the feelings of the time for the whole county:

> Cheer Up, Basin Folks! We should consider ourselves among the more fortunate ones in the entire U.S., or in fact the whole world—and we'll tell you why! Last week was the breaking point of the depression in the Uintah Basin, when the news broke telling us that the state and government had decided to construct the Moon Lake Water Storage Project. . . . It will give hundreds of jobs, bring more land under cultivation, and create a chance for a sugar factory with plenty of water.[28]

As the weeks went by, hopes continued, and farmers were sure that they could protect themselves against future drought. Two more dry years passed, however, before funds were appropriated by

Congress, and yet another year passed before groundbreaking officially started the project.[29]

State, federal, and local officials and dignitaries including
Governor Henry H. Blood were present for the groundbreaking ceremony. "Moon Lake Day Celebration" was a special day for the entire
county. In addition to speeches, ball games, and other community
activities, the day lifted the spirits of the farmers in the county.

As discussed in an earlier chapter, the Civilian Conservation
Corps provided a great deal of work clearing the land. The dam and
spillway on the south side of the lake were completed in 1937. The
lake's surface nearly doubled and its storage capacity reached nearly
30,000 acre-feet of water.

In the twenty-five years following the completion of Moon Lake
the Moon Lake Water Users Association consolidated its holdings
in high mountain reservoirs. Located on the Lake Fork and
Yellowstone drainages are the following reservoirs: Kidney Lake
with 4,000 acre-feet capacity, Island Lake with 700 acre-feet, Brown
Duck Lake with 300 acre-feet, Clement Lake with 700 acre-feet,
Give Point Lake with 475 acre-feet, Drift Lake with 160 acre-feet,
Bluebell Lake with 250 acre-feet, Superior Lake with 340 acre-feet,
Miller Lake with 25 acre-feet, Deer Lake with 130 acre-feet, Farmers
Lake with 120 acre-feet, Twin Potts Reservoir with 3,800 acre-feet,
Midview Reservoir with 5,200 acre-feet, Big Sand Wash with 6,500
acre-feet, and Moon Lake with 30,000 acre-feet. This comes to a
total of 52,700 acre-feet of water-storage capacity. Presently the Dry
Gulch Irrigation Company, with 32,800 shares, is the largest partic-
ipant in the Moon Lake Water Users Association. Dry Gulch
Irrigation Company bought out the Farmers Irrigation Company,
complete with their high mountain lakes, on 18 May 1945.[30] Others
holding shares include the Farnsworth Irrigation Company, the
Lake Fork Irrigation Company, the Lake Fork Western Irrigation
Company, the Monarch Canal and Reservoir Company, the South
Boneta Irrigation Company, the T.N. Dodd Ditch Company, and
the Uteland Ditch Company.

Water users faced other challenges in their efforts to use the
Uinta Mountains lakes. Up to the end of World War II the primary
concern of the U.S. Forest Service was the management of timber

Jesse Knight. (Utah State Historical Society)

reserves, watersheds, and grazing. However, beginning in the late 1940s the public began to demand more recreational use of the national forests. These new demands increasingly clashed with traditional uses of the national forests. In the early 1960s the Forest Service adopted a broader multiple-use management scheme which included consideration of outdoor recreational enthusiasts as well as the protection of big-game habitat. In 1960 Congress passed the Multiple-Use Sustained Yield Act, which was the first act to mandate a more environmentally responsible management system for the national forests.

Among the outdoor recreational enthusiasts were a growing number of people concerned with the ecological protection of the national forests and other public lands. Their concerns were marshaled in protecting wilderness areas from further intrusion by economic interests. In 1961 hearings were held by the U.S. Senate Committee on Interior and Insular Affairs on a proposed bill to create wilderness areas in the United States. A central section of the Uinta Mountains was eyed for possible wilderness designation. The water users of the county understood this designation to mean no further development or maintenance of the important high Uinta Mountains lakes.

Earlier, in 1931, approximately 250,000 acres in the Ashley and Wasatch national forests between Hayden and Kings peaks, roughly the same area as the proposed new wilderness designation, was designated the High Uintas Primitive Area. There had been little opposition to the High Uintas Primitive Area, especially when it was reported in the local newspapers that no water, timber, or forage resources were to be withdrawn from public use.[31] The *Uintah Basin Record* did grumble about it, however. The newspaper and many county residents were already upset about the plan to divert water from the upper Duchesne River to the upper Provo River for use in Salt Lake City and Provo.

> Here in this Uintah Basin we should have something to say about this entire matter. If Salt Lake City is going to take our water, or the water naturally belonging to our lands yet unreclaimed while large tracts are "sewed up" in federal, "proposed" projects, we deserve something for it.[32]

Congress authorized the Provo River project in 1933, and two years later President Roosevelt approved the project. In 1938 work began on the Deer Creek Dam in Wasatch County; three years later, work commenced on the six-mile-long Duchesne Diversion Tunnel. It was completed in 1942.

The purpose of the High Uintas Primitive Area designation was to provide an opportunity "to the public to observe the conditions which existed in the pioneer phases of the Nation's development, and to engage in the forms of outdoor recreation characteristic of that period."[33] At the hearing for the new wilderness plan, Utah Senator Wallace F. Bennett spoke out for most people of the county and many other Utahns regarding the wilderness bill:

I have been a consistent supporter of our Forest Service and Park Service wilderness programs, and I do not propose weakening them now. The real question, then, is not whether we shall have wilderness but how much wilderness shall we have, and where will it be, and who will create it?[34]

Bennett stated that only Congress should be authorized to create wilderness areas. "Surely wilderness areas should enjoy the same stature as national parks, which are created by act of Congress."[35] The bill failed.

Two years later, a second wilderness bill was introduced and hearings held in the U.S. Senate. This time Congress passed the bill known as the Wilderness Act of 1964. The draft of the bill also authorized the president of the United States to safeguard interests of various natural resource users:

The President may, within a specific area and in accordance with such regulations as he may deem desirable, authorize prospecting (including but not limited to exploration for oil and gas), mining (including but not limited to the production of oil and gas), and the establishment and maintenance of reservoirs, water-conservation works, transmission lines, and other facilities needed in the public interest.[36]

Since the passage of the Wilderness Act, some environmentally conscious individuals have put increasing pressure on the Forest Service to stop the Moon Lake Water Users Association from repairing its dams, hoping the lakes could be restored to their original state. Many fishermen and hikers also want the reservoirs to remain in a pristine state. The draw down of water from the reservoirs each late summer leaves unsightly mudflats down to the water's edge at the lakes. Just what is the best balance between users of natural resources and recreationists and conservationists remains a heated issue.

To provide additional storage of water and provide additional water for Indian water users, the 5,200-acre-feet Midview Reservoir (Lake Boreham) was constructed downriver and off stream from the Lake Fork River. The storage dam was completed in 1938.

A later project that added storage in the Upalco region was Big Sand Wash. Located between Upalco and Mount Emmons, the reservoir added irrigation water for the areas of Upalco and Ioka. Ground was broken for this $650,000 project in June 1963, and it was completed two years later.[37]

Central Utah Project

From the time of the opening of the Uintah Indian Reservation, Duchesne County's history has been largely impacted by various congressional actions. Perhaps no other project has impacted the county more than the development of the Central Utah Project.

Interest in Uinta Basin water increased soon after the completion of the Strawberry Valley project in 1913. Within a decade there was talk of enlarging it. This did not sit well with county residents, especially when the *Roosevelt Standard* in 1928 published an erroneous news article in which the editor claimed that Salt Lake City had already diverted water from the upper Strawberry River and now wanted more water.[38] The newspaper was only partially correct in its claim. Water from the Strawberry River was diverted to water users in the southern portion of Utah County. More than a decade earlier than the Strawberry Valley project, farmers from Heber Valley successfully constructed a 1,000-foot diversion tunnel through the Wasatch Mountains to divert water from the upper Strawberry River to a small tributary to Daniels Creek. Strawberry River water was used to augment irrigation needs for farmers at the south end of Heber Valley.

Early in the century it was recognized that the Colorado River was of vital interest to the growth and development of the states of the southwest. As related earlier, in 1922 representatives from Colorado, Nevada, New Mexico, Wyoming, Utah, Arizona, and California agreed to the Colorado River Compact which provides for a division of the water of the Colorado River. The compact divided the river into the upper (Wyoming, Utah, Colorado, and New Mexico) and lower (California, Nevada, and Arizona) basins. Each basin was to receive 7.5 million acre-feet of water annually. The river compact also worked to prevent future contentions and expensive interstate legal wars over the water.

California and Nevada moved quickly to develop their portion of water. In 1928 Congress passed the Boulder Canyon Project to construct the giant Boulder Dam—later renamed Hoover Dam—which was completed in 1935.

The upper basin states were not as quick to the water tap. The Depression and World War II seriously interrupted their plans. However, during the interim, Utah officials began to formulate a massive reclamation project known as the Central Utah Project (CUP).

Following the war, Utah was prepared to move ahead with its plan. However, before any development of Colorado River water could take place among the upper basin states, they had to agree among themselves to an equitable sharing of the river water. In 1948 representatives of the upper basin states met in Santa Fe, New Mexico, where they agreed to the Upper Colorado River Compact. Utah's share of the upper Colorado River water allotment was set at 23 percent of the 7.5 million acre-feet.

That same year, Congress passed the Colorado River Storage Project (CRSP), which included the CUP.[39] However, the project faced several delays. The most troublesome battle was over a proposed Echo Park Dam located just across the state line in Colorado. A nationwide debate ensued over the Echo Park Dam and the companion Split Mountain Dam. Both the Echo Park and Split Mountain dams were located within or very near the boundaries of Dinosaur National Monument. Early opposition to the dams was led by author, historian, and Ogden native Bernard De Voto. California water users, eastern interests, conservation groups, and others joined the debate. Lack of public support nationwide for the projects halted plans for the two dams and threatened the CRSP and the CUP.

The Echo Park Dam was an important part of the overall CUP and, as a result, Utah congressmen fought long and hard for the dam. However, they and other upper-basin states congressmen and senators failed to win enough support for the Echo Park Dam. They did, however, manage to maintain support for the CRSP; in April 1956 Congress passed a $760 million appropriations bill for the CRSP and its participating projects, including the CUP—the largest single participating project in the Colorado River Storage Project. With appropriations now in hand, construction began in the fall of 1956 on dams at Flaming Gorge and Glen Canyon.

The Central Utah Project was meant to organize and centrally develop Utah's water allotment of Colorado River water. A massive system of storage reservoirs and water transportation systems of canals and tunnels and an intricate arrangement of water transfers and substitutes was planned and agreed to by various water users, government entities, the state of Utah, and the Ute Tribe. The CUP's objective is to provide water for industrial and municipal uses along the Wasatch Front as well as irrigation water for 200,000 acres of new farmland and supplemental irrigation water for an additional 239,000 acres of farmland.

The CUP was divided into seven units. The Bonneville, Upalco, and Uintah units directly impacted water development and use in Duchesne County. Out of a need for better centralized and coordinated management of the CUP, the Fourth District Judicial Court in 1964 organized the Central Utah Water Conservancy District, directed by a board of seven men from Duchesne, Uintah, Wasatch, Utah, Salt Lake, and Summit counties. Duchesne County was represented by Leo Haveter for a one-year term, Leo Brady for a two-year term, and William J. Ostler for a three-year term. Later, Weber, Juab, Millard, Davis, Sanpete, Sevier, Garfield, and Piute counties were added as participants in the CUP.

The Central Utah Water Conservancy District serves as the local organization that deals with and enters into contracts with the Bureau of Reclamation. As part of the budgetary process, each project within the CUP required separate appropriations from Congress, which has extended the development of the project by many years. Repayment has been scheduled over several decades.[40] As ideas of water use were expanded, the CUP also has included plans for fish and wildlife management and habitat enhancement and for recreational use.

The Bonneville Unit

The Bonneville Unit is the keystone as well as being the largest and most expensive unit of the Central Utah Project. Its objective is to transfer water from the south slope of the Uinta Mountains to the Wasatch Front, especially the Salt Lake Valley. The Bonneville Unit is designed to impound an additional 600,000 acre-feet of water in the

enlarged Strawberry Reservoir and the newly constructed Soldier
Creek Dam nine miles downstream. Water is collected at the Upper
Stillwater Reservoir on Rock Creek and on Current Creek collection
reservoirs, and through a series of tunnels and canals water is
diverted from the West Fork of the Duchesne River, Rock Creek, Wolf
Creek, and Water Hollow to the enlarged Strawberry Reservoir. From
there, water is carried through a new transmontane diversion and
delivery system to water users in Juab, Salt Lake, Utah, Garfield,
Millard, Piute, and Sevier counties. The Bonneville Unit also provides
for the exchange of water for Duchesne, Wasatch, and Summit counties.

The diversion, storage, and trans-basin conveyance of Rock
Creek and upper Duchesne River water to the Great Basin was the
most ambitious portion of the Bonneville Project.[41] In exchange for
water being diverted from the watersheds in Duchesne County, water
users in the county were promised additional storage units, canals,
and additional water from Flaming Gorge Reservoir as well as water
storage at Starvation Reservoir.

As elements of the Bonneville Unit progressed, they exceeded
both cost and time projections. When the Duchesne County portion
of the Bonneville Unit was completed, the proposed Taskeetch Dam,
located on the Lake Fork River downstream from Moon Lake, the
Uinta Reservoir, located on the Uinta River, and other features of the
Upalco Unit—primarily designed to serve the needs of Duchesne
County—were dropped or drastically modified. In fact, the proposed
Upalco Unit was abandoned, including the Whiterocks project in
Uintah County. This has caused major frustration and created a feeling of betrayal by the CUP in many county water users. They believe
that the completion of the Bonneville Unit satisfied the water needs
of a great portion of the state's voters but has left them high and dry.

Although not all of the elements of the Bonneville Unit have
been completed, the significant number that have been completed
have improved the water situation in the county. These elements
include the Upper Stillwater Dam, Docs Diversion and Feeder
Pipeline, Stillwater Tunnel, North Fork Siphon, Hades Diversion and
Feeder Pipeline, Hades Tunnel, Rhodes Diversion and Feeder
Pipeline, Win Diversion and Feeder Pipeline, Wolf Creek Siphon,

Rhodes Tunnel, West Fork Pipeline, Vat Diversion Dam and Feeder Pipeline, Vat Tunnel, Currant Creek Dam, Currant Tunnel, Water Hollow Diversion and Feeder Pipeline, Water Hollow Siphon, Water Hollow Tunnel, Open Channel No. 2, Soldier Creek Dam, Knight Diversion Dam and Starvation Conduit, and Starvation Dam. The Bonneville Unit serves a much larger geographical area than Salt Lake City alone; however, this distinction is rarely voiced—if understood—by county residents when water issues and the CUP are discussed. The Bonneville Unit has been expanded as far south as Piute County.[42]

With the CUP only partially completed as stated in its original plans, there remains thousands of acre-feet of water allotment not being utilized, and many Utahns fear that the water will be lost forever. Further, many residents of the county question if there is any difference between losing water to Salt Lake City or losing it to California.

Starvation Reservoir

The Starvation Reservoir and collection system is important to the diversion of water from the Strawberry River and Current and Rock creeks through the Strawberry Aqueduct. Both are vitally important to farmers in the Myton, Pleasant Valley, and Bridgeland areas of the county as well as to Indian farmers in the Midview area. Starvation Reservoir provides them with a dependable water supply which heretofore they have not had.

Starvation Reservoir, the first feature of the Bonneville Unit, was begun in March 1967 and completed in November 1970. The project's construction, the largest such effort in Utah up to that point, was initiated with an old-fashioned public barbeque and a program of Ute tribal dances. The county had not witnessed such a gathering of dignitaries in its history; included on the list were Congressman Wayne Aspinall of Colorado, chair of the important House Interior and Insular Affairs Committee; Governor Calvin L. Rampton; Senators Wallace F. Bennett and Frank E. Moss; Congressmen Laurence J. Burton and Sherman P. Lloyd; U.S. Bureau of Reclamation Commissioner Floyd E. Dominy; former U.S. Senator Arthur N. Watkins; and former governor George D. Clyde.

Located about three miles upstream from the town of Duchesne on the Strawberry River, the earth and rockfill dam is 155 feet high and has a crest length of 2,900 feet. The total capacity of the reservoir is over 165,000 acre-feet, of which 152,320 acre-feet is active. The Knight diversion tunnel diverts water into the Starvation feeder canal from the Duchesne River.[43]

The name "Starvation" came from early times of the area's history. A.C. Murdock had wintered a herd of cattle in the area when a severe blizzard snowed-in the town, making it impossible for his men to check the cattle. The entire herd starved to death before they could be driven to feed. Residents of Duchesne City embrace the name with some humor, often wearing tee shirts or hats printed, "Duchesne— On the verge of Starvation."

Upper Stillwater Dam

The dam at Upper Stillwater on Rock Creek is one of the most impressive structures in the county. The concrete dam, wedged between a sharp-walled canyon, is 292 feet high and 2,650 feet wide. It has a total storage capacity of 35,253 acre-feet. Due to the narrowness of the canyon, the spillway is an uncontrolled ogee with a stepped chute and drowned hydraulic jump basin. When the dam is completely full, the water tumbling down the spillway makes an impressive sight. Construction began in 1983 and was completed in November 1987. The road from Mountain Home to Rock Creek was upgraded and paved for use by heavy construction equipment. A side benefit of the road improvement is that it provides improved access to some of the county's best camping and fishing areas.[44]

Some of the original features in the Uinta and Upalco units of the CUP have never been built. Other important features of the Uinta and Upalco units have been included as part of the Bonneville Unit. However, many of the irrigators in Duchesne and western Uintah counties have been left with unfulfilled dreams and promises. The Uinta Basin lacks the strong political voice and muscle to help force the completion of the two reclamation units for the basin. The farmers of the Tabiona, Utahn, Duchesne, Bridgeland, Myton, and Pleasant Valley areas are more fortunate; they now have sufficient water from the completed parts of the Bonneville Unit to carry them through drought years. The overall results of the CUP for the county therefore are mixed.

CUPCA and the UBRP

Knowing that the original CUP was never going to be completed as planned, and also due to the increased concern of environmental problems caused by the CUP, Congress passed the Central Utah Project Completion Act (CUPCA) in 1992. In the Uinta Basin the deployment arm of CUPCA is the Uinta Basin Replacement Projects (UBRP).

There are a total of nine replacement projects under consideration as Central Utah Water Project alternatives. On the Upalco Unit, these considered projects include enlarging the Big Sand Wash Reservoir to nearly double is present size; building Cow Canyon Reservoir of 20,000 acre-feet in Yellowstone Canyon; building the Crystal Ranch Alternative, which would create a 30,000-acre-foot on-stream reservoir on the Yellowstone River; building the Twin Potts alternative, which calls for the completion of the above projects and repairing the earthen dam at Twin Potts; and constructing the South Clay Basin Reservoir.

The Uintah Unit proposal includes the Lower Uintah alternative, which would consist of three new storage reservoirs. The first would be a 45,000-acre-foot on-stream reservoir on the Uinta River approximately one mile upstream from the Uintah Power Plant; the second reservoir would be of 20,000 acre-feet on the Whiterocks River some two miles north of the U.S. Forest boundary at Red Pine Canyon; and the third a 5,800-acre-foot reservoir at Merkley Drop, about 2.5 miles northeast of the town of Whiterocks. Also under consideration are reservoirs at Clover Creek on the Uinta River and at Coyote Basin.[45]

Other elements of CUPCA which affect the Uinta Basin are the settlement of water-rights disputes with Ute Indians, with a projected cost of $199 million, and the stabilization and rehabilitation of the High Uinta lakes for fish and wildlife habitat. Finally, the troubled administration of the CUP has been transferred from the Bureau of Reclamation to the Central Utah Water Conservancy District.

Even after the passage of CUPCA several troublesome issues remain. One is the unkept promises of the CUP with the Ute Tribe.

Earlier the tribe had agreed to relinquish its claims to Rock Creek water of the Bonneville Unit in exchange for what would be more usable water from the promised Upalco and Uintah units to irrigate 30,000 acres of additional land owned by the Ute Tribe. In 1994 the Ute Tribal Council presented a $33 million bill to the Central Utah Water Conservancy District for diverting water without authorization from the tribal council. Tribal leaders claimed that until the CUP meets its obligations to them it has no legal right to the Rock Creek water. The bill has yet to be paid by the conservancy district and will likely be a point of contention well into the next century.

Soil Conservation Service and Salinity Control

To state the obvious, the Colorado River system is critically important to millions of people in the American West and Mexico. In addition to its heretofore unpredictability, the Colorado River presents another serious problem—the quality of its water. Water quality problems of the river were recognized as early as 1903. However, due to the increased manipulation and use of the river, its water quality for irrigation, drinking, and industrial uses has been placed in serious jeopardy. High salinity concentrations in Colorado River water have adversely affected downstream irrigated crop yields, altered crop patterns, and increased culinary water-treatment costs.

The Colorado River carries about 9 million tons of salt annually into Lake Mead and the lower Colorado River Basin. Upstream irrigators are significant contributors to the water quality of the river. Areas being irrigated that have underlying saline formations add about half of the total salinity to the river, as the runoff picks up some of that salt as it returns to the river system. In an attempt to solve the problem, Mexico and the United States entered into a treaty in 1973 that commits the U.S. to maintain a basic salinity of water arriving at the Mexican border.[46]

Features of the CUP and CUPCA strive to reduce the salts carried from the various projects to the Colorado River. These features have also improved the quality of water in Duchesne County. The Soil Conservation Service (SCS) in the state and the county has played a significant role as technical advisor to county farmers and water developers to reduce salinity outflow. The Soil Conservation Service estimates that as much as 111,000 tons of salt per year will be kept out of the Colorado River system due to its efforts.[47]

The Soil Conservation Service's salinity-reduction project is also having a significant impact in the county, creating more and better farmlands. It is estimated that more than 18,000 acres of land currently in pasture, alfalfa, and grain will be improved in the county under the salinity-reduction project. This will be accomplished by means of increased irrigation efficiency, including deep percolation irrigation. Yield estimates for alfalfa are nearly double—from 2–3 tons per acre to 3–6 tons per acre. Some alfalfa farmers claim yields as high as ten tons to the acre. This creates an estimated $840,000 increase in dollar-value yield—$441,000 in direct farm benefits and $399,000 in downstream benefits saved in cleaner water to users on the lower Colorado River.

Any farmer who wants to participate in the program can usually qualify for assistance in financing a high-efficiency sprinkling system through this program. The SCS funding pays for 70 percent of the system and the landowner's share is 30 percent. It is hoped that the increased efficiency and resulting yields will easily pay for the installation of the systems and also show higher profits for the farmers.[48]

Wetlands

Another water issue that faces Duchesne County residents is Section 404 of the Clean Water Act of 1972 and subsequent amendments which pertain to wetlands. Wetlands administration and wetland determination is directed by the Army Corps of Engineers. Only a few years ago wetlands were regarded by some people as health hazards and a nuisance. Those who took the time and effort to drain them were applauded for improving the country. But more recently attitudes have changed, as wetlands have become recognized as important to the overall environmental health of a region. Still, there is the feeling of many nationwide, including many county residents, that the involvement of the federal government in overseeing wetlands has become a burden. Wetlands can and do serve as habitat for some wildlife and help with erosion control. The passage of Executive

Order 11990, "Protection of Wetlands," during President George Bush's administration set the goal of "no net loss of wetlands." With this the government was seen by many to create problems for private property owners.

Most of the natural wetlands in the Duchesne area are in the Ouray National Wildlife Refuge. Another 2,295 acres of wetlands are located primarily along the Duchesne and Strawberry rivers, Currant Creek, and the oxbows of the Green River and other low-lying depressions. There also are some 5,030 acres of artificial wetlands in the county. These wetlands have been created due to irrigation and man-made changes in the water system of the region.[49] Some of the wetland designations were made during wet years.

Section 404 means a net loss of useable land for Duchesne County farmers who can no longer dig drainage ditches in swampy areas or convert marshlands into pasture land. If farmers attempt to do so they are in violation of the law and must restore the lands to a wetland status at their own expense. In other instances, during dry years county farmers are required to direct some of their irrigation water to designated wetlands to maintain the water levels of the wetlands, some of which are created by irrigation. Many county residents deeply resent this preemptive use of their own lands.

Conclusion

Some people call the Uinta Basin and Duchesne County Utah's "last watering hole." More rivers flow through the Uinta Basin than through any other region in the state, and because of the county's abundance—when compared with the rest of the state—much of the county's history has been driven by water issues. The growth and stability of the county are inseparably tied to the availability of water resources, and, because of the geological setting of the county, those resources involve people as distant as California and Mexico.

The ever-increasing complications of water issues makes the voice of the county one that is heard. Water has shaped the history of the county and there is little doubt that it will continue to be an important element in shaping the county's future, as increased demands for water likely will continue in Utah and the American Southwest.

ENDNOTES

1. See Donald Worster, *Rivers of Empire, Aridity, and the Growth of the American West* (New York: Pantheon Books, 1985).

2. For an in depth study of the development of the Colorado River see Norris Hundley, Jr., *Dividing the Waters: A Century of Controversy Between the United States and Mexico* (Berkeley: University of California Press, 1966).

3. George H. Dern, "Utah's Interest in the Colorado River," statement at the hearings before the Committee on Irrigation and Reclamation, U.S. Senate, 17 December 1925.

4. Harold T. Brown, "Early History of Water Development in the Uinta Basin," paper presented at the third annual Uinta Basin Water Conference, 12 February 1991, Vernal, Utah, 1; "Agricultural Census for Duchesne County, Utah" 18 August 1997, available on Internet at http://govinfo.kerr.orst.edu/cgi-bin/ag-list.

5. Gregory D. Kendrick, ed., *Beyond the Wasatch: The History of Irrigation in the Uintah Basin and Upper Provo River Area of Utah* (Washington, D.C.: U.S. Department of the Interior/National Park Service, 1986), 18.

6. Ibid., 22.

7. Ibid.; E.C. La Rue, *The Colorado River and Its Utilization,* United States Geological Survey Water Supply Paper 395, Washington, D.C.: United States Geological Survey, 1916), 130. For more information on the Indian Canals see Cyrus Cates Babb, *The Water Supply of the Uintah Indian Reservation, Utah,* Doc. 671, 57 Cong., 1st Sess., 1902; and Journal History of the Church of Jesus Christ of Latter-day Saints, 25–27 August 1861, LDS Church Archives.

8. William L. Woolf, *The Autobiography of William L. Woolfe* (n.p., 1979), 82–83.

9. See Michael C. Meyer, *Water in the Hispanic Southwest* (Tucson: University of Arizona Press, 1984), chapter eight.

10. *Roosevelt Standard,* 24 March 1915.

11. For additional information see William Smart, Diaries, vol. XVI, pp. 110–12, Special Collections, Marriott Library, University of Utah.

12. The first board of directors of the Dry Gulch Irrigation Company included R.S. Collett, John Glenn, Ed Harmston, Hyrum Baird, George F. Merkley, N.J. Meagher, Herbert Tysack, John N. Davis, J. Garnett Holmes, Henry J. Harding, William G. Fell, and John W. Roseberry. Harmston was not a member of the LDS church but as founder of Roosevelt City was a major factor in all the early interests in the area. See Dry Gulch Irrigation

Company Minutes, 1 December 1905; and Dillman, *Early History of Duchesne County*, 22.

13. Kendrick, *Beyond the Wasatch*, 48; Dillman, *Early History of Duchesne County*, 17.

14. Record Book A, Dry Gulch Irrigation Company, Roosevelt, Utah, pp. 46–48.

15. The establishment of national forests in Utah and subsequent careful use of them was strongly advocated by U.S. Senator Reed Smoot and various LDS church leaders. See Thomas G. Alexander, *Utah, The Right Place* (Salt Lake City: Gibbs Smith, 1995), 226.

16. Quoted in Kendrick, *Beyond the Wasatch*, 62.

17. Kendrick, *Beyond the Wasatch*, 72–76.

18. All the dams constructed by the Farmers Irrigation Company were on lakes on the Yellowstone/Swift Creek drainage. For more information, including acre-feet of storage of these lakes, see Kendrick, *Beyond the Wasatch*, 76–81.

19. Woolf, *Autobiography*, 87–89.

20. See "Records of Minutes of the Blue Bench Irrigation District No. 1," Jesse Knight Papers, Special Collections, Harold B. Lee Library, Brigham Young University, Provo, Utah.

21. Ibid.

22. Quoted in Diane L. Mangum, "Jesse Knight and the Riches of Life," *Ensign: The Ensign of the Church of Jesus Christ of Latter-day Saints* (October 1993): 554–59.

23. Woolf, *Autobiography*, 72. This was the year before Woolf was hired by the Dry Gulch Irrigation Company. His hiring by Dry Gulch was at least partially due to his experience with Knight's company. Woolf was significant in the county's water development. He selected the sites and oversaw the construction of dams at the Chain Lakes, Atwood Lake, and Fox Lake. He also settled many of the early water disputes in the county.

24. See Jesse Knight Papers.

25. Gary Fuller Reese, "Uncle Jesse: The Story of Jesse Knight, Miner, Industrialist, Philanthropist" (Master's thesis, Brigham Young University, 1961), 82, 83.

26. William F. Gettleman, "Report on the Lakes and Reservoir on the Headwaters of the Uintah, Whiterocks and Lakefork Rivers, Uintah Project, Utah: Feb. 1932," Uintah Irrigation Project, BIA Offices, Uintah and Ouray Agency, Fort Duchesne, Utah.

27. William Smart to Mildred Miles Dillman, cited in Dillman, *Early Duchesne County History*, 22.

28. *Roosevelt Standard,* 2 July 1931. The hoped-for sugar factory was not built. It had been hoped that with more water for industry and farming a sugar beet industry, complete with a sugar factory, could be started in Duchesne County.

29. *Roosevelt Standard,* 23 November 1933, 15 November 1934, 27 June 1935.

30. See Dry Gulch Irrigation Company, Minute Book, number 2, 1945, 53–54.

31. *Duchesne Courier,* 15 May 1931.

32. *Uintah Basin Record,* 18 September 1931.

33. Thomas G. Alexander, *The Rise of Multiple-Use Management in the Intermountain West: A History of Region 4 of the Forest Service* (Washington, D.C.: U.S. Forest Service, 1987), 113, quoting from Blaine Bettenson, "Report on Grandaddy Lakes Primitive Area," 18 December 1929, File 2320, High Uintas Primitive Area, Lands and Recreation Library, Ogden Regional Office, U.S. Forest Service.

34. U.S. Congress, Senate, Committee on Interior and Insular Affairs, "Hearings on S. 174, A Bill to Establish a National Wilderness Preservation System for the Permanent Good of the Whole People, and for Other Purposes," 87th Cong., 1st Sess., 1961, 34, Utah State Historical Society Library.

35. Ibid.

36. U.S. Congress, Senate, Committee on Interior and Insular Affairs. "Hearings on S.4, A Bill to Establish a National Wilderness Preservation System for the Permanent Good of the Whole People, and for Other Purposes," 88th Cong., 1st Sess., 1963, 6, Utah State Historical Society Library.

37. *Uintah Basin Standard,* 27 June 1963. Big Sand Wash Dam was a CUP project and the only finished reservoir on the Upalco Unit of the CUP.

38. *Roosevelt Standard,* 7 June 1928.

39. For a concise outline of CUP and CRSP see Craig Fuller "Central Utah Project," *Utah History Encyclopedia,* 82–85; and Hundley, *Dividing the Waters.*

40. Repayment for the CUP is still a raging controversy throughout the state. In 1965 voters in seven counties approved of the repayment plan for the $325 million Bonneville Unit of the CUP. The ratio to approve the plan was 13 to 1. Duchesne County voters approved of the plan, 673 to 80 votes. However, Uintah County voted against the repayment plan, 351 approval to 804 negative votes. See *Salt Lake Tribune,* 15 December 1965.

41. U.S. Bureau of Reclamation, "Brief Overview of The Central Utah

Water Conservancy District," (Washington, D.C.: U.S. Department of the Interior, 1963), 4.

42. In 1993 preparations were made by Millard and Sevier counties to withdraw from the CUP and in 1995 both counties made it official. For a discussion of Sevier County's withdrawal see Guy M. Bishop, *History of Sevier County*, (Salt Lake City: Utah State Historical Society/Sevier County Commission, 1997), 262–69.

43. Central Utah Project, "Fact Sheets," unnumbered information material issued by CUP, 25, in author's possession. Using Starvation Dam as an example, repayment schedules for construction costs include: $931,000 to be repaid by water users amortized over fifty years, $4,698,100 from ad valorem taxes levied by the Central Utah Water Conservancy District; and approximately $9,400,000 from power revenue. For more information see Bureau of Reclamation, Central Utah Water Project, "Benefits of the Bonneville Unit to Non-Indian Water Users on the Duchesne River," (Washington, D.C.: U.S. Department of the Interior, 1963), point 6a.

44. Central Utah Project, "Fact Sheets," 1, in author's possession.

45. *Uintah Basin Standard,* 8 November 1994.

46. See Soil Conservation Service, "Salinity Update; Special Edition" (Washington, D.C.: U.S. Department of the Interior, 1994), I.

47. Soil Conservation Service, "Framework Plan for Monitoring and Evaluation of Colorado River Salinity Control Program," (Washington, D.C.: U.S. Department of the Interior, 1991), 66.

48. *Vernal Express,* 8 June 1994.

49. Francis T. Holt to Wayne Urie, 18 September 1991, quoted in the *Vernal Express,* 16 February 1994.

CHAPTER 10

DUCHESNE COUNTY ECONOMICS: THE 1960S TO THE 1990S

The backbone of Duchesne County's economic development is its natural resources: water, land, oil, minerals, and timber. Because of this, the county's economic development is greatly influenced by national economic trends and, especially in the last half of the twentieth century, by international political and economic developments. Although the county is rich in many natural resources, it lacks capital to fully develop them. As much as the county residents pride themselves on being self-reliant, rugged individualists, willing to work hard; many economic developments of the county have come to rely on outside financial assistance, including direct or indirect state and federal government financial aid. A primary example of federal financial aid is the construction of the Upalco Unit of the Central Utah Project. As it was originally planned in 1956, the Upalco Unit was to impound 19,900 acre-feet of water annually for irrigation, municipal, and industrial use. Millions of government dollars have been spent on reclamation and irrigation projects in the county since the turn of the century. During the Depression there were cattle buyouts and other federal programs such as the CCC, WPA, and the

Rural Electrification Administration that provided relief and encouraged economic development. Since World War II crop subsidies have been common.[1]

From settlement times to the Great Depression and through World War II to the 1960s the county experienced economic fluctuations. Through these economic changes, the average personal income in the county remained below the state average. Industry and big business have not located in the county during most of its history. For more than one-half century agriculture on small land holdings has been the mainstay of the county's economy.

County farmers and ranchers have become more experienced, more aggressive, and have adopted advanced agricultural methods to survive in a very competitive world. No longer can a million dollar investment be run without a keen business sense and up-to-date methods in every facet of agriculture.

Important to the change in agriculture is its labor force. As the children of Duchesne County farmers have graduated from the local high schools, many have left the country for better employment opportunities. Unless their fathers were ready to retire, there was little opportunity for children to assume the family farm or ranch. For much of the last forty years the existing non-agricultural job market has been unable to absorb the excess labor pool. Some county residents have opted to take poorer paying jobs in order to stay in the region rather than leave for better employment elsewhere. Some who have left have found ways to return to take up residence again in the county.

Changing Agriculture

In the 1970s, a newly inspired economic optimism was generated by the oil boom in the county. However, this optimism laid the foundation for economic disappointment for many in the county later. For some farmers and ranchers newfound wealth came from oil that was being pumped from their land. Flush with capital for the first time, many moved rapidly to acquire more land even as land prices were on the rise. Some farmers and ranchers doubled or even tripled their land holdings. The sharp escalation of land prices led many to believe that the trend would continue indefinitely. Other county

Early oil exploration and drilling in the Uinta Basin, 1913. (Uintah County Library–Regional History Center, Neal Collection)

farmers negotiated loans to expand their farms with land that came available as elderly farmers retired or died. Collateral for the loans was based on rapidly rising land prices. Farm land sold in the late 1960s for between $300 and $400 an acre; by the mid-1970s area farm land was selling for $1,000 to $1,500 an acre. Smaller pieces of land sold for as much as $3,000 an acre. Some of the older farmers and ranchers sold out as land prices continued to rise; however, when oil-royalty checks doubled and even quadrupled other farmers' incomes in the 1970s many looked to buy yet more land. Consolidation of some smaller farms took place.

Overall, the number of farms in the county declined from 635 in 1964 to 534 in 1974. Ironically, although there was some consolidation, the average size of farms in the county was reduced. In 1964 the average size of a county farm was slightly under 822 acres; ten years later, the average size was less than 742 acres. The amount of land farmed dropped from 521,806 acres in 1964 to 396,025 acres in 1974.[2]

Inflation and interest rates soared during much of the decade of the 1970s, placing an increased financial burden on many farmers in the county. The inflation rate in 1967 was at 3 percent; seven years later it climbed to 12 percent and would remain in double digits for the remainder of the decade. The high cost of machinery was also crippling; to try to stay competitive many farmers purchased bigger and better equipment. In 1970 an average tractor cost about $8,000, a bailer $3,500, and a swather $6,000. Most farmers hauled their hay by hand without a bail-wagon. In the 1990s, if a farmer was to purchase the same size and quality of equipment, a tractor would be about $18,000; but most farmers would increase the size of their tractor and purchase a four-wheel-drive tractor, which brings the average cost to $40,000; a bailer's cost is $14,000, and swather $35,000. Most farmers now use bail-wagons to pick up the bales of hay, with a cost of $20,000 for the wagon.[3] To meet their debt obligation county farmers raised more cattle and milked more cows at a time when prices were unstable.

As with cattle and milk prices, hay prices also fluctuated. Even with the consolidation of some of the smaller farms and the purchase of more land, most farmers lost money raising hay in the 1970s; as a result, many continued to carry a heavy debt through much of the 1970s. It was not until the 1980s that hay producers in the county approached the break-even mark. The average price per ton of hay in the 1970s was about thirty-five dollars; during the 1980s the price of hay ranged from about sixty dollars a ton to more than eighty dollars a ton.[4]

Between 1982 to 1985 area land prices fell. As land values fell, so too did beef and milk prices. Statewide, the price per head of cattle dropped from $505 in 1980 to $395 in 1985 and 1986; it then made a steady climb to over $660 by 1991.[5]

To maintain the same income, county farmers and ranchers were forced to expand their operations by buying more land and often incurring a larger debt load. As a result, many county farmers had a debt greater than the combined value of their land and machinery. Some of the county's farmers did not economically survive. The number of farms in the county continued to decline—from 534 in 1974 to 465 in 1982. Some farmers sold out to avoid foreclosure or auction. Some of the farmers continued farming only because they were fortunate to have other incomes from oil royalties or a second job.

During the remainder of the 1980s the average size of farms slowly increased. In 1987 there were approximately 658 farms in Duchesne County, with an average size of 486 acres. Roughly thirty percent of the average farm, or about 149 acres, was irrigated. In 1987, 38 percent of the farms in the county were less than 100 acres and 39 percent of the farms were larger than 260 acres. A total of 320,446 acres were being farmed in 1987.[6] In 1992 there were 733 county farms, with a total of 399,011 acres being farmed. The average farm in the county presently is just under 500 acres. When the price of stocking it with cattle and the cost of farm equipment and machinery is added in, the average investment is about $600,000 at 1994 prices.[7]

More land is being farmed today than when the Uintah Indian Reservation was opened to homesteading in 1905. Mechanization, the development of irrigation, and improved markets have significantly contributed to the increased size of farms in the county.

As discussed in previous chapters, farmers in Duchesne County have moved away from growing a variety of crops and are now concentrating on livestock and growing hay and silage for their livestock. The consolidation and expansion of farms, the climate, and market forces all have significantly contributed to this shift. In 1959 there were only 35,530 cattle (beef and dairy combined) raised in the county. The 1992 census of agriculture showed 103,443 beef cattle, 4,600 milk cows, and 65,645 sheep in the Uinta Basin. The annual market value of agricultural products sold in the basin is about $38 million.[8]

In 1987 cattle production accounted for nearly 60 percent of the agricultural income of the county, followed by dairying at 24 percent, sheep (lamb and wool) at 6 percent, hogs less than 0.5 percent, and other livestock about 1.5 percent. Hay and silage accounts for only 6 percent of the agricultural income, and the other agricultural crops account for less than 3 percent.[9] The average farm in the county presently has 35 percent of its land in alfalfa, 5 percent in grains, and 60 percent in pasture.

In 1992 county producers of livestock, poultry, and livestock products received more than $19 million for their agricultural commodities, placing the county eighth in the state in that category.[10] Agricultural commodity prices received by county producers closely paralleled prices received elsewhere in the state. Prices paid farmers for milk, beef, lambs, and hay have not increased in terms of real dollars during the past twenty years. Milk prices twenty years ago averaged around nine dollars per hundredweight. In November 1994 milk prices had climbed to $11.90, but, as a result of static prices in real dollars, farmers have had to increase yields through increased efficiency in order to survive.[11]

According to Ronald Peatross, in 1970 at 80 cents per pound and 500 pound shipping weight, it took 13–18 calves to pay for a new four-wheel-drive truck that cost $5,000–7,000. In 1994, with calf prices somewhere near the same, it takes 67 calves to purchase an equivalent four-wheel drive pickup, which now costs $27,000.[12] This same trend holds true for sheep producers. Lamb prices in 1994 were sixty-eight cents per pound, and wool sold for fifty-three cents a pound, virtually the same as twenty years ago. In 1966 Alton Moon, a prominent sheep and cattle rancher, sold his wool for sixty-one and one-half cents per pound in the county. He recalls, "Twenty-five years ago there was probably ten to twelve herds of sheep going on the winter range south of Myton. Now there are only three."[13] Sheep herds, unlike those of cattle raisers in the county, have not significantly increased in size from those of several years ago.

Along with increased production costs and inflation during the past twenty years, farmers in the county faced another serious problem—drought. Between 1979 and 1994 the Uinta Basin received about 20 percent less rainfall than normal. The 1991 growing season was particularly difficult for many farmers in the Upper Country as well as in the Neola and Roosevelt areas. Some drought relief was obtained from the federal government. Many farmers in these areas have become disenchanted with the Central Utah Project, portions of which have yet to be completed. They hope that the replacement projects will make the needed difference in getting water to all county farmers in years of shortages.

One of the small yet significant businesses in the county is Yack Honey, a small family-owned business recognized for its quality honey. The same alfalfa and clover fields that brought brief prosperity to a number of farmers in the county with the seed industry in the 1920s and early 1930s provided the necessary ingredients to produce some of the finest honey known. The business was started by Frank and Joe Yack (Yaklovich) in the 1930s, and it is now run by the second generation of family members. Members of the Yack family immigrated to the United States and the Intermountain West near the turn of the century. Several male family members took up jobs in the coal mines of Wyoming, Colorado, Montana, and Utah. George and Frank Yack eventually settled in the Uinta Basin, George as a homesteader.[14] Yack Brothers honey has won prizes for color and flavor at the Utah State Fair for a number of years. When Pete Harmon, Utah's first franchisee of Colonel Sanders Kentucky Fried Chicken, began his restaurant in Salt Lake City in 1951, Harmon used Yack Brothers honey with his homestyle biscuits and remained one of Yacks' best customers until the franchise rights in Utah were sold.[15]

Oil Boom

As discussed earlier, oil became an important element in the county's economy in the 1970s. As early as 1917, county residents were excited with the prospects of oil being developed in the Uinta Basin. In the early spring of 1917, the *Roosevelt Standard* reported that as many as six different companies were planning to drill for oil during the summer.[16] However, the oil excitement was short-lived when the oil companies failed to make an appearance.

During the next several years the *Standard*'s headlines made wild claims about oil possibilities including "Mountains of Oil in the West," "Riches In Oil Shale," and "The Uintah Basin is the Greatest Underdeveloped Oil Field in the West."[17] But no drilling took place. In the 1920s Earl Douglass, the famed paleontologist who discovered a cache of dinosaur bones in what is now Dinosaur National Monument, spent considerable time and effort touting the oil potential of the Uinta Basin.

An oil well was first drilled in Duchesne County in 1928, but there was no follow-up drilling for twenty-one years. Elsewhere in the Uinta Basin a few oil holes were drilled, but as the Depression deepened drilling ground to a halt. Again in the 1940s, with the outbreak

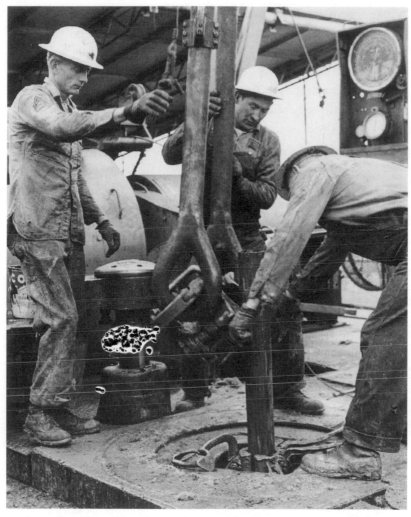

In the early 1970s oil production boomed in the Uinta Basin and brought a decade of economic growth followed by a bust in the mid-1980s. (Utah State Historical Society)

of the war, there was some excitement that oil drilling would add jobs and augment the agricultural economy of the county; however, it was not until 1949 that serious oil exploration took place and the Roosevelt oil field was developed. In 1955 limited drilling had begun in the Bluebell field, but this brought little follow-up drilling for another fifteen years.[18] Then, in 1970, Miles No.1 Well was drilled in the Altamont/Bluebell oil field. The success at Miles No. 1 and the growing oil crisis overseas stimulated a full-blown oil boom in the county.

The discovery of large quantities of oil excited the entire county about the possibilities of the oil industry and the potential wealth it would bring to the area. No other segment of the county's economy has had such wide swings as has oil. Nationally and internationally the oil market has gone from scarcity to glut, and the prices of oil have reflected those extremes. By 1978, the Greater Altamont/Bluebell field produced 33,607 barrels of oil daily, which amounted to 39 percent of the oil produced by the state. This percentage dropped as drilling in the 1980s extended to additional counties in Utah.[19]

Oil exploration and production in the Uinta Basin and elsewhere in the West increased significantly in 1973 when the nation and most of western Europe felt the sting of the oil embargo established by the Organization of Petroleum Exporting Countries (OPEC). Oil speculation and development in the county reached unprecedented proportions during the next several years. The decade of the 1970s saw boom times in most of the oil-producing states: Texas, Alaska, Oklahoma, Colorado, Wyoming, Montana, and, to a lesser degree, Utah. Utah is not usually thought of as an oil state, and the Uinta Basin is the major exception. Additional limited drilling has occurred in several other counties in the state.

Overnight, high-paying jobs became available in the county. Scores of drilling rigs moved into the area and hundreds of new jobs were created, some in the public sector, such as in education and road construction, and others in the private sector, including the establishment of new commercial businesses and oil-field support services. The increased demand for shopping, eating, and housing facilities and services dramatically impacted the area and each was being stretched to fill the burgeoning needs.

As a result of the oil boom, the county's population increased from 7,299 in 1970 to 12,537 in 1980—a 58 percent increase. Large numbers of men were hired as roustabouts, as construction workers, in related services, in trucking companies, building pipelines and pump stations, and in building a refinery in Roosevelt.

Real estate prices doubled in just a few years and then continued to rise due to the inflation and high interest rates of the 1970s. Sales of mobile homes boomed. Grocery stores and restaurants added new shifts, and many built additions to accommodate the growing needs of the county. Many new businesses were started. Teachers were added to meet the growing enrollment of students. More professional services—doctors, lawyers, realtors, and insurance personnel—were in demand with the increased population.

The county accounted for 18 percent of the state's total oil production in the 1970s.[20] In the period of the last thirty-five years, the state's oil production peaked in 1974 at 39.36 million barrels, with an estimated value of just over $1 billion. The greater Altamont-Bluebell Duchesne Field reached 12.26 million barrels in 1978. The cumulative production total through 1978 for the greater Altamont-Bluebell field was 115.14 million barrels, making it the second-largest oil field in the state.[21]

The Utah Division of Oil, Gas, and Mining reported forty-six new wells in the county in 1981, five of which were dry holes.[22] The Utah Energy Office also reported that there were 367 oil and natural gas wells in the county, ranking it third in the state behind Uintah (672) and San Juan (619) counties. Duchesne County was second in the state in the production of oil for 1981, producing over 7.7 million barrels; San Juan County remained the leader in the state, producing over 8.1 million barrels in 1981. The Greater Altamont-Bluebell field located in Duchesne and Uintah counties led all oil fields in the state in oil production with nearly 7.6 million barrels.[23]

By the middle of the 1980s several dozen energy companies were actively involved in Duchesne County. They included AFE Management Ltd. of Canada; TCPL Resources; Japex Corporation; Stauffer Chemicals; International Goldfields; Utex Oil; Chevron; Bow Valley Petroleum; and Proven Properties, Inc., owned by Pennzoil Company.

A huge percentage of the world's oil reserves is locked in sand and shale deposits. In the Uinta Basin lies a wealth of yet untapped oil—shale oil. The Arab oil embargo of the 1970s prompted an effort to develop the oil shale, most of it located in Uintah County. In 1980 President Jimmy Carter created the Syn Fuels Corporation to promote the extraction of oil from shale and tar sands. This oil, though as pure and refinable as any other, was far too costly to extract to be competitive on the open market and five years later the project was terminated. The region's large oil shale deposits must wait for another time to be fully developed. When they are developed, Uintah and Duchesne counties will doubtless experience a rapid expansion of the local economy similar to that of the oil boom of the 1970s.

As the oil boom struck the county quickly, so too did the oil bust develop rapidly. A drop in international oil prices changed the economic structure for drilling and developing Uinta Basin oil. Beginning in 1985 the price of crude oil fell in just a few years to twenty dollars a barrel from a record of nearly forty dollars a barrel. Just as the international oil market brought about the conditions that resulted in the oil boom, so too did it contribute significantly to the bust. In 1985 several member nations of OPEC reshaped the oil market with overproduction, causing an oil glut in the international market. The relatively high production costs associated with Duchesne County oil severely reduced new oil drilling in the county. In 1984, 37.9 million barrels of oil were produced in the state; in 1988, production had declined to about 33 million barrels. However, the value of that oil was significantly different. The 1984 oil was valued at more than $1 billion while the 1988 oil production, while only 4.88 million barrels different, was valued at only about $470 million—less than half—due to the decline in oil prices.[24]

The total number of rigs drilling in the county plummeted as petroleum companies cut back their exploratory activities. Many workers lost their jobs and a devastating ripple effect set in as oil and service companies, restaurants, retail stores of all types, banks, real estate companies, city and county governments, schools, and social service agencies were all impacted by the oil price drop. Surcharges and fees imposed by the state and federal government coupled with high drilling costs made oil exploration and production less profitable in the county. For example, in 1994 the average cost per foot for drilling for oil in Utah was $87.68; the national average was $67.87. Drilling costs are higher in Utah than in any onshore state except Alaska and Louisiana.[25]

Uinta Basin crude oil also has another element which causes higher than average costs for its production and shipping—it contains a high percentage of wax, which requires that the crude oil be heated during the winter months in order for it to flow. This adds to the overall cost of production.

The high production costs of oil forced large international oil companies such as Shell, Gulf, and Chevron to sell their local oil fields to smaller companies including Linmar and Keystone. By 1986 new oil drilling in the county was nearly at a standstill, and by 1992 only forty-four new wells were being drilled in the county.[26] Many oil-field service companies were forced to leave the county; some filed for bankruptcy, leaving many local businesses financially impaired. The downturn of the county's oil industry coupled with a winding down of the construction of the large water reclamation projects in the west end of the county resulted in a countywide economic recession. The total gross taxable sales and use-tax in Duchesne County demonstrate the extent of the recession. The $134,586,446 gross taxable sales in 1984 was recorded at the peak of the county's growth. Four years later, the figure had fallen to $71,468,095—a 53 percent decrease.[27]

Homes sales also dropped. In 1978, for example, a typical newly constructed house sold for $65,000; by 1987 the price of those houses dropped to between $20,000 and $30,000. Many houses were abandoned as bankers and mortgage companies were left with vacant houses and a housing surplus. In 1985 there were only sixty-seven new dwelling-unit permits granted for the county. In Duchesne City there was not a single new home built between 1988 and 1992.[28] There were virtually no new housing starts in the county during this five-year period.

The rapid decline in oil exploration and production left the county financially strapped. Concerned with the heavy tax burden incurred during the early 1980s, county officials turned to the state for relief. In a political battle that many throughout the state thought futile, the gas and oil industry got a much-needed tax break for new and existing wells. As oil prices fell it simply was not worth the oil companies' time and effort to keep local wells producing while paying high taxes to the state.

State Representative David Adams along with Representative Beverly Evans from Mt. Emmons, Representative Dan Price from Vernal, and State Senator Alarik Myrin from Altamont joined their legislative efforts in 1990 to pass House Bill 110, providing a tax waiver based on the international price of oil and tax exemptions for oil-producing regions of the state, including Duchesne County.[29] The bill also provided incentives to stimulate existing well production and promote new drilling.

The free fall of the county's economy was halted with the passage of House Bill 110. The local housing market was revitalized in the months that followed. By 1993 and 1994 real estate prices had increased by as much as 40 percent and the total number of real estate sales approached the high mark of 1985.[30]

A part of the revitalization of the housing market in the early 1990s was fueled by social concerns elsewhere. Perhaps the greatest number of new people to the county came from California, many of whom found it easy to pay cash for their houses. A typical house in California sold for over $200,000, and a similar house in the Uinta Basin could be purchased for $44,000. This subtle growth in the county's economy was not dependent solely upon extractive uses of the land. The economic growth is less volatile and is much more stable. Wages and salaries in the mid-1990s are not as high as they were in during the earlier oil boom, but they are higher than they were immediately following the oil slump.

Post-High School Education

In a recent statewide study, counties with the highest percentage of college graduates per capita were Cache, Salt Lake, Summit, Utah, Davis, Box Elder, and Washington. The lowest percentage of college graduates was found in Beaver, Tooele, Piute, Emery, Uintah, and Duchesne counties. In the same study, the seven highest and lowest counties per capita were computed related to state welfare assistance. Those counties with the highest number of college graduates had the lowest percentage of welfare recipients, and the counties with the lowest number of college graduates had the highest percentage of welfare cases.[31]

For a number of years prior to World War II, the Uintah Basin

The pristine beauty of the Uinta Mountains offer some of the best hunting and fishing in the state. (Utah State Historical Society)

Industrial Convention and the extension program of Utah State Agricultural College filled part of the area's needs, especially when it came to agricultural education and improvements. Since the end of World War II, however, education and post-high school educational opportunities have been seen as vitally important to the economic development of the county.

The geographical isolation of the Uinta Basin has had a signifi-

cant role in its lack of educational opportunities. The establishment
in Price of Carbon College (later renamed the College of Eastern
Utah) in 1938 by the state provided some opportunity for qualified
students from the county to continue their education closer to home;
yet this opportunity was limited.

A year later, Rulon V. Larsen, Republican House representative
from the county, and George V. Billings, Democratic senator from the
county, introduced legislation to create a junior college in Roosevelt.[32]
Local newspapers expressed a great deal of excitement, but in the end
the proposal was vetoed by Governor Henry H. Blood, as was a similar bill to create a junior college in Sevier County.[33]

A second attempt to establish a junior college was launched by
Uintah and Duchesne counties in 1959. In Duchesne County one of
the groups that supported the idea of a junior college was the
Roosevelt Chamber of Commerce. Its chair, Cliff Memmott, held a
number of community meetings to bring together the county's interests in a junior college. After great effort on the part of the legislative
higher education committee chaired by Dr. R.V. Larson of Roosevelt,
and with the strong support of state representative Bennie Schmiett
and Glen Hatch of Heber City, a bill was passed for a junior college
and approved by the governor. However, no funds were appropriated
for the college.

During that same legislative session, the Coordinating Council
on Higher Education was created. Its function was to coordinate the
direction of higher education in the state. Nearly a decade later, however, it would snuff out the county's dreams of a junior college. Many
feel that the coordinating council during much of its life failed to
fully function as the legislature had intended. For the next several
years hopes ran high, but funding failed to gain legislative approval
even though the college had been authorized.[34] Meetings were held
and studies conducted to convince the state legislature to fund a college in the Uinta Basin. The economic vitality of the basin rested in
part on its having a well-educated public, yet fewer than 25 percent
of Duchesne County high school graduates were going on to some
type of post-high school training.

In 1967 State Representative Daniel Dennis of Roosevelt introduced yet another bill to fund the earlier-authorized creation of

Roosevelt Junior College, and $300,000 was appropriated for the new junior college. Political pressure came to bear on Governor Calvin Rampton not to sign the funding bill, however. Newspapers along the Wasatch Front were opposed to the college, arguing that it would be a big mistake if the governor signed the bill. On 16 March 1967 the *Uintah Basin Standard* announced that Governor Rampton had signed the bill appropriating $300,000 for the Roosevelt Junior College. Rampton placed a provision on the bill, however; funds for the college would not be released for a year. During that time, the Coordinating Council on Higher Education was to study the situation and issue its recommendations to the governor.

The coordinating council and local supporters acted quickly. By April the Uintah Basin Junior College Committee was organized. It was chaired by Hollis G. Hullinger, with an executive committee composed of Daniel Ennis, D. Blayne Morrill, Alva Snow, Francis Wyasket, Arvin Bellon, Ed Emmons, Merrill Millett, and an advisory committee composed of nearly forty citizens from the community.[35]

However, there was growing competition of interests in Duchesne and Uintah counties over post-educational opportunities. Both county school districts had made applications to establish vocational education institutions. The Uintah County School District was fearful that if it didn't apply for federal funds for a vocational school it would be at least six years before such an opportunity would present itself again. The Duchesne County School District was equally fearful that if it didn't support the idea of a vocational school the message might be sent to the state legislature that it was not fully supportive of a junior college. The question was raised whether the basin could support both a junior college and a vocational education institution.

Following a two-day on-site review and meetings by the Coordinating Council on Higher Education in April, the council decided unofficially to recommend the establishment of a "teaching station" rather than a junior college. It argued that the station would be less costly, would provide a broader curriculum, and that it would be managed by Utah State University.

The unofficial announcement was met with mixed feelings. The editor of the *Uintah Basin Standard* wrote:

Cattle grazing on public lands is a multi-generational way of life for Duchesne County ranchers. (Utah State Historical Society)

> As we look over the past two months, it is heard [*sic*] to realize that such a turn of events could be perpetrated right under our nose, while we were so trusting and naive to believe that someone had our interest at heart. We were lulled to sleep by the soft music of promises and reassurances, then the bed was kicked out from under us. . . . The law as passed, establishing and financing a junior college in the Uintah Basin, stipulated that the school should be established and supervised by the state school board. This, we feel, should done NOW![36]

By the summer of 1967 the coordinating council had officially made its recommendation. No junior college was to be established in the Uinta Basin. Instead, it recommended that an extension branch of Utah State University be located in Roosevelt and that the first classes be offered beginning in the fall of 1967. In July, officials at Utah State University, with the approval of Governor Rampton, moved to establish a branch of the university in Roosevelt. Delbert Purnell was hired as coordinator for what became known as the

Uintah Basin Center for Continuing Education. Purnell previously had been county agent in Sanpete County and at the time of his hiring was working towards a doctorate in education.

The speed with which Utah State University moved to establish the Uintah Basin Center was encouraging to many in the county, and county residents were encouraged to support the Uintah Basin Center. The editor of the *Uintah Basin Standard* stated:

> We are on the threshold of a great opportunity. We can either bow our heads and say, "That [the Uintah Basin Center] isn't what we wanted! Give us a full junior college!" Or we can push open the door which has been placed before us, and build on our opportunities.[37]

The extension center began in a small one-room office. Classes were held in high school and junior high school buildings in the evenings, with professors flown in from Logan. During the next few years two resident teaching faculty members were added, Bruce Goodrich in mathematics and Nels Carlson in theater arts. Classes and degree offerings were expanded.

An innovative program pioneered at the school in Roosevelt was concurrent enrollment. It took general education courses to the local high schools and offered seniors the chance to begin their collegiate studies, thereby giving many qualified students a head start. This instilled confidence in many students that they could perform on a college level.

The Uintah Basin Center provided educational opportunities for many adults who otherwise could not go to college. Local school districts had a hard time filling teaching positions with qualified people; few teachers were willing to move to the basin and make it their permanent home. The turnover rate of teachers was alarmingly high. Now county residents who loved the area, armed with a Utah State University degree, could apply for local teaching positions and help stabilize the district. Many adults enrolled at the center, which has changed the lives and educational opportunities of many residents of the county.

The growth and identity of the USU extension center reached a significant milestone in 1989 with the dedication of a new 25,000-

square-foot office, administrative, and classroom building in Roosevelt. Funding for this project was obtained from a state Community Impact Board grant. Roosevelt City, Duchesne County, and Uintah County combined their efforts to secure the grant. With the building's completion, area residents had more visible evidence of the university's presence in the community. Two years later, a 40,000-square-foot building was purchased in Vernal, which more than doubled the classroom and office space available for the USU extension program in the Uinta Basin. And, in 1993, with a generous donation by First Security Bank, an additional building was purchased in Roosevelt for an administration building. In 1994 the Utah Board of Regents approved a name change for the institution to Utah State University Uintah Basin Branch Campus.

Presently the Uintah Basin Campus serves more than 1,100 students a quarter. There are about 230 courses taught per term, and there are over twenty full-time faculty employed. Distance education through computer and television classes accounts for about one-third of all courses taught, a number that will likely grow as technology advances. Planes still deliver professors three or four nights a week, and qualified adjunct instructors augment the teaching at the campus. Utah State University Uintah Basin Campus offers four associate degrees, sixteen bachelor's degrees, and eight master's degrees.

The local economic impact of Utah State University Uintah Basin Campus is significant. At present over 50 percent of high school graduates in the county continue on to some type of post-high school training. The average cost per year of schooling away from home—tuition, fees, books, room, and board—ranges from $6,500 to $9,000. Local students who stay home and attend the school can do so for $2,500. In the 1993–94 school year there were 155 college freshmen who stayed in the basin to attend college, saving their families hundreds of thousands of dollars total on higher education costs. Many of these families could not afford to send their children to college were it not for the Uintah Basin Campus.

Since the establishment of the campus in 1967 the number of college-bound students has increased steadily, as has the number of college graduates from the county. With the educational opportunities presently available and the increasingly educated local work force, county and city officials hope to attract more corporate and industrial jobs to the area.

The technological education needs of the Uinta Basin and Duchesne County are met by the Uintah Basin Area Technology Center (UBATC). In 1969 the state legislature approved funding for a vocational center to be built near Union High School to assist with the vocational needs of high school students. Duchesne County School District donated land just south of the high school, and a building was completed in 1970. In 1977 a 79,000-square-foot building was completed at a cost of over $2 million. It too was funded by the state legislature. With the completion of the new building, the role of the technology center was enlarged to serve the educational needs of adult learners not seeking degrees as well as providing vocational high school classes.

In 1988 the name of the center was changed to the Uintah Basin Area Technology Center, and in 1993 an additional wing of 23,000 square feet was completed. Presently the UBATC serves more than 1,000 students and offers over twenty-five programs including farm management, diesel mechanics, six different business programs, a licensed practical nursing program, emergency medical technician certification, auto mechanics, computer-aided drafting, welding, cabinetry, hazardous materials training, petroleum technology, and machine manufacturing programs.

The technology center contracts with Duchesne County School District to run the adult education program. Special programs and services offered at UBATC include a basic skills (GED) program, regional test assessment, a small business development center, and day care for children. Educational telecommunications broadcasting for the Uinta Basin originates from the studio at the technology center. This up-to-date telecommunications studio utilizes both microwave and fiber-optic transmissions. UBATC, working closely with USU and the Duchesne County School District, gives educational opportunities to the county's residents that are many times enhanced from what was possible just a few decades ago. Many individuals now can get the education and training to enable them to seek the more highly paid skilled jobs that were closed to them in the past.[38]

Economic Impact of the Central Utah Project

Duchesne County residents, and in particular those in the city of Duchesne, have been direct beneficiaries of the Central Utah Project. The Bureau of Reclamation mobile-home camp in Duchesne City housed nearly 100 full-time employees for more than a decade. Many of the technical jobs were filled by people transferred to the Duchesne Bureau of Reclamation office; however, a significant number of the jobs went to residents of the county.

Population in the city of Duchesne increased from approximately 800 in 1966 to 1,300 three years later with the influx of Bureau workers and construction crews and their families. School enrollment nearly doubled in that time. In 1977, $200,000 was paid by the Bureau of Reclamation to construct additions to the elementary, middle, and high schools in Duchesne City. From the mid-1970s until closure of the camp and offices in 1988 nearly $40,000 a year was allocated by the Bureau of Reclamation to supplement teacher salaries in the county school district.

The establishment of a project office and the arrival of dozens of Bureau of Reclamation workers and their families also placed a great deal of strain on the public utilities and social facilities of Duchesne City. To mitigate the impact, the Bureau agreed to help with a new sewer system, a new water-treatment plant, and recreational opportunities for the community. It assisted in building a community swimming pool and bowling alley. These facilities were turned over to the city to manage.[39]

The county's share of repayment to the government for the CUP from 1968 and 1978 was $943,543. However, the county recouped this expenditure from the jobs the CUP created, the purchase of goods and services by Bureau employees and construction workers, and the money spent by approximate 100,000 visitors to the newly established Starvation State Park.

The completion of the various CUP projects greatly enhanced the outdoor recreational facilities in the county and has had a significant positive economic impact on the county. Fishing and boating opportunities in 1977 drew 106,247 visitors to Starvation Reservoir. That number declined in the late 1980s and early 1990s due to a

Utah State Univerity Uintah Basin Branch Campus and the Uintah Basin Area Technology Center offer several degrees and programs that assist in the overall economic development of the region. (John D. Barton)

decline in the quality of the trout fishing coupled with poor maintenance of the facilities. However, with the introduction of walleye and bass to the reservoir by the Utah Fish and Game Department, fishing has improved and fishermen and other visitors are returning to Starvation Reservoir. Newly improved recreational facilities also make coming to Starvation more attractive, and more than 100,000 people came there in 1994.[40]

In 1988 the last major CUP project in the county, the Upper Stillwater Dam, was completed. The Bureau of Reclamation pulled out of the county, leaving a small crew to maintain its various projects. As mentioned, the withdrawal of construction workers coincided with an already serious economic turmoil in the county—the local oil bust. County revenues and budget were increasingly tight and the unemployment rate skyrocketed.

Unemployment rates have continued to run high for the past two decades. Unemployment in the county fell from 10 percent in 1970 to less than 5 percent in 1972. It continued at about 5 percent until 1980, when it rocketed to 13 percent between 1981 and 1983. In 1985 the county's unemployment rate stood at 10.5 percent, eighth highest in the state. (Juab County's unemployment rate was the highest in the state at 15.5 percent.) In 1987 unemployment rose to a peak of 16.4 percent during the county's economic recession following the oil bust and the winding down of construction of CUP projects in the county. The state average unemployment in 1987 was 6.0 percent. The state unemployment rate for 1987 was 6.4 percent.[41] County unemployment declined to 10.6 percent in 1989 and to 7.5 percent in 1990; it then remained near that rate for the next four years. In 1994 unemployment fell to just below 7 percent.[42]

Recreation and Tourism

A resurgence of travel and outdoor recreation occurred following the end of oil crisis of the 1970s. Duchesne County has benefited from this and from the completion of various CUP projects, the changing focus of the U.S. Forest Service to promote recreational opportunities, and the promotion of the state's natural wonders.

The Uinta Mountains include some of the classic wilderness and recreational areas in the West. With better access roads to trailheads and new public campgrounds and parking areas at some of the sites, Stillwater, Rock Creek, Moon Lake, Yellowstone and Uinta canyons are experiencing increased usage each year. The Uinta Basin offers some of the finest fishing and hunting in Utah. Each year greater numbers of hikers and horsemen visit the Uinta Mountains. By 1983 recreational use of the national forests in Region 4 of the United States Forest Service (which includes Duchesne County) eclipsed timber and grazing uses.[43] In 1994, 70,000 visitor days, figured as one person spending a twelve-hour day, were spent in the forest in the county, which computes to 140,000 individual visitors.[44]

In Duchesne County there are approximately 2.1 million acres of land. The U.S. Forest Service manages about 35 percent, the Ute Tribe owns 18.8 percent, and the BLM manages 9.7 percent; only 28 percent of the county is privately owned.[45] With a large segment of the county owned by the public, it makes sense for county residents to focus on the newly evolving economic activities of outdoor recreation and tourism to create income rather than to weep over a diminished tax base from non-taxable lands.

The U.S. Forest Service in lieu of taxes pays the county about fifteen cents per acre of land it manages, or about $105,00 annually for the more than 700,000 acres of forested land. In addition to in-lieu payments, the Forest Service also pays the county 25 percent of all receipts collected from grazing permits, mining leases, oil and gas leases, and timber sales.[46] These revenues then are respent several times in the county, adding to the county's economy. For example, there are nearly sixty grazing permits in the Roosevelt and Duchesne forest districts. The cattlemen pay about two dollars a month per cow/calf unit. However, the cattlemen generate a living from those cattle that graze on forest land and put many times the two dollars per month into the local economy. The same is true with timber sales. The trees are felled and hauled, logs are cut into boards and sold, and men are employed as a result of the resource coming from the forest. There is only one sawmill in operation in the county, located in Tabiona. Most of the timber cut in Duchesne County is hauled to sawmills in Uintah County.[47]

Statewide, tourist-related jobs have increased from 41,700 in 1981 to 69,000 in 1994.[48] Duchesne County motel and hotel room rents collected $341,000 in 1981, and the figure grew to over $1 million in 1992.[49] Still, the county remains near the bottom, ranking twenty-sixth of the twenty-nine counties in the state for gross room rents. Currently there are nine establishments that provide a total of 162 rooms in the county.[50] Tourists and visitors who rent rooms are apt to buy gasoline and groceries from local merchants, which generates hundreds of thousands of dollars annually to the county's economy.

In recent years several county residents have recognized the economic potential of the county's outdoor recreational possibilities. In 1988 Howard Brinkerhoff, an elementary school teacher living in Altamont who had a passion for fly-fishing and falconing, started a small fishing-guide business to the Uintas. He soon joined with Nick Stevenson's L.C. Ranch and Ned Mitchell's Dave's Ranch, both of which had private ponds ideal for the large-trout fishing needed to attract fishermen. From this merger Altamont Fly Fishers was born.

Jim Beal, part owner of Novell Netware Systems, was enthralled with Brinkerhoff's idea for a business based on a 1990s concept of eco-tourism and nonconsumptive utilization of the outdoor wonders of the region. Together they turned Falcon Ledge Lodge into a reality in 1992. This ultra-modern destination resort offers world-class catch-and-release fishing and wing shooting that attracts sportsmen from all over the nation as well as a growing number of international customers.

Falcon Ledge also provides a unique attraction—raptor hunting and observing. Brinkerhoff, an avid falconer, has an average of three or four raptors in residence at the lodge and additional falconers on call with unique and varied hunting birds including peregrine falcons, goshawks, redtailed hawks, and prairie falcons. The lodge is built with the most modern environmentally benign innovations, complete with passive solar design and biodegradable soaps. Beal's marketing skills include computer network marketing to attract high-profile customers such as film star Tom Selleck and professional basketball player Shawn Bradley. The purpose of Altamont Fly Fishers and Falcon Ledge Lodge is to bring to the region sportsmen who wish to enjoy without consuming the fauna of the area.

Also available in the county is pheasant hunting on farms where the ecological concept is to raise and release more pheasants than the number that are hunted. Other recreational activities at the Falcon Ledge Lodge and elsewhere in the county are snowshoeing and cross-country skiing. Currently, guided flyfishing costs are about $400 a day with a three-day minimum, and wingshooting is $800 a day with a similar minimum. Thus, this type of eco-business greatly adds to both the economy and quality of life in the region.[51]

Duchesne County's Finances

The county's financial condition has experienced a rocky road since the bust of the oil boom and the winding down of the Central Utah Project. An additional problem was the Utah State Tax Commission's decision in 1992 to slice the taxable rates of oil wells. In 1992 this loss to the county of tax revenue from oil wells amounted to over $300,000—one of the single greatest blows to the county's coffers ever. Oil companies operating in the state were successful in lobbying the state tax commission to revise the method for figuring the taxing base of oil wells. This new method allowed oil companies to discount the expenses of production (which are high in the Uinta Basin) before determining the profit margin and thus the taxes to be paid. For instance, if the cost of oil well drilling and pumping facilities such as tanks, pumps, and buildings is greater than the cash flow from the oil being pumped, then the well is taxed on only the property value of the oil well.

In 1992 this taxation method reduced the property value of the county's oil wells by approximately 30 percent. Also, the tax commission not only lowered the rate but also made it retroactive to 1987. This not only reduced the income of the county but also required it to pay rebates to the oil companies for the excessive taxes collected.

To make the tax picture worse in the county, the Bureau of Land Management in 1992 recalculated its in-lieu payments to the county and determined that it had overpaid the county by as much as $67,000. This required the repayment of the sum to the BLM. In 1995 the county secured a loan to pay the BLM for excess in-lieu funds received as well as to remit to the oil companies the excess taxes collected.

The loss of collectable taxes has kept the county commission scrambling to provide the necessary services to county residents as well as keep its long-term commitments. For example, in 1993 the county's property tax declined by more than one million dollars, from $2.8 million in 1992 to $1.7 million. In recent years, the county commission has been forced to cut programs and services and to increase property taxes to the full assessed value. Of all the county services, perhaps the road department has been hit the hardest.[52]

The overall economic picture of the county is best measured by the individual financial status of its residents. The per capita personal income (PCPI) for county residents was only $235 in 1929—the second-lowest of any county in the state, Kane County residents being lower by only three dollars. In 1940 the PCPI for Duchesne County was $241, the lowest in the state. By 1950 the PCPI in the county had increased to $846, which was the fifth lowest in the state. Nineteen years later the PCPI was at $2,130, but was still in the bottom four counties statewide. In the inflationary years of the 1970s, which were also the boom years for the county, personal income rose to $6,262, ranking the county fifteenth in the state. In 1979 the average per capita income for Duchesne County residents was $6,514—nearly $1,000 below the state average of $7,407. In 1984 Duchesne County peaked with a PCPI of $9,083; it declined the next year to $8,689. For the most part, personal incomes in the county over the years have not matched the average personal income for the state. For example, in 1992 the per capita income in the county was $13,600 while the state average was $15,600.[53] The oil boom with its new jobs and high wages did significantly raise the standard of living in the county. It has taken several generations, turmoil in the international oil market, and a heavy infusion of federal expenditures—the planning, construction, and management of the Central Utah Project—to lift personal income in Duchesne County to near the state average. In 1989 the median household income in the county was $23,653 ranking the county seventeenth in the state. The state median income for 1989 was $29,470. That same year, Duchesne County ranked fourth in the percentage of residents in poverty—18.7 percent for the county compared to the state average of 11.4 percent.[54]

In the last third of the twentieth century the county's population has steadily increased. In 1970 the county's population stood at 7,500; it then increased to a high of 14,500 in 1984. However, since 1984 the population of Duchesne County has fallen, levelling off at about 12,500 people.[55] Of the 12,654 people residing in the county in 1990, 2.8 percent were Hispanic, 0.2 percent Asian or Pacific Islander, 4.9 percent Native American, and 0.1 percent black, the balance (about 92 percent) being white.[56]

The largest employer in the county in 1993–94 was the Duchesne County School District with over 400 employees, followed by Duchesne County Hospital with over 200 employees. Penzoil employed a few less than 200, followed by Duchesne County with around 150. No other single employer had more than 100 employees in the county.[57]

Total employment in the mid-1990s in the county is just over 4,000 jobs, with a current unemployment rate of about 7 percent. In 1993, new jobs were created in retail, construction, and government sectors. The total gross taxable sales from purchases in the county presently come to nearly $90 million.[58]

Conclusion

The economic story of Duchesne County is one of hard work and dedication to the land. From the time the first homesteaders came to the Uinta Basin in 1905 hoping to turn their dreams of farming and ranching into reality, their labor outpaced their economic rewards. However, most people who have spent their lives in the county would not live anywhere else. Having survived the boom-bust cycles of the past eighty-five years, and once again experiencing an economic rebound, most county residents are cautiously optimistic as they look to the future.

ENDNOTES

1. See *Upalco Unit: Central Utah Project Draft Environmental Statement* (Washington, D.C.: Bureau of Reclamation, 1979).

2. Rondo A. Christensen and Stuart H. Richards, *Utah Agricultural Statistics Revised 1924–1965* (Logan: Agricultural Experiment Station, Utah State University, 1967), 20, 24; *1979 Utah Statistical Abstract* (Salt Lake City: Bureau of Economic and Business Research, University of Utah, 1979), xv-15, xv-16.

3. Ronald Peatross, interview with John D. Barton, 23 November 1994, Roosevelt, Utah, transcript in possession of the author.

4. *1991 Utah Agricultural Statistics* (Salt Lake City: Utah Department of Agriculture 1991), 41.

5. Ibid., 53.

6. U.S. Department of Agriculture and Soil Conservation Service, *Final Environmental Impact Statement; Uintah Basin Unit Expansion— Colorado River Salinity Control Program* (Washington, D.C.: U.S. Department of Agriculture, 1991), 14. Figures from the 1987 Census of Agriculture.

7. *Statistical Abstract of Utah, 1996* (Salt Lake City: Bureau of Economic and Business Research, University of Utah, 1996), 302.

8. U.S. Department of Agriculture, *Final Environmental Impact Statement; Uintah Basin,* 21.

9. U.S. Bureau of the Census, *U.S. Census of Agriculture, 1987* (Washington, D.C.: U.S. Department of Commerce, 1988), 27–33.

10. *Statistical Abstract of Utah, 1996,* 304.

11. Mark Monson, 12 November 1994, Bluebell, Utah,. The Monson family has been in the dairy business for three generations in Duchesne

County. When inflation is figured in for the past twenty years, the milk price has actually decreased.

12. Peatross, interview.

13. Alton Moon, interview with John D. Barton, Duchesne, Utah, 11 November 1994, transcript in possession of the author. See also *Uintah Basin Standard*, 26 May 1966.

14. For a brief history of the Yack family see *From then Until Now: 75 Years in Central Uintah Basin, 1905–1980* (Roosevelt, UT: Ink Spot, 1987), 1033–34.

15. Lawrence Yack, interview with John D. Barton, Roosevelt, Utah, 9 December 1994, transcript in possession of the author.

16. *Roosevelt Standard*, 18 April 1917.

17. *Roosevelt Standard*, 24 September 1919; 10 March 1920; 23 March 1921.

18. See *Beehive History* 16:23; and George H. Hansen and H.C. Scoville, compilers, "Drilling Records for Oil and Gas in Utah," Utah Geological and Mineralogical Survey Bulletin 50 (February 1955).

19. Wayne L. Walquist, ed., *Atlas of Utah* (Provo: Weber State College/Brigham Young University Press, 1981), 211.

20. Ibid., 110.

21. *Beehive History* 16: 23; Walquist, *Atlas of Utah*, 211.

22. *Utah Energy Statistical Abstract* (Salt Lake City: Utah Energy Office, n.d.), 68.

23. Ibid., 174.

24. *Vernal Express*, 28 September 1994.

25. Ibid.

26. Ibid.

27. See *Statistical Abstract of Utah, 1990*, table 8.

28. Ibid., tables 12, 13, 17, 37. See also Gerald Wilkerson, interview with John D. Barton, 24 November 1995, transcript in possession of the author.

29. *Utah House Journal, 1990* (Salt Lake City: State of Utah, 1991), 121; See also *Utah Code Unannotated*, Title 59, chapter 5, paragraphs 101 and 102; Beverly Ann Evans, interview with John D. Barton, 5 December 1994, transcript in possession of the author.

30. Wilkerson, interview.

31. The statistics were presented by Dr. Laird Hartman, USU Uintah Basin Campus Director, to President George Emert, 4 May 1994, Roosevelt, Utah, copy in possession of the author.

32. Rulon V. Larsen taught school in the county before passing the state

bar and becoming an attorney in 1924. He served as the city attorney and later mayor of Duchesne before being elected to the Utah House of Representatives. George Victor Billings also served as mayor of Duchesne as well as a four-year term as county commissioner, two terms as a member of the Utah House of Representatives and one term in the Utah Senate.

33. *Roosevelt Standard,* various issues from March 1939 through February 1940.

34. *Uintah Basin Standard,* 22 January 1959, 26 March 1959, 23 April 1959, 23 February 1961.

35. *Uintah Basin Record,* 27 April 1967.

36. *Uintah Basin Record,* 6 July 1967.

37. *Uintah Basin Record,* 21 September 1967. The trouble over the junior college in part led to a review of the role and function of the Coordinating Council on Higher Education. In 1969 the state legislature enacted the Higher Education Act of 1969 creating a fifteen-member State Board of Higher Education.

38. Mark Rose, superintendent, and Richard Jones, assistant superintendent, UBATC, interview with John D. Barton, 15 December 1994, Roosevelt, Utah, transcript in possession of the author.

39. "Economic Benefits of the Central Utah Project on the Economy of Duchesne County," (Provo: Central Utah Project, 1985), 1–3.

40. Richard Redmon, Manager of Starvation State Park, interview with John D. Barton, 28 October 1994, transcript in possession of the author. If each visitor spends an average of eight dollars in the county, it provides $849,976 annually for county merchants.

41. *1996 Economic Report to the Governor* (Salt Lake City: Office of Planning and Budget, 1996), 67.

42. State Economic Coordinating Committee, "Economic Report to the Governor, 1991," table 2; and Basin West 2000 packet, Utah Department of Employment Security.

43. Alexander, *The Rise of Multiple-Use Management in the Intermountain West,* 226.

44. Recreation Information Management Report, U.S. Forest Service, Roosevelt and Duchesne Districts, 1994, 3–8.

45. "Federal Land Payments in Utah," *Utah Economic and Business Review* 52 (September 1992): 2.

46. Recreation Information Management Report, 2.

47. Ibid.

48. *1996 Economic Report to the Governor,* 209.

49. *Statistical Abstract of Utah, 1993* (Salt Lake City: Bureau of Economic and Business Research, University of Utah, 1993), 463.

50. State of Utah Department of Community and Economic Development, "Uintah Basin: Outdoor Education Institute," 1994, 10–12.

51. Howard Brinkerhoff, interview with John D. Barton, 23 November 1994, Talmage, Utah, transcript in possession of the author.

52. Curtis Dastrup, Duchesne County Commissioner, interview with John D. Barton, 15 December 1994, Ioka, Utah, transcript in possession of the author.

53. Kenneth E. Jensen, "Utah Personal Income, 1929–1985," (Salt Lake City: Utah Department of Employment Security, 1986), 19–20.

54. *Statistical Abstract of Utah, 1993*, 164, 167.

55. Information packet prepared for the Basin West 2000 Committee, 1994, in possession of the author.

56. See 1990 U.S. census, *General Social and Economic Characteristics: Utah*, vol. 1, part 46 (Washington, D.C.: U.S. Department of Commerce, 1993).

57. Basin West 2000 packet, quoting from the *Utah Directory of Business and Industry, 1993–1994.*

58. "Utah's Uintah Basin District: Daggett, Duchesne, and Uintah Counties," Utah Department of Employment Security quarterly newsletter (Second Quarter 1993): 2, 3, 17.

CHAPTER 11

WHOSE LAND?

W ith the complexities of an ever-changing society, yesterday's maligned and mistreated are sometimes the winners in today's court battles. Ute tribal members, having been the losers in nineteenth- and early-twentieth-century land disputes, more recently have found themselves victors in the federal courts.

Those who came and homesteaded the county at the government's invitation in 1905 had no idea of the problems later generations would face over land and jurisdictional issues. However, these issues are far from the only ownership and land use concerns facing county residents. As the nation's land and natural-resource policies have evolved since the Great Depression, the same government agencies that were established with policies to promote development now create polices that seem to many county residents to limit the use of federal lands to specifically mandated and increasingly restrictive ways.[1] As populations increase throughout the region and state, so too does tension over land use. The differing land users feel that their own opinions and views are correct and others are wrong, archaic, or misinformed, leading to increasing polarization of groups and viewpoints.

Battle lines have been drawn for new range wars, and ownership and control over the land and other resources are being challenged on several fronts.[2] Replacing the shootouts of the past century's range wars, lawyers now are hired to fight land and other natural-resource battles in courts of law. In addition, lobbyists have been hired to lobby state and federal politicians, hoping to sway lawmakers to their points of view. The trend of the last decade has been to create environmental legislation in the courtrooms rather than in state and federal capitol buildings.

There are some extreme environmentalists trying to stop ranchers from using public land for grazing; others want more limited grazing use of the land or for ranchers to pay higher permit fees. Environmentalists employ a myriad of state and federal rules and laws—wilderness acts, antiquities acts, wetlands acts—to try to protect and control the land, alienating long-time residents and other users of the land who feel that they are better able to manage the land or that they are entitled to continue using what they have worked to develop. There also are other more radical political groups who have purchased land in Duchesne County in the belief that American society will break down soon and that the isolation of the county will provide them some security as they reorder their society.

Many county residents want to see the archaeological wonders of Nine Mile Canyon preserved and protected from vandals, but many of these centuries-old remnants of past cultures are on private land.

These and other contending interests are at work in the county, and their interests raise a number of questions. Should a government agency step in and oversee Nine Mile? Who should control and manage the land presently owned by the Ute Tribe—the tribe? the Bureau of Indian Affairs? What role do the terminated Utes play in the control and development of Ute lands and resources? And, most significantly of all, who owns and/or controls the land that was once set aside as a reservation for the Ute Indians by President Abraham Lincoln but which was later opened for homesteading.

Federal, State, and County Lands

With a population of fewer than 13,000 individuals in the county, and with 72 percent of the county being public land managed or controlled by the federal government, many county residents often feel they have little voice in the direction and management of much of their county. State legislator Beverly Evans explained: "Most local people are distraught. They have concerns over land use and feel that they haven't had access or input on multiple use issues. The bureaucracy allows little input when federal planners over-ride local concerns." Evans lamented, however, that many of her legislative colleagues have the attitude, "We don't care about what the Uinta Basin wants, we'll do what is good for Utah," and their concept of Utah is often only the Wasatch Front.[3]

At present, about 77 percent of Utah's population resides in urban areas, primarily in Utah, Salt Lake, Weber, and Davis counties. There has been a huge shift from the rural agricultural lifestyles of our parents and grandparents to the urban lifestyles of present times. In the last two generations most Utahns have moved from farms to urban centers, echoing a national trend. The once-traditional values and uses of land have come into question by even Utah city-dwellers, especially as they have come to have an increasing interest in recreational use of the land.

The trend increasingly has been to preserve public lands for multiple-use purposes, including hiking, sightseeing, camping, catch-and-release fly-fishing, and other non-consumptive uses. This trend greatly affects hunting, grazing, timber, oil exploration and production, and mining uses of the land in Duchesne County. The nationwide trend is against these extractive uses of public land. This is the opinion not just of Utahns but of people nationwide, who feel they should have as much say in what occurs in western lands as the people who live there, because such lands are in the public domain and are the property of all Americans.

As the population of the state increases, coupled with increasing numbers of tourists who come to the state and county, the debates about land use will continue to increase. In the 1970s and 1980s there was a strong movement called the Sagebrush Rebellion that was led by Nevada and joined by Utah and other western states. Although this movement was not successful in shifting ownership and control of federal lands to the states, it centralized and brought into focus for many westerners the issues at hand. A central issue is, Who will determine how public land in the West and in Duchesne County will be used: those who have made a living from it for several generations or those who want it preserved to be used only in non-consumptive ways?[4]

Duchesne County officials are concerned with these questions and want a voice in land use issues in the county. That voice has solidified in recent land-use planning. After almost two years of meetings and discussions by county officials, involved citizens, and state and federal agency representation, the Duchesne County General Plan was finalized in 1995. In it the county's objectives on policy and economic growth are clearly outlined. Of primary concern are public land management, recreation, and tourism questions.

On the issue of public lands—both federal and state—the county's objectives include: active county participation in the federal and state planning process, county support for maintaining public multiple-use land-management practices, participation by county leaders in public land classification and use designations, and finally, strong county support for "no net increase" of public land within the county.[5] These objectives clearly demonstrate that county officials and a majority of residents desire to have a strong voice in the policies and management of the land within the county and that they wish to stop, or at least slow down, the increasing federal management of land and resources in the county.

One of the focal points of use and control of federal lands that impacts Duchesne County is grazing. Duchesne County cattlemen voice concerns over this issue and most county residents, with their roots closely tied to the land, believe that multiple-use concepts should include grazing. Since the nineteenth century, cattlemen and sheepmen have grazed their herds on public lands. Nearly a century ago most of the large ranchers in the county owned only a small portion of the land they used to graze their livestock. Due to concern with watersheds and the overgrazing and deterioration of land in the West, Don B. Colton and others encouraged a better system of grazing on public land through the establishment of local grazing districts. From this came a better-managed grazing program on public lands using the grazing permit system common today.

The movement of the past few years to rid federal lands of cattle and other livestock is almost beyond comprehension to most county livestock growers. Although movements to ban grazing with the slogans "No Moo in 92" and "Cattle Free in 93" have failed, similar efforts by environmentalists continue. Arguments posed by those wanting to rid federal land of stock vary by degrees. Some desire to restore a more pristine land to provide more homeland for natural species. Others move a step farther in their arguments, claiming that cattle are hard on delicate ranges and destroy many species of flora, which in turn negatively impacts natural fauna species. Some think that the cattle destroy the riparian lands, those delicate lands along streambanks and lakes; and others go so far as to believe that the flatulence and belching of cattle are creating too much methane, one of the elements destroying the ozone layer of the earth's atmosphere. Cattlemen have a hard time accepting most of these challenges to their way of life and livelihood.[6]

The Peatross Ranch in Strawberry and Avintaquin provides an example of a county cattleman caught in this conflict. When William Peatross began expanding his ranch in 1942, he purchased seven original homesteads. The homesteaders' animals had overgrazed the land so badly that the lower Avintaquin property would only support thirty cow/calf units during the summer months. Currently William's son Kent runs about 250 cow/calf units on the same land and cuts over 100 tons of hay each summer. In addition, the land supports between 600 and 800 deer for six weeks each spring on sprouting alfalfa, and more than 100 elk pasture there in the fall. In the 1940s and 1950s there were very few deer and almost no elk along Avintaquin Creek, as there was too little feed to support them.

For more than fifty years the Peatross family has worked on the riparian lands along Avintaquin Creek and Strawberry River at their expense, knowing it was vital to their own interests to develop and improve the land for grazing purposes. In recent years, however, they have had their fences cut and stock watering troughs destroyed by vandals who think cattle on public lands are damaging the forest and land. Kent Peatross said of the situation: "There is so much federal land around us we are dependant upon the multiple use of it. The environmentalists are out of touch with how we use it. We are healing the land from the abuses of the past."[7]

At present there are sixty grazing permits, varying in number of cow/calf units from fifteen to fifty, given to stockmen in Duchesne County on U.S. Forest lands. The present cost of the permits are two dollars per cow/calf unit per month.[8] To many this seems far below market value—and it may be. However, Duchesne County cattlemen maintain that they not only graze cattle on public lands but also develop the land and springs for their cattle, which has assisted the habitat, allowing expansion of large game such as elk. Prominent area cattle rancher and high school teacher Brent Brotherson explained this position:

> Most of the decisions are made on emotion by those who want to lock-up land for their own use. If they relied on science it allows room for grazing, timber, mining, as well as recreation in the multiple use concept. Lots of grazing lands are in better shape today than 100 years ago. We've had land in the area for three generations now and the range is better now than when my grandparents homesteaded. Wildlife has also benefited. There are far more deer and elk now because of improved range.[9]

In the last few years the number of laws and restrictions that apply to land use and ownership have greatly increased. Many feel that even these restrictions are barely sufficient to protect archaeological sites as well as flora and fauna species from further destruction. Others see the many laws as an effort to restrict their freedom and use of the land and its resources.

Since 1931, when the U.S. Forest Service designated the High Uintas Primitive Area, there has been concern over the management of public lands in the county. The primitive area encompassed more than 240,700 acres. In 1964 Congress passed the Wilderness Act. Its stated purpose is to secure some federal lands in order to provide "for the American people of present and future generations the benefits of an enduring resource of wilderness."[10] Twenty years later, Congress passed the Utah Wilderness Act of 1984 that set aside thousands of acres of roadless national forest land in the state, including much of the area known as the High Uintas. These laws prohibit motorized vehicles from entering lands designated as wilderness. They, of course, are not popular with mining and timber users of the national forest, who feel restricted by the federal laws and mandates.

Other federal laws which restrict land use include the Wetlands Act, discussed previously. This law restricts how wetlands can be developed by private landowners. The Endangered Species Act passed in 1973 is a move by the federal government to protect animals and plants from extinction—certainly a laudable motive. Among its provisions, any new construction site must provide one-half mile clearance to a raptor nest. Oil drilling south of Myton was halted for a time because the potential migratory routes of mountain plovers may have been disturbed by the drilling rig.[11] Construction activities also may be halted to allow for environmental impact studies to ensure that construction activities will not harm any endangered species. Some extreme environmentalists believe that the dams on Uinta Basin rivers should be removed, among other reasons, to restore original river flows to protect endangered fish species. The razor-backed sucker, bony chub, and Colorado squawfish are all endangered fish species that are found in the Green and Duchesne rivers. Environmentalists argue that these species are dependant upon an unrestricted water flow in the spring for spawning and that humans need to consider other creatures and the established ecosystem as a whole.

Hunting rights (or privileges, as some view them) are also being challenged by animal-rights groups throughout the nation. As one of the best hunting regions of the state, these concerns over land use impact the county. Presently the hunting population is a very small percentage nationwide. In Utah less than 10 percent of the population took out a license to hunt deer in 1990. Again, if the lands are to be controlled by the voice of the majority, whose concerns and rights should control federal land: the majority of those who live in the region or the majority of the nation as a whole? Another concern of the hunting population of the county is the rapid rise in the number of hunters from the Wasatch Front coming to the area to hunt. In the last few years the Division of Wildlife Resources has drastically reduced the number of regions for open bull elk hunts. The Uinta Mountains is the best and largest open bull hunt region left in the state. This has attracted thousands of hunters to the area, which has angered and frustrated many county residents who have felt that their interests and concerns have not been taken into account.

There are acts mandated by the federal government which are not totally funded by the federal government. Such acts force areas like Duchesne County to raise taxes to comply with their provisions. The Clean Air Act and the Pure Water Act are two examples. The purposes of these acts are laudable, but they often have negative ramifications on the county's economy. For instance, the Environmental Protection Agency succeeded in closing down the Pennzoil Refinery in Roosevelt because of its failure to comply with clean air standards. The owners simply could not afford to meet new regulations and keep the refinery profitable. As a result, the county lost over 150 of its best-paying jobs; yet no one can argue with the desirable concept of having clean air. What is the proper balance between families' livelihoods and environmental issues?

Many county officials as well as members of the state legislature representing voters of the county at times despair over how to deal with these issues. Any attempts to impose new and stricter regulations anger constituents with opposing points of view, yet to uphold and protect the status quo alienates and angers large numbers of voters who are demanding change. Ignoring the issues and passing no new legislation angers all sides. From a political point of view it is seen as a no-win situation. Radicals on both sides of the issues—environmentalists on one side and ultra-conservatives on the other—feel their own points-of-view are right and that legislation should be implemented to protect their interests. Finding a consensus seems impossible, and finding compromises is difficult. These efforts will be important in the coming years.

Nine Mile Coalition

A major concern of many in the county is protecting the fragile cultural elements of the county's very early residents. In Nine Mile Canyon is found some of the best archaeological evidence of the Fremont culture. The many pictographs and petroglyphs on the canyon walls fires the imagination of many and causes all who see them to wonder about the people who drew them and lived in the region centuries ago. The Nine Mile rock art panels have been called the "longest art gallery in the world." In addition to the rock art, there also are many structures and caves used by the prehistoric people.

In addition to the prehistoric artifacts found in the canyon, there are many historic sites, including the Nutter Ranch, homesteaders' cabins, the Price-Fort Duchesne stage route, telegraph poles, a telegraph relay station, and late nineteenth- and early twentieth-century graffiti—names of wagon freighters written with axle grease. Many of the archaeological and historic sites are being vandalized or are slowly disintegrating due to the lack of care and protection from the natural elements provided them. A number of the prehistoric and historic cultural sites also are found on private land and therefore are not protected by federal or state laws. The loss of pottery, tools, and other cultural artifacts to pot hunters and others is incalculable.

As greater numbers of people become aware of Nine Mile Canyon, due largely through the promotion of the area by regional travel councils, the cultural sites are threatened even more. There are no public facilities of any kind in Nine Mile Canyon for the public. Although the area is somewhat isolated, many feel that the canyon's cultural sites should be preserved and interpreted for the public. In 1991 discussion was initiated by the Duchesne County Historic Preservation Committee on the possible preservation of Nine Mile Canyon. The Duchesne County Historical Preservation Committee was organized in September 1991 under the direction of the Duchesne County Commission. The author, John D. Barton, was elected chairman of that committee; H. Bert Jenson was appointed chairman of the Nine Mile Canyon Committee. From that small beginning, a much larger Nine Mile Canyon Coalition developed whose goal is to preserve as much as possible the scenic wonders and cultural sites in Nine Mile Canyon for study and enjoyment by future generations.

In January 1993 the Nine Mile Canyon Coalition was formed with the support of the Moab and Vernal districts of the Bureau of Land Management, Duchesne County, Carbon County, Utah State University, the College of Eastern Utah, the Ute Tribe, and various historic organizations, tourism councils, chambers of commerce, and private citizens. It was proposed that a study be conducted on the feasibility of trading private land containing cultural sites for land of similar or greater grazing and ranching value in Argyle Canyon. All archaeological and historic sites in the canyon would then be managed and protected by the BLM.[12] State and county governments are concerned in their interactions with federal agencies that control land that there be no net loss of additional lands, and no net loss of private land would occur under terms of this proposal. If the Nine Mile Coalition is successful, the canyon's scenic and historic past will be better preserved. Businesses also may offer concessions and services for the many interested visitors to the canyon. If not, at the present rate of destruction, much will be lost forever and landowners, angered by abuse and trespass of their property, will make access to the cultural sites ever more difficult.

A County Divided

Land and water issues, legal jurisdictions, the definition of membership in the Ute Tribe, and federal land policies have divided the residents of the county during the last quarter of the twentieth century. Among the two most serious of these issues that have caused confusion, mistrust, anxiety, fear, lawsuits, hefty legal expenses, and economic and educational boycotts among various groups of county citizens are the ownership and management of assets between mixed- and full-blooded Utes and the question of the legal jurisdiction on the Uintah Indian Reservation.

The roots of these two issues are found in laws passed by Congress and policies established by the Ute Tribe since the passage of the Dawes Act more than a hundred years ago. As discussed in an earlier chapter, the Dawes Act and subsequent congressional acts passed around the turn of the twentieth century allotted lands on the Uintah and nearby Uncompahgre reservations to Indian families, placed thousands of acres in a national forest reserve, set aside hundreds of acres for reclamation projects, and opened the balance of the land on the two reservations to non- Indian homesteading and mining.

In 1934 Congress passed the Wheeler-Howard Act (the Indian

Reorganization Act) which formally ended the allotment of Indian land in the West and reconstituted Indian tribes and reservations. Reconstituted Indian tribes adopted their own constitutions and defined membership in their tribes. In 1937 the Ute Indian Tribe wrote its own tribal constitution and established eligibility for membership in the Ute Tribe, which generally meant one had to be at least 1/8 Indian by blood heritage. Membership eligibility in the Ute Indian Tribe was limited to persons of Indian blood whose names appeared on the census rolls in 1935 and children born to any member of the Ute tribe who was residing on the reservation at the time of birth. The tribal constitution gave power to the tribal business committee to prepare ordinances covering future membership requirements.

On 27 May 1953 the Ute Tribe passed Resolution 600, which changed membership eligibility requirements; the tribe now stipulated that one must be one-half Indian to be a member of the Ute Tribe.[13] That same year Congress enacted Public Law 280, which attempted to end or terminate federal assistance and involvement with several Indian tribes. The act called for the ending of Bureau of Indian Affairs involvement in the lives and affairs of individual Indians and tribal governments. Health, education, and other services once provided by the federal government to the Indians were now to be the responsibility of state and county governments. The act was aimed at mainstreaming Indians into the non-Indian society. Tribal resources could either be divided and distributed to the members or the tribe could form a corporation and divide the assets of the tribe by means of stock certificates issued to tribal members.

A year later, members of the tribe voted to terminate and remove from tribal rolls all former members with less than one-half Indian blood. There were 490 mixed-blood Utes as well as fifteen full-blood Utes who accepted termination, leaving about 1,500 tribal members on the Ute roll. The Ute Tribe then adopted as membership qualifications the present "5/8 plus a drop" as well as the need for the member to live on the reservation.

Those membership qualifications remained until 1984, when Haskel Chapoose, a full-blood Ute who had married a non-Indian and had children, sued the tribe for discrimination against his half-blood children. He argued that he was a member of the tribe and that his children should be eligible for all benefits of a tribal member. Chapoose was victorious and the decision opened a window for about 1,500 children of non-terminated Utes to become Ute Tribe members.

In 1958 the government's policy of forced termination ended. In the meantime, the terminated Utes had organized, called themselves Affiliated Ute Citizens (AUC), and established their own board of directors to manage slightly more than 27 percent of the assets of the Ute tribe. The AUC organized the Ute Distribution Corporation (UDC) to manage non-dividable assets, particularity mineral, water, oil, and natural-gas resources.

Most of the land that the AUC members controlled was located in the Rock Creek and Antelope areas of the county. To manage these assets the AUC formed two other organizations, the Rock Creek Cattle Corporation and the Antelope Sheep Corporation. These two corporations failed within a few years, however, and the assets were sold, with the proceeds going to the members of the AUC. The Ute Distribution Corporation continued to manage the affairs of the AUC. To protect AUC members' assets, no shares in the UDC could be sold or traded until 1964, after which the Ute Tribe was given the right of first refusal to shares of AUC members.

In 1956, just two years after the termination of mixed-blood Utes, Congress restored to the Utes the mineral, oil, and gas rights to 36,000 acres of land taken from them by Congress in 1905.[14] When oil and gas were found on this land in the 1970s and 1980s hard feelings occurred once again between the two groups of Indians. Lawsuits followed as the AUC sued the Ute Tribe over payment of its share of oil and gas revenues.

Hunting and fishing rights also were a bone of contention between the two Indian groups. This issue was resolved in 1985 when the Tenth Circuit Court ruled "that mixed-blood Indians retained their own rights to hunt and fish on the reservation." However, those rights were considered "not assets that could be divided fairly" and therefore hunting and fishing rights cannot be passed down to the children of mixed-blood Utes.[15]

The second issue which divided the county was over jurisdiction on the Uintah Reservation. More specifically, it involves what actually is Uintah Indian Reservation land and who has legal control of activities on the reservation. This issue was raised by the Ute Tribe in 1975 when it sought to exercise jurisdiction over all lands that originally had encompassed the Uintah Valley Indian Reservation. In 1975 the Ute Tribe established its own law and order code. The Ute Tribe filed a suit in U.S. District Court to seek clarification and a resolution to their claim of legal jurisdiction on their land. For the next several years extensive research of historical documents was conducted to find a resolution to this very complex question.

While the 1975 suit was being studied, the criminal arrests and convictions of two Indian residents of Myton occurred in the 1980s. Both men appealed their convictions before the Utah Supreme Court, arguing that the non-Indian court system lacked legal jurisdiction of their cases because Myton was still part of the Uintah Indian Reservation. The Utah Supreme Court invited the United States Department of Justice to file a brief as a friend of the court because of its involvement with the 1975 legal suit involving reservation boundaries. The court ultimately ruled that Myton was not a part of the reservation and upheld the convictions and sentences.

In the Ute Tribe case concerning reservation boundaries, Judge Bruce Jenkins of U.S. District Court for Utah ruled that the Uintah Reservation had not been diminished in 1905. The decision was appealed to the Tenth Circuit Court. At issue was the question of what Congress really intended when it passed the 1902 and 1905 acts which forced the Utes into compliance with the Dawes Act and which returned the "surplus" reservation lands to the public domain.[16]

During the next decade, the case bounced around in the federal courts, and each time a decision or an opinion was rendered it gave hope to one side or the other. Finally, in 1993 the case was heard by the United States Supreme Court. In its decision the U.S. Supreme Court upheld only part of the state supreme court's earlier ruling that the communities of Roosevelt, Duchesne City, and Myton were outside the limits of the reservation. The Supreme Court cited the act of 27 May 1902 that provided for allotments of some Uintah Reservation land to Indians, and said that "all the unallotted lands within said reservation shall be restored to the public domain."[17]

There remained numerous questions concerning reservation boundaries, and the Supreme Court asked the lower courts to reexamine these questions.

The decisions from the various courts caused further problems and confusion in the county. For instance, on 21 September 1994 Ute students attending Union High School walked out in protest over what they voiced as unfair and prejudicial treatment. District school officials met with Ute tribal leaders to hear their concerns. Ute students later resumed attending school with no further incident.[18]

On the positive side of this lengthy legal confrontation which has divided the county, tribal leaders and elected officials from Duchesne and Uintah counties have met to talk and arbitrate issues and concerns rather than seek to settle them in the courtroom. For the first time, the Ute Tribal Business Council invited anyone interested to attend and give input in their meeting on 22 March 1994. The leaders of both groups hope that a new era of mutual trust and understanding can evolve.

Attempts were made by Beverly Ann Evans and other legislative representatives from the Uinta Basin to solve the vexing problem to the county of the state's severance tax on oil and gas. They have been partially successful in the past several legislative sessions to have some of the oil and gas severance taxes deposited in a special Uinta Basin revitalization fund. In recent years this has added up to several million dollars to be used in the basin.[19]

With the depletion of Ute tribal funds due to the decrease in oil and gas revenues since 1985 and the doubling of enrolled members, in recent years the Ute Tribe proposed to tax businesses and charge business licenses for those businesses located on what they considered to be tribal land. Tribe officials also proposed billing the Central Utah Project for $33 million for water reclamation projects not completed and for water from the Stillwater Dam the tribe claimed and for which it had not received any compensation. Further, the tribe looked to market its water to the thirsty desert states of California and Arizona.[20]

In May 1997 the Tenth Circuit Court of Appeals issued what many believe to be a "finality" to the twenty-five-year Ute tribal suit. The court ruled that the Ute Tribe and the federal government retained jurisdiction over all Indian trust lands, the national forest lands, and the Uncompahgre Reservation in Uintah County as well as several categories of non-trust lands that are within the boundaries of the 1861 Uintah Valley Indian Reservation. The court also ruled that state and local governments have jurisdiction over lands removed from the reservation under the 1902 and 1905 allotment legislation, which includes settled communities.[21]

In June 1997, officials of Duchesne and Uintah counties announced that they would ask for a rehearing of the May decision before the Tenth Circuit Court. Fearing more legal costs to protect their legal gains, the Ute Tribe Business Committee agreed to discuss with the two counties an agreement that it would not impose taxes, hunting or fishing restrictions, or other regulations on non-Indians living on former Indian allotments on condition that the counties would never again litigate the issue of exterior reservation boundaries.

By late summer of 1997 negotiations between the counties and the Ute business committee had broken down. Duchesne County Attorney Herb Gillespie in a letter to the tribal business committee said of the tribe's negotiating position:

> The tribe's proposal, as we view it, does not give any guarantees against the exercise of tribal authority upon non-Indians which do not already exist under present law. What we sought is guarantees that the tribe will never tax or regulate non-Indians on non-Indian lands even in situations where they may have the right to do so.[22]

Late in September 1997 Duchesne County and Uintah County lawyers asked the U.S. Supreme Court to review the appeals court decision of May that upheld the original boundaries of the reservation. The tribal council once again stated that it would not impose jurisdiction on non-Indians living on former Indian allotments if the two counties agreed never again to litigate the question. The counties invited the state of Utah and the city of Roosevelt to ask the U.S. Supreme Court to reexamine the boundary issue. Roosevelt City and the state decided that they would not join the appeal but agreed to negotiate with the tribe's business committee. The Supreme Court subsequently declined to consider the two counties' petition to rehear the boundary dispute.

The response from the two counties after receiving word of the Supreme Court's decision was basically, "We've all had our day in court and now it's time to get together and go forward."[23] There remain many issues, including water allocation, mental health, education administration, and wildlife management, that still need to be addressed and resolved to everyone's satisfaction.

Conclusion

Duchesne County's history can be seen as a microcosm of the history of the American West. It has included settlement by prehistoric Indians and later by other Native Americans and white immigrants, Spanish explorers, lost Spanish mines, mountain men, fur trade forts, an Indian reservation, and a nearby military fort complete with cavalry troops. There have been land rushes and homesteaders, droughts, boom-bust cycles in an extractive-based economy, and legal battles between individuals, the Ute Tribe, and county, state, and federal governments. Each has its own story as part of the larger Duchesne County story. Various groups and individuals have sought control and ownership of the land in the county; control of the land and its resources has been sought as a means to wealth and power. Beginning with the displacement of the early Fremont culture by the Numic-speaking Native Americans and continuing to the jurisdictional and federal-mandated policies and issues of today, the central issue has been control of the land.

As the county moves into the twenty-first century, these land ownership and/or control questions most likely will be solved, although perhaps not to the liking of all parties. It is quite likely that some solutions will be viewed by some county residents as unfair. Many issues already have been settled, but new concerns will certainly arise. The issues had their beginnings with historical events, and the seeds of tomorrow's issues in the county have already been sown. The harvest of today's history awaits a future historian with the truest and best perspective of all—that of time.

ENDNOTES

1. Clyde A. Milner, ed., *Major Problems in the History of the American West* (Lexington, MA: D.C. Heath and Company, 1989), 629.

2. Barry Sims, "Private Rights in Public Lands? The New Range War moves to a Familiar Battleground—The Courts," *The Workbook* 18 (Summer 1993): 50–58.

3. Beverly Ann Evans, interview with John D. Barton, 30 December 1996, Mt. Emmons, Utah, transcript in possession of the author.

4. See Michael P. Malone and Richard W. Etulain, *The American West; A Twentieth Century History* (Lincoln: University of Nebraska Press, 1989), 286–88; and Milner, *Major Problems in the History of the American West,* 561–73, 654–81.

5. "Duchesne County General Plan," Bear West Corporation in conjunction with Duchesne County, 1996, 2–5. See also *Uintah Basin Standard,* 6 February 1996.

6. Brent Brotherson, interview with John D. Barton, 30 December 1996, Boneta, Utah, transcript in possession of the author.

7. Kent Peatross, interview with John D. Barton, 30 December 1996, Strawberry, Utah, transcript in possession of the author.

8. Recreational Information Management Report, U.S. Forest Service, 1994.

9. Brotherson, interview.

10. Public Law 88–577, 88th Congress, 3 September 1964.

11. *Uintah Basin Standard,* 4 May 1994.

12. "Recreation and Cultural Area Management Plan: Nine Mile Canyon, Special Recreation and Cultural Management Area," (Bureau of Land Management, 1993), 2.

13. *Roosevelt Standard,* 8 April 1954.

14. Information from Chris Denver. See also *Uintah Basin Standard,* 30 January 1958.

15. *Salt Lake Tribune,* 22 October 1997.

16. The only exception was the case *Clifford Washington v. Duchesne County.* In 1965 attorney George Stewart argued in the Clifford Washington case that the court proceedings were occurring on a reservation and that the court system, being a regular court and not the tribal court, did not have jurisdiction over his client. The case was dismissed without any ruling on the argument.

17. The information on the jurisdiction issue was prepared from materials given the author by Herb Gillespie, Duchesne County Attorney. For more information on the actual Supreme Court ruling see Supreme Court

of the United States, Syllabus, Hagen v. Utah, Certiorari to the Supreme Court of Utah, No. 92–6281, I-iii. Justice O'Conner delivered the opinion of the Court, in which justices Rehnquist, Stevens, Scalia, Kennedy, Thomas, and Ginsburg agreed; justices Blackmun and Souter dissented.

18. *Uintah Basin Standard,* 27 September 1994.

19. *Vernal Express,* 7 December 1994.

20. *Uintah Basin Standard,* 2 February 1994; *Vernal Express,* 9 February 1994.

21. *Deseret News,* 9 May 1997.

22. *Deseret News,* 1 September 1997.

23. *Salt Lake Tribune,* 24 February 1998.

Selected Bibliography

Alexander, Thomas G. "An Investment in Progress: Utah's First Federal Reclamation Project, The Strawberry Valley Project." *Utah Historical Quarterly* 39 (Summer 1971): 286–306.

Alley, John R., "Prelude to Dispossession: The Fur Trade's Significance for the Northern Utes and Southern Paiutes." *Utah Historical Quarterly* 50 (Spring 1982): 104–23.

Alter, Cecil J. "W.A. Ferris in Utah 1830–1835." *Utah Historical Quarterly* 9 (1941): 81–108.

Barton, John D. *Buckskin Entrepreneur: Antoine Robidoux and Fur Trade in the Uinta Basin 1824–1844*. Vernal: Oakfield Publishing, 1996.

———. "Fort Uintah and the Reed Trading Post." *Montana Magazine of Western History* 43 (Winter 1993): 50–57.

Bolton, Herbert E. *Pageant in the Wilderness*. Salt Lake City: Utah State Historical Society, 1951.

Conetah, Fred A. *A History of the Northern Ute People*. Fort Duchesne, Utah: Uintah-Ouray Ute Tribe, 1982.

Degler, Carl N. *The New Deal*. New York: New York Times, 1937.

Dillman, Mildred Miles, compiler. *Early History of Duchesne County*. Springville, UT: Art City Publishing Company, 1948.

Ferris, Warren A. *Life in the Rocky Mountains.* Denver: Old West Publishing Company, 1968.

Fisher, Louise Larsen. *Family Courageous.* Salt Lake City: Deseret Book Company, 1957.

Fremont, John C. *Narrative of the Exploring Expedition to the Rocky Mountains.* London: Wiley & Putnam, 1846.

Fuller, Craig. "Land Rush in Zion." Ph.D. dissertation, Brigham Young University, 1990.

Gunnerson, James H. *The Fremont Culture.* Cambridge, MA: Peabody Museum, 1969.

Hafen, LeRoy R., and Ann W. Hafen. *The Old Spanish Trail.* Glendale, CA: Arthur Clark Co., 1954.

Hanks, J. Whitney. "Personal Income In Utah Counties: 1962–1966." Bureau of Economic and Business Research, University of Utah.

Hundley, Norris. *Dividing the Waters: The Colorado River Compact and the Politics of Water in the American West.* Berkeley: University of California Press, 1975.

Jackson, Donald, and Spence, Mary Lee, eds. *The Expeditions of John Charles Fremont, Travels from 1838 to 1844.* Urbana: University of Illinois Press, 1970.

Jennings, Jesse D. *Prehistory of Utah: The Eastern Great Basin.* University of Utah Anthropological Papers, No. 98. Salt Lake City: University of Utah Press, 1978.

Jenson, H. Bert, "Smith Wells: Stagecoach Inn on the Nine Mile Road," *Utah Historical Quarterly* 61 (Spring 1993): 182–97.

Kendrick, Gregory D., ed., *Beyond the Wasatch: The History of Irrigation in the Uintah Basin and Upper Provo River Area of Utah.* Washington, D.C.: U.S. Department of the Interior/National Park Service, 1986.

MacKay, Kathryn L. "The Strawberry Valley Reclamation Project and the Opening of the Uintah Indian Reservation." *Utah Historical Quarterly* 50 (Winter 1982): 68–89.

Malone, Michael P., and Etulain, Richard W. *The American West; A Twentieth Century History.* Lincoln: University of Nebraska Press, 1989.

Meldrum, Evva LaMar. *The Girl On The Milk-White Horse.* New York: Vintage Press, 1975.

Metcalf, Warren. "A Precarious Balance: The Northern Utes and the Black Hawk War." *Utah Historical Quarterly* 51 (Winter 1989): 24–35.

Milner, Clyde A. II, ed., *Major Problems in the History of the American West.* Lexington, MA: D.C. Heath and Company, 1989.

Morgan, Dale L., ed. *The West of William Ashley.* Denver: Old West Publishing Company, 1964.

Pearce, Finley. *O My Father: A Biography of Joseph Harold Eldredge.* Yorba Linda, CA: Pearce, 1980.

Pattie, James O. *The Personal Narrative of James O. Pattie.* New York: J.P. Lippincott Company, 1962.

Peterson, Charles S. *Utah: A History.* New York: W.W. Norton & Company, 1976.

Powell, Allan Kent, ed. *Utah History Encyclopedia.* Salt Lake City: University of Utah Press, 1994.

Price, Virginia N., and Darby, John T. "Preston Nutter, Utah Cattleman, 1886–1936." *Utah Historical Quarterly* 32 (Summer 1964): 232–51.

Quaife, Milo Milton, ed. *Kit Carson's Autobiography.* Chicago: R.R. Donnelly and Sons, 1935.

Russell, Osborne. *Journal of a Trapper 1834–1843.* Lincoln: University of Nebraska Press, 1965.

Spangler, Jerry D. *Paradigms & Perspectives: A Class I Overview of Cultural Resources in the Uinta Basin and Tavaputs Plateau.* Salt Lake City: Bureau of Land Management, 1995.

Stewart, Omer. "Ute Indians: Before and After White Contact." *Utah Historical Quarterly* 34 (Winter 1966): 38–61.

Van Cott, John W., *Utah Place Names.* Salt Lake City: University of Utah Press, 1990.

Walker, Gary Lee. "History of Fort Duchesne Including Fort Thornburg: The Military Presence in Frontier Uinta Basin, Utah." Ph.D. dissertation, Brigham Young University, 1992.

Warner, Ted J., ed. *The Dominguez-Escalante Journal.* Provo: Brigham Young University Press, 1974.

Weber, David J. *The Taos Trappers.* Norman: University of Oklahoma Press, 1968.

White, Richard. *"It's Your Misfortune and None of My Own": A History of the American West.* Norman: University of Oklahoma Press, 1991.

Worster, Donald. *Rivers of Empire, Aridity, and the Growth of the American West.* New York: Pantheon Books, 1985.

Index